Rebuilding the Celtic Languages

Rebuilding the Celtic Languages

Reversing Language Shift in the Celtic Countries

Diarmuid Ó Néill (Ed.)

with a preface by Joshua Fishman

First impression: 2005

Cover map: Jakez Derouet

ISBN: 0 86243 723 7

Published and printed in Wales
by Y Lolfa Cyf., Talybont, Ceredigion SY24 5AP;
e-mail ylolfa@ylolfa.com
website www.ylolfa.com
tel. +044 (0)1970 832 304
fax 832 782.

"When I think of my tongue being no longer alive in the mouths of men, a chill goes over me that is deeper than my own death, since it is the gathering death of all my kind."

– David Malouf, Australian author (1985)

Copyright

ISBN 0-9689552-0-7

National Library of Canada

Contents

The soft smile and the iron fist

Prefatory remarks by Joshua Fishman

Yeshiva University (New York), New York University (NY)
and Stanford University (California)

In a sense, small languages without state apparatuses of their own had it better when the iron fist was still in fashion. Basque advocates (and even simple Basque speakers) could be imprisoned and even executed for their offense against public peace and order in Franco's Spain. Ukrainian could be barred from publication in Czarist Russia. Yiddish newspaper stands could be set on fire and speakers at public lectures be drowned out by hooligans on the streets of Tel Aviv. Hebrew could be banned for over half a century, both in public and private ("little pitchers have big ears"), in the USSR. Korean could be similarly erased from any overt use during the years of Japanese rule. Totalitarian social planning has always included language planning and punitive and prohibitory policies were the order of the day. Nevertheless, the little languages knew where they stood and realized that no mercy would be shown to them and that their salvation depended on their own dedication, wits and slender resources. Many lived entirely underground, behind locked doors and doubly curtained windows, printed clandestinely and distributed by hand, from one trusted hand to another. It was a hard life but hope for better days, for liberation, for reform of the oppressive regime kept a small band of intellectuals and a larger circle of rank and file supporters ready, willing and able to spring into action in the public arena as soon as ameliorative circumstances presented themselves.

However, totalitarian regimes are no longer in fashion and even those that do still exist clothe themselves (and their policy rhetoric) in softer hues. This complicates things for regional and smaller non-state languages, because the source of their misfortunes is no longer so clearly and obviously defined. Ostensibly permissive "hands off" policies no longer fulminate against antiquarian, primitive or otherwise uncivil "disturbers of the peace". They simply smile benignly and invite the benighted and presumably intrapunive outsiders into the co-prosperity and co-civility tent under Big Brother's beneficent protection. It does not take long for the band of true defenders to realize that to follow such blandishments is tantamount to succumbing to slow-paced euthanasia rather than to the firing squad. "Permissive" policies often overtly prohibit no languages nor do they openly support any. They merely support education, the media (print and non-print, public and private), theatre and all other expressions of culture (even signage, which is after all, the public recognition of local history) in accord with the wishes of the majority of the citizenry. Such a stance is much harder to resist than oppression, because it is interpretable as resisting prosperity, enlightenment and civility. It also pauperizes human identity, both that of the minority and of the majority. Both are considered incapable of acting on any motivational bases other than those of material rewards and incapable of complex identities at the level of culture. Of course, it does make a difference whether minorities are hounded by the military or "merely" laughed off the scene for being "parochial", "ungrateful" and unconcerned about their own children's chances in the greater community, not to mention in the world at large. Assimilation is "white death" and genocide is "black death". They are quite different along an overt-covert dimension, but they both lead to the same bleak conclusion, namely the dislocation, attrition and termination of minority language-in-culture-and-identity.

Of course, there is a third policy possibility, namely a genuinely "supportive" stance toward minority languages and cultures. I say "genuinely" to differentiate it from most of the Soviet policies which were "prohibitive" at their core while being "supportive" via a temporary sugar-coating. In Western minority language policies, "supportive" approaches have just begun to become visible during the past half century and are still tentative and experimental, on the one hand, and meagerly implemented (by and large), on the other. They are often little more than promissary notes, commitments made to international bodies that cannot enforce them. They are often suspected of being fancy window-dressing, without budgetary specificity and without clear lines of communication and implementation within the minority communities themselves. One does not "send lettuce via a rabbit", an Afro-American proverb states, and it is at least somewhat dubious that the same states that only belatedly transitioned from "prohibitive' to "permissive" policies will really undertake genuinely "supportive" ones before it is too late for them to do any good, let alone to do so on a stable and reliable basis. As a result, I have counselled the supporters of threatened languages all over the world not to place their "trust in princes", but to primarily undertake efforts that they can implement themselves, by their own sweat, tears and resources. I have tried to suggest a carefully prioritized approach to such efforts. I have suggested a stagewise approach, in which the foundation is erected first and more broadly than the superstructure that rests upon it and that must always be conscientiously linked back to it.

Most importantly of all, I have cautioned that minorities cannot merely be miniaturized versions of the majorities that surround them, but must also be multilingual and multicultural carriers of a life-style that is distinctively and historically their own. They must be able to confidently compete with the majority on selected genuinely "open turfs", not compete on others, and studiously look and listen inward, toward their drummers, on yet others.

I congratulate Diarmuid Ó Néill for taking on France and Great Britain, on behalf of the Celtic Six, just as I have taken on the USA and the Global Community on behalf of threatened languages and cultures everywhere. I hope that others will emulate his example, both with respect to case studies of other minorities in France and Britain, who with all of their delicacy and cultivation have been grossly reluctant for many centuries to do anything genuinely supportive for their linguistic minorities. Their signed international commitments, conventions, charters and proclamations notwithstanding, they basically remain deeply sceptical as to whether little peoples, cultures and languages are even in their own members' best interests, just as they very definitely remain sceptical about such "little peoples" being in the centre's national interest. They are smugly self-satisfied about their "open door policy" and consider it to be a free gift of love rather than a lion's den from which no small language and culture (or even larger ones throughout the world) can return unscathed. Under such circumstances, it is far better to be cautious and to make progress slowly, particularly when budgets are tight (as they must be when one cannot put one's hand into the public till), than to be assertive and to work on all fronts simultaneously, without being able to learn what is working and when. I consider intergenerational mother-tongue transmission to be the core and the bedrock of security for threatened languages, while fancy footwork and computerized theatrics are marginal. While Ó Néill and I agree on most points, we may nevertheless disagree here and there. Nevertheless, we are both united in our efforts for a multicultural and multilingual humanity and for a world rendered "safe for threatened languages" everywhere, first and foremost within ostensibly democratic states. The Celtic Six are obviously important cases to receive international attention, precisely because they are enveloped in the soft gloves that mask but do not change the iron fists that are still there inside.

Joshua Fishman

Notes and acknowledgements by the editor

Notes

This has been a challenging work to edit and coordinate, largely because of the diversity of the Celtic world and the widely differing political and sociolinguistic circumstances of the six Celtic countries, not to mention of the two Celtic-speaking areas in the Americas treated here (Welsh in Argentina and Scottish–Gaelic in eastern Canada). At first glance one might wonder what mainly Catholic Ireland has in common with Presbyterian Scotland, Nonconformist and Methodist Wales or a largely French-speaking Brittany? However, as we shall see, all six languages find themselves facing a very similar threat not only to their cultural development but to their very survival, locked in a contest, as they are, with three of the most powerful and influential languages in history: English, French and Spanish. All six languages are presently making a certain degree of progress, thanks to the efforts of both voluntary and government agencies, owing to the Celtic cultural renaissance that dates to the 1970s, and yet their re-establishment on a widespread scale continues to elude the revivalists. We will attempt here to examine why and will also attempt to make recommendations in each case which are likely to lead to the desired recovery of healthier status in all six cases.

The recommendations made in this work are based on the theories of the sociolinguist Joshua Fishman, in particular his eight-stage GIDS Scale which theoretically can be applied to any language and was first published in 1991 in his work *Reversing Language Shift*. Joshua Fishman's approach places heavy emphasis on the rebuilding of family and community life in the threatened language. In the case of the Celtic languages, all six languages have suffered massive erosion over the past several centuries in all domains where they were formerly used, from the family and community to education and government administration.

In this work, Welsh in Wales is tackled by Colin Williams of Cardiff University and the Welsh Language Board, while Welsh in Argentina has been examined by Paul Birt of Ottawa University. Irish or Irish Gaelic in the Irish Republic as well as Ireland generally is treated by the editor with the assistance of Seán De Freine, as is Irish in Northern Ireland, while Manx-Gaelic is treated by Brian Stowell, the retired Manx Language Officer, and Philip Gawne (also presently appointed by the Manx Government to work for Manx). Cornish is dealt with in a report submitted by Wella Brown of the Cornish Language Board commissioned by the Government Office of the Southwest (the report itself is done by Ken MacKinnon of Edinburgh University), while Scottish-Gaelic in both Scotland and Nova Scotia is also treated by the editor; and finally, the Breton section is the Nominoë Study of Breton carried out in Brittany also by the editor and Marcel Texier in February 2000, with some updates but largely based on interviews with individuals and agencies working for the Breton language, as well as substantial research.

It is hoped that this work will shed light on a very difficult problem – how to bolster receding languages for those who are presently and in the future labouring on their behalf.

Acknowledgements

I am very pleased to say that throughout the three-year project of putting this book/report together (some might label it a report or snapshot of the situation today) on the Celtic languages and what status planning might best assist their survival and growth, I encountered pretty much universal goodwill towards the project. The finished product could truthfully be called a bipartisan effort by people of widely divergent political views in Britain, Ireland, Brittany and elsewhere. Both Nationalist – and Unionist – minded people contributed in the interest of making the project work and it is fair to say that they put the higher cause of preserving the Celtic languages first. Joshua Fishman himself was both supportive of the project and of great assistance. Multilingual Matters of England was of assistance in several matters. The Office of the French Language/Office de la Langue Française in Québec also provided important assistance regarding French in Canada, as well as Aboriginal languages. The Basque and Catalan Governments provided statistical information, as did the Ministry of Culture of the Government of Nova Scotia. During the Breton field research, Marcel Texier (ICDBL), Pierre Lemoine (Kuzul ar Brezhoneg), Lena Louarn (Ofis ar Brezhoneg), Andrew Lincoln (Diwan), Per Denez (Kuzul ar Brezhoneg), Yoran Delacour (Coopérative Breizh), Annaïg Renault (Skol Uhel ar Vro/The Cultural Institute of Brittany), and others kindly donated their time to be interviewed for the Breton case study and give their viewpoints.

Regarding the other languages, I always encountered a cooperative attitude from such bodies as the Welsh Language Board, Gaelscoileanna (Irish), Údaras na Gaeltachta, Foras na Gaeilge (Irish), CLI, short for Comann an Luchd Ionnsachaidh (Scottish-Gaelic), Bord na Gàidhlig, Comunn na Gàidhlig (Scottish-Gaelic), Yn Cheshaght Ghailckagh (Manx-Gaelic), The Welsh Books Council, Kesva An Taves Kernewek/The Cornish Language Board, regarding any enquiries I had regarding statistics and other information in general.

I must also extend a special thanks to certain individuals without whom this book could not have happened, such as my brother Seán Ó Néill, Eilish Flood, Robert Flood, Mary Dewane, Patrick Flavin, Joan Flavin, Margaret Kraul, Shane Kraul, Mairead Bradley and Gerry Bradley and countless other souls in the Celtic countries, who are too numerous to be mentioned here.

Also I must mention the assistance of the Celtic League and two of its leading members, Patricia Bridson (editor of Carn) and Cathal Ó Luain (convenor of the Celtic League). In addition, Lois Kuter and the US ICDBL consistently came through with needed statistics and the other ICDBL branches in Europe also provided financial and logistical support for the book. In addition, translations into Breton by Tangi Louarn and into Cornish by Ray Edwards were particularly helpful.

Diarmuid Ó Néill

I. Introduction

The purpose of rebuilding the Celtic languages

Diarmuid Ó Néill

Since the publication in 1991 of *Reversing Language Shift*[1] by the sociolinguist Joshua Fishman there has been a great deal of debate among Celtic language activists as to how they might apply the Fishman GIDS scale or model to their own beleaguered languages. In this fascinating work, one Celtic language – Irish – was among those studied. The other languages examined were Basque, Frisian, Navajo, Spanish, Yiddish, Maori, Hebrew, Catalan, Quebec French and the Aboriginal languages of Australia. More recently Joshua Fishman has revisited the issue of aid to threatened languages in *Can Threatened Languages Be Saved?* New languages examined include the Native American Quechua language of South America, the Oko language of Africa, the Andamanese language of India and the Ainu language of Japan.

This particular work is an attempt to apply the Fishman model to the Celtic languages. It is not a new departure in sociolinguistics. The goal of Celtic language activists is to strengthen and enhance the spoken Celtic languages rather than preserve these languages in mummified fashion in university courses or library records or in limited school programmes. Joshua Fishman's fundamental point is that the threatened language must be strengthened at the family, community, and neighbourhood levels. This is the sixth point in his eight-point Graded Intergenerational Disruption Scale (GIDS). Otherwise, as Fishman accurately observes, all other higher levels of attainment are superficial and are effectively only buying time for the said language, be they media in the language, adult literacy courses or even higher order activities such as university courses or official status or recognition for the language.

The position taken by this work – *Rebuilding The Celtic Languages* – is a maximalist one. The aim is not only to explore the strengthening of existing Celtic-language communities and Celtic-speaking networks in the six Celtic countries but also to explore how the Celtic languages can be re-established on a much wider scale than is presently the case.

This book is about the rebirth of the spoken Celtic-languages and their repossession of their rightful patrimony as the dominant, if not exclusive languages, in the Celtic lands. English, of course, would be retained in Ireland, Scotland, Wales, Cornwall and the Isle of Man, just as French would be retained universally in Brittany. English and French are important world languages, necessary for economic survival in the twenty-first century. What public opinion in the Celtic countries does question, however, is whether there is no place in the modern world for their traditional Celtic tongues.

Polls have indicated consistently that over 30 per cent of parents in Ireland and Brittany want to see their children being educated in Irish- and Breton-medium schools. The equivalent percentage for Welsh is 50 per cent, and in Wales about 20 per cent of children already are in Welsh-medium schools. There is increasing grass roots pressure in Cornwall, Scotland and Man for more schooling in their respective languages.

The traditional establishment viewpoints emanating originally and mainly from London and Paris but also aped by local economic establishments in the Celtic lands themselves (Dublin, Edinburgh, Rennes, etc.) that English and French alone were/are the only ticket to modern civilization and culture as well as to economic survival and prosperity, have been patently rejected by the Celtic peoples today in 2005 at the beginning of the new millennium.

The virtual destruction of the Breton language in the twentieth century, when it declined from 1.5 million speakers in 1900 to 240,000 in 1997, by a French government purportedly only interested in spreading education, social benefits and French culture to all, is now recognized for what it really was and essentially still is – masked imperialism and internal colonization. Ireland's horrific ordeal in the 1800s of mass starvation and mass eviction, halved the population by 1900 from 9 million to 4.5 million and reduced the Gaelic-speaking population from 4 million in 1840 to about 400,000 in 1910. Gaelic Scotland similarly was singled out for fairly brutal treatment with the Highland Clearances which commenced in the mid–1700s, thus reducing a Gaelic-speaking population of perhaps 700,000 in 1740 to

231,000 in 1901. Wales, Man and Cornwall also underwent early military subjection.

The situation of Welsh in Argentina is somewhat different, as the Argentine Government encouraged Welsh immigration in the mid-1800s, but later insisted on Spanish-medium education. Likewise, the Gaelic colonization in Nova Scotia and Canada at large was actively encouraged by the Canadian authorities, and Canadian Gaels, while subject to pressures for assimilation, were never viewed as politically suspect surplus tenantry, best got rid of as they had been in Scotland.[2] Nevertheless, Wales, Cornwall and Man have also paid a heavy price, not only through economic exploitation by the London regimes which supported the then expanding British Empire but also through what one might refer to as the morally corrupting effect of having to compromise one's own cultural values over and over again in the face of external pressure. One might also make the point that not only the Celt but the Saxon ended up making moral compromizes in the cultural trade-off, as in the process of colonization the English (and French) became just as morally corrupted as those who were forced to compromise their traditional Celtic culture. Regardless of when or where or how it happened, the underlying motive was imperialism and economic expansionism rather than some altruistic desire to spread the benefits of the English and French languages and cultures.

The above-mentioned cultural and political subjection at the hands of London and Paris has made the story of the Celtic peoples a rather tragic one. The Celtic cultural and linguistic renaissance since the 1970s has also been accompanied by political progress, with recent calls for Breton and Cornish devolution (over 50,000 signatures have been collected in Cornwall out of a population of 502,000 at the time of writing, requesting a Cornish Parliament) along the lines of either the Welsh Assembly or the Scottish Parliament, which were established in 1999. A Manx Government is already in place with its ancient Norse-derived Tynwald Parliament. The conflict in Northern Ireland may be on the road to resolution and a ceasefire is presently in effect. Northern Ireland may or may not unite with the Irish Republic in the future, although one would suspect a gradual fusion of Protestant and Catholic into one society at some point (just as the medieval Norse and English colonists eventually fused with the native Irish population). However we do not yet know the final outcome. We do know that the existing political/linguistic status quo in the six Celtic nations is altering and it is clear that these ancient nations are reasserting themselves both politically and linguistically.

This work is an attempt to analyse the unique historical circumstances and present-day situation of each Celtic language and then to put forth proposals as to what may be done to further the recreation of Celtic language-speaking societies in each of the six Celtic countries. It recognizes that the goal of language restoration in the Celtic countries is to arrive at a point of bilingualism.

This work questions and challenges the often held viewpoint that the dominant usage and position of English and French today in the six Celtic countries is already a *fait accompli* and that nothing could or should be done to restore the Celtic languages to their former positions of more widespread usage in daily life. Strangely enough, the holders of this viewpoint are as likely to be inhabitants of the six Celtic countries, as outsiders. As Fishman correctly put it, "we have met the enemy and it is us". While the 18 million inhabitants of the Celtic countries have plenty of external opponents, Fishman's analysis nevertheless holds up.

There are plenty of Bretons who actually do see Breton as an obstacle to economic and cultural progress. The economic establishment in Ireland and other Irish institutions such as the Roman Catholic Church have consistently opposed steps to strengthen the position of Irish in society, as they clearly believe that English and English alone can be relied upon for international trade and cultural contacts with the outside world, as well as for internal purposes.

In Northern Ireland too there is scepticism among both Catholics and Protestants about the role of the Irish language for different reasons which add up to the same negative thumbs down on serious efforts on the language's behalf. Many Catholics or Nationalists also regard Irish as something ancient and disconnected from themselves, despite their more ardent professions of loyalty to this language. This viewpoint conveniently forgets that up until the early 1800s a majority of the population of Ulster still spoke Irish. Further than this, many Protestants, also, were Irish-speaking out of necessity, particularly in western and southern Ulster, where the native Irish and Irish-speaking population remained dominant. In general, Protestant or Unionist attitudes in Ulster have, in the past century, tended to regard Irish as something which was the preserve of the Catholic/Nationalist tradition and ethos. In addition, as mentioned, many Protestants learned Irish, once they had settled in Ulster during the 1600s and 1700s, for practical reasons and indeed Presbyterian ministers in Ulster were required to study Irish-Gaelic as recently as 1831. Despite the heightened nationalism of Ulster no political party in Ulster has any language policy which would seriously challenge the status quo of English monoglotism.

Many Anglophone Welsh citizens sympathise with the Welsh language but worry about it being imposed on them and their children, for employment purposes among others, in an increasingly nationalistic Wales. In Lowland Scotland there is still the widely held misconception that Gaelic was always a Highland language and is no concern of theirs when, in reality, much of Lowland Scotland was also Gaelic-speaking until the 1400s when the Scots or Lallans dialect began to spread to the north and west at the expense of Gaelic.

In Cornwall and Man also, there is a certain amount of doubt as to whether these ancient Celtic languages really are relevant to present circumstances, let alone languages that should be promoted as vehicles of everyday speech in the community. Firstly, Cornish still had native speakers well into the 1700s (a thousand years after Celtic speech had died out in other parts of southern Britain) and secondly, western Cornwall was still a mainly Cornish-speaking place as recently as the early 1600s, so Cornish does have a claim on the modern and everyday life of that Celtic country.

With Manx, the case is even more emphatic. Most Manx people could not even speak English as recently as the early 1800s and Manx-Gaelic remained a strong community language as late as the 1920s with several thousand speakers, with the last native speaker dying only in 1974.

This work excludes from its consideration three non-Celtic speeches indigenous to the Celtic nations. They are the Gallo dialect of Romance spoken in eastern Brittany, the Scots or Lallans dialect of Lowland Scotland and the closely related Ulster-Scots dialect still spoken in Ulster. The latter two forms of speech are closely related to, and evolved in a parallel manner to, the Anglo-Saxon dialects of eastern Britain from the fifth century to the present day. They are just as deserving of financial and moral support from the Celtic peoples but they lie outside the scope of this work.

Most minority language activists, aware as they are that they are almost always challenging a more powerful political establishment, are often at pains to insist that their particular language movement is not a political one but a cultural one. Such pragmatism is probably necessary for tactical reasons, as long as activists do not actually start believing, themselves, that the status of their language is unrelated to the political status of their political sociolinguistic or ethnic group.

The gains made by Quebec French since the 1960s would not have been possible without the political gains and language legislation in both Quebec and Canada at large, by more assertive and nationalistic French –Canadian politicians and the legislation they enacted. Likewise, the impressive advances made by Basque, Galician and Catalan since 1979 are not unrelated to the political advances made by the Basques, Galicians, and Catalans with their achievement of political autonomy within Spain. The more modest but not insignificant achievements of Irish since 1921 would not have been possible without Irish political independence. The recent establishment of Devolution in Wales should help the Welsh language and empower the agencies working on its behalf. Similarly, the lack of real political clout for regions such as Brittany, Cornwall, Corsica, Friesland, and others has clearly weakened the position of language agencies in these lands because of their lack of a solid political support base.

As far as Celtic nationalism in particular is concerned, however, the horse is clearly already out of the stable, if indeed it ever was in the stable to begin with. There is a possibility of Scottish independence in the future, while in Northern Ireland no one can truly say what the future holds (demographic trends point to a Nationalist majority within the coming decade but whether this will lead to joint sovereignty or a united Ireland is uncertain). Wales, Man, Cornwall and Brittany may or may not pursue outright political independence but the possibility of greater autonomy for them is entirely plausible and might even be more desirable, within a European framework, than full-blown independence. In any case, not for many centuries has the political situation in the Celtic countries been so fluid. (In addition, events such as the Québecois march to sovereignty and possible future independence, and recent moves by the Basque Government towards a referendum on independence from Spain, have also helped shape thinking in places like Scotland, Wales and Brittany). It is beyond doubt, however, that all the Celtic nations will be pursuing greater autonomy and control over local affairs, including cultural and linguistic matters.

The Celtic languages and intergenerational dislocation

Language planning has, during the last fifty years, become an increasingly important sphere of activity for local, regional or national governments which have in their care a threatened language. It involves matters concerning the corpus of language – the language's vocabulary, construction and grammar – as well as the status of a language – the way in which it is used at various levels of government and public life. It is also interested in the use of language in community, neighbourhood and home.

A language is considered to be threatened when it is used less frequently by the younger generation than the elder generation; when it loses its dominant presence in various domains, e.g. for religion, education, work or home; when levels of literacy in the language decrease; when it loses its geographic presence; when it fails to be transmitted in homes, and when it fails to develop linguistically.

In discussing language shift, and the relation of a threatened language to its dominant neighbour, Joshua Fishman uses "X" to denote the threatened language, and "Y" to denote the dominant language. Thus Xmen are people who belong to the ethnic group of the threatened language and Ymen are those who belong to the ethnic group of the dominant language. Xish is the threatened language, and Yish is the dominant language. XSL denotes the threatened language as a person's second language.

Joshua Fishman has put forward an eight-point scale for considering the efforts necessary for reversing language shift. These vary from a need to reconstruct a dead or almost dead language, to the use of language in the higher spheres of society and government. He has argued that stage 6 is of utmost importance. This involves the successful transmission of the threatened language in homes. Any success at higher stages, e.g. obtaining official status for the language at government level, will be in vain if the use of the threatened language in the home and community is disregarded.

Diglossia – the use of one language for some spheres of life (domains), and another language for others – is thought to be a requisite in the development of a threatened language to become a generally widely used language in most or in all domains.

As this book discusses the position of the Celtic languages in relation to the eight stages of Fishman's GIDS, it is worth reproducing it here:[3]

Stages of Reversing Language Shift: severity of intergenerational dislocation

(read from the bottom up)

1. Education, work sphere, mass media and governmental operations at higher and nation-wide levels.
2. Local/regional mass media and governmental services.
3. The local/regional (i.e. non-neighbourhood) work sphere, both among Xmen and Ymen.
4B. Public[4] schools for Xish children, offering some instruction via Xish, but substantially under Yish curricular and staffing control.
4A. Schools in lieu of compulsory education and substantially under Xish curricular and staffing control.

II. RLS to transcend diglossia, subsequent to its attainment

5. Schools for literacy acquisition, for the old and for the young, and not in lieu of compulsory education.
6. The intergenerational and demographically concentrated home-family-neighbourhood: the basis of mother tongue transmission.
7. Cultural interaction in Xish primarily involving the community-based older generation.
8. Reconstructing Xish and adult acquisition of XSL.

I. RLS to attain diglossia

(assuming prior ideological clarification)

Some terms need further explanation. 4B schools are schools which primarily use the outside language such as English or French and are under the control of Yish staff also. 4A schools are schools in which the local language is the main medium of instruction and which are administered under Xish control. In Ireland, the Gaelscoileanna schools would be classified as type 4A schools because their medium of instruction is Irish and they are administered by Irish speakers. Likewise in Brittany, the Diwan, Div Yezh and Dihun schools would also be classified as type 4A schools because the medium of instruction is Breton and they are administered by Breton speakers. Those schools in Brittany which use French for both the medium of instruction and administration would be classified as type 4B schools.

Advocates of bolstering retreating languages such as the Celtic languages or other threatened minority languages have to do more than merely launch new schools in these languages and campaign on their behalf in other fields. They have to be prepared with a good ideological argument as to just why monoglot English, French and Spanish speakers should repossess their linguistic patrimony. The Celtic languages in particular are severely dislocated and with only about two million of the 18 million inhabitants of the six Celtic countries still conversant in their respective Celtic languages.

Because the languages which have supplanted the Celtic tongues are of greater currency in the world today, it is particularly important that RLS advocates have their positions well thought-out, particularly because the primary adversaries they face will be unconvinced relinguified fellow Celts. Living in a globalistic world as we do, it is becoming difficult even for languages like French and German to hold their own.

Celtic RLS advocates might adopt as their strongest card the moral upper ground. The centralistic British and French states imposed artificially stifling conditions from outside which strangled languages that otherwise would have continued with a healthy existence. Irish, with its 3–4 million speakers in the 1830s, was not particularly a minor language by nineteenth-century standards. However, it was a persecuted one. Over half the population of Brittany spoke Breton in 1900 (about 1.5 million people). So the suppression of Breton in this century was a completely artificial and unnatural undertaking by the French state. The assault on Gaelic Scotland, beginning in earnest in the 1740s, eventually brought an end to most of the Scottish Gaedhealtachd, something which was by no means inevitable. Equally, Manx-Gaelic was rooted out and almost destroyed, with the same questionable motives, by a highly centralistic state during the 1700s and 1800s. While Cornish, the last vestige of British Celtic in lowland Britain, suffered to a certain extent from an almost inevitable retreat westwards (which lasted for 1,300 years), the past hostility to the Cornish nation by London is unmistakable, hence the consequent Cornish uprisings in the 1500s. Welsh, too, was the victim of attempted murder by a centralizing state which has, only in the past century, made concessions to the Welsh language. In short, Celtic RLS advocates hold the moral high ground.

Finally, it should be pointed out that Celtic RLS advocates need not go to the elaborate rationalizations adopted by their opponents. Apart from the moral high ground argument, defending a Welsh-speaking lifestyle or a Gaelic-speaking one requires less justification than the opposing position – that these languages should be abandoned as redundant (which they are not) and that there is no other option (there IS another option) in the modern world. In addition, it is very true that the six Celtic languages express traditional and other concepts that cannot be translated into English or French, there is more than traditionalism on the side of Celtic idioms. A modern life can be lived just as productively through Breton, Irish or Gaelic. Those who argue otherwise have adopted or co-opted not just a defeatist mentality but the ideology of those who sought to assimilate and destroy the Celtic languages in the first place. This is hardly a position which is in the interests of the Celtic peoples, whether on linguistic, political or economic grounds.

This book includes separate chapters for each of the six Celtic languages, and a further chapter on Welsh in Patagonia, and Gaelic in Nova Scotia. It is no surprise that each is at different stages of the RLS GIDS and of language restoration in general.

Welsh/Cymraeg

Of the six Celtic languages Welsh remains the most intact in community use. While still not out of danger, Welsh may, like Catalan, Basque and Quebec French, achieve stability within the next two decades, provided it can hold its present ground and, equally important, go over to the offensive and attract new speakers in the urban south and among younger families, who must be persuaded to include Welsh in the child-rearing process. In short, stages 6, 5 and 4 are the crucial ones here. Wales has already also partly progressed to stages 3–1.

Among the greatest cause for optimism are the programmes launched by the statutory Welsh Language Board, financed by the Welsh Assembly Government, urging young parents to raise their children in Welsh, the expanded usage of Welsh-medium schooling (now about 20 per cent) and the establishment of a Welsh-medium television network. It remains to be seen if all these programmes can come together to get Welsh off life-support to a point where it is once again safely and securely occupying its rightful position as one of the two major community languages of Wales.

In the traditional Welsh-speaking communities of the Chubut region of Argentina, Welsh has largely retreated to the older (above 30) generations, so Welsh RLS here will be a matter of reaching out to the younger child-rearing generation, with a greater effort to strengthen Welsh language media and perhaps even focus on new Welsh-speaking communities.

Irish/An Ghaeilge

Although often written off as a lost cause in past decades, Irish is in fact, after Welsh, the Celtic language which is now coming closest to re-establishing itself in community life. The establishment of new urban Irish-speaking communities in Belfast and Cork makes it clear that the Irish language movement contains people who understand clearly the critical importance of community use and not merely school use of the language. The increase in Irish-medium schooling to about 6 per cent of primary students (in the Republic) and continued expansion of Irish-medium schooling in the North (in the Gaeltacht levels remain steady) has also strengthened the position of Irish but Foras na Gaeilge and Gaelscoileanna must realize that Irish-speaking students are not enough (there is reason to believe that they do not actually comprehend the life-or-death importance of new Irish-speaking communities, and Foras na Gaeilge, for example, does not at present support new Irish-speaking communities, although there is talk it may reverse this position). Within five years of graduation, most Gaelscoileanna children lose their Irish-speaking ability. Similarly, policies being pursued in Northern Ireland must also be re-examined (likewise for a lack of any substantial commitment to expansion of Irish usage in the community, in the family or anywhere else). The Official Languages Bill which has at last been passed into legislation by the Irish Government has already been assailed by even Foras na Gaeilge as insufficient. What is needed both north and south is:

- Recognition of the nature of the problem (need for community Irish)
- A commitment in principle to its achievement.
- The establishment of an action plan coordinating Gaelscoileanna, Foras na Gaeilge, Conradh na Gaeilge, Comhdháil Náisiúnta na Gaeilge, the Ultach Trust and other language bodies in the formation of new Irish-speaking communities around the country (stages 6 and 4) and new programmes to expand Irish in the workplace, as well as other areas such as higher education and the government (stages 2 and 1).

The Irish Government and language movement have yet to embark upon a path which could make Irish widely spoken again. Nevertheless, Irish today has about 414,000 or so functional-to-fluent speakers, so past and present policies have made a certain amount of progress but future progress must lay the foundations for the language's future survival and continuity.

Breton/Brezhoneg

Breton was, until recently, a very widely spoken language and in fact was the most widely spoken Celtic language as recently as 1960 (about 800,000 daily speakers) but has undergone catastrophic decline in both community and family usage and has seen Herculean efforts at revival in the past three decades. Despite an uncooperative French state, Breton-medium schools have been established (Diwan, Div Yezh and Dihun), Breton radio stations have been established, as well as a Breton language television service – Télé Breizh – and many initiatives have been launched by Ofis ar Brezhoneg/Office of the Breton Language, Skol Uhel ar Vro/The Cultural Institute of Brittany, and Kuzul Sevanadurel Breizh/the Cultural Council of Brittany which have established hundreds of adult literacy classes in Breton, posted thousands of new road signs in Breton, and launched other programmes to increase publishing in Breton and, most recently, the YA D'AR BREZHONEG programme (Yes to Breton) whose goal has been to increase the usage of Breton in business life and in the workplace and even in the civil service. Although the position of Breton is still serious, with the number of speakers having fallen to about 304,000 out of 4.1 million people in Brittany in 2003 and with the French Government fighting tooth and nail against every advance made by Bretons, the Breton language clearly has made progress, not just in the lower order 8–5 stages of the GIDS scale but also even in the higher order 4–1 stages. However, it must be said that in Brittany, unlike in the other five Celtic nations, the failure to establish a strong local Breton political party or voice is an issue which remains to be addressed and, some might say, is essential to any possible further progress for the Breton language. In short, Bretons continue to avoid facing the political question – a luxury they cannot afford.

Scottish-Gaelic/An Ghàidhlig

In the Middle Ages this language was the official tongue of a powerful, independent commercial and maritime kingdom in northern Europe, whose population in 1300 was over 90 per cent Gaelic-speaking. Today, in 2003, the Gaelic-speaking population has declined to less than 2 per cent and revival efforts seem, on the surface, to trail those in other Celtic nations. Clearly RLS efforts in Scotland face some serious challenges.

The implications for the Gaelic language of phenomena such as increased Scottish nationalism in the past decade are difficult to guess, as many Scots identify with the English and Scots languages rather than Gaelic, even if they are nationalistic (reminiscent of Navarese rejection of its Basque language heritage). In general, however, a rising tide lifts all boats, so it is not unreasonable to hope that devolved Scottish governments in the future will be more open to funding for Gaelic language programmes.

As far as the present state of the language is concerned, it is clear from the 2001 census (58,652 speakers) that the language continues to suffer erosion in the Western Isles and the western Highlands, until recently the stronghold of the language. Unfortunately, Gaelic is barely present in stages 3–1 of the GIDS scale and has only recently begun to break into education (stage 4). Stage 6 was never lost, while stages 8, 7 and 5 remain firmly planted, so the Scottish RLS scene is not as grim as some would think.

In Nova Scotia, belated efforts at Gaelic RLS are now underway through joint government and voluntary auspices. The challenge will be great. Spoken by 80,000 people in Nova Scotia in 1890, Gaelic in 1991 had only 452 speakers. Nevertheless, a recently released report, "Gaelic Nova Scotia", seems to have a grasp of the need to focus on such basics as pre-school in Gaelic, Gaelic immersion schools, greater media in Gaelic as well as adult literacy.

Cornish/Kernewek

As mentioned above, Cornish activists themselves regard Cornish as having advanced to stage 5 of the Fishman GIDS scale. Recent attempts to have Cornish included within the British Government's interpretation of the European Charter of Minority Languages have finally borne fruit and, at the time of writing, the UK minister of local regions is preparing to include Cornish in the Charter. Cornish, however, has made strides in the past century, despite a perpetual lack of government funding. Although Cornish has not been introduced into the schools, either as a subject or as a medium of instruction, it is considered a matter of time before this happens.[5]

Only when greater progress is made between stages 8–4, can Cornish try to break into stages 3–1, entailing greater use in business, higher education and government administration. Clearly, these are on the Cornish agenda. Another issue is the final adoption of one standard Cornish dialect. At present, three Cornish dialects are vying for supporters and scarce funds (*Unified, Common* and *Modern*). When the Cornish have decided on one dialect they will have surmounted an obstacle which has been a drag on their movement's progress.

Manx-Gaelic/Yn Ghailckagh

It will come as a surprise to many, but the Manx language movement is now on the cutting edge as far the Celtic language movements go. Indeed, because of the limited use of Manx in government (in the Tynwald or Manx Parliament to give one example), one could even say Manx is present at almost all eight of the Fishman GIDS scale stages. In September of 2002 the first Manx-medium school was opened, while, for many years now, Manx has been offered as a subject in the schools of the island. This progress has been due to the fact that a Manx Government administers the island. This fact has facilitated funding of Manx language initiatives, such as the appointment of Manx Language Officers and publishing of school texts in the language. Also, the census of 2001 has shown a sharp increase in the number of Manx speakers (in contrast to some other Celtic languages). Just how far the Manx Government is prepared to allow the language movement to go towards re-establishing a Manx-speaking society, remains to be seen. For now, perhaps Manx activists should focus their energies on greater home, school and community uses of the language (stages 8–4) where there is still plenty of room for improvement in any case, before tackling issues such as Manx in government and business (although these must be addressed eventually).

Table 1.1
Population and language statistics for the Celtic countries

Country	Population	Speakers of a Celtic Language	Percentage of Population
Alba/Scotland	5,062,011	58,652 (2001)	1.15%
Breizh/Brittany	4,123,795 (2004)	304,000 (2002)(est)	7.37%
Cymru/Wales	2,903,085 (2001)	659,213 (2001)	23%
Éire/Irish Republic	3,917,336 (2002)	339,541 (2002)	8.65%(est)
Ulaidh/N. Ireland	1,685,267 (2001)	75,125 (2001)	4.8%
Total Ireland	5,620,603	414,666 (2001)(est)	7.37%
Kernow/Cornwall	501,267 (2001)	500 (2002)(est)	0.01%
Mannin/Isle of Man	76,315 (2001)	1,689 (2001)	2.2%
Alba Nuadh/Nova Scotia	943,000 (2001)	415 (2001)	0.044%

II. The Brittonic/ Brythonic languages

Explanatory note

Three examples of Brittonic/Brythonic (or British) speech are examined in this volume: Welsh, Breton and Cornish. (A fourth British language, Cumbric, was spoken in north-western England and south-western Scotland until the 1300s.) British was the language of the ancient Britons, and was a member of the Celtic branch of the Indo-European family of languages. This branch had two divisions: the 'P' division, consisting of Gaulish and the British group, and the 'Q' division, consisting of dialects in Gaul and Spain, and the Gaelic or Goidelic group, which consists of Irish, Gaelic and Manx. Cornish remained in regular use into the late 1700s and has since been restored to some extent.

Both Welsh and Breton have continued in use to the present day. Welsh today is the strongest Celtic language numerically with 575,640 speakers being recorded in the census of 2001, with a further 222,077 possessing other Welsh language skills. Breton has diminished with about 304,000 speakers today according to the Office of the Breton Language.

i.) The Case of Welsh/*Cymraeg* in Wales

Colin Williams
University of Wales, Cardiff, and The Welsh Language Board

Rhagair

HEDDIW rydym ar drothwy cyfnod newydd yn hanes y berthynas rhwng yr iaith Gymraeg a'r wladwriaeth. Yn sgîl datganoli a mesur o ymreolaeth, mae Pwyllgor Iaith a Diwylliant y Cynulliad Genedlaethol yng nghanol arolwg eang iawn o bolisi tuag at y Gymraeg. Bydd y Pwyllgor yn awgrymu strategaeth genedlaethol a fydd yn talu sylw arbennig i alluogi pobl i ddefnyddio naill ai'r Gymraeg neu Saesneg ymhob agwedd ar fywyd cenedlaethol ac yn eu cymunedau – cefnogi Cymraeg fel iaith y teulu a'r gymuned – a darparu cyfleoedd i bobl ddysgu Cymraeg, a'i defnyddio. Yn yr un modd mae Pwyllgor Addysg y Cynulliad hefyd ar fin adrodd am y ffordd y mae'r llywodraeth yn bwriadu "Creu Cymru Ddwyieithog" oddi fewn i strategaeth y Cwricwlwm Cenedlaethol, addysg ôl-16, hyfforddi athrawon a strategaethau diwygiedig ELWa, ACCAC, y Cyngor Addysg Cyffredinol.

Erbyn diwedd y flwyddyn bydd canlyniadau cyfrifiad 2001 ar gael. Rhain fydd sail ystadegol ein cynllunio ond ni fyddant yn ddigonol. Felly mae Bwrdd yr Iaith Gymraeg wedi argymell y canlynol:

- Dylid gwneud y Gymraeg yn bwnc llorweddol i ystadegwyr y Cynulliad a'r Swyddfa Ystadegau Gwladol;
- Mae angen syncroneiddio data ar yr iaith Gymraeg gyda ffynonellau eraill;
- Mae angen cydweithio agosach rhwng y Bwrdd a'i bartneriaid a'r Cynulliad, a chyrff ac arbenigwyr eraill sydd yn dadansoddi data ystadegol, er mwyn sicrhau cynllunio ieithyddol holistaidd.

Mae gweithgareddau'r Bwrdd yn allweddol er mwyn sicrhau rhyw elfen o gysondeb yn y broses o lunio dyfodol mwy ffyniannus i'r Gymraeg. Dyma y blaenoriaethau:

- Cynllunio caffaeliad iaith: maes sydd yn cwmpasu trosglwyddiad iaith, addysg cyfrwng Cymraeg a dwyieithog as addysg gydol oes;
- Cynllunio defnyddio'r iaith: gyda phwyslais arbennig ar ddatblygu defnyddio'r iaith gan y sector preifat, marchnata'r iaith i bobl ifanc a datblygu gweithgarwch ieithyddol yn y gymuned, yn enwedig yng nghyd-destun y mentrau iaith;
- Cynllunio statws i'r iaith: maes sydd yn cynnwys hybu defnyddio'r Gymraeg mewn gweinyddiaeth gyhoeddus yng Nghymru;
- Cynllunio corpws: sydd yn cynnwys datblygu'r diwydiant cyfieithu a chysoni a safoni termau.

Wrth gwrs cynnig arweiniad yn y maes ydi cyfrifoldeb y Bwrdd, mater arall ydyw newid agweddau, ymddygiad a chreu cyfleoedd i'r cyhoedd. Ond os gwireddir hanner yr hyn a gynigir gan wahanol gyrff yn y maes, gan gynnwys cymunedau blaengar ar lawr gwlad, wedyn bydd defnydd y Gymraeg yn ehangu. Ond yn y pen draw, fel pob prosiect cenedlaethol, mater i drigolion Cymru gyfan ydi.

Am fwy o fanylion parthed syniadau diweddar y Bwrdd, gweler "Rhagolygon yr Iaith", darlith a draddodwyd ar ran y Bwrdd gan Gadeirydd y Bwrdd, Rhodri Williams, Caerdydd, 26/2/2002.

Cydnabyddiaeth

Dymunaf ddiolch i'r Wasg a'r golygyddion am eu caniatâd i ddefnyddio fy ngwaith a gyhoeddwyd yn gyntaf fel "Adfer yr iaith", G.H. Jenkins a Mari A. Williams (gol.), (2000) *Eu Hiaith a Gadwant?, Y Gymraeg yn yr Ugeinfed Ganrif*, Gwasg Prifysgol Cymru, Caerdydd.

Foreword

Today we stand at the threshold of a new relationship between the Welsh language and the State. Following devolution and a measure of self-government, the Culture Committee of the National Assembly for Wales is conducting a comprehensive review of the Welsh language. The Committee will recommend a strategy to realize the aims of enabling people to use either Welsh or English in all aspects of national life and in their communities – supporting Welsh as the language of the community – and for providing opportunities for people to learn Welsh and use it. Similarly, the Education Committee is due to report shortly on its recommendations for realizing the "Creation of a Bilingual Wales" within the revised strategies of the National Curriculum, the post-16 education sector, training, Welsh for adults, teacher training – ELWa, ACCAC, the General Funding Council.

By the end of this year we will have the full results of the latest Census Survey of 2001. Although this data will constitute the statistical basis for our planning, it will not be enough. Consequently the Welsh Language Board has recommended that:

- Welsh should be a cross-cutting theme for the Assembly's statisticians and the Office of National Statistics;
- There is a need to synchronise data about the Welsh language with other data sources;
- Closer co-operation is required between the Board and its partners and the Assembly, and other bodies and specialists that analyse statistical data, to ensure holistic language planning.

The activities of the Welsh Language Board are critical in determining the future success of the Welsh language. Here are its current priorities:

- Language acquisition planning: a field that includes language transmission, Welsh-medium and bilingual education and lifelong learning;
- Language usage planning: with particular emphasis on developing the use of the language by the private sector, marketing the language to young people, and developing language activities in the community, particularly in the context of Mentrau Iaith (see below, p65.).
- Language status planning: a field that includes promoting the use of Welsh within public administration in Wales.
- Corporate planning: which includes developing the translation industry and the regularization and standardization of terms.

Of course, the Board has a statutory obligation to provide professional leadership in this field. It is quite a different matter seeking to change attitudes, behaviour and creating new opportunities to use the language.

But even if only half of the current initiatives, including those communal enterprises working closest with the target groups, are realized, then the scope of Welsh will have been extended considerably. Yet, ultimately, as with all such national projects, it is a matter for popular assent and Welsh national conviction.

For more information on the Board's current thinking, see "The Prospects for the Welsh Language" a lecture delivered by the Chairperson of the Board, Meri Huws, Cardiff, 26/2/2002.

Reversing Language Shift: Wales

Introduction

The process of language revitalization or RLS (reversing language shift) is an exercise in social engineering requiring both determination and delicacy if it is to succeed in convincing recalcitrant or hesitant citizens that the acquisition of a non-dominant language is worth the effort. Normally, language planning strategies adopt a technical-bureaucratic discourse, as befits official government pronouncements. However, Joshua Fishman has encouraged students of reversing language shift to be far less objective and scientific when interpreting issues such as a commitment to the national struggle. He avers that "language is part of a felt moral sensitivity to the past and a felt moral dedication to the future that are but dimly and indirectly illuminated by the economic, political, demographic and historical data that "external" theories marshal in explaining socio-cultural phenomena."[6] Thus, in order to evaluate fully the experience of involvement within the Welsh language struggle, one would do well to move beyond statistics and political rhetoric and celebrate the wisdom of Waldo Williams's poetry or the cheeky joy of W. R. Evans's comic verses.[7]

I have described the history of reversing language shift in Wales as a struggle for survival, recognition and equality (Williams, 2000a). Although the infrastructural developments necessary to enable Wales to function as a bilingual society have been assembled, individual and social behaviour has yet to take advantage of the increased opportunities available. Consequently, the current challenge is to encourage the public's greater use of Welsh. This involves both greater institutionalization, i.e. ensuring that the language is represented in key strategic agencies of the State, i.e. the law, education and public administration, together with parallelism/normalization, i.e. extending the use of the language into the optimum range of social situations as a normal medium of communication in, for example, the private sector, entertainment, sport and the media.[8]

Historical context

Following the Edwardian conquest of Wales after 1282 AD, English colonial control turned to a form of shared power with the accession of the Welsh nobleman, Henry VII in 1485. His heir, Henry VIII, enacted the Acts of Union 1536 and 1542, which formally incorporated Wales into the legal and political realm of England. The Acts' most significant clause in terms of the future of the language was to exclude Welsh from official life and require all public officialdom that was transacted in the "principality" to be in English. State policy sought to develop an indigenous, Anglicized ruling class, which built upon the established practice of the Welsh gentry being incorporated within an English hierarchical stratification system. The practice of sending sons of the Welsh gentry to English public schools and of encouraging inter-marriage between landed families either side of the border accelerated this assimilation process. As Janet Davies has reminded us, "the process took at least 250 years and was virtually complete by the late eighteenth century. It had profound consequences. Linguistic differences reinforced class differences. Welsh culture, which had been essentially aristocratic, came into the guardianship of the peasantry and the "middling sort of people" – craftsmen, artisans and the lower clergy. As the inhabitants of the gentry houses ceased to speak Welsh, the system of patronage which had maintained the Welsh poets over the centuries collapsed, and the standardized Welsh they had jealously defended came into peril of deteriorating into an assortment of mutually unintelligible dialects" (Davies, 1993, p.23).

However, the same Tudor State also sanctioned the translation of the New Testament and Prayer Book by William Salesbury in 1567 and the complete Bible into Welsh by William Morgan in 1588.[9] This provided an elegant standard form of Welsh, which has provided the bedrock for subsequent linguistic accretions and is a key factor in interpreting the survival of Welsh.

Some degree of autonomous cultural reproduction was encouraged in the seventeenth century by the emergence of new religious movements, such as the Independents (Yr Annibynwyr) and the Baptists (Y Bedyddwyr), which paved the way for non-Established religious affiliations with their own social organizations, networks and denominational presses. Calvinistic Methodism dominated the next century with its emphasis on order, sobriety, piety and learning. The Methodist Church soon became established as the dominant religious force in large parts of the country. In the succeeding centuries, despite discrimination and persecution, dissenting religious groups flourished and encouraged a trans-Atlantic, Welsh-medium network of correspondents, journalists, teachers, social and spiritual interpreters that culminated in a period of late-nineteenth-century liberal radicalism during which the lasting values of modern Wales were formed.

Late-nineteenth-century Wales experienced a population explosion fuelling industrialization, urbanization and Anglicization. An unprecedented demographic growth was based on the mineral exploitation of iron and coal, together with steel and engineering production, which meant that bilingualism became a mass phenomenon. It was reflected in new codes of worship, of work, leisure and political beliefs, which were transmitted to an increasingly literate workforce by a mass media created by print capitalism. In the midst of this upheaval, the Welsh language was undoubtedly saved, according to Brinley Thomas (1959) and Glanville Williams (1971), because of the internal redistribution of a growing population consequent with industrial expansion. The Welsh, unlike the Scots or the Irish, did not have to abandon their homeland and language for employment abroad, particularly by emigrating to the New World. Consequently, the large-scale rural-urban shift was capable of sustaining a new set of Welsh organizations, which gave a fresh impetus to the indigenous language and culture, institutionalizing them within modernizing industrial domains.

This may be the principal reason why modern Welsh identity is more closely linked to the maintenance of language than the other Celtic cases treated in this volume. Welsh culture was not reliant on formal agencies and is reflected more through popular involvement in chapel-based social activities, choral festivals, Eisteddfodau – competitions in music, drama and poetry – a brass band tradition, miners' libraries, and early national sporting federations. These manifestations were as much a redefinition of indigenous Welsh culture as they were the sharpening of a distinctly Anglo-Welsh identity and tradition best represented in the literary work of

Dylan Thomas, Gwyn Thomas and R.S. Thomas. However, this mutually-dependent Welsh and Anglo-Welsh popular culture has heavily influenced the nature of urban Welsh-medium culture, for, unlike rural Wales, such changes were operative within a set of formal, English-medium public sector and commercial domains.

At the beginning of the twentieth century, English had emerged as the dominant language in Wales, primarily as a result of in-migration and state policy. Imperial economic advances and state intervention following the Education Act of 1870 and the Welsh Intermediate Education Act of 1889, bred a new awareness of English values, culture and employment prospects and gave a powerful institutional fillip to the process of Anglicization, which encouraged the process of transmitting Welsh identity predominantly through the medium of English.

Closer economic and administrative association with the rest of the UK followed the standardization of education and local government. Modernization reinforced English and denigrated Welsh. Refusal to speak Welsh with one's children was a common enough reaction to the status differential, which developed between the languages. How the masses welcomed this "liberation" from traditionalism and conservatism is best evidenced by the wholesale generational language shift in the period 1914-1945 (Pryce and Williams, 1988). English was perceived (and still is to a large extent) as the language of progress, of equality, of prosperity, of commerce, of mass entertainment and pleasure. The wider experience of empire-building, understandably, made acquisition of English a most compelling instrumental motivation, and the key to participation in the burgeoning British-influenced world economy. Added to this was the failure to use Welsh in the wide range of newer speech domains which developed in all aspects of the formal and social life of the nation. Whether by policy choice or the habit of neglect, Welsh became increasingly marginalized. It lost ground among groups most exposed to the opportunities of an improved standard of living in the urban culture of the south and north-east.

A prime vehicle of modernization was the rapidly expanding communication network, which intensified in the late nineteenth century. Social communication theorists stress the importance of physical and social communication in the development of self-conscious nations and in the process of cultural reproduction and replacement. In Wales, relative geographic isolation had provided some basis for cultural differentiation both within and between the socio-linguistic communities. However, the development of an externally derived transport and communication system served to reduce that isolation. Technology promised to overcome the friction of distance. The critical factors influencing the development of the transport system were defence and commerce, in that it was designed to facilitate through -traffic from England to Ireland via Wales. The main railway routes ran east–west through the centre and along the northern and southern coasts respectively, with branch lines penetrating the resource-rich hinterland, allowing the exportation of slate, coal and iron and steel products. This had the effect of integrating South Wales economically with the Bristol region, the Midlands and London, and North Wales with Chester together with the Lancashire conurbations focussed on Manchester and Liverpool. Wales's poorly developed internal road and rail system did not conduce to the creation of a nationally shared space and territorial identification, and led to post-1945 economic initiatives being located either in better served British regions or attracted to Wales largely as a result of government subsidies and regional development grants.

Rapid industrialization and the closer integration of Wales into the burgeoning state and its attendant Anglicized culture during the latter part of the nineteenth century resulted in massive language shift a generation later, during the period 1914–45.[10] As a consequence of both industrialization and modernization, political life in Wales reflected the radicalism of a working-class mass struggling for representation, equality of opportunity and decent working and living conditions for themselves and their dependants. At the turn of the twentieth century the majority of voting males supported the Liberal Party. It was dedicated to social justice, to educational and health improvements under statutory regulation, to the Disestablishment of the Church of England in Wales, and to Home Rule all round for the Celtic nations, particularly in Ireland. In the Welsh-speaking parts of Wales, Liberalism was a vehicle for cultural nationalism and for the development of a Nonconformist-influenced moral and social order. More prosaically, it was a mass movement within which ordinary people could achieve some degree of upward social mobility. Its strength lay in its ability to represent marginalized people and places, particularly those drawn from the Celtic periphery and from the burgeoning urban settlements that were under-represented in the Tory dominated shire counties and long-established market towns.

The foundations of the language movement were laid down during the period c. 1890 – c. 1945, although two quite distinct phases were involved. In the first, 1890–1914, Cymru Fydd and elements of the Liberal Party sought to mobilise aspects of Celtic nationalism to secure the national recognition of Wales. In the second period, c. 1921–39, Dissenting intellectuals and, more particularly, Plaid Cymru sought to anchor the fate of the language to the establishment of an independent nation-state. Though such ambitions always overreached the achievement, the campaign for recognition of the separate, national character of Wales was realized in the establishment of a range of national institutions and cultural organizations.

During the early part of the twentieth century, under its charismatic, Welsh-speaking Prime Minister, David Lloyd-George, the Liberal Party was arguably the most influential political party on the world stage, reflecting British Imperial power and interests. It was simultaneously the national party of Wales, advocating self-government at home, whilst enslaving more and more indigenous people abroad in the name of God, King and Country. In the Liberal heyday, Wales established a set of national institutions that paralleled those in Scotland and Ireland. These included the federal University of Wales (established 1883); the National Library of Wales at Aberystwyth and the National Museum of Wales at Cardiff, which were established in 1907; and the Church in Wales, which was created following the Act of Disestablishment in 1920. A variety of cultural movements flourished, such as Undeb Cenedlaethol Y Cymdeithasau Cymraeg (the National Union of Welsh Societies, formed in 1913) and Urdd Gobaith Cymru in 1922.

At the local level, the main conduit for spreading the Liberals' message of social reform and democratic representation was the Free Church or Nonconformist Chapel system which pervaded almost every settlement in Wales. The spectacular growth of the Nonconformist denominations following on from the Great Religious Revival of 1905 not only made Wales an outwardly more Christian society than hitherto but also influenced nearly every aspect of public behaviour and private life.[11] Both in literary and scholarly terms, Welsh popular culture owes a great deal to the opportunities for self-expression and publication afforded by the various denominations. Despite the ravages of secularization, the church and chapel system has long been a pillar of support for Welsh cultural maintenance and its impact even today should not be underestimated.

However, this impressive political-cultural infrastructure was still largely dependent upon external factors and it was soon concluded that the forces which militated against the reproduction of a Welsh culture could only be mediated by a form of genuine self-government or home rule.

In 1925 Plaid Genedlaethol Cymru (The Welsh National Party) was formed in Pwllheli by a small group of bourgeois intellectuals which included Saunders Lewis, a University lecturer and playwright, the Reverend Lewis Valentine, a Baptist Minister, and D. J. Davies, an economist. Their initial concerns were the preservation of Welsh cultural and spiritual values, primarily through the maintenance of a small-scale, predominantly rural, communitarian lifestyle. The nationalist movement sought to differentiate itself from political movements based upon imperialist or social class appeals. It sought to do so primarily through a series of prescient policy initiatives, mostly related to the restitution of Welsh as the national language. It is no exaggeration to claim that much of the language-related activity since the 1920s has been a playing-out of the agenda set by early Plaid Cymru leaders.

For the intellectual figures in the early language movement, culture, history and education were constant reference points.[12] Their collective search for identity was predicated on a platform of struggle, recognition and legitimacy, as realized in a plethora of social reforms and cultural initiatives, such as the establishment of Urdd Gobaith Cymru (The Welsh League of Youth) founded in 1922, in the development of the Welsh University and College sector, in the Disestablishment of the Church of England to become the Church in Wales in 1920, in the formation of Plaid Genedlaethol Cymru at Pwllheli in 1925, in the Tân yn Llŷn episode of 8 September 1936 when three leading Nationalists – Saunders Lewis, D. J. Williams and Lewis Valentine – set fire to buildings at the RAF bombing school in the Llŷn peninsula, in the presentation of a language petition to Parliament in 1941, and in the Welsh Courts Act of 1942 which eradicated the "language clause" in the original Act of Union of 1536 and gave limited statutory legitimacy to the use of Welsh in the courts of Wales.

The principal concerns of the original nationalist movements were the Welsh language, national identity and Christianity. The three aims of Plaid Genedlaethol Cymru in 1925 were all related to the promotion of Welsh.[13] It was only after 1932 that self-government was adopted as party policy as a means of achieving national self-respect and some semblance of autonomy. Although preoccupied with questions of cultural defence, the nationalist intelligentsia did not adopt a narrow conception of their predicament.[14, 15] Control of the local state apparatus, so as to make it more accountable and more reformist, was the principal goal. Early Welsh nationalists sought a redefinition of the evolving European order in moral, not in materialistic, terms. However, whilst in the main the intelligentsia turned to the Celtic realm for moral inspiration and to post-Civil War Ireland as an example of a successful national struggle, Plaid Cymru's president, Saunders Lewis sought his authenticity in the larger context of a European, Catholic and Latin civilization.[16] This was because he believed that medieval Europe possessed a unity of spirit and of law, which protected and nurtured small nations. Diversity could only be accommodated within a universal European civilization. In his seminal lecture "Egwyddorion Cenedlaetholdeb" [17] he outlined his conception of Welsh national history, which was to be influential in subsequent justifications, both of the language struggle and party strategy.

He argued, perhaps ironically, that it was nationalism which had destroyed the civilization of Wales, and of other small countries in Europe. In medieval Europe, individual cultures were nurtured and protected because their rulers deferred to a higher authority, for "every nation and king recognized that there was an authority higher than state authority, that there was a law higher than the king's law, and that there was a court to which appeal could be made from the State's courts. That authority was the moral authority, the authority of Christianity. The Christian Church was sovereign in Europe, and Church law was the final law."[18]

When state nationalism emerged in the sixteenth century, it ushered in the era of state building and tolled the death-knell of smaller national-regional cultures, for state uniformity could not tolerate cultural differentiation and ethno-linguistic challenges to its hegemony. Having usurped the moral Christian order, state authority inaugurated a programme of state-nation congruence in the name of the people, covering a systematic expurgation of minorities under a veil of democratic rhetoric which, in time, emphasized the principles of liberty and equality, if not always brotherhood, within the state's aegis. *Table 2.1* is a summary of Saunders Lewis's conceptualization of history.

Lewis sought to counterpoise state nationalism, which, he argues, emerged in the sixteenth century to challenge the universal moral order of the Church, with organic nationalism, which was a revised version of an earlier form of political doctrine developed under medieval Christendom. In order that his compatriots deliver themselves from the false consciousness of British imperialism and state nationalism, he advocated that they rediscover this pre-existent nationalism.

Nationalism was advocated as a necessary means by which Welsh culture would be nurtured within its own political institutions. The keystone of this culture was the promotion of the Welsh language, an issue that came to be central to the activities of Plaid Cymru between 1925 and 1974. Lewis justified the selection of Welsh as the critical battleground for political action because its continuance, despite centuries of state-inspired Anglicization, was proof of the Welsh having kept faith, so to speak, with traditional European values. At a time when Britain was acutely conscious of its role in maintaining a world empire, and of nurturing trans-Atlantic connections by virtue of its "special relationship" with the emerging super-power of the USA, Lewis sought to remind the public that there was a pre-existent Europeanness to be found in the history of these isles. He declared that Wales should "demand a seat in the League of Nations, so that she may act as Europe's interpreter in Britain, and as a link to bind England and the Empire to Christendom and to the League itself".[19]

Exaggerated though Lewis's claims were about the importance of the relationship between Wales and Europe, he did, at least, seek to challenge the Welsh into choosing between the Empire and the League of Nations. In this re-direction of Welsh politics, away from the Empire and towards contemporary Europe, Lewis set the tone for a long-standing debate within Welsh nationalism, the strains of which echoed until his death in 1985.[20] It concerned his drawing upon Catholic Europe, rather than Socialist Britain, for inspiration and his personal advocacy of social and political policy, for Lewis had converted to Catholicism and been received into the Roman Catholic Church on 16 February 1932.[21] Ostensibly radical, dissenting and Nonconformist, the Welsh populace (let alone his own party supporters) did not approve of his political convictions and personal style. The Nationalist Party was criticised for being elitist, intellectual, and unpatriotic because some members appeared to support quasi-Fascist movements in Europe.[22]

Lewis's successor as President of Plaid Cymru in 1945, Gwynfor Evans, reflected a more representative strata of Welsh nationalism, although his

Table 2.1

A summary of Saunders Lewis's interpetation of Welsh history (based on Lewis, 1926)

Roman Europe
Condition: unity enforced by a dominant Christian, Latin civilization which induced a European moral integrity
Result: minority peoples, though conquered, were elevated by sharing a powerful, civilizing tradition

---

Medieval Europe
Condition: the one and indivisible church exercising supra-national authority
Result: local cultural diversity nurtured and protected within a framework of spiritual and legal unity

---

Reformation Europe
Condition: successive challenges to the universal Christian order by individual and institutional interests
Result: Church authority denied; the King's sovereignty and writ established; the State replaces the Church as the supreme sovereign body, leading to confusion, disintegration, and the genesis of the State's drive towards unitary principles

---

Sixteenth-Century Nationalism
Condition: unification and integration sought within states by establishing one government, one language, one state law, one culture, one education, one religion
Result: "the triumph of materialism over spirituality, of paganism over Christianity, of England over Wales"

Contemporary Britain (1926)
Condition: imperialistic and Marxist challenges within an advanced industrial order
Result: a materialistic spirit of narrow and godless nationalism destroying the individuality of Wales

---

Prescription
The establishment of a central Welsh authority exercising self-government and guaranteeing the primacy of the Welsh language in all aspects of public life.

Source: Williams, C.H., 1988, pp.210–11

background was far from typical.[23] His Christian commitment to pacifism marked him out as a principled leader of his party, who earned grudging respect from his opponents for his consistency and strong moral demeanour, which he had displayed both in opposition to the Second World War and to the various state-sanctioned projects to harness Welsh resources for English metropolitan needs. In the post-war period, a large number of capital-intensive projects initiated by the state so as to provide water, hydro-electric power, etc. resulted in some Welsh communities being transformed and several Welsh valleys being drowned to provide water for English cities.[24] There followed a sporadic bombing campaign directed against symbolic targets and state property. Within this context, Evans, in 1973, was invited to deliver the Alex Wood Memorial Lecture, organized by the Fellowship of Reconciliation. He chose as his theme "Non-violent Nationalism" a concept which he had practised and preached all his life. Here Evans expounded on his conviction that "will, not force, is the basis" of popular social change, and demonstrated why the Irish adoption of violence as a means of resisting incorporation into the British state was tragically misguided. It is a persuasive argument for a small country so intrinsically incorporated within one of the world's major powers.[25] It is in keeping with the fate of many minority nations in the twentieth century, although it is not an inevitable fate.[26] Evans acknowledged that "if I thought violence could ever be justified in the pursuit of any social objective, it would be to secure freedom and full nationhood for Wales, the cause in which most of my life has been spent. But even this noble cause, on which the survival of the Welsh nation depends, does not in my view justify the use of violence".[27]

How the national movement, especially Plaid Cymru, developed these principles has been the subject of much debate and analysis.[28] Since the early 1970s, Plaid Cymru's justification for advancing the cause of national autonomy has been broadened to reflect a Wales in Europe manifesto. While recognizing the constitutional salience of the British context, the party has placed an increased emphasis on European commonalities and on working with other members of the Greens/Free Alliance group of the European Parliament. The party currently returns four MPs to the Westminster Parliament, all representing heartland constituencies, and usually claims the political affiliation of about 10 per cent of the Welsh electorate for parliamentary contests. Within the first term of the National Assembly

(1999–2003) it was the second largest party, with 17 of the 60 available seats, and senior figures in the party chaired several of the Assembly's key committees.[29] Currently, it retains its opposition party status, having returned 13 AMs in the May 2003 Assembly election.

A more focussed attempt to make Welsh an essential concern of public policy was the emergence of the Welsh Language Society in October 1962. Created, in part, in reaction to Saunders Lewis's seminal radio lecture, *The Fate of the Language*, broadcast on the BBC on 13 February 1962, the Welsh Language Society's primary aim was to have the Welsh language recognized and used as an official language, equal with English in all matters of state and local authority administration in Wales.[30] A longer-term aim was to effect a transformation in the Welsh psychology, to strengthen national consciousness and "to inject... a new reality into nationalism by bringing to light, through the language struggle, the hidden oppression in the relationship of Wales and England".[31] The Society saw itself as the radical, anti-establishment arm of Welsh nationalism, willing to take risks and to mobilize young people in defence of their threatened culture. In the initial five years there was little consensus over means and ends but under the influence of leaders such as Ffred Ffransis, one of the chief characteristics of the Society was the conscious refusal to engage in violence against persons, preferring to highlight the perceived structural inequality between Wales and the British state by engaging in non-violent direct action.

In keeping with Saunders Lewis's declared aim that the achievement of freedom was a prerequisite for the maintenance of a distinct Welsh culture, the Welsh Language Society was always self-consciously nationalist.[32] It is often argued that it was a conservative movement by fiat, for the early campaigns appeared to have little to do with the wider issues which animated so many of their cohort among the socialist, the international student, anti-apartheid and fledgling green movements.[33] In departing from the orthodox view, I have always maintained that major issues such as decolonization, social justice for beleaguered peoples and a programme for global economic equalization have figured strongly in the Language Society's justification for direct action to redress local injustices as part of a global pattern of social reform.[34] In emphasizing the local urgency of their plight, the Society's goals were internally consistent and recognisable to a Welsh audience. Society members felt that Plaid Cymru's insistence on social-political change through constitutional means was insufficient to redress the declining fortunes of the Welsh language. Thus, they began to advocate a policy of non-violent direct action, whereby language-related grievances might be publicized through acts of civil disobedience, which was largely justified by reference to the inspired examples of Gandhi, Martin Luther King and Gwynfor Evans. The leaders had quickly recognized the dependency of any government in Britain upon the mood of the electorate and had deduced that the consent of the governed has a profound effect on the formulation and discharge of the processes of political change. They thus hoped that a prolonged period of active pressure on the language front would force a change in government policy toward the legal institutionalization of the language, as being co-equal with English. The situation, which led to the decline of the language, was recognized as being complex. Whilst the Society's most appealing rationale in terms of invigorating the language movement was cultural in origin, members also saw themselves as forming a radical element within the broader nationalist spectrum.[35] Their answer to the crisis was that the Welsh language was the political weapon by which support for an independent, self-governing Wales would be mobilized. In many ways it was the only logical choice. Wales had no serious race question, unlike South Africa and the Southern States of the USA. It had no imprisoned dissident artists like Czechoslovakia and Hungary. But it did have equally pernicious threats in the form of a gradual extinction of a national culture by powerful, and attractive, external forces.[36] Plaid Cymru projected itself as the defender of Welsh language, culture and society, while the Language Society was perceived as a radical fringe group of young nationalists, whose reforming spirit had not yet been tempered by reality.[37] Consequently, the Society had great difficulty in impressing its claims on an unresponsive bureaucracy and adopted direct-action campaigning between 1963 and 1965, when the Society sought to persuade local authorities and public bodies to adopt a policy of bilingual service to consumers. In July 1963, the Society had announced an abstention from direct action in response to the establishment by Sir Keith Joseph, the Minister for Welsh Affairs, of a committee under the chairmanship of Sir David Hughes Parry to "clarify the legal status of Welsh Language and to consider whether changes should be made in the law".[38] In retrospect, it would appear to be an astonishingly accommodating response by the Society, but its adherence to its strategy of public persuasion carried the day. The pressure on public institutions was made in emotional, neo-spiritual terms, appealing to those in authority who had lost their proficiency in Welsh not to encourage the further decline of the language by not recognizing its place in the official transactions of the nation. The public institutions were seen as essential agents for the establishment of the conditions which would allow the remnant to use Welsh as a matter of course. Clearly, their appeals echoed the ideas of Saunders Lewis and Professor J. R. Jones, whose writings had provided a philosophical rationale for the existence of the movement. One of J. R. Jones's central themes, *cydymdreiddiad iaith a thir*, a form of "mutual interpenetration" between land and language, was consistently stressed by the Society's literature.[39]

As a consequence of a failed campaign to persuade the Post Office to adopt the language, and the relative lack of progress, a vociferous minority called for a reappraisal of the total strategy of non-violent direct action, arguing that it was an excuse for inaction, a form of weakness in the face of confrontation and, consequently, the Society was in danger of disintegrating.[40] In addition, it had still not convinced most of the target group of the legitimacy of their claims to speak as representatives for the Welsh language.[41] In 1971, the presence of over a hundred Welsh defendants in jail for language-related offences was an emotionally charged issue which was not helped by the publication of the 1971 census figures relating to the Welsh language, which indicated that the Welsh-speaking proportion had fallen a further 5.4 per cent in the preceding decade, from a figure of 26.06 per cent in 1961 to 20.84 per cent in 1971. This represented an actual population of some 431,245 Welsh speakers.

It is not an exaggeration to say that a Cultural Revolution has occurred in Wales since the launch of the Welsh Language Society.[42] The most successful campaigns concerned the introduction of a bilingual road-fund licence disc, the adoption of bilingual road signs and public information signs and a commitment to the increased transmission of Welsh-medium broadcasts. The broadcasting authorities had long recognized the need for an extension of Welsh-medium broadcasting, but had done little to implement such a conviction. Consequently, the Society's attacks on production equipment and occupation of broadcasting studios introduced an element of urgency into their deliberations.[43] Nevertheless, the introduction of Sianel Pedwar Cymru (S4C) in 1982 has heralded a new era, both in the opportunity for self-expression through Welsh and in the associated

Figure 2.1
Welsh speakers, 1961

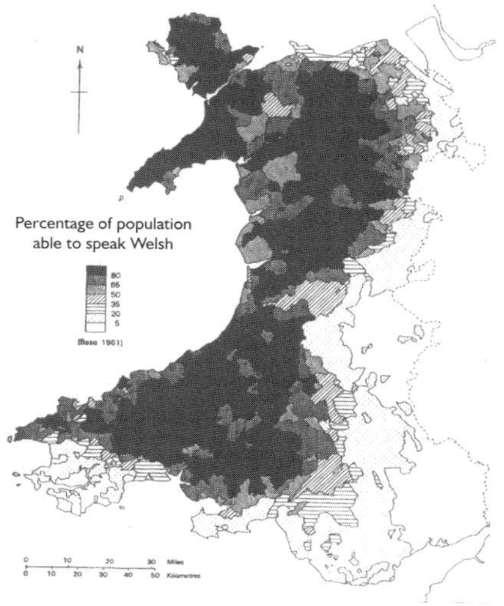

Figure 2.2
Welsh speakers, 1971

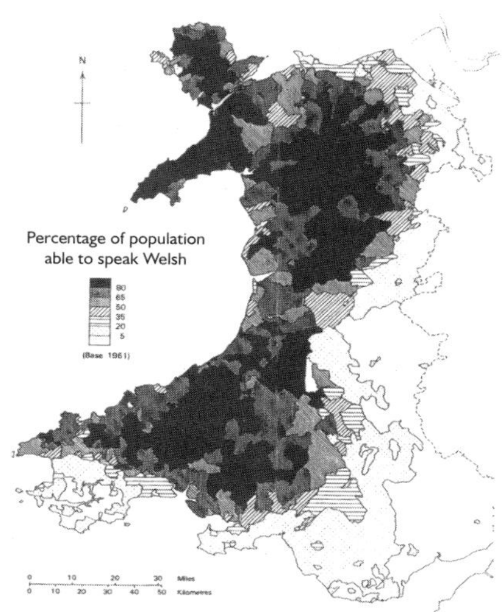

Figure 2.3
Welsh speakers, 1981

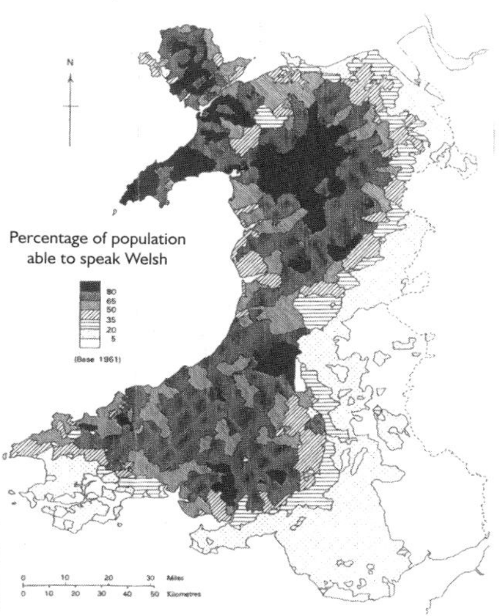

Figure 2.4
Welsh speakers, 1991

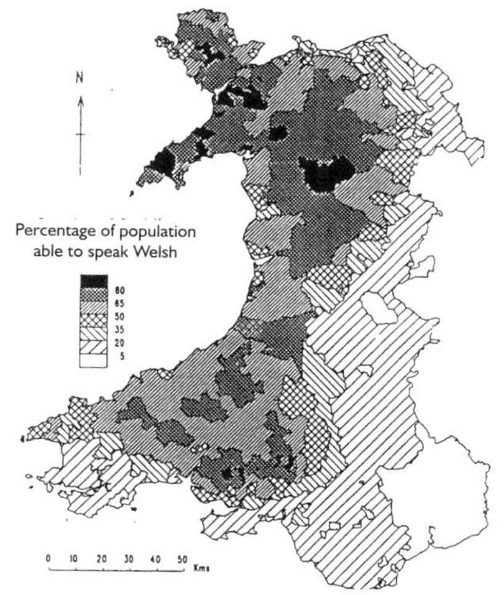

Source: University of Wales Press, 1993, The Welsh Language, Janet Davies

nurturing of talent, business and enterprise which an independent television and media industry creates. It has become one of the central pillars of cultural reproduction and offers a broader representation of Welsh within an increasingly plural society. Consequently, there are new opportunities for networking in Welsh, new challenges in maintaining attractive and informed Welsh-medium programmes, and a new instrument by which the communicative skills of linguistically mixed family and community structures may be boosted.

Despite the growth in numbers of young Welsh speakers and the increased opportunity to use Welsh in new locales such as a diversified workplace, there remains a structural tension as to how limited energies and resources might best be expended in support of Welsh as a community language. Those who advocate strengthening the core areas of Welsh constitute an honourable lineage of language campaigners, who, while pleased at the success of the bilingual schools initiative, the media developments and the greater status accorded to Welsh in official circles, nevertheless insist that unless sufficient attention is paid to the myriad problems of *Y Fro Gymraeg* we may not have an autonomous culture left to celebrate in the medium-term future. The most strident variant of this concern, the "Fortress Wales" mentality, is most closely identified with Adfer and its leading advocate was Emyr Llewelyn.[44] The foundation of this appeal is territorial control, initially through private economic and community endeavours, and only once this has been established, can one exert a legal recognition of the wider Welsh value system through formal boundary demarcation. The rationale for this drive, in the late-1960s to late 70s, was the economic and social undermining of rural Wales by undifferentiated state policies, the uneven effects of regional development and capitalist penetration, tourism and the growth of second-home-ownership. In reaction, a crisis mentality was being formed whose chief concern was the preservation of an extensive Welsh-speaking zone.[45] In the past few years, a modern variant of this acute anxiety over local control, housing policies, inadequate employment, in-migration and creeping Anglicization, has resurfaced in Gwynedd and Ceredigion with the formation of Cymuned (Community). This is a civil action interest group, inspired by the public protestations of a Plaid Cymru councillor, Seimon Glyn, against the influence of English in-comers in small, predominantly Welsh-speaking communities. The concern is that many of these new residents do little to integrate themselves within the local community. Their lack of commitment to learn Welsh and their insistence on the primacy of English in their dealings with the local state serves to undermine the presumption that Welsh is the locally dominant language, the norm, the default tongue. Coupled with this is a progressively spiralling housing market, which disadvantages local purchasers and forces younger families to move from the community to less attractive locations in market terms. As a consequence of these demographic forces, the socio-linguistic nature of many predominantly Welsh-speaking communities, including their social networks, is undergoing a profound transition. Remedial action has been halting, even though as a result of political pressure some professional attention is now being paid to the development of appropriate, economic housing and planning policies, as discussed below. Groups such as Cefn, Cymuned, Rhag, CYD have supplemented the Language Society in terms of a collective pressure to advocate reforms in the field of civil rights, housing, tourism, planning, education, a new Language Act, a Property Act and the promotion of the bilingual character of the National Assembly. In short, many within the wider language movement have adopted an ecological and holistic approach to language defence, and are no longer as reliant on either Plaid Cymru or Cymdeithas yr Iaith to advance their cause.

A century of demo-linguistic change

Welsh society is characterized by a unilingual majority and a bilingual minority, which is gradually benefiting from institutionalized recognition by the State. However, the Welsh language faces severe difficulties in being recognized as an essential language even within its own national territory, for the twentieth century has witnessed the collapse of the language as a popular medium of communication in most parts of Wales. In 1901, the census recorded 929,824 of the population as able to speak Welsh and 1,577,141 as able to speak English. Of these, 280,905 were Welsh-speaking monoglots, 648,919 were bilingual Welsh-English speakers, and 928,222 were monoglot English-speaking residents. English had become pervasive and advantageous in most spheres of life. Successive inter-censal decline has been the marked feature of census evidence on Welsh speaking. The peak was 1911, when 977,400 persons were returned as able to speak Welsh, 190,300 of whom were monoglots. The recent low (1991) was 590,800, hardly any of whom were adult monoglots. This represents a decline from 43.5 per cent of the population in 1911 to only 18.7 per cent in 1991, a loss of 24.8 per cent. Explanations for this decline focus on the inter-war period when stigmatization, a collapse in confidence and depression-induced population out-migration encouraged widespread language shift. 1921–39 was the crisis turning-point as a generation was denied the opportunity to learn Welsh. This reflected parental rejection of the language and an unresponsive education system, which reproduced imperial values, and attitudes, which deemed that Welsh was irrelevant in a modernizing world order. Such convictions have waned since the 1950s, for the rate of decline has been more moderate, reflecting a reversal in the language's fortunes. Changes between 1981 and 1991 were minimal, while the current bilingual population is growing. (*Table 2.2*)

Bilingualism represents a series of social choices for the *c.*590,800 individuals, who switch language by domain, by interlocutor and by preference, as the opportunity allows. The census does not probe deeply into the social context or use of bilingualism. An alternative is the Welsh Office Welsh Social Survey (1993) which contains details of 19,056 households interviewed between September and December 1992. The survey revealed that Welsh speakers represent 21.5 per cent of the total population. Disaggregating the ability factor, we find that the highest incidence is in the youngest age range, 3–15, with 32.4 per cent of the population fluent in Welsh. The proportion drops dramatically in the age range of 16–29, at 17.8 per cent, and for the 30–44 age range falls further to 16.7 per cent. For the age range 45–64 the figure rises to 18.7 per cent and reaches 24.2 per cent for those aged 65 and over. Clearly this bodes well for the future, but in- and out-migration, marriage patterns and a host of other reasons preclude any firm prediction that the youngest cohort will necessarily maintain their reasonable levels of fluency into adulthood. We need to know far more about the details of first- and second-language patterns and, in this respect, the survey revealed that 55.7 per cent of Welsh speakers considered it to be their mother tongue. They represent 12 per cent of the national population.

The balance between first- and second-language speakers is a delicate issue. Very often, one hears about the need to encourage language reproduction within predominantly Welsh-speaking families and communities. However, language production through the education system, rather than

Table 2.2
Proportion of the population speaking Welsh, by county, 1921–1991

	% of all persons speaking Welsh							% of all persons speaking Welsh only					
	1921	1931	1951	1961	1971	1981	1991	1921	1931	1951	1961	1971	1981
Wales	37.1	36.8	28.9	26.0	20.8	18.9	18.7	6.3	4.0	1.7	1.0	1.3	0.8
Clwyd	41.7	41.3	30.2	27.3	21.4	18.7	18.2	5.8	3.4	1.3	0.8	1.4	0.8
Dyfed	67.8	69.1	63.3	60.1	52.5	46.3	43.7	15.3	9.6	4.1	2.4	2.4	1.6
Gwynedd	5.0	4.7	2.8	2.9	1.9	2.5	2.4	0.2	0.1	0.1	0.2	0.1	0.1
	78.7	82.5	74.2	71.4	64.7	61.2	61.0	28.1	22.1	9.1	5.2	4.9	6.2
Mid Glam.	38.4	37.1	22.8	18.5	10.5	8.4	8.5	2.3	0.8	0.3	0.4	0.8	0.5
Powys	35.1	34.6	29.6	27.8	23.7	20.2	20.2	6.1	3.9	1.6	0.9	1.0	0.9
South Glam.	6.3	6.1	4.7	5.2	5.0	5.8	6.5	0.2	0.1	0.1	0.1	0.4	0.2
West Glam.	41.3	40.5	31.6	27.5	20.3	16.4	15.0	3.6	1.3	0.5	0.5	1.0	0.8

Source: Census, 1981, *Welsh Language in Wales*, p.50

Table 2.3
Welsh speaking characteristics by unitary authority, 1991–200

Speak Welsh [a]	Thousands	*Per cent* [b]
Isle of Anglesey	39	*60*
Gwynedd	77	*69*
Conwy	31	*29*
Denbighshire	24	*26*
Flintshire	20	*14*
Wrexham	18	*14*
Powys	26	*21*
Ceredigion	38	*52*
Pembrokeshire	24	*22*
Carmarthenshire	84	*50*
Swansea	29	*13*
Neath Port Talbot	23	*18*
Bridgend	13	*11*
Vale of Glamorgan	13	*11*
Cardiff	32	*11*
Rhondda Cynon Taff	28	*12*
Merthyr Tydfil	5	*10*
Caerphilly	18	*11*
Blaenau Gwent	6	*9*
Torfaen	9	*11*
Monmouthshire	7	*9*
Newport	13	*10*
Wales	**576**	***21***
National Park		
Snowdonia	15	*62*
Brecon Beacons	5	*15*
Pembrokeshire Coast	5	*23*

Source: Welsh Language Board, April 2003

language reproduction through local community socialization, seems to characterize the younger elements of the population. The Survey shows that only 27 per cent of the total Welsh speakers in the 3–15 age range considered Welsh their mother tongue. Presumably the remainder consider Welsh fluency to be a school-acquired competence rather than their first, instinctive language of daily life. Each successive age cohort recorded higher proportions of mother-tongue speakers, reaching a peak of 79.3 per cent for the 65-and-over group. Older age groups learned Welsh at home within the family and, for some linguists, this is a significant feature, for their use of Welsh is likely to be natural, richer, more idiomatic and colloquial than the rather formal, English-influenced style and patterning of younger Welsh speakers. This raises difficult questions of interpretation, for, in terms of vocabulary and domain confidence, the quality of Welsh spoken by the youngest group may be superior to that of the eldest group, even if it is less idiomatic. It may also be suggested that for the younger age groups their language loyalty/affiliation may not prove to be as resolute in the future, if Welsh represents for them a predominantly second language: a useful means of communication, rather than an automatic first choice language of expression.

The Social Survey also indicates that 368,000 (13.4 per cent) are fluent in Welsh. A further 94,900 (3.5 per cent) described themselves as able to speak quite a lot of Welsh, and 467,300 (17.0 per cent) described themselves as speaking only a small amount of Welsh. Thus, 930,200 (33.9 per cent) were able to speak a little Welsh and 462,900 (16.9 per cent) were capable of speaking a considerable amount of Welsh. These figures surpass the census figure of *c.* 590,800 Welsh speakers and offer a rough guide to the potential Welsh-speaking population able to use government services or consumer/audience opportunities. Of those who claimed to be fluent, 80.5 per cent came from families where both parents spoke Welsh, 7.2 per cent from where the mother was fluent, 4.6 per cent from where the father was fluent and 7.7 per cent from families where neither parent was fluent.

Welsh speakers, asked to describe one statement which best represented their current use of Welsh (*Table 2.3*), reflected interesting county variations, with former Gwynedd and Dyfed recording the highest usage of Welsh at 79 per cent and 71.1 per cent respectively. Lower proportions are recorded for Powys and Clwyd at 51.5 per cent and 40.9 per cent, while West Glamorgan and the amalgamated category of the three counties of the south-east record 32.8 per cent and 33.1 per cent respectively. Significantly, whilst only 6.9 per cent of fluent Welsh speakers in West Glamorgan would claim that they rarely use the language, as many as 15.3 per cent in the industrial south-east found little reason or opportunity to use Welsh (*Table 2.3*).

The most recent Census results for 2001 are encouraging. The Census question asked: "Can you understand, speak, read or write Welsh?" This is the first time the Census has collected information on understanding spoken Welsh and clearly enlarges the numbers capable of answering positively. Also, the question in 2001 was "Can you...?" rather than the "Do you... ?" as used in previous censuses.

The Census results show the proportions of those aged 3 and above who can understand, speak, read and/or write Welsh, irrespective of the level of ability or usage (*Figure 2.5*). 21 per cent – or some 580,000 – can speak at least some Welsh. Of these, 16 per cent can understand, speak, read and write Welsh, i.e. they have the full range of skills (but without any indication of the level of ability or usage). Five per cent can understand spoken Welsh only, i.e. have no other skills in the language. 72 per cent declared they had none of the skills in the language; conversely, 28 per cent indicated that they had a single skill or several skills.

In comparison with the 1991 data this is encouraging because, in both numerical and proportional terms, the trend of decline has been reversed. Thus the percentage of people able to speak, read and write Welsh has increased from 13.6 per cent in 1991 to 16.3 per cent.

Because the overall data have not been completely disaggregated, the Welsh Language Board has provided a minimum and a maximum threshold for the 2001 data. These figures display long-established spatial variations in the distribution pattern, with a marked preponderance of speakers in the north and west. Yet this is also the area where the greatest proportional decline in speakers has been recorded. If we use the minimum threshold, we see that several local authority areas have experienced decline over the past decade, particularly Anglesey, Gwynedd, Ceredigion and Carmarthen. Three factors account for this. The first is the continued out-migration from these areas of relatively young, well-educated Welsh speakers, many of whom relocate to the rest of the UK consequent to finding employment, a sizeable minority of whom relocate to south-east Wales. The second

Figure 2.5
2001 Census of Population, proportion aged 3 and over who can speak Welsh

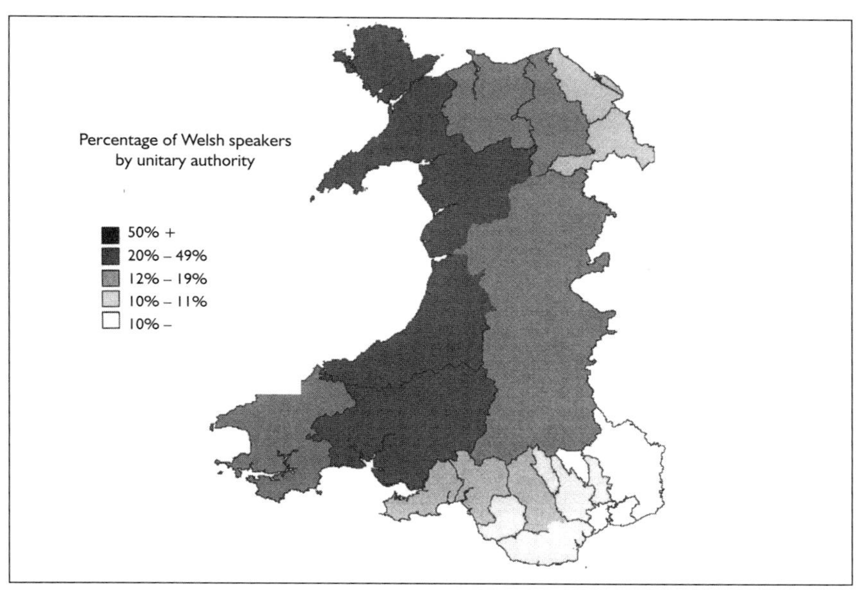

Census figures:	2001[a]	1991[b]	Change from 1991[c]
	per cent	per cent	percentage points
Gwynedd	69	72	-3
Isle of Anglesey	60	62	-2
Ceredigion	52	59	-7
Carmarthenshire	50	55	-5
Conwy	29	31	-2
Denbighshire	26	27	-1
Pembrokeshire	22	18	4
Powys	21	21	0
Wales	**21**	**19**	**2**
Neath Port Talbot	18	18	0
Wrexham	14	14	0
Flintshire	14	13	1
Swansea	13	13	0
Rhondda Cynon Taf	12	9	3
Vale of Glamorgan	11	7	4
Caerphilly	11	6	5
Torfaen	11	3	8
Cardiff	11	7	4
Bridgend	11	8	3
Merthyr Tydfil	10	8	2
Newport	10	2	8
Blaenau Gwent	9	2	7
Monmouthshire	9	2	7

Table 2.4
Proportion of Welsh speakers by local authority area, residents aged 3 and over, ranked in descending order of 2001 proportion

factor is the continued in-migration of non-Welsh speakers, either for employment reasons or as a consequence of having retired. The ensuing tension over issues such as house prices and property values, appropriate forms of economic development, community viability, increased drugs trafficking and levels of serious crime are linked in the public discourse to issues of local control and language rights campaigning. The third factor is that, unlike the 1991 census, university and college students in 2001 were registered at their college address rather than at their home address. Thus, in Ceredigion alone, over 9,000 students, the overwhelming majority of whom were non-Welsh let alone non-Welsh-speaking, were added to the local population. A similar trend was observed in the other areas of Anglesey, Gwynedd and Carmarthen. A positive, partial effect on the local Welsh-speaking population data would obtain for Swansea, Cardiff and Rhondda Cynon Taf.

A stage-by-stage analysis of current RLS efforts on behalf of Welsh[46]

Stages 8 and 7: Reassembling the language and bringing it to adults, some of whom once learned it and still remember it marginally, and others who never acquired it before

The vast majority of Welsh citizens do not speak Welsh, even though their English may be heavily influenced by Welsh idioms and forms of expression, yet clearly they feel themselves to be very Welsh. In previous times, when migrants moved into predominantly Welsh-speaking communities, local demographic and social pressure was sufficient to incorporate newcomers into Welsh-medium social networks. By the late sixties, this was no longer feasible as the *Fro Gymraeg* began to shrink. Thus, greater emphasis was placed on teaching the language to adults. Steve Morris (2000) has recently described how the seventies were a turning point for the part which adult education played in language acquisition. This decade saw the construction of a network of Welsh classes for adults developed through the extra-mural departments of the University of Wales, further education colleges, the Workers Education Association, local education authorities, numerous voluntary movements and courses offered

Table 2.5
Language attributes and household type

Household types		% of households
Type 1 All households		
(i)	Households without Welsh speakers	73.6
(ii)	Households with Welsh speakers	26.4
Type 2 Households with Welsh speakers		
(i)	Households wholly Welsh-speaking	53.6
(ii)	Households partly Welsh-speaking	46.4
Type 3 Household composition and Welsh speech		
a	Households wholly Welsh-speaking	
(i)	With children	10.9
(ii)	Without children	42.7
b	Households partly Welsh-speaking	
(i)	With Welsh-speaking children	18.9
(ii)	With non-Welsh-speaking children	5.8
(iii)	With no children	21.7
Type 4 Household size, composition and Welsh speech		
a	Households wholly Welsh-speaking	
(i)	With children	10.9
(ii)	Single-person households	21.3
(iii)	Without children	21.5
b	Households partly Welsh-speaking	
(i)	Households with Welsh-speaking children – single speaker	6.2
(ii)	Households with Welsh-speaking children – more than one Welsh speaker	12.7
c	Households partly Welsh-speaking but with non-Welsh-speaking children	
(i)	Single Welsh speaker	4.9
(ii)	More than one Welsh speaker	0.9
d	Households partly Welsh-speaking without children	
(i)	Single Welsh speaker	18.6
(ii)	More than one Welsh speaker	3.1

Source: Aitchison and Carter, 1997. Each type is a successive division of the previous type, thus Type 2 is a subdivision of Type 3. Each Type (1-4) therefore sums up to 100.

through the media. A turning point was the establishment of the first "Wlpan" courses held in the early seventies in Cardiff and Pontypridd in South Wales and Aberystwyth in Mid Wales (Rees 1974 and James 1974). This was modelled on intensive teaching methods developed in Israel which sought to linguistically – and culturally – assimilate non-Hebrew-speaking Jewish incomers and to ensure that Hebrew would be the main language of the new state (Crowe 1988, p.17). Pioneers in the field, such as my former colleague, the late Chris Rees of the University Centre for Teaching Welsh to Adults in Cardiff, adapted the intensive methods of the "Wlpan" course which was based on the following principles: (i) intensive, functional-structural drilling, (ii) emphasis on oral skills, (iii) emphasis on Welsh as the principal teaching and class language, (iv) attending classes five times a week for a period of three to four months at a time. It is only after fully mastering the basic principles and patterns of the oral language that students move on to the formal written language. Morris avers that this development was a critical step forward in the organization of Welsh for adults in Wales, giving a better opportunity for students to succeed in learning to speak basic Welsh in a comparatively short period and enabling them to use it like first-language speakers.

A general provision for adults therefore evolved in Wales, whereby the intensive course provision was – on the whole – the responsibility of the departments of adult continuing education in the University of Wales and the University of Glamorgan and the once-a-week provision was located in the further education colleges, local education authorities and various other providers. This situation was to some extent formalized during the mid-nineties when the Further and Higher Education Funding Councils for Wales, having undertaken a comprehensive review of Welsh for adults provision, gave responsibility for planning that provision and formulating development plans to eight consortia, broadly based on the county boundaries prior to local government reorganization in Wales in 1996. In general – although this has not always been the case in all parts of Wales – there is a holistic provision, where the adult student can choose at what pace she/he would like to study, and at which level they should begin. Consortia were also charged with ensuring adequate systems of educational guidance and support for those unsure of where they should "fit in" or how to progress. A structure and system of quite specific progression routes has evolved and developed, in addition to nationally recognized systems of accreditation of the various levels available. Yet the system remains inadequate, poorly funded and without strategic leadership.[47] ELWa is currently attempting to restructure the sector, and the first results of its reforms should be in place during 2004.

In the past, a lack of clear Welsh Office or National Assembly planning in the field of Welsh for adults and devolvement down through quangos – quasi-autonomous non-governmental organizations – such as the Funding Council and the Welsh Language Board, has militated against the full realization of the potential of Welsh for Adults. Fragmented responsibility for this area continues to undermine the development of a comprehensive adult immersion programme in Wales and its location within a coherent language planning policy for the country. Morris argues that this is in stark contrast to the Basque system, where HABE – the Institute for Literacy and Re-Basquization of Adults – is located with those responsible for Language Planning, Culture, Promotion of the Basque Language and Linguistic Normalization programmes in the Department of Culture of the Basque Autonomous Community (Gardner, Puigdevall i Serralvo and Williams, 2000). Where coherent planning in the field of Welsh for Adults does exist in Wales, it is primarily at the level of those immediately responsible for the delivery of the provision, i.e. the tutor/organizers at local level, who work together on an all-Wales level with the national officer for Welsh for Adults who is located within ELWa. The WLB has demonstrated a commitment to tackle questions such as lack of basic research on the motivations, aspirations, drop-out rates of adult Welsh learners and their chances of subsequently integrating into a series of Welsh-medium social networks. Thus, it is likely that this stage of RLS will receive far more attention and resources than hitherto has been the case.

Stage 6: Establishing the vital linkage with youth, family, neighbourhood and community

As has been noted elsewhere in this volume, family and community life are the cornerstones of any language restoration efforts. For decades, this activity has been largely untrammelled by formal language planning considerations. Nevertheless, there is acute cause for concern and direct social intervention in favour of reversing language shift because:

1) In many families where only one parent can speak Welsh, the children are unable to speak it.

2) A large percentage of children who complete primary education as first-language Welsh speakers commence their secondary education as second-language Welsh speakers and take their curriculum through the medium of English.

3) The Welsh Language Board's commissioned surveys show that more than forty per cent of Welsh-speaking adults lack confidence in using the language, and therefore use it infrequently.

4) During adolescence, many bilingual teenagers use the language less frequently as they grow older (though this trend may be reversed in later life).

5) Geographically, the Welsh language has tended to decline by a westward movement, with many communities lessening in their everyday use of the Welsh language.

Family/household composition

Language survey data suggest that social context, family language transmission and exposure to formal bilingual education are key factors in language reproduction. Yet community and family are less powerful agents of language reproduction than they were previously. Analysis of family/household composition patterns by Aitchison and Carter (1997) reveal significant and possibly damaging trends. Their analysis of SARs data shows that an extremely high proportion of Welsh speakers is linguistically isolated within their home environments. *Table 2.5* describes a nested hierarchy of four types of households, based on the language ability of household members. A basic distinction was drawn by Aitchison and Carter between Type 1(i) – those households that have at least one Welsh speaker (defined as "Welsh-speaking households"), and Type 1 (ii) – those that have no Welsh speakers. Twenty-two per cent of all households belong to the first of these two types, but over half (51 per cent) of the households contain only one Welsh speaker within them and many of these are elderly persons living alone. This does not bode well for the future.

A second distinction is that between households which are wholly or partly Welsh-speaking, Types 2(i) and 2(ii), just over half of Welsh-speaking households are wholly Welsh-speaking (54 per cent) but they represent only 14 percent of all households in Wales. Wholly Welsh-speaking households can be further sub-divided into those with and those without children (aged 3-17 years) – Types 3a(i) and 3a(ii). Aitchison and Carter (1997) aver that such a pattern is disconcerting for Welsh, as the data show that a very high proportion of such households have no children within them; furthermore, almost half are single-person households (Type 4(ii)). Similarly, of partly Welsh-speaking households, nearly two thirds (64 per cent) have just a single Welsh speaker (Types 4a(i), 4b(i) and 4c(i)), the majority of whom are in households which have no children. Encouragingly, 41 per cent of the households that are partly Welsh-speaking have one or more children who are able to speak Welsh. More sobering is the realization that some 70 per cent of the Welsh-speaking households have no Welsh-speaking children within them. Welsh households are, in the main, linguistically fractured and structurally diverse in composition. Despite this decline, it is possible to argue that conscientious efforts to erode elements of fragmentation have been successful. For example, the Welsh Language Board's Strategy for the Welsh Language (1999) summarizes recent achievements as follows: "The Welsh Language Act of 1993, the Mentrau Iaith (*see below*), the spread of bilingual education at primary and secondary level, Welsh as a compulsory subject in the National Curriculum, the vitality of movements such as Mudiad Ysgolion Meithrin, Urdd Gobaith Cymru, local and national eisteddfodau, Welsh language schemes, increasing use of bilingualism and business and the economy are just a few of the many examples where language planning has successful bucked the trend of downward shift."

Community language revitalization

A unique experiment in Wales concerns the development of community language enterprise agencies, known as Mentrau Iaith. There are now 23 Mentrau Iaith and several more in the process of being established. The original Mentrau Iaith, dating from 1991–1993, were established in predominantly Welsh-speaking communities. Their aim is to stimulate the development of Welsh within a wide social context, and one might almost define them as community regeneration movements with a linguistic cutting edge. They are funded mainly by the National Assembly through the Welsh Language Board, which in the late nineties amounted to £1.3 million per annum, together with some ancillary funding by Local Authorities, which amounted to £310,384 per annum. They provide one model of interventionist language planning at the community level. As all have

Figure 2.6
Welsh-speaking population percentage change, 1991-2001

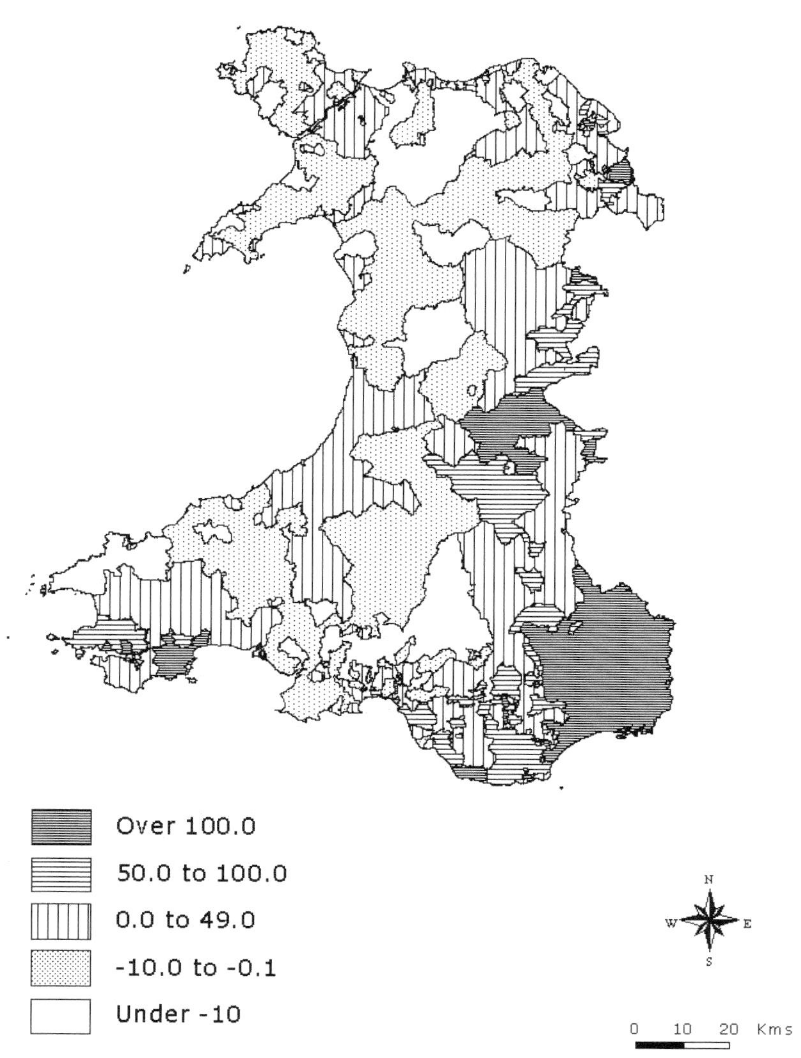

Source: Y Lolfa, 2004, *Spreading the Word,* Aitchison and Carter

Figure 2.7
Percentage population able to speak Welsh, 2001 proportion

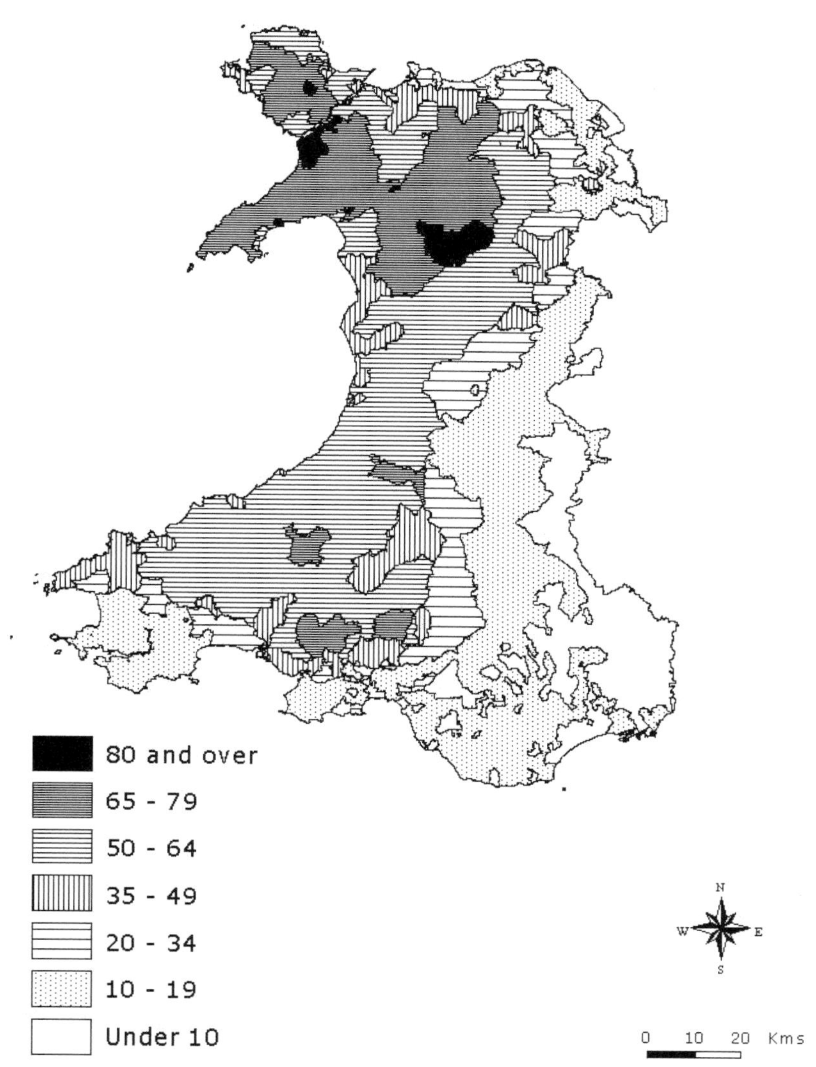

Source: Y Lolfa, 2004, *Spreading the Word*, Aitchison and Carter

Figure 2.8
Percentage population with knowledge of Welsh, 2001

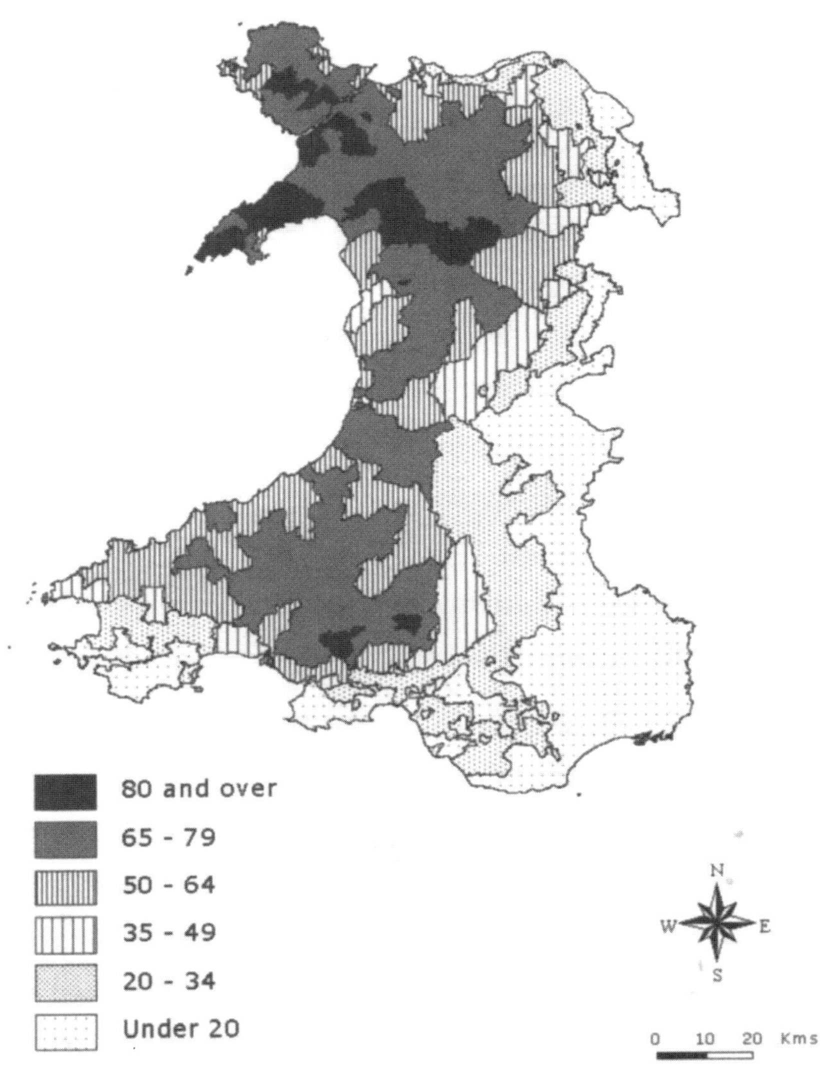

Source: Y Lolfa, 2004, *Spreading the Word*, Aitchison and Carter

been established within the past decade, it is difficult to measure their long-term impact on language use, although the WLB has preliminary evidence on such trends through its commissioned reviews in this field (Williams and Evas, 1997; Iaith Cyf, 2000).

Two compelling reasons for supporting Mentrau Iaith are that:

- In situations which are characterized by strong language potential but a weak sociolinguistic network, they offer a significant socio-psychological fillip for Welsh maintenance in contexts which would otherwise lead to fragmentation;
- In respect of their remit as local language planning bodies, they can function as a focus to create a new set of partnerships between the central government in the form of the National Assembly, the Welsh Language Board, local government, statutory public bodies, health trusts and a variety of other voluntary agencies and private companies, so as to extend the domains within which it would be possible to use Welsh.

Mentrau Iaith have a significant advantage in that they can shape a new role for Welsh in hitherto limited domains, without constituting part of the official administration of any district.[48] This relative autonomy enables the Mentrau to initiate novel and pioneering forms of encouraging the use of Welsh, and to take advantage of successive opportunities as they arise. However, in order to maximize this autonomy, Mentrau have to display a considerable degree of political acumen and inter-personal skills. As such, they may operate and be perceived as highly respected coordinating bodies, without necessarily accruing any political status or power. As currently constituted, Mentrau Iaith will continue to depend on other, more established agencies both for their existence and for their shared success. However, as they seek to extend their remit and co-operate with others within the system, they will have to be wary of being assimilated and of losing sight of their original linguistic focus.

The great strength of Mentrau Iaith is that they seek to serve the needs of the local community, but that increasingly they do so within an agreed national framework. Their success, however, raises a new round of questions. The first is whether or not one should establish a specifically Language Enterprise or a broader Community Enterprise. The second is whether or not the Mentrau Iaith should be temporary adjuncts to other community initiatives. If a Menter is to be a pioneering, interventionist agency, created so as to change expectations, create new networks and enable communities to regain ground which they have lost in linguistic terms, does it follow that any Language Enterprise should be a short-term or a medium-term agency? Does it follow that other agencies, which seek to improve the situation of Welsh through improving the sociolinguistic nature of the community, should also become permanent entities? Should such entities be primarily community enterprises or economic enterprises or a combination of both? Or should a model be developed, which is closer to that of an agency charged with the coordination and encouragement of Welsh-medium activities initiated by others?

It follows that a Menter Iaith should encourage the community to appropriate the language, including transferring responsibility for its continued survival back to community volunteers.[49]

The prime aim of the Mentrau Iaith is to normalize the Welsh language. Currently the Mentrau Iaith and their partners are seeking to refine their national framework and core mission, based in part on the Community Language Planning Report (Williams and Evas, 1997) recommendations that Mentrau should undertake several of the following tasks depending on the exigencies of the local situation:

- urge and encourage community ownership of the language, together with a transference of responsibility for it back to volunteers and the Menter's community partners
- by means of social and leisure activities, increase the opportunities available for people to use Welsh
- work for the promotion of Welsh in the community, through co-operation with movements, institutional representatives and other individuals at local and national level
- raise the profile of Welsh in business in the local area
- promote bilingualism in the workplace
- encourage Welsh speakers to use the language and to make use of existing bilingual opportunities
- improve the command of fluent speakers
- regain uncertain speakers, or those who have lost their Welsh for whatever reason
- offer practical assistance to adult learners and pupils who are

learning Welsh as a second language

- assimilate new speakers to the Welsh-medium community and inform the mother-tongue speakers about their needs
- lobby training agencies to prepare professional bilingual and language-friendly materials
- disseminate information about local Welsh-medium education and training
- if appropriate, promote issues which will lead to local economic development.

Consideration should also be given to several administrative issues when planning and launching a new Menter Iaith:

- an appropriate management structure for each new situation;
- a robust financial plan for the likely life-span of the Menter (initially some 2-5 years would seem appropriate)
- practicable formulations as to how to "normalize" the Mentrau Iaith, so that they gradually lessen their dependence upon government direct grant as they seek to become self-sustaining agencies, genuinely working within the community they serve and from which they sprang
- detailed consideration of the target area's networks, together with a consideration of the sociolinguistic nature and wishes of those who might be described as "the invisible Welsh speakers" i.e. those citizens who currently do not constitute an element of the existent Welsh-medium networks
- consideration of the role and possible efficacy and/or baneful effects of recent forms of telecommunications in maintaining newer networks
- consideration of the attractions that would accrue, following the establishment of cultural resource centres, which would not necessarily constitute an integral part of the Mentrau: they could be an additional element, in which case the element of co-operation in any proposed relationship should be stressed
- consideration should be given to convening a series of seminars in association with the agencies, the local authorities and disciplinary

specialists in order to discuss and evaluate the experience gained hitherto

- preparation of an information pack which would review the concept of community planning; provide an overview of the strategies and efficacy of the current Mentrau; offer examples of successful and unsuccessful features together with a detailed interpretative account; give an outline of the probable annual investment, so that all decisions are made upon a realistic basis.

The Strategy of the Language Board (1999) gives a prominent place to the extension of the Mentrau. The Strategy maintains that Mentrau Iaith "are becoming highly effective means of engineering bespoke language planning, tailored to the needs of the communities they serve. They are achieving much in terms of the marketing of the language and empowering Welsh speakers and revitalizing the use of the language in the communities. We regard the development and expansion of the work of the Mentrau Iaith to be a priority". Recent increases in the WLB's annual budget have allowed it to plan two new Mentrau Iaith by the end of 2004.

In March 2001 the WLB committed itself to the establishment of a Community Language Planning Partnership involving all the major players, and sought to implement most of the recommendations relating to training, a national database, advice and guidelines and monitoring, as suggested by the two strategic reports it had commissioned from specialists in the field (Williams and Evas, 1997, 1998; Jones and Ioan, 2000).

Language action plans

A recent addition to the range of planned activities are the Language Action Plans which operate in more localized bilingual areas where there has been a recent sharp decline in the proportion of people who speak Welsh. These are aimed at drawing together local people and several of the WLB's partners to facilitate the use of Welsh locally. By 2004 it is intended that eight such LAPs be established. The first Language Action Plan was developed in the Fishguard area during 2001–02 in partnership with Menter Iaith Sir Benfro. Five other LAPs operate in Ammanford, Corwen, Ruthin, Pwllheli and Pen Llŷn, and in the present financial year, 2003–04, LAPs will be established in Llanrwst, Cardigan and Newport.[50] The Newport Area Plan is an important experiment, targeting as it does an area of significant potential, which hosted the National Eisteddfod in 2004.

LAPs mirror, at a local level, the initial motivation of the Mentrau Iaith, namely to empower local communities to revivify their Welsh language networks. The WLB defines its own role as "to act as a catalyst to bring local people and organizations together in order to establish a dynamic partnership that gives local people the opportunity and the ability to recognize the linguistic needs within their communities, together with the influence to make decisions and take actions that promote the use of Welsh" (WLB, 2003).

An important by-product of these Plans is to strengthen the practical co-operation at the local level between the Board and its main partners, especially the Mentrau Iaith together with the Urdd, Mudiad Ysgolion Meithrin and the Young Farmers. The details of such operations may be gleaned from a snapshot view of the activities of the Fishguard LAP during 2003:

- opening new Cylchoedd Ti a Fi (parent and toddler groups) in Fishguard, Mathry and Letterston. A further Cylch Ti a Fi is about to open in Goodwick and a Cylch Meithrin in Fishguard
- continued support for the work of the Language Unit at Ysgol Bro Gwaun (formerly Fishguard High School) and to the teacher's liaison with local parents
- developing the work of the Twf project in the area, including the provision of Welsh taster classes for young parents
- establishing an *Aelwyd* of the Urdd which meets regularly
- organizing fun days and sports events for local children of primary school age
- the local comprehensive school launching its new name, Ysgol Bro Gwaun, and an increase in the numbers studying subjects through the medium of Welsh
- support for the local CYD branch to organize new social events for learners to practise their Welsh
- organizing gigs with Welsh-language bands and supporting other forms of entertainment, e.g. the Wes Glei quiz nights held in local pubs
- increasing the profile of Welsh among local businesses through

distributing business packs, organizing seminars, and through the development of the Welsh B&B Scheme

- contributing to relevant socio-economic initiatives, e.g. the Fishguard and North Pembrokeshire Regeneration Plan (WLB, 2003).

The Board recognizes that it is critical that the LAPs be evaluated both in terms of the effective means of measuring language use at the community level and also in engaging the community itself in the evaluation process as a core and continuous activity under the Plan.

Community development capacity building is realized through raising the awareness of the linguistic situation in the area, the networks where Welsh is used, organizations that help maintain the use of Welsh or which have a responsibility to treat the language on a basis of equality, and the specific social networks where the need to act is most critical in order to safeguard the future of Welsh as a social and community language. This is achieved primarily through the consolidation of the activities of the Board's partner – organizations. The WLB recognizes that "where the responsibility for maintaining social networks and opportunities to use Welsh is solely in the hands of organizations, and where there is not a sense of shared ownership between organizations, service providers and the community, the foundations for the future use of Welsh as a social and community language are weak and untenable" (WLB, 2003). The Board is also conscious that it must develop usage planning through a number of marketing initiatives and projects aimed at increasing the use of Welsh in areas such as the private sector and the workplace. Again, the key priority areas are the private sector, young people, and persuading Welsh speakers to use the language in every aspect of their lives.

In the field of status planning, the Board's main efforts are concentrated on the statutory work on Welsh language schemes, which increases both status and opportunities.[51] A second growth area has been the provision of Welsh-medium software in Information and Communications Technology.

In the field of corpus planning, the Board coordinates projects in the areas of standardization of terminology and place-names. It also provides core funding to the Association of Welsh Translators and Interpreters, and is advizing government on the regulation of the translation profession.[52]

Stage 5: The attainment of literacy, independent of the public education system

In the past, it was the various religious and charitable foundations which promoted literacy in Welsh. Today, a more linguistically self-conscious focus is the Welsh for Adults sector discussed under Stages 8 and 7. This sector operates through Wlpan and related schemes, which are geographically widespread and reasonably well subscribed. These, in turn, often feed Welsh clubs and social centres, which may have sport, folk dancing or music as their focus but offer a wider entree into the indigenous culture. The cutting-edge of such classes is the provision made for non-Welsh-speaking in-migrants and their children, who may attend Language Centres designed to speed up their integration into the local community, and literacy is certainly a prime element of their instruction. However, as in most unbalanced bilingual countries, there are severe difficulties in reconciling the rights and obligations of indigenous citizens with those of incomers, many of whom are antagonistic or hostile to the legal requirement that their children attend a bilingual school.[53]

Stage 4: Education in Welsh and learning Welsh at school and at other institutions

Education, the bedrock upon which the language movement has flourished, has fulfilled five functions.[54] It has legitimized Welsh bilingualism as a social phenomenon within this most critical agency of socialization.[55] Secondly, it has developed the value of bilingual skills in a range of new domains, especially in terms of meeting some of the demands of the burgeoning bilingual economy and public-sector labour market. Thirdly, it is a focus of a national project of identity reformulation. For many engaged in the language struggle, education was the principal focus and justification for their involvement. For such individuals the advancement of Welsh-medium education was both a personal and a national cause and not only an extension of state educational policy, the more so as it required tremendous energy, conviction and perspicuity in arguing the case for the provision of bilingual education, often in the face of a hostile and unsympathetic response from politicians, local authorities, fellow-professionals and many parents.[56] Fourthly, the Welsh-medium educational infrastructure, from the nursery school level right through to the university sector, provided a series of distinctive, interlocking socio-cultural networks which validated and reinforced developments at each level in the hierarchy. This was crucial in the cultivation of a sense of national purpose for professional bodies such as Undeb Cenedlaethol Athrawon Cymru, Mudiad Ysgolion Meithrin, and for pioneering local education authorities such as Flintshire, Glamorganshire, and since 1974, for Gwynedd Education Authority, which has had the most complete bilingual system of all local authorities.[57] Fifthly, as bilingual education has been both academically and socially successful, it has served as an additional marker of the country's distinctiveness within both a British and an international context.

The schools' role in reproducing Welsh language skills has increased following the reforms of the 1988 Education Act which insisted that Welsh be a core subject in the National Curriculum.[58] A wider range of subjects including Maths and Science, Design and Computing are now capable of being taught through the medium of Welsh. Consequently, a far greater number of pupils are exposed to the language and culture of their homeland, and this may serve to reduce somewhat the latent tension which has long existed between fragments of the two language communities. However, such reform also requires a huge investment in teachers and resources to be successful. In the Further and Higher Education sectors there is a wide range of vocational and non-vocational courses available to full- and part-time students, even if the numbers involved within any particular course are small. Even so, the trend and direction of change is significant, for it extends both the domain use and practical utility of bilingualism in society.

The use of Welsh

From 1990–97 the proportion and number of pupils in formally designated Welsh-medium primary and secondary schools had grown very slowly. Of the 1,718 schools in 1990, designated Welsh-medium schools where Welsh was the sole or main medium of instruction accounted for 25.9 per cent (445) of the total. The number in this category had risen slightly to 26.7 per cent, (449) schools by 1997. However, it is in the non-conventional Welsh-medium sector that the most significant changes have been recorded. In 1990, 50.7 per cent (870) of schools had classes where Welsh was taught as a second language only. By 1997 this proportion had risen to 67.6 per cent (1,136). Most of the increase was due to the curriculum impact of the 1988 Education Act and the social effects of the Welsh Language Act, 1993, which in effect abolished Category D schools. While, in 1990, 14.2 per cent (244) of primary schools were not obliged to teach any Welsh, by 1997 only one school was exempted from this statutory requirement. The nineties were thus a crucial decade for laying foundations for an increased bilingualism within statutory education.

A different method of measuring the impact of the reformed curriculum is to analyse changes in the numbers of children able to speak Welsh as a direct result of being exposed to the school influence, in addition to any home or parental fluency in Welsh. Both at the beginning and end of the period 1990–97, about the same number of children (aged 5–11) (c.14,500) speak Welsh at home. But there has also been a steady increase in the number of children who can speak Welsh fluently, but who do not speak it at home, from 15,181 to 21,221. Similarly, the numbers who can speak Welsh, but are not completely fluent, doubles during the period, from 30,753 in 1990 to 67,666 in 1997, and consequently there has been a corresponding drop in the numbers who cannot speak Welsh at all, from 155,796 to 124,682.

Alternative evidence of the same structural change may be presented in relation to the organization of teaching through the medium of Welsh in maintained primary schools, by class and by pupil distribution. There has been a general increase in the range and number of classes taught through the medium of Welsh and a corresponding absolute drop of four fifths in those classes wherein Welsh is taught, down from 2,455 in 1990 to only 550 in 1997. Similarly, there has been a significant growth in the number of pupils in classes where Welsh was the sole or main medium of instruction, from 38,404 in 1990 to 50,392 in 1997. Conversely, there has been a sharp decline in the numbers of pupils in classes being taught no Welsh, from 62,245 in 1990 to 14,553 in 1997.

At the secondary level a similar picture obtains but we may trace the trend over a longer time period: 1980–97. Here, a more structured and linguistically differentiated pattern of school type becomes apparent. The composite school category, where Welsh was taught as both a first and second language, has shrunk, while there has been a corresponding increase in the number of schools where Welsh is taught as a first language only, from the five pioneering schools which existed in 1980 to the 18 such schools by 1997. A larger number of secondary schools are now classified

Table 2.6
Primary schools, by the use of Welsh as a teaching medium

	School year (a)				
	1994/95	1995/96	1996/97	1997/98	1998/99
Schools having classes where:					
A: Welsh is the sole or main medium of instruction (b)	453	455	449	446	445
Percentage of schools	26.8	27.1	26.7	26.7	26.8
B: Welsh is used as a medium of teaching for part of the curriculum (c)	120	106	95	94	82
Percentage of schools	7.1	6.3	5.7	5.6	4.9
C: Welsh is taught as a second language only	1,091	1,109	1,136	1,133	1,133
Percentage of schools	64.5	66.0	67.6	67.8	68.3
D: No Welsh is taught	27	11	1	-	-
Percentage of schools	1.6	0.7	0.1	0	0
Total schools	1,691	1,681	1,681	1,673	1,660

Source: Schools' Census and Jones and Williams, (2000), p. 65.

(a) At January each year. Includes grant maintained schools. The mode of instruction in primary schools varies widely according to linguistic background and a school may have classes in more than one category. However, each school appears once only in this table, under an appropriate heading.

(b) i.e. more than half of curriculum teaching is through the medium of Welsh

(c) i.e. Welsh is used as a medium for less than half of curriculum teaching.

as equipped to teach Welsh as a second language, from 116 in 1980 to 161 in 1997. As a consequence, the final category of schools (35) where no Welsh was taught in 1980 has been eliminated from the classification by 1997. Most of these 35 schools were either state-funded Catholic schools or secondary schools located within long-Anglicized areas of Wales, mostly in the border counties abutting England.

What is the current situation as we address the needs of the twenty-first century? The percentage of primary pupils who can speak Welsh fluently is increasing, though the percentage that speaks Welsh as a home language is decreasing. About 2 per cent of pupils assessed as fluent Welsh speakers at the end of their primary education do not study Welsh as a first language when they start in secondary school. In the primary sector, the percentage of pupils assessed in Welsh as a first language in National Curriculum assessments is higher than the percentage fluent in the language (Jones and Williams, 2000).

Welsh in schools at the beginning of the twenty-first century

Pupils

In 2002, 1 in 6 primary school children were fluent in Welsh (16.8 per cent) which included 6.2 per cent who spoke Welsh at home. The percentage of primary school children speaking Welsh fluently has increased, from 13.2 per cent in 1988 to 16.8 per cent in 2002. The percentage of primary school children speaking Welsh at home fell over the same period, from 7.1 per cent to 6.2 per cent, while the percentage speaking Welsh fluently but not as a home language rose from 6.0 per cent to 10.5 per cent.

1 in 5 primary school pupils are taught in classes where Welsh is used either as the main medium of teaching or for teaching part of the curriculum. At the end of Key Stage 1, 18.9 per cent of pupils were assessed in Welsh, although head-teachers thought only 16.9 per cent of that age group (7-year-olds) spoke Welsh fluently. On average, over the period 1998–2002, the percentage assessed in Welsh at the end of Key Stage 1 was about two percentage points higher than the percentage considered by head-teachers to be fluent in the language.

At the end of Key Stage 2, 17.6 per cent of pupils were assessed in Welsh, although of that age group (11-year-olds), head-teachers thought only 16.7 per cent spoke Welsh fluently. On average, over the period 1998–2002 the percentage assessed in Welsh at the end of Key Stage 2 was just over 1 per cent higher than the percentage considered by head-teachers to be fluent in the language. Just over 1 per cent of fluent speakers did not continue to learn Welsh as a first language when they transferred from primary to secondary school. 15.3 per cent of pupils were learning Welsh as a first language in their first year in secondary school but 16.5 per cent of 11-year-old pupils were considered as fluent speakers by primary head-teachers in the previous year. 1 in 7 secondary school children were taught Welsh as a first language, 14.4 per cent of pupils in year groups 7–11 (compulsory school age) in maintained secondary schools.

Each year since 1978, when the comparable figure was 9.8 per cent, the percentage of secondary school children taught Welsh as a first language has increased. By 2002, 15.3 per cent of pupils in Year 7 were being taught Welsh as a first language.

At January 2002, 14.3 per cent of pupils in Year 9 studied Welsh as a first language and a similar percentage were assessed in Welsh first language at the end of Key Stage 3 (13.9 per cent). At January 2002, 4 in 5 secondary school pupils were taught Welsh as a second language, 84.5 per cent of secondary school pupils in Years 7–11. Major growth has occurred since 1978 (40.4 per cent) and even 1987 when the comparable figure was only 42 per cent.

Schools

Of all primary schools, 27 per cent (442 schools) are mainly Welsh-medium schools. A further 80 schools, (4.9 per cent of the total), use Welsh as a teaching medium to some extent. In the remaining 1,102 schools, (67.9 per cent of total), Welsh is taught as a second language only. The percentage, and number, of primary schools where Welsh is used as a medium to teach only a minority of pupils, or to teach less than half of the curriculum, has been falling in recent years.

The number of Welsh-speaking secondary schools increased from 44 in 1990/91 to 53 in 2001/02. This type of school is a major resource for language reproduction and is set to grow steadily. However, as a result of increased demand for bilingual education, falling rolls in some English-medium schools and the financial costs of starting new bilingual secondary schools, it is likely that more formally unilingual English schools will incorporate a bilingual stream within their provision. As a consequence, we are likely to see a more diverse range of bilingual teaching opportunities, especially within Anglicized areas.

This geographic diversity is evident in the existing provision. When the data are placed in rank order, we see that the vast majority of pupils in Gwynedd (78.9 per cent) and Anglesey (63.0 per cent) are taught Welsh as a first language, some 54.5 per cent in Ceredigion, 29.4 per cent in Carmarthenshire, followed by smaller proportions for Rhondda Cynon Taf (19.4 per cent), Denbighshire (18.5 per cent), Conwy (13.2 per cent) and successively fewer for the remaining fifteen local education authorities. The Welsh average is 14.4 per cent of all secondary school pupils in year groups 7–11.

That the position of Welsh-medium education has been strengthened, is a significant development in its own right and is recorded in much more positive attitudes towards bilingualism and the construction of a bilingual society *per se*. However, beneath this positive trend, there remains for many a grumbling doubt as to the real worth of bilingualism, for it is argued that once many pupils have left the confines of the school classroom there is little economic and instrumental justification for maintaining fluency in Welsh. Such judgements have far less purchase now than a decade ago, for, as we shall see below, there has been a corresponding growth also in the value of bilingual skills within the workplace.

Stage 3: Welsh in the worksphere and economy

A major feature of language revitalization has been the attempt to harmonize both language reproduction and regional development as mutually supportive community enterprises. Too often in the past, it was assumed that the price of successful economic development was the denial of socio-cultural separateness and, in consequence, a perception had grown among some influential leaders, that all externally-derived development was antipathetic to the best interests of the threatened ethno-linguistic community. Cultural defence was essentially conservative activity, which hindered the unfettered modernizing impulse of regional development. The current challenge is to encourage appropriate development, which is sensitive to the needs of the threatened community and takes account of holistic arguments and integrated planning policies.

Language revitalization schemes should give considerably more attention than hitherto to the impact of linguistic and cultural considerations on economic development and the impact of economic initiatives on language maintenance. Key aspects of these relationships include an increased appreciation of the role of language planning in regional economic development, community regeneration, questions of accessibility (Wessels and Beck, 1994), in accommodating in-migrants (Dafis, 1992; van Langevelde, 1993, 1999), in the pioneering work of Grin (1996, 1999), Vaillancourt (1985, 1996) and in relating questions of community leadership, social cohesion and confidence in language-use to the formal framework of bilingual public services, the operation of the voluntary sector and the increased penetration of Welsh speakers within the private sector workplace.

A second theme is the management and exploitation of regional environments. This is an especially critical issue for those local authorities who seek to use statutory measures to restrict deleterious influences on the local community, which James and Williams (1997) have examined within the statutory framework of town and country planning legislation in Scotland and Wales. There is a dualism between arguments which stress that the region has been structurally discriminated against because of its relatively weak position vis-à-vis the hegemonic culture, and counter-arguments that, despite relative disadvantage, the region in question offers sufficient advantages to attract external investment in an increasingly competitive market situation.

The Welsh Development Agency Economic Panel (Hill, 1999) has described the prosperity gap between Wales and the rest of the UK and the EU as stemming from a structural problem which is that: "a) Given existing conditions, policies and expectations, the 'prosperity gap' is likely to widen in the short term; b) Demand efficiency is a major part of the economic problem in Wales; c) Supply-side policies can help, but Wales does not have control of its macroeconomic environment; d) Continuing over-reliance on slow-growth, mature sectors and too few high-growth sectors; e) Enterprise continues to be under developed in Wales; f) Too few people at work in Wales." (p.13). The implications in terms of solutions are: "a) The need is for an imaginative, radical long-term policy response to change in the path of development; b) Export-led economic growth is crucial, which can only result from enhanced competitiveness across all sectors; c) Foreign Investment is a significant demand stimulus, but Wales must get better at maximizing its impacts; d) Wales must diversify its industrial structure onto high-value 'tradable' sectors, especially into those that are fast-growth, skills-demanding, value-adding and knowledge-based; e) The social and economic obstacles to work must begin to be addressed and overcome at the same time as the opportunities for work are increased across Wales" (Hill, 1999, p.13).

I have recently added a fresh dimension to this on-going discussion by placing a greater emphasis than is normal in conventional economic analyses on factors which are internal to Welsh society, particularly those related to cultural factors and to the charge that enterprise is underdeveloped in Wales (Williams, 2000b). Along with European regions, several Welsh local authorities and enterprise agencies are currently examining the role indigenous culture can play in encouraging sustainable development. For the first time, the relationships between culture and business formation, product innovation, risk-taking and enterprise are being systematically analysed. It is claimed that if one can understand the inner workings of a culture, then strategic intervention can direct underperforming regions to become more concerned with economic success and indigenous development. This would involve examining the ideological basis of Welsh social values to ascertain how messages relating to business, enterprise, political representation, regional development and planning are constructed and diffused.[59]

The central question which revisionist economists ask is, what socialization processes predispose individuals and cultures to gravitate towards or away from entrepreneurial business skills and acumen? However, a more pluralist post-modern perspective seeks to reduce the interpretative power of structure and agency by focusing on key questions, such as whether belonging to an additional language group or maintaining a high level of fluency in two or more languages is going to return an extra value in the market place? Additional issues concern the adaptation of lesser-used-language speakers to the opportunities afforded by changes in global-local networks, the growth of specialized economic segments or services and of information networks which are accessed by language-related skills. Accessibility to or denial of these opportunities is the virtual expression of real power in society, which must be taken on board in any discussion of the politics of cultural representation.

Economic strategies and language initiatives

Williams (2003) has identified five alternatives and, as yet, only partially related approaches to the question of economic development and language regeneration. These are:

1) Community-level involvement as represented by Mentrau Iaith
2) International- and national-level initiatives represented by the Welsh Development Agency and European Union sponsored activities
3) Regional-level involvement represented by Menter a Busnes and Antur Teifi initiatives and activities
4) Objective 1 Funding for Regional Regeneration
5) National Assembly for Wales-led integration of the language-economy nexus.

Welsh-European partnerships are the most significant example of fresh economic initiatives, yet there is little formal recognition of a linguistic dimension in such planning, even though the socio-cultural character of Wales is offered as a consideration for inward investment. However, as with Brittany, Catalonia, Flanders and Scotland, Wales represents a particular configuration where regional innovation has also led to a renewed sense of confidence in European-level institutions and networks. By relating Welsh events to European currents of thought and praxis, new opportunities are created for the development of so-called "problem regions". There is a considerable debate as to how one should play the European dimension, precisely because Wales simultaneously wishes to be seen as both a dynamic leader of post-industrial development, as witnessed by its active participation in the Four Motors Programme, and as an eligible member for European Regional Development Funding (ERDF). Up until the late 1980s massive dislocation in the traditional industrial sectors of mining, steel making and textiles had dealt a body blow to Welsh economic performance. However, following the 1988 reforms, Wales has obtained an average share of 12.5 per cent of all UK ERDF funds, and 8.6 per cent of all UK ESF funds. Commenting on this trend, Mathias (1995) argues that this is a considerable success when one takes the restrictions in eligibility into account. Evidence of the reconstruction of the Welsh economy is provided by the increase in levels of inward investment from around £30m in 1985 to around £230m in 1992, most of which is private overseas capital (Cooke, 1993a).

Five European Union Initiatives have been of relevance to Wales. RE-

CHAR (I/II) was significant as the mining industry sought to adjust to the massive haemorrhage of men, following the ruthless downsizing of the middle Thatcher years. RETEX was aimed at textile-manufacturing regions and did not perform well in Wales, even though the industry continues to struggle, especially in the north and west. LEADER was concerned with strengthening agencies of rural development and has been a considerable success, particularly in terms of local infrastructural development and introducing new farming practices. KONVER was established to assist areas in coping with problems stemming from the decline of the defence industry. Both Pembroke and Anglesey have benefited from compensation for the decommissioning of RAF production and maintenance facilities. INTERREG, aimed at facilitating cross-border co-operation, has become the most significant initiative, used extensively by local authorities in West Wales dealing with Irish partners and with Pembroke's new partnership with the Greater Amsterdam region (Mathias, 1995).

Recent expansion in the use of European funds has seen a shift from investment in capital infrastructure, such as transport and physical communication, to the creation of community projects which provide a network of support for sustained development and enhanced quality of life, including housing, education, access to information and telecommunication facilities (Mathias, 1995). Thus the Welsh RELAY Centre was established in 1993 with the express purpose of helping industry take advantage of the EU programmes such as ESPRIT, BRIDGE, BRITE/EURAM and STRIDE. In addition, the EU and the Welsh Development Agency have jointly funded the UK's first Electronic Data Interchange (EDI) Awareness Centre, in Wales. Late in 1995 Wales was nominated as one of the newly-created Regional Technology Plan (RTP) regions. Participants recognize that this is not a panacea for the long-term complications of structural adjustment because of the difficulty in meeting all the requirements of, additionally, consolidating networks and harnessing the potential of the region. In that sense, like many other EU programmes in Wales, it is essentially an exercise in network-construction and access to technology rather than an income-generating programme. But, over time, synergy becomes crucial as a trigger to innovation and mini-technopoles may develop as a result of the strategies identified in Castells and Hall (1994).

The discussion to date has tended to focus attention on aggregate structural factors which relate either to a predominantly rural economy or to the downturn effects of a post-industrial landscape, as in Cwm Gwendraeth and Aman-Tawe. Issues of external investment, control and policy implementation have gradually given way to a concern as to how Welsh national agencies such as the Welsh Development Agency and other interventionist arms of the state can regenerate such communities, either through pump-priming schemes or infrastructural improvements.

Menter a Busnes

A key question is to what extent there is a significant economic difference if the language promotion is undertaken on behalf of a target group by a state agency, and to what extent are the considerations altered if the promotional work is undertaken by the minority speakers themselves within the community and local economy?

Since its establishment in 1989, Menter a Busnes has adopted innovative approaches to the challenge of promoting self-directed and targeted economic development and cultural change which aims to:

- maximize the economic potential of Welsh speakers
- create and operate a long-term, action-based programme to make sure that Welsh-language culture adapts itself creatively in terms of economic attitudes and activities
- increase considerably the number of Welsh speakers who develop companies that already exist; work in and manage businesses of all kinds; invest in businesses; establish new ventures; initiate economically-based activities in the community; operate in a wider range of sectors; and manage effectively in a variety of situations.

The practical means by which Menter a Busnes translates these aims into reality include: comprehensive business and management training programmes; school and adult education seminars on business enterprise opportunities; vocational training; agricultural enterprise and marketing information packs; promoting empirical research and policy initiatives; EU inter-regional projects coordinated by AGORA, with an emphasis on cultural tourism and farm diversification; promoting new forms of bilingual intervention in both the rural and urban contexts (Menter a Busnes, 1997). Currently Menter a Busnes is the lead organization in a NAfW-sponsored project to harmonize government economic and sustainable community policies for Welsh-speaking areas and is set to play a critical role in the implementation of Iaith Pawb's strategy as it relates to Welsh-medium entrepreneurship (*see p. 100*).

Antur Teifi

Antur Teifi was founded in 1980 as a private company to stimulate economic enterprise in the Teifi Valley. An underlying concern was to revitalize aspects of the local economy so as to maintain a viable community in what was then one of the strongest Welsh-speaking areas in Wales. Its great strength is that it was grounded in the aspirations of local community activists to improve their region's economic condition. Initially it concentrated on diversifying the agro-economic base and providing telematic training and facilities to a hitherto poorly served rural area. The interventionist strategy has operated through the improvement of the local infrastructure, through the provision of professional marketing advice and economic development information, through a commitment to joint venture partnerships and through experimental methods of restructuring local-global economic networks. Welsh is a natural means of communication, for over 90 per cent of the staff are Welsh-speaking, but the language is an extension of local involvement, not an end in and of itself. The value added in operating in a bilingual context may be itemized as follows:

- it assists effective local and regional networking
- it attracts backing from other agencies such as the Welsh Development Agency, the Development Board for Rural Wales, and European support through the Leader Project
- it facilitates Antur's ability to respond quickly and effectively to local community needs, especially the demand for skills training
- it assists the company to adopt a holistic and flexible approach to a rapidly changing economic context
- by encouraging local people to seek employment within the region, it is perceived as a community asset
- local support for the aims and methods of Antur Teifi have allowed it to penetrate into other neighbouring regions and to become a significant actor in the local economy of south-west Wales.

The company has realized much of its potential as a dynamic, self-sustaining enterprise agency. It has countered much of the traditional prejudice against a Welsh-medium enterprise culture, and is expanding its range of activities. The experience of Antur Teifi is obviously of great significance to others seeking to harmonize economic development and language regeneration and, given its success, is likely to act as a role model for new ventures within the SME sector.

The Objective I programme

A major initiative has been the granting of EU Objective 1 status to large parts of Wales, which over the seven years 2000–06 is providing an additional £1.3 billion of development funding. This is a mixed blessing, for, although it is a financial boost, it is also a socio-economic indictment that regional deprivation has been allowed to slip so far behind the UK and European thresholds. The West and Valleys designated area, which qualified for Objective 1 support, is characterized by:

- extremely low and declining GDP which was 72 per cent of the EU average, reflecting the Welsh national average, which is 17 per cent below the UK average. Many parts of Wales fare much worse, for example the Central Valleys figure is 64 per cent of the EU average, while Anglesey is 68 per cent of the EU average
- unemployment, especially the long-term
- declining economic activity rates
- high levels of social deprivation, with 82 of the 100 most deprived wards in Wales being within the designated area
- an over-dependence on declining industries, e.g. energy, defence, slate and oil refining
- a region dominated by the crucial role of the agricultural industry which has been hit by a number of crises in the past decade
- relatively few dynamic indigenous medium-sized businesses with growth potential
- a region which is economically isolated, with poor communication network and infra-structure.

The Single Programming Document for the period 2000–06, gives prominence to culture and language. Welsh is described as a "critical element, which underpins the region's identity with nearly 75 per cent of the Welsh-speaking population living in the region" (Wales European Taskforce, 1999, p. 5). However, the results to date in terms of practical and measurable change have been limited, to say the least.

Nevertheless, measures to enhance the economic performance of the region, which include a specific linguistics/cultural dimension, include: 1) business development and enterprise priorities, which will be influenced by Menter a Busnes planning and policy; 2) a competitive environment, which will seek to enhance the enterprise initiatives; 3) community regeneration initiatives, which will likely be modelled on the Mentrau Iaith experience; 4) promoting employability and a learning society based, in part, on bilingual skills training programmes; 5) rural development and sustainable use of natural resources, which will adopt more ecological and holistic approaches to the social and economic needs of the rural communities within the region.

Wales is beginning to mobilize the key structural determinants of economic performance, environmental sustainability and cultural reproduction within one integrated programme. When allied with the mainstreaming intent of Iaith Pawb, the Objective 1 spin-off could be of far greater significance in terms of strengthening communities, than was initially appreciated.

This is more true once the full impact of a new set of players in the regional development-language enterprise nexus is realized. These new actors include: a) Newidiem, a spin-off from Menter a Busnes, which seeks to concentrate in the short term on promoting bilingualism within the workplace, especially the major retail and service sectors; b) refashioned Mentrau Iaith – Language Enterprise Agencies – of which the most recent have a far more hard-headed economic rationale to their work and engagement in community development; c) major UK economic development agencies recognizing the significance of bilingualism in Wales as an economic value, rather than a social cost in the labour market; d) the growth of a significant number of consultancies spawned by devolution and constitutional change which seek to advise on Wales in UK, Irish-British context and European sphere of economic interest.

Additional promising trends include the initial success of language marketing and promotion in three sectors: a) elements of the agricultural sector, dairy products, food marketing and eco-business activities; b) small and medium-sized enterprises; c) information technology and communication/

media companies. Major barriers remain to the widespread introduction of Welsh/bilingual skills in the manufacturing and retail sectors, outside the predominantly Welsh-speaking areas. The major difficulty in normalizing Welsh is enabling it to go beyond the formal patina of bilingualism in activities such as banking, specific services and insurance sectors. This involves more than the provision of opportunity and an ancillary right to language choice. It requires investment, training, encouragement and conviction, for the development of a thoroughgoing bilingual employment market is a novel trend as yet. It is likely that it will take another generation before we see the full effects of the current round of strategic interventionist language planning. National Assembly initiatives are best represented by the strategy adopted in Iaith Pawb which will be discussed below.

Stage 2: Local government services and the media

Beyond the educational and economic spheres there remains the vibrancy of popular Welsh culture. Mass literacy and the development of a lively and innovative publishing sector have contributed greatly to the promotion of Welsh since the mid-nineteenth century. By comparison with English, the range and overall quality of production leave much to be desired; although given the constraints, which face any lesser-used language, the output is remarkable.[60] Broadcasting is a more accurate test of the contemporary social worth and adaptability of Welsh culture. Radio had paved the way with a limited range of Welsh-medium transmissions, largely devoted to religion, children or issues of daily life. In 1977–9, as a result of the development of VHF wavebands, an English-medium Radio Wales and a predominantly Welsh-medium Radio Cymru service were launched. The latter provides some 127 hours per week, 90 of which are in Welsh. One could almost describe this service as a "friend of the family" to many Welsh speakers, for its presenters are regular household names whose aim is to present musical and contemporary items in a manner which is simultaneously both intimate and professional. Thus, Radio Cymru serves as a national communication network for many, as it encourages audience participation to a far greater extent than do its far more diverse – and, hence – specialist English counterparts.

At a number of key turns in the seventies, it became obvious that there was a growing support in favour of a fourth TV channel being devoted in whole or in part to Welsh-medium services. The absence of such a channel had clear implications, not only for language reproduction, but also for sustained dissatisfaction on behalf of the unilingual English-speaking majority in Wales.[61]

The 1974 Crawford Committee endorsed this view, as did the Conservative manifesto pledge of 1979. However, within a few months of taking office, the new administration withdrew their commitment, preferring to improve the existing broadcasting arrangements. This policy change engendered the largest mass protests witnessed in post-war Wales, with a plethora of social movements, political parties and non-aligned interest groups all campaigning in tandem to force the government to honour its pledge. The focus of this campaign was the decision of Gwynfor Evans, on 5 May 1980, to fast to death unless the government announced the creation of a body akin to S4C.[62] To the great relief of all, on 17 September 1980 the government reversed its decision and S4C was established on 1 November 1982, as a major boost to the promotion of Welsh through popular and varied Welsh-medium broadcasting. Some 30 out of 145 hours per week are transmitted in Welsh, mainly at peak time. The channel reaches a relatively high percentage of its target audience and is facing a rather unpredictable future with more confidence now than was true of the mid-eighties. S4C is a commissioning rather than a production organization, and, in consequence, has spawned a network of independent film and programme makers, animators, creative designers, writers, etc., who can convert their original Welsh-language programmes into English or "foreign" languages for sale in the international media market place. Cardiff ranks second to London as a media production centre in the UK, with all the technical, economic and post-production facilities and infrastructure associated with the media industry.

Four issues have dominated recent debates in Welsh broadcasting: 1) financial self-sufficiency versus subsidy; 2) the relaxation of certain linguistic conventions and rules regarding the appropriate mix of Welsh and English within and between programme schedules;[63] 3) the "multicultural" nature of S4C which transmits European soccer and sport, repackaged documentaries, full-length films and co-production series in Welsh. In part, this is to attract new viewers to the channel and in part it reflects S4C's participation in the European Broadcasting Union and commercial marketing of international television material; 4) the impact of digital technology and the advent of multi-channel broadcasting which has given S4C, new challenges for widening its remit within a consortia of broadcasters, established to take advantage of the new opportunities available.

The populist base of Welsh culture can too often be ignored in comparison with the more innovative and professional representations of material culture, as transmitted by the mass media. Nevertheless, there remains, at a more voluntary level, a very active network of Eisteddfodau (competitive cultural festivals) which nurture school-based and community-based performances of musical items, poetry, Welsh plays and plays in translation, craft work, art and design and scientific projects. Unique in British life as an agency of social integration, this network starts at the local level and the successful competitors progress through intervening stages to reach the National Eisteddfod and the Urdd National Eisteddfod. During the twentieth century it was the Eisteddfod system which acted both as a champion for Welsh-language rights and as a vehicle for national culture, both setting the standards and prioritizing certain themes in the popular representation of Welshness. Recently, the Urdd (The Welsh League of Youth) has modernized its image by adding to its conventional activities, go-karting, tenpin bowling, discos, and surfing "in Welsh". An additional voluntaristic element are the myriad organizations representing sub-sections of life, such as Merched y Wawr, Mudiad Ffermwyr Ifainc Cymru, many religious societies, Welsh folk dance and musical groups. Such has been the collective force of all these organizations and movements, that the legitimacy and social acceptance of Welsh–English bilingualism is rarely seriously challenged today. Indeed there has been a profound turnaround in the social perception of and range of favourable attitudes towards Welsh, in marked contrast to the climate which prevailed in the immediate post-war period.

Local government has also made a significant contribution to increasing the possibility of RLS, initially through its bilingual education policies (see Baker and Prys Jones, 2000) and more recently through its adoption of Welsh-language schemes as specified by the Welsh Language Act, 1993, and under the influence of the Welsh Language Board (WLB 2000). One of the Board's first tasks in 1993/4 was to prepare guidelines on the form and content of language schemes. The Board's draft guidelines were presented to Parliament in March 1995 and approved in July 1995, with further guidance as to the form and content of schemes following in March 1996. Taken together, they clearly illustrate the close links between planning and policy in the context of scheme preparation. The first statutory notices to public bodies, informing them of the requirement to prepare language schemes, were sent in the Autumn of 1995. Since then, the language has been on the public sector agenda throughout Wales. Up to 31 March 2000, 134 schemes had been agreed, with over 120 others at various stages of preparation, covering a wide range of areas of public service provision, including Local Government, Health, Education, Police, Magistrates Courts, Central Government executive agencies and, most notably, Government Departments.

The WLB's own perception is that this is very much a planned process. The Board, from the first, has targeted organizations on the basis of a schedule it prepared, giving precedence to agreeing schemes with bodies which have contact with a substantial number of Welsh speakers, or which provide services that give rise to the greatest demand for Welsh-medium provision, or which have a high profile in Wales, or are influential because of their status or responsibilities. Of the 350 organizations identified initially as priorities, over two-thirds have either prepared a language scheme, or are in the process of doing so. As a result, the Board is now giving greater priority to monitoring and reviewing existing schemes (as opposed to agreeing new schemes) in order to ensure that those already in place operate effectively and continue to develop to meet the needs of their bilingual customers. The real question, of course, is how effective such language schemes are in changing the behavioural patterns of both employees and customers. Having raised the profile of Welsh, it is now likely that many local authorities will seek to implement a more thoroughgoing bilingual administrative system wherein the macro-relationship with the National Assembly and the micro-relationship with local partnerships will be critical.

Stage 1: Welsh in the higher spheres of work, education and government

Wales has a long history of initiating domain-related language policies, but specific enactments of language legislation are rare. A trio of Acts in the decade 1988–1998 provides a new statutory infrastructure and institutional context to enable social reform in the field of language policy and planning to be realized. The domains are education, language rights and governance, as represented in turn by the Education Act of 1988, the Welsh Language Act of 1993 and the Government of Wales Act of 1998, which authorized the establishment of a National Assembly for Wales following elections in May 1999.

Following the passage of the Welsh Language Act (1993) and the establishment of the statutory Welsh Language Board, Welsh is increasingly identified with government support, being designated a co-equal working language of the National Assembly, which promises to be the most important instrument for democratic representation in Welsh history.

The role of education, as a key agency of socialization, has become central to the language struggle. It is the most fundamental feature of language revitalization in Wales and has been very well documented (Williams, 1998; Baker, 1993; Jones and Ghuman, 1995; Williams, 1999a). But the role of Welsh in Higher Education is both limited and disappointing. A real opportunity to build on the reforms within the statutory educational system has been lost. The granting of core status within the National Curriculum recognizes the reality of bilingualism in Wales. The diffusion of Welsh as a subject in all schools makes it more likely that all children will have experience (and, for many, some real competence) of the language as they enter adulthood. But the transference of this potential into the reality of taught courses in Further and Higher Education has just not happened. The most recent data available paint a sad picture.

Statutory obligations

A cumulative history of tackling language issues in a positive manner has given Wales a wealth of experience as regards language policy, though to what extent this could be called self-conscious integrative language planning is doubtful, as specific enactments of language legislation are rare.

Legislation is critical, not only in authorizing linguistic rights, but also in establishing the infrastructure wherein such rights can be exercized without let or hindrance. Too often, individuals and groups have a titular right to certain services, but such rights are held in abeyance because of a lack of commitment to honour language choice rights at the point of local contact. Thus, the current challenge is to realize a fully functional bi/multilingual society through creating new opportunities for language choice within the public, voluntary and private sectors of the economy.

The Welsh Language Act (1993) provided a statutory framework for the treatment of English and Welsh on the basis of equality and inaugurated a new era in language planning. Its chief policy instrument is the re-fashioned and strengthened Welsh Language Board, established on 21 December 1993, as a non-departmental statutory organization. Initially funded by a grant from the Welsh Office, it is now funded by the National Assembly Executive which, in the year ending 31 March 1998, totalled £5,756,00.[63] It has three main duties: 1) advizing organizations which are preparing language schemes on the mechanism of operating the central principle of the Act, that the Welsh and English languages should be treated on a basis of equality; 2) Advizing those who provide services to the public in Wales on issues relevant to the Welsh language; 3) Advizing central Government on issues relating to the Welsh language.

The Welsh Language Act 1993 details key steps to be taken by the Welsh Language Board and by public sector bodies in the preparation of Welsh language schemes. Since 1995, a total of 67 language schemes have been approved, including all 22 local authorities. By 1998, notices had been issued to a further 59 bodies to prepare schemes.[64]

The Welsh Language Board's primary goal is to enable the language to become self-sustaining and secure as a medium of communication in Wales.[65] In 1993 it set itself four priorities: 1) to increase the numbers of Welsh-speakers; 2) to provide more opportunities to use the language; 3) to change the habits of language use and encourage people to take advantage of the opportunities provided, and 4) to strengthen Welsh as a community language. (For details on how it has met these goals see Williams, 2000d).

In order to increase the numbers speaking Welsh, it has focused its efforts on normalizing the use of Welsh among young people by seeking to ensure that the provision of Welsh-language and Welsh-medium education and training is planned in conjunction with the key players. It also seeks to ensure an appropriate level of provision to obtain Welsh-language education services for young people, to formulate policies and effective initiatives which ensure the proper provision of public and voluntary services and to provide grants for initiatives which promote the use of Welsh among young people.[66]

The Board's second objective is "to agree measures which provide opportunities for the public to use the Welsh language with organizations which deal with the public in Wales, giving priority to those organizations which have contact with a significant number of Welsh speakers, provide services which are likely to be in greatest demand through the medium of

Welsh or have a high public profile in Wales, or are influential by virtue of their status or responsibilities".

A third objective is to change the habits of language use and encourage people to take advantage of the opportunities provided. This is done through an innovative marketing campaign, including attractive bilingual public display signs, the development of a Welsh spellchecker and on-line dictionary, a direct Welsh Link Line for queries regarding the Welsh language and language-related services, a language in the workplace portfolio/file, a Plain Welsh campaign with excellent guidelines for writing Welsh, and the recent release by Microsoft of a Welsh version of Windows XP. Such improvements to the infrastructure are necessary before a real language choice can be made by the general public.[67]

The WLB's fourth objective is "that Welsh-speaking communities be given the facilities, opportunities and the encouragement needed to maintain and extend the use of Welsh in those communities".[68] This aspect of language planning is concerned with participation and community-level language empowerment which was given a policy dimension by the recommendations of the Community Language Report (Williams and Evas, 1997). The essence of regenerating Welsh as a community language is to inculcate a shared responsibility for its condition and to promote its use in those daily tasks which are so psychologically important for increasing confidence and changing behaviour patterns.[69]

The number of domains in which Welsh is used has increased significantly over the past thirty years, especially in education, the media, leisure and selected public services. However, there has also been a corresponding intensification of the influence of the English language, particularly in relation to new technology.[70] But this is not an inevitable trend, for once the infrastructure is in place, the same technology can be used to facilitate the internal communication of a predominantly Welsh-medium network. A virtual community has been created via E-mail and the World Wide Web with an increasing, though inadequate, range of software available. Today it is the home and the education system, rather than the community *per se*, which share the task of nurturing new speakers. However, the community context is still vital for the social realization of bilingualism.

Additional work is needed on a range of factors which influence the transmission and use of Welsh, such as:

- occupational structures and local economic development

- unorthodox social networks, especially in urban contexts
- research on the implications of telematic networks and the digital economy
- demographic trends and age/sex differences by language acquisition and maintenance
- a lucid understanding of rural community changes which may be independent of, though contributing to, those conditions which maintain Welsh as a dynamic element in society
- an analysis of the contemporary Welsh way of life
- consideration of the available methods whereby the linguistic abilities of Welsh speakers could be improved
- research on how the Mentrau may evolve as agencies in the field of social development.

It is a little premature to assess the full regenerative impact of the Mentrau Iaith but one should not underestimate their potential. Mentrau are likely to become the key instruments for stabilizing linguistic fragmentation, especially in areas where there is a high proportion of Welsh speakers. The core question is to what extent the National Assembly should be thinking of extending this form of LP intervention into many other Welsh-speaking communities, or are there better, alternative models available which should be promoted? Still in its infancy, the promotion of a robust national language-planning framework, including a central role for Mentrau and LAPs, will be able to calibrate their achievements. This will lead to the establishment of a database of good practice, by which one may formulate more dependable methods of predicting the outcome of language intervention measures. Without such a national framework, it is hard to envisage how the Welsh Language Board's Strategy will be realized.

The Government of Wales Act 1998

The high point of the language struggle towards normalization was the establishment of the bilingual National Assembly for Wales in May 1999.[71] Bilingual or multilingual decision-making assemblies are the norm in contemporary world politics, whether within European regional legislatures, such as in Catalonia and Euskadi, within the organs of the European Union or within other supra-national organizations, such as the Council of Europe, NATO and the United Nations.[72] In conforming to this international norm, the National Assembly in Wales is signalling its intention of being a modern, representative political institution and committing itself to serving its constituents in both of the languages of Wales. This is why language legislation and the establishment of a set of modern bilingual institutions are fundamental. Of itself, it does not guarantee success, but it does enable selected initiatives to be realized, and authorizes new patterns of language choice as a result of changes in the infrastructure.

The National Assembly for Wales and the Welsh language

The Government of Wales Act 1998 makes several references to the Welsh language. The most significant and potentially most far-reaching is in section 32, which states that "The Assembly may do anything it considers appropriate ... to support the Welsh language". The Act also established Welsh and English as the working languages of the Assembly.

The Assembly's first term (May 1999 –April 2003) produced a number of important structural initiatives, among which are: a) a powerful economic committee; b) structural change and internal merging of key agencies to produce a more powerful and integrated Welsh Development Agency; c) the bilingual structure and operation of the Assembly; d) vigorous education, training and language policies; e) resources from the National Assembly to a range of agencies and former quangos, including the Welsh Language Board, to engage in more medium-term holistic language planning and community development programmes.

Community language policies, the development of bilingual education, bilingual service provision in local government, health and social services are a major feature of current policy. Secondly, there are the proposed economic policies and regional development initiatives, which seek to stabilize predominantly Welsh-speaking communities, to create employment, and to promote bilingual working opportunities. Thirdly, there is to be serious consideration of the interests of Welsh language and culture as they are impacted upon by town and country structure planning and improvements to the transport system.[73] This will include a review of the pressing housing, property control and rural service issues highlighted by Cymuned and Cymdeithas yr Iaith.[74] The central political issue is how the Assembly itself both operates as a bilingual institution and implements its intended revitalization policies for Welsh-speaking citizens.

The Assembly Government's Welsh language scheme was recently approved by the Board. Following the comprehensive review of the language by the Culture and Education Committees, summarized in its final report Our Language: Its Future (June 2002), the Assembly declared its aim of creating a bilingual Wales. This is a highly significant statement of policy intent and, if implemented fully, could be the most prescient advance yet in official thinking on language-related issues. The Board, along with other participants, had pressed the National Assembly:

- To take ownership itself of the principles of holistic language planning
- To treat bilingualism as part of its equal opportunities agenda, across all policy fields
- To encourage every body which the NAfW sponsors to do likewise; and
- To investigate the true potential of existing legislation – both specific and non-specific to language.

The Government's immediate and positive response was its policy statement, Dyfodol Dwyieithog: Bilingual Future which reiterated that the Assembly Government was "wholly committed to revitalizing the Welsh language and creating a bilingual Wales". Moreover, it committed the Government to supporting the language in a number of positive ways, including the following:

- Providing strategic leadership to sustain and encourage the growth of the Welsh language "within a tolerant, welcoming and open Wales"
- Mainstreaming the Welsh language into the work of the Assembly Government and its agencies
- Providing support for communities, including primarily Welsh-speaking communities, by pursuing policies which seek to create economically and socially sustainable communities; and
- Ensuring that effective structures are in place to enable people to acquire or learn Welsh.

Iaith Pawb: Recommendations and criticism

In December 2002, the Assembly Government produced a comprehensive document, Iaith Pawb (Everyone's Language), which provides a National Action Plan for a Bilingual Wales. Following on from its earlier policy statement, Iaith Pawb sets out in detail the specific actions and initiatives by which the Government will seek to increase bilingualism and strengthen the Welsh language. If we focus only on the rhetoric, as opposed to the possible implementation, we can state that it is the most far-reaching document yet published on official language promotion. The measures set out in the Action Plan are to be assessed against a number of key targets.

The five main aims are to:

- increase the proportion of Welsh speakers by 5 per cent by 2011 from the 2001 Census baseline
- arrest the decline in heartland communities, especially those with close to 70 per cent+ Welsh speakers
- increase the percentage of children in pre-school Welsh education
- increase the percentage of families where Welsh is the principal language
- mainstream Welsh-medium services.

Its principal policy options for achieving these aims are:

- the NAfW Welsh Language Unit
- mainstreaming Welsh into policy development
- developing national language planning through Bwrdd yr Iaith
- developing the Government's research and analysis capacity
- creating evidence-based policies in the field of language revitalization.

In affirming the WLB's central role as the national language planning body and giving the Board a central role in delivering the Plan, the Assembly Government has increased the Board's total grant by £16 million over the next three years. In 2003–04, the Board's total budget will rise to £11.6 million, an increase of over £4.7 million on 2002–03.

Iaith Pawb devotes considerable attention to the principal fields of government activity within which bilingualism might be encouraged. Thus, within the economic development portfolio, it suggests that bilingualism could be mainstreamed in the various initiatives of Finance Wales plc; the Community Loan Fund; the Community Development Financial Institutions and integrated more fully within the Wales for Innovation strategy. The bilingual elements of an entrepreneurial culture are to be harnessed through Potentia; the Business Gateway; the Enterprise Factory; through Cwlwm Busnes programmes and, most critically, through an enhanced role for Menter a Busnes.

Within tourism, the Welsh culture is seen as an added attraction to be marketed through such devices as the "Wales" Tourism Product, various Cultural Tourism Strategies and through the Destination Management System, while the lead bodies identified are the familiar litany of the National Assembly, the Welsh Development Agency, Menter a Busnes, the Wales Tourist Board and ELWa. The latter agency has a vital role in meeting the training needs of the industry. For not only is tourism seen as a means of showcasing the distinct socio-cultural regions of Wales, the sector also enables local residents with a variety of skills to be gainfully employed in relatively disadvantaged regions. But if the pattern of seasonal under-employment in tourist-related activities is to be supplemented by better-paid, higher-quality jobs, then the necessary value-added skills training courses need to be put in place.

A third element is community development, which is why Iaith Pawb highlights the relevance of schemes such as Communities First programme, the WDA Regeneration Framework and "toolkit", the various initiatives such as Farming Connect, Retail Outlets, the Post Office Development Fund, and the Wales Rural Observatory. Proven initiatives such as LEADER+ have already been useful for the Mentrau Iaith and now an attempt is being made to harmonise their actions within both the Rural Community Action scheme and the Rural Development Programme.

In submissions to the Culture and Education Committee's review of the Welsh language, individuals, agencies and interest groups stressed the need to examine the planning and housing systems, for, as currently constituted, they had a damaging effect on the maintenance of viable Welsh-speaking communities. The government's reaction was to hint that the existing arrangements would have to be revisited in the light of commissioned research but, in the interim, pointed to various schemes such as "affordable housing", the Homebuy scheme – with grants of 50 per cent in rural areas, the Social Housing Grant programme, which is funded to the tune of £56.4m in 2003/4, the operation of the Housing Needs Assessment scheme, increased levels of research on second and holiday homes, together with studies on the planning implications of changing housing ownership legislation. Non-Welsh-speaking newcomers in specified areas would be provided with "welcome packs", while the education system, the Mentrau Iaith and the Urdd were all encouraged to help integrate new residents.

In recognizing that both community fragmentation and failure to transmit Welsh within the family were serious issues, Iaith Pawb rehearsed existing remedial solutions but stressed that more money would be made available over the medium term to extend the effectiveness of language acquisition agencies such as formal education, Lifelong-Learning and especially latecomer centres within predominantly Welsh-speaking areas. The successful Twf – Family Language Transfer programme – was to be expanded. But the two significant initiatives were to target an increase in the functional bilingualism of services and employees of NHS Wales and Iaith Gwaith, a scheme to promote Welsh in the workplace. Providing increased opportunities is an essential part of any language promotion scheme but so is equipping personnel to deal with the increased bilingual demand in its myriad forms. Thus, Iaith Pawb also discusses the measures by which language tools are to be made available to turn opportunities into social practice. This is to include a national database of standardized terms, lexicographical and machine translation aids, a rigorous translation strategy and a plethora of IT advances.

When the draft of Iaith Pawb was circulated for improvements and refinements I responded that, had this been declared as government policy twenty years ago, it would have been the most radical and far-reaching of documents. However, the language issue has moved on and although many of the key issues are addressed by fine rhetoric which legitimizes policy, the current policy is characterized by ill-defined mechanisms, with far too little detail on the monitoring effects of policies, together with insufficient additional resources. Most of the remedial answers on offer are but slight extensions to existing programmes, reflecting an unconvincing political will to implement a radically new total strategy as a coherent package.

Several specific weaknesses are likely to command attention in the short term. The most significant is education, which is a major weakness. If the target is to increase the proportion able to speak Welsh by 5 per cent by the next census, then substantial sustained investment in bilingual teacher training must begin forthwith, let alone curriculum and resource development for all age groups. Secondly, there is little detail *in* Iaith Pawb on developing Welsh within the statutory sector, whether in terms of the provision of additional bilingual schools, or in the boosting of the Welsh L2 sector, or using Welsh as the medium for the teaching of a wide range of subjects. Neither is there any informed attention paid to the rates of language attrition between primary, secondary and tertiary levels. Some focus on Welsh for Adults in the document has been accompanied by a recent ELWa-inspired review of the system and, dependent on the recommendations, this could provide a consistent basis for additional growth. However, the use of Welsh within the Higher Education sector remains woefully inadequate, particularly in the light of a needs-based assessment of the likely skills required of an increasingly bilingual professional work force.[75]

Thus, despite the apparent extra energy to be expended on creating a bilingual society, Iaith Pawb is seriously handicapped in reaching its own declared aims by a lack of structural capacity to influence language behaviour modification. The most far-reaching change to date within the public sector was initiated by statutory legislation, thus it is even more surprising that Iaith Pawb does not contain a stronger commitment to investigating any proposed consideration of a stronger Welsh Language Act which would oblige large elements of the private sector to initiate bilingual working practices. Indeed, the treatment of the private sector by this and previous government documents is minimal and cursory at best. Thus, there needs to be a far more professional commitment to policy formulation to create a bilingual economy so as to make the rest of government language policy convincing to economic interest groups.

One positive element which the NAfW is advancing is an additional review of the Town and Country Planning Process and its effects on the Welsh language. Thus, Iaith Pawb makes extensive reference to national planning policy, to revisions of Technical Advice Note 20 and other related guidance to the planning profession, to housing development guidance, to the need to develop appropriate methodologies for conducting linguistic impact assessments (LIAs) to be devized in a joint-venture including 13 local authorities, two National Parks, the Welsh Language Board and commissioned academics. All of which is to dovetail with the strategies outlined in Wales Spatial Plan.

Nevertheless, Iaith Pawb has adopted many of the fine recommendations put to the Assembly reviews during 2002, the most notable of which are:

- the operation of the principle of language equality
- devizing an effective in-house bilingual culture
- deciding how Welsh will be a crosscutting issue in all aspects of policy
- producing bilingual legislation
- developing a professional bilingual legislative drafting team of jurilinguists, as in Canada
- developing innovative IT translation procedures
- prioritizing the NAfW's translation needs
- finessing its relationship with Welsh Language Board and its many partners
- relating its bilingual practices to other levels of government, institutions and to civil society.

However, the NAfW still needs to attend to unfinished business as proposed in Williams, 2000d; 2003:

- a National Data Centre for analysis, evaluation, monitoring
- a National Language Planning and Resource Centre
- priority action in the designated "Bro Gymraeg" districts
- action on the Concordats related to integrated planning and policy already entered into by the WDA, WLB, WTB, ELWa and related agencies
- consideration of a powerful Language Authority based on the statutory force of a new Welsh Language Act, which dealt with the rights of consumers and workers within designated parts of the private sector
- urgent consideration to the need to expand the bilingual education and training opportunities afforded by the Welsh University and Further Education sector.[76]

Finally, let us place the RLS lessons in an international Celtic context.

A pressing need is comparative work on bilingual policy and language equality issues within the UK, Ireland and Brittany.

RLS policy implications in comparative context

Future policy could be directed towards instigating research-based answers, which sought to:

1) Contribute both a theoretical and a practical element to language planning and language policy in the UK, Ireland, Brittany and within member states of the EU and the Council of Europe.
2) Assess the character, quality and success of the institutional language policies of the political assemblies in Scotland, Wales and Northern Ireland.
3) Investigate the complex nature of bilingual educational and administrative systems in Wales, together with regional specific systems in Scotland, Northern Ireland and Brittany.
4) Assess the role of cross-border arrangements for the increased recognition of Irish on the island of Ireland, together with Northern Irish, Gaelic and Ulster Scots links with Scotland. This involves the role of the underutilized Irish–British Council in terms of cooperation, and political bargaining at the UK and European level, together with bilingual education, civil rights and group equality issues in Northern Ireland.
5) Gauge the degree to which the information technology and media opportunities developed in connection with the National Assembly of Wales and the Northern Irish Assembly are capable of sustaining a wider range of bilingual practices in public life.

   (It is noteworthy that the development of Sianel 4 Cymru, and, to a lesser extent, the Gaelic-medium television service, has created a self-confident and pluralist bilingual workforce which sustains a wide range of media activities. It is possible that both Assemblies will have a similar impact in relation to the information society as it relates to matters of public administration, education, legal affairs and the voluntary sector.)
6) Investigate what effect the arrangements for the bilingual servicing of the National Assembly will have on the legitimization

of bilingualism as a societal norm, both in Wales and other British contexts.

7) Assess how the experiences generated within the National Assembly will impact on the bilingual character of educational and public administrative services, together with the local government and legal system.

8) Investigate to what degree the institutionalization of Celtic languages vis-à-vis the established dominance of English/French can be a model for the relationship of other lesser-used languages worldwide, in their relationship with English/French. Potentially, this issue is of global significance if one can transfer several of the lessons to be learned from the survival of the Celtic languages to multilingual contexts as varied as contemporary India, and much of Sub-Saharan Africa, let alone the evolving European political system.

9) Analyse the economic demand for a skilled bilingual workforce in several sectors of the economy; determine to what extent bilingual working practices in Wales offer a model for subsequent parallel developments within a range of multilingual contexts within the English regions, e.g. either in respect of several European languages or selected non-European languages such as Arabic, Urdu, Hindi or variants of Chinese languages of wider communication.

10) Analyse the extent to which European Union and Council of Europe language initiatives related to both the RM and IML are adopted in the various political contexts which comprise the UK and Ireland (Williams, 2003).

Conclusion

The National Assembly, Welsh Language Board, Welsh Development Agency, ELWa and Wales Tourist Board (among others) have a critical role as legitimizing institutions constructing new forms of partnership through their statutory obligations and pump-priming initiatives. Quite radical initiatives to strengthen the role of Welsh both as a community language and as a language of the workforce are underway following the recommendations of Williams and Evas (1997) and the Wales European

Task Force (1999) and, more significantly, the implementation of Iaith Pawb (2003). But the long-term, infrastructural support and dynamism will be non-governmental, largely located within the private sector and grounded within local communities who have already exhibited remarkable initiative in supporting regional economic enterprises. Charitable assistance and support is easy enough to offer when no one knows the full extent or the demands of the policy of creating a bilingual society. It will get tougher as the details unfold. Thus, committed political leadership and adequate resources are crucial, if the process of reversing language shift outlined in this chapter is to be fully realized.

Acknowledgements

The historical material based on my "Restoring the Language" in G.H. Jenkins and Mari A. Williams (eds.), *Let's Do Our Best for the Ancient Tongue: The Welsh Language in the Twentieth Century*, The University of Wales Press, (Cardiff, 2000), is used with permission of the University of Wales Press. I am also grateful to the ESRC for their support through grants No. R000 22 2936 and No. L219 25 2007.

Proposals for the Future of Welsh

August 2001: Policy Options

Colin H. Williams
Cardiff University

Several priorities in terms of policy initiatives

(N.B. policies should be accompanied by the specification of realisable targets within a reasonable timescale)

- economic development and job-creation programmes, a priority to tackle the fragmentation of Welsh-speaking communities
- holistic language planning which ties language goals to other socio-economic currents and regional development initiatives
- Welsh for Adults national plan and learning programme, geared towards integrational immersion
- a national strategic plan for bilingual skills in education which will bring bilingual education into mainstream provision, and build on a linguistically integrated education and training system for Wales
- the promotion of bi- and tri-lingualism to make Wales an "intelligent region"
- to build on the partial success of consumers' rights to bilingual services in several sectors of the economy it is necessary to ensure that workers enjoy similar rights
- revised Welsh Language Act to establish the statutory framework within which the pressing concerns of economic change, local property market fluctuations and migration issues may be addressed
- extending Welsh Language Board language schemes to appropriate elements within the private sector
- the National Assembly for Wales to formulate, adopt and revise a comprehensive language plan for its internal procedural and administrative operation
- the National Assembly for Wales to develop a national language

policy in order to realize its stated goal of creating a bilingual nation

- develop a national language plan for young people and youth culture
- small and medium-sized enterprises to develop bilingual schemes and working practices
- promote IT developments which offer bilingual choice as a norm rather than as an add-on extra.

References

Aitchison, J. W. and Carter, H. (1993) "The Welsh Language in 1991 – a broken heartland and a new beginning?" *Planet*, 97, pp.3–10.

Aitchison, J. W. and Carter, H. (1994) *A Geography of the Welsh Language*, 1961–1991, Cardiff, University of Wales Press.

Aitchison, J. W. (1995) "Language, Family Structure and Social Class, 1991 Census Data", presentation to The Social History of the Welsh Language Conference, Aberystwyth, 16 September.

Baker, C. (1993) Foundations of Bilingual Education and Bilingualism, Clevedon, Avon, Multilingual Matters.

Bellin, W. (1989) "Ethnicity and Welsh bilingual education", *Contemporary Wales*, Vol. 3, pp.77-97.

Casson, M. (1993) "Cultural determinants of economic performance", *Journal of Comparative Economics*, Vol. 17, pp.418-42.

Castells, M. and Hall, P. (1994) *Technopoles of the World: The Making of 21st Century Industrial Complexes*, London, Routledge.

Cooke, P. (1989) "Ethnicity, Economy and Civil Society: Three Theories of Political Regionalism", in C.H. Williams and E. Kofman, (eds.), *Community Conflict, Partition and Nationalism*, London, Routledge, pp.194-224.

Cooke, P. et al. (1993a) "Regulating Regional Economies: Wales and Baden-Württtemberg in Transition", in R. Rhodes, (ed.), *The Regions and the New Europe*, Manchester, Manchester University Press.

Cooke. P. (1993b) "Globalization, economic organization and the emergence of regional interstate partnerships", in C.H. Williams, (ed.), *The Political Geography of the New World Order*, London, Wiley, pp.46–58.

Council of Europe (1992) European Charter for Regional or Minority Languages, Strasbourg, Council of Europe.

Crowe, R. (1988) *Yr Wlpan yn Israel*, Aberystwyth, Canolfan Ymchwil Cymraeg i Oedolion.

Cynulliad Siroedd Cymru (1992) *Cyfarwyddyd Cynllunio Strategol yng Nghymru*, Yr Wyddgrug, Cynulliad Siroedd Cymru.

Davies, J. (1993) *The Welsh Language*, Cardiff, University of Wales Press.

Fforwm Iaith Genedlaethol (1991) *Strategaeth Iaith, 1991–2001*, Aberystwyth, Fforwm yr Iaith Gymraeg.

Gardner, N., Puigdevall i Serralvo, M. and Williams, C. H. (2000) "Language Revitalization in Comparative Context: Ireland, the Basque Country and Catalonia", in C. H. Williams, (ed.), *Language Revitalization: Policy and Planning in Wales*, Cardiff, University of Wales Press, pp.311–61.

Grin, F. (1996) "Economic Approaches to Language and Language Planning", *International Journal of the Sociology of Language*, Vol. 121, pp.1–16.

Grin, F. (1999) *Minority Languages and Regional Economic Activity*, mimeo, Flensburg, ECMI.

Grin, F. and Vaillancourt, F. (1997) "The Economics of Multilingualism", *Annual Review of Applied Linguistics*, Vol. XVII, pp.43–65.

Hechter, M. (1975) *Internal Colonialism: The Celtic Fringe in British National Development*, London, Routledge.

Hill, S. (1999) "Understanding the Prosperity Gap", *Agenda*, Summer, pp.12–13.

Huggins, R. and Morgan, K. (1999) "Matching a National Strategy with European Intervention", *Agenda*, Summer, pp.15–18.

James, C. and Williams, C. H. (1996) "Language and Planning in Scotland and Wales", in H. Thomas and R. Macdonald (eds.), *Planning in Scotland and Wales*, Cardiff, University of Wales Press, pp.264–330.

James, D. L. (1974) "Wlpan Cymraeg Aberystwyth" *Yr Athro*, 26 (December), pp.106–16.

Jones, H. and Williams, C. H. (2000) "The Statistical Basis for Welsh Language Planning: Data Trends, Patterns, Processes", in C. H. Williams, (ed.), *Language Revitalization: Policy and Planning in Wales*, Cardiff, University of Wales Press, pp.48–82.

Jones, K. and Ioan, G. (2000) *Mentro Ymlaen: Arolwg o'r Mentrau Iaith*, 2000, Castell Newydd Emlyn: Cwmni Iaith Cyf.

Jones, R. M. and Singh Ghuman, P. A. (eds.), (1995) *Bilingualism, Education and Identity*, Cardiff, University of Wales Press.

van Langevelde, A. P. (1993) "Migration and Language in Friesland", *Journal of Multilingual and Multicultural Development*, Vol. 14, No. 5, pp.393–411.

Mathias, J. (1995) *Wales – The Shift From Nationalism to Regionalism*, mimeo, European Studies, University of Wales, Cardiff.

Menter a Busnes (1993) *Nodweddion siaradwyr Cymraeg mewn busnes*, Aberystwyth, Menter a Busnes.

Menter a Busnes (1994) *A Quiet Revolution: The framework of the academic report*, Aberystwyth, Menter a Busnes.

Menter a Busnes (1997) *Success Story: A Report on the Work of Menter a Busnes 1995–6*. Aberystwyth, Menter a Busnes.

Menter Cwm Gwendraeth (1991) *Strategaeth, Menter Cwm Gwendraeth*, Cross Hands, Menter Cwm Gwendraeth.

Minority Rights Group, (1991) *Minorities and Autonomy in Western Europe*, London, Minority Rights Group.

Mlinar, Z. (ed.) (1992) *Globalization and Territorial Identities*, Aldershot, Avebury Press.

Morgan. K. and Price, A. (1998) *The Other Wales: The Case for Objective 1 Funding Post-1999*, Cardiff, The Institute for Welsh Affairs.

Morris, S. (2000) "Adult Education, Language Revival and Language Planning", in C.H. Williams, (ed.) *Language Revitalization: Policy and Planning in Wales*, Cardiff, University of Wales Press, pp.208–20.

Morris Jones, R. and Ghuman Singh, P. A. (eds.) (1995) *Bilingualism, Education and Identity*, Cardiff, University of Wales Press.

O'Riagain, D. (1989) "The EBLUL: its Role in Creating a Europe United in Diversity", in T. Veiter, (ed.) *Fédéralisme, régionalisme et droit des groupes ethniques en Europe*, Vienna, Braümuller.

O'Riagain, P. (1992) *Language Planning and Language Shift as Strategies of Social Reproduction*, Dublin, Instituid Teangeolaiochta Eireann.

Osborne, D. and Gaebler, E. (1992) *Reinventing Government: How the Entrepreneurial Spirit is Transforming the Public Sector*, London, Addison Wesley.

Puigdevall i Serralvo, M. (1999) "Politica linguistica al Pais de Galles" in *Politiques Linguistiques a Paisos Plurilingues*, Barcelona, Institut de Sociolinguistica Catalana, pp.97–111.

Rees, C. (1974) "Wlpan", *Barn*, 145, (November/December), pp.563–5.

Thomas, H. (1993) "Welsh planners voice some lingering doubts", *The Planner*, 22 October, pp.41-2.

Vaillancourt, F. (1985) *Economie et langue*, Québec, Conseil de la Langue Française.

Vaillancourt, F. (1996) "Language and Socioeconomic Status in Québec: measurement, findings, determinants and policy costs", *International Journal of the Sociology of Language*, 121, pp.69–92.

Wales European Task Force (1999) West Wales and the Valleys Objective 1, Cardiff, European Affairs Division, National Assembly.

Wales European Task Force (1999) *A Prosperous Future for Wales*, Cardiff, European Affairs Division, National Assembly.

Welsh Office (1993) "Welsh Social Survey", Cardiff, The Statistical Section, The Welsh Office.

Welsh Office (1995) "The Welsh Language: Children and Education", Cardiff, Welsh Office Statistical Brief SDB 14/95.

Welsh Office (1998) Statistics of Education and Training in Wales: Schools, 1998, Cardiff, The Statistical Section, The Welsh Office.

Welsh Language Board (1999) "A Strategy for the Welsh Language: Targets for 2000-2005", Cardiff, The Welsh Language Board.

Williams, C. H. (1986) "Language planning and minority group rights" in I. Hume and W. T. R. Pryce (eds.) *The Welsh and Their Country*, Llandysul, Gomer Press and Open University, pp.253-72.

Williams, C. H. (1988) "Addysg Ddwyieithog yng Nghymru Ynteu Addysg Ar Gyfer Cymru Ddwyieithog?", Canolfan Astudiaethau Iaith, 1, 1–28, Bangor, Canolfan Astudiaethau Iaith.

Williams, C. H. (1989) "New Domains of the Welsh Language: Education, Planning and the Law", *Contemporary Wales*, Vol. 3. pp.41–76.

Williams, C. H. (1993a), "Towards a New World Order: European and American Perspectives" in C.H. Williams (ed.), *The Political Geography of the New World Order*, London, Wiley, pp.1–19.

Williams, C. H. (1994) *Called Unto Liberty: On Language and Nationalism*, Clevedon, Avon. Multilingual Matters.

Williams, C. H. (1998) "Operating Through Two Languages" in J. Osmond (ed.) *The National Assembly Agenda*, Cardiff, The Institute of Welsh Affairs, pp.101–16.

Williams, C. H. (1999a) "Legislation and Empowerment: A Welsh Drama in Three Acts" in *International Conference on Language Legislation*, Dublin, Comhdháil Náisiúnta na Gaeilge, pp.126–59.

Williams, C. H. (1999b) "Bilingual Education in the Service of Democracy", *Annales di Studi istriani e mediterranei*. Koper, ZRS, pp.89–110.

Williams, C. H. (2000a) "Governance and the Language", *Contemporary Wales*, Vol. 12, pp.130–54.

Williams, C. H. (2000b) "Regional Development, Enterprise and Cultural Reproduction in Wales" in F. Grin and B. Winsa, (eds.) *Minority Languages and Regional Economic Activity*, Stockholm, UNESCO.

Williams, C. H. (2000c) "Restoring the Language" in G. H. Jenkins and M. A. Williams (eds.)*Let's Do Our Best For The Ancient Tongue*, Cardiff, University of Wales Press, pp.657–81.

Williams, C. H. (ed.) (2000d) *Language Revitalization: Policy and Planning in Wales*, Cardiff, University of Wales Press.

Williams, C. H. and Evas, J. (1997a) *The Community Research Project*, Cardiff, The Welsh Language Board.

Williams C. H. and Evas, J. E. (1997b) *Crynodeb Y Cynllun Ymchwil Cymunedol*, Caerdydd, Bwrdd yr Iaith Gymraeg.

Williams, C. H. and Evas, J. (1998) *Community Language Regeneration: Realizing the Potential*, Cardiff, The Welsh Language Board.

Y Swyddfa Gymreig (1992) *Arolwg Teuluoedd*, Caerdydd, Y Swyddfa Gymreig.

ii.) The Welsh Language in Chubut Province, Argentina

Paul W. Birt
University of Ottawa

The existence of Welsh communities and the survival to this day of the Welsh language in Chubut Province, in southern Argentina, may seem unexpected at first, given some of the more familiar nineteenth-century immigration patterns in the northern hemisphere. However, if we consider the economically-driven need to emigrate from mid-nineteenth-century Wales, and the successful drive on the part of the Argentine authorities to attract immigrants from western Europe during that period, the choice soon assumes a more integral place within the migratory patterns of Europeans in the mid-nineteenth century.[77]

Background

The Welsh people underwent considerable cultural changes during the course of the eighteenth century, partly initiated by industrial development and demographic growth but also by a new sense of self-awareness as a nation.[78] These changes came in conjunction with religious and educational ideas rooted in evangelical Nonconformity that were set to become the defining force of Welsh culture for the next two hundred years. The sense of Welsh identity predicated upon the nonconformist chapel tradition, dates largely from this sea-change in Welsh culture which also saw a renewed interest in the history of the Welsh people. The Welsh language was also central to this new direction since it was the primary, if not the only, language of the majority of Welsh people well into the nineteenth century. Within a context of religious enthusiasm, literacy in the language was achieved well before the advent of state education. New spiritual values played a central role in the evolving national ideology that was formed during the first half of the nineteenth century, yet despite this, inevitably, economic depression, coupled with a minoritized status for the Welsh language and élite prejudice against religious nonconformity, led many Welsh individuals and families to seek better opportunities overseas. New Welsh communities grew up especially in the Americas,[79] where it soon became apparent that by the second and third generation exogamous marriages were undermining the hope of ensuring language maintenance for the future.[80] This was of importance clearly in new Welsh communities because of the high prestige given to the Welsh language as receptacle of Welsh spiritual and communal values.

The problem of acculturation of Welsh people into the mainly English-speaking majority in North America and its attendant drift away from traditional linguistic and religious norms, led eventually to discussions about ways of obviating these tendencies.[81] The fact of emigration from Wales was accepted as a consequence of economic and other factors, but also the hostility of the state authorities in Wales towards largely non-Anglican religious practices and towards the Welsh language itself, created a situation where the concept of creating a New Wales seemed worthwhile and necessary. Not surprisingly, given the experience of new Welsh communities abroad, the idea of promoting Patagonia had its roots in the United States. One prerequisite in their choice was that the new Welsh community would not be immediately integrated into the larger anglophone community. One of the most active in the search for ways of channelling Welsh emigration, and for ways of creating a New Wales, was Michael D. Jones.[82] He, together with Lewis Jones, Edwin Cynrig Roberts and others, considered a number of places where a viable community in both economic and cultural terms could be founded. Amongst the places considered were Vancouver Island, Brazil and Argentina. The emigration company eventually made an application to the Argentinian authorities for a tract of land in the southern part of the country, initially in the Lower Chubut Valley area near the eastern coast. This was indeed an area which the Argentines wanted to populate with people of European stock. Prior to the arrival of the first contingent of Welsh colonists in 1865, the Argentine authorities had engaged in a genocidal war against the indigenous peoples of Patagonia, often euphemistically called the Desert Campaign. This, in theory, left the lowlands in Chubut open for colonization. This policy of attrition against the indigenous peoples of Tehuelche and Mapuche origin continued during the 1880s in the upper Chubut valley close to the lower reaches of the Andes near the disputed Chile-Argentine border. To their credit, the early Welsh colonists maintained good relations with the increasingly dispossessed natives, and Lewis Jones, in particular, frequently made overtures to the central government in Buenos Aires that fair provision be made to protect the rights of the native population.

The first contingent of nearly 160 Welsh colonists arrived on board the *Mimosa* from Liverpool on the evening of 27 July 1865.[83] After a difficult trek by some members of the group of some forty miles from New Bay to the northern Chubut riverbank, they subsequently experienced a period of extreme hardship as they established a network of small homesteads close to what would develop as the town of Rawson. Without help from the central government and local indigenous people they would almost certainly not have survived, and indeed several relocated almost immediately. Yet, despite setbacks, they succeeded in creating the nucleus of a self-sufficient Welsh colony, which, largely isolated from the central authorities in Buenos Aires except by sea, was able to develop its own institutions uniquely through the medium of the Welsh language. The concept of the colony as a self-sufficient and self-governing community is clearly reflected by the kinds of institutions that were created in the earliest years of the colony. The community gave itself a constitution, two types of law (*deddf athrywyn* and *deddf rhaith*), a local governing council and the beginnings of the Welsh chapel religious system. The constitution and law structure were without doubt innovations in modern Welsh life, since, in Wales, the law was the law of England and Wales administered in English, native Welsh law having been supplanted in the sixteenth century. In stark contrast, the English language during the earliest years of the Welsh colony was all but absent. In the first years, a basic school system evolved, usually attached to a chapel or the home of a schoolmaster, in which elementary education was given through the medium of Welsh. Although rudimentary, this system provided the basis for a wider provision in Welsh-medium elementary education that held sway until the mid-1890s.

The colonization initially took place entirely in the lower Chubut valley region. Small urban centres soon evolved, especially Rawson (known in Welsh as Trerawson) on the coast, which was to become the regional capital in later years, but also Gaiman, which today is still the focal point of Welsh language and culture in the locality. Eventually, when the building of a railway was undertaken to carry agricultural goods to the coast for export mainly to Buenos Aires, a new town of Trelew[84] founded in 1886, grew in size and population until it became the largest town in the area by the 1890s. These three semi-urban concentrations remained predominantly Welsh until about the late 1880s and early 1890s by which time in-migration, generated by the economic success of the Welsh colony, began to transform the demographic features of the urban areas of the colony. Rawson, the centre of local administration where the centrally appointed territorial governor resided, soon assumed a multi-ethnic identity, as it became the political focus of regional authority. The Welsh settlers in the first few decades, certainly, and for many decades subsequently, identified themselves territorially in terms of the patchwork of farms along the north and south sides of the Chubut river and their culture was defined in terms of the bonds of kinship and cultural ties that held the fabric of the new community together, with the Welsh language as the link that ensured the cohesion of those bonds.

Expeditions by members of the community such as Lewis Jones, Aaron Jenkins and John Murray Thomas into the hinterland had been undertaken since the 1870s partly in search of more fertile land but also in search of precious minerals. The latter interest gave rise eventually to a mini-goldrush in the region in the 1890s especially amongst those who, having come to the settlement, had difficulties securing viable farming land. The native peoples had talked about the forests and lakes of the Andean region in the west, and this was also fuelled by the writings of several earlier explorers, especially George Chaworth Musters, whose book about Patagonia was certainly well known in the colony.[85] The first official expedition, which did not have the previous military aim of rounding up the native peoples, took place in 1885, and was led by the new Governor of Chubut, Luis Jorge Fontana. This first expedition was made up mainly of Welshmen led by officers of the Argentine Army. This, and further expeditions to the Andean foothills along the upper reaches of the rivers Chubut and Tecka, led to the creation of a new Welsh colony with its eventual small urban centres of Esquel and the village of Trevelin.[86] Several of the original expeditions to the area by young Welshmen in the early 1880s had been in search of gold[87] but it was the lush and potentially attractive agricultural land that led to the new communities there, since available farm land within contact of the network of irrigation ditches in the east had become scarce. Newer settlers in the 1890s and afterwards were encouraged to work on farms in the new Andean colony. Although in smaller numbers and in many ways more isolated from centres of administration, the Welsh who settled there recreated the Welsh life that was already flourishing in the Lower Chubut Valley. This colony, generally called Cwm Hyfryd (or Cwm Hydref) in Welsh and Colonia 16 de Octubre in Spanish, came to prominence especially in 1902 when a plebiscite was held in the Welsh colony where they voted in favour of remaining Argentinian rather than becoming Chilean, thereby ensuring the border between the two countries, following a long period of contention regarding the issue of which country would have sovereignty over Patagonia.[88]

The influx of Welsh people into the Lower Chubut Valley can be seen as a very uneven process over a period of some fifty years from the date of the first landing in 1865. The *Mimosa* had on board approximately 160 passengers; few arrived again until 1874 and 1875 when over 500 came, not only from Wales, but from smaller Welsh communities in the USA. Another peak in the immigration numbers occurred in the early 1880s with the building of the local railway between Puerto Madryn and the newly created Trelew. The last major influx of 120 Welsh immigrants arrived in November 1911 on board the *Orita*, after which Welsh immigration into Patagonia ends, except for a continuing trickle of individuals who came as pastors for the colony's chapels or individuals who came for health reasons to a drier climate. The colony also lost some of its members for mainly economic reasons, the most notable being those 259 who left in 1902 on the *Orissa* for Canada, where they settled in Saskatchewan.[89] This occurred after the extremely destructive flooding that affected the Lower Chubut in the late 1890s, but also the growing involvement (some might call it interference) in the affairs of the colony by central government created an atmosphere of uncertainty and disaffection amongst some of the settlers. Some ideas of the numbers of Welsh speakers in the most affluent period of the colony can be extrapolated from some of the census figures for the area. The Lower Chubut Valley (including Rawson and Puerto Madryn) had a population of about 1,650 in the mid-1880s,[90] almost all of whom must have been Welsh-speaking. By the year 1893, it was estimated that Chubut Territory had a population of 2,513, not counting the indigenous peoples. Of these, there were 2,010 Welsh people and the remaining 503 were mainly "Argentine".[91] In 1895, the census reveals that in the rural areas of the valley 97 per cent of the 1,540 population were Welsh and, we can presume, Welsh-speaking. The Welsh population of Cwm Hyfryd was 166 at the same census.[92] In the urban sectors, namely Gaiman, Trelew, Rawson and Puerto Madryn, the Welsh population remained in the majority in the first two settlements but were in a minority of around 20 per cent in the latter. This tendency towards minoritization of the Welsh in the urban sector become a feature of the demography of Trelew, which was to become, within two decades, the largest town in the region.

Evolution of Welsh in Patagonia

Research conducted especially during the 1970s revealed a basic linguistic uniformity of the Welsh language throughout the Welsh communities, both in the Lower Chubut valley and the Andean colony of Colonia 16 de Octubre.[93] This is argued to be relevant in sociolinguistic terms, since uniformity, especially in the lexicon, can be viewed as a result of the unifying force of the language of chapel and education even though the direct influence of these two forces for normalization waned in the first decades of the twentieth century. Certainly the chapels, which only used Welsh, exerted a major influence in the formation of this spoken norm. The Sunday school system which was an integral part of the chapel organization in Wales also became, in Patagonia, the forum for discussion in which largely "higher" forms of the language would be used. In Wales, differences in lexicon tend to be most noticeable on a north-south axis. The Welsh language in Patagonia demonstrates a bias towards northern forms in the lexicon which might initially suggest a preponderance of immigrants from northern regions of Wales. In fact, it would seem that the majority came from the south and, in particular, from the south Wales industrial belt.[94] The 1875 and 1876 arrivals were specifically from the Rhondda valley and Aberdâr. Although not all inhabitants of these localities were necessarily from those areas originally, it does seem that the language of the first generation was moulded towards a norm that has its roots in the language of the chapel and the newfound prestige of the language in the public domain in Patagonia, which was lacking in parallel domains in Wales at the time. It should be noted, in addition, that the most prominent of the leaders in Patagonia in the first decades of the settlement tended to be from the north, although not without some prominent exceptions. This tended again to give a higher status generally to north-Walian speech forms. This normalization may have taken place quite quickly.[95] John Daniel Evans (1863–1942), one of the members of the original *Mimosa* contingent and who grew up in Patagonia, wrote graphically about the first years of the colony in Welsh and occasionally reflects the industrial south-Walian dialect of his parents (which would have been a familiar dialect amongst many of the *Mimosa* contingent) but in his later writings of the 1920s and 1930s his Welsh shows a very clear tendency to use forms associated with northern speech and no doubt reflects what had become a well-established norm. This diglossic situation would have been very prominent in south Wales in the nineteenth century where the language of chapel and the language of ordinary discourse would have displayed considerable divergence. This diglossic situation seems, from the writings of John Daniel Evans, to have existed in the earliest years[96] but evidently gave way to a new norm that brought the high and low forms of the language together. A reference to the language and distinctiveness of the earliest settlers described in the autobiography of John Coslett Thomas (1863–1936) and based on his firsthand experience after coming to Patagonia in 1875, is instructive.

> Be that as it may, my candid opinion is that the "polite and enlightened" new settlers had nothing to teach the old settlers, though they had spent ten years having hardly any communication with the world at large. Considering the hardships the old settlers had endured, they had done wonderfully well industrially and mentally. Their language was superior to that of the new settlers, irrespective of where the new settlers came from. Their speech was less vulgar, due to a ten-year fusion of dialects and the elimination of incorrect diction.[97]

Welsh toponymy

In common with other European settlers in the Americas and elsewhere, the Welsh gave names to locations in their new environment in their own language. Where indigenous names had long been used they tended to be kept, as in the case of Gaiman in the Lower Chubut Valley and Esquel in the Andean colony of Cwm Hyfryd. However, in the areas where the Welsh established themselves in the Lower Chubut Valley, the toponymy rapidly reflected the unilingual nature of the new society. Far larger numbers of indigenous names seem to have survived in the western areas where independent native settlements lasted longer. This new toponymy concerned, in the first place, prominent geographic features, farms and certain field names. Some were then also utilized as chapel names.[98] These chapel names then frequently became the name by which a particular locality or "zona" was known along the north and south banks of the Chubut river valley. Amongst these zones are Ebenezer, Bethesda as well as the more secular names of Glan Alaw, Tir Halen, Bryn Crwn, Lle Cul, Bryn Gwyn, Drofa Dulog, Treorki, and Tair Helygen. In modern times, several of these names, where possible, have become hispanized to Tres Sauces, Lomo Blanco, Tierra Salada etc.

Several urban and semi-urban conglomerations have Welsh names, the most obvious being Trelew, the largest town in Lower Chubut Valley, and named after the town's founder, Lewis Jones. Rawson, named after Dr Guillermo Rawson, was widely referred to as Trerawson (*tre*=town) in the nineteenth century and this Welsh form is still sporadically used. Further up the valley there is the village of Dolavon (River meadow); on the Atlantic coast, Porth Madryn (Puerto Madryn – Madryn Port) and in the Andean colony, apart from the larger town of Esquel, the village of Trevelin (Milltown) was founded in the later nineteenth century and in many respects acts as a focus of Welsh language and culture, not unlike Gaiman in the Lower Valley. Many other Welsh names were forged out of the Welsh experience of exploration along the Chubut River. Some names reflect historic or anecdotal events, Dyffryn Y Merthyron (the Valley of the Martyrs), Hirdaith Edwyn (Edwin's Trek), Dôl yr Ymlid (Meadow of the Chase). The descriptions in Welsh of the expeditions by the first Governor of Chubut, Luis J. Fontana, give an insight into the creative act of naming places as a way of assuming possession of the land; amongst the many names coined during that period, one can mention: Hafn Halen, Dyffryn yr Eglwys, Dyffryn Triphysg, Dyffryn Coediog, Yr Allorau, Craig yr Eryr, Hafn yr Aur, Nant yr Eira, Colofn y Llaw, Aber Gyrants, Dyffryn y Mefus, Cors Bagillt, Craig Goch, Nant y Fall, many of which occur along the northern stretches of the Chubut and the Andean foothills. The many Welsh place-names would easily run into the hundreds and some would be better known to those who made the longer journeys between the Andean colony of Cwm Hyfryd and the Lower Valley. However, the Welsh names of the colonies themselves were well-established by the end of the nineteenth century and afterwards, but the process of hispanization meant that many of these Welsh names, coined in the period when Welsh was the language of the majority, were translated into Spanish with the result that it is these forms today which are most frequently used and found on official maps. Some of the most prominent in this category are: Las Plumas (Dôl y Plu), Valle de los Mártires (Dyffryn y Merthyron), Paso de Indios (Rhyd yr Indiaid), Rio Corrintos (Aber Gyrants), Valle Frio (Dyffryn Oer), Arroyo Pescado (Nant y Pysgod), La Angostura (Lle Cul), Fuerte Aventura (Caer Antur). The most common Welsh names (which have also been translated into Spanish) are still known by many of the Welsh speakers of Patagonia; members of the older generation can sometimes give detailed information on specific names of a particular locality.

Welsh language education

The importance of education in Wales meant that the Welsh community in Patagonia was equally determined, even given the very restricted resources at hand, to provide the rudiments of elementary education. A Welsh-medium elementary school existed from 1868 in Rawson, the only village at the time, and later a small network of day schools following the same pattern arose in tandem with the more traditional Sunday schools, the latter being divided into classes for young people and adults.[99] The teaching of literacy in the Welsh language was of paramount concern, and, in this sense, the first and most influential Patagonian pioneer in this sphere, Richard J. Berwyn, was continuing the work of several generations of Sunday school teachers in Wales. He was, in addition, the author of an influential book in Welsh for teaching literacy in the colony. Day schools in the Welsh language, which spread during the following three decades throughout the colony, represented an initiative in terms of the Welsh language that was all but absent in Wales itself, where the only Welsh-medium education was the Sunday school. John Daniel Evans, who arrived in 1865 on board the *Mimosa* as a three-year-old, describes in his autobiography[100] the conditions that prevailed in the day school he attended and refers to another well-known teacher, T. Dalar Evans, who taught in the Glyn Du district near Rawson. He describes the situation at the school in the mid-1870s where the teacher used the Welsh Bible, the hymn-book and R. J. Berwyn's book to teach the young first generation of Welsh Patagonians. Another teacher from the period was R. J. Powel[101] (also known as Elaig) who later taught at the same school. A Welshman brought up in London, he had learned Welsh and other languages; he was the author of a book in Welsh, this time to help Welsh-speakers learn Spanish through the medium of Welsh. Since he was sent in the first instance by the authorities to teach in the colony, this probably represents the first clear indication that attempts would be made to ensure that new Argentines (i.e. those born in the country) would be strongly encouraged to learn Spanish. He was sent by the central authorities in Buenos Aires to teach at the Glyn Du school through the medium of Spanish, which was not eagerly accepted by the Welsh-speaking colonists. Efforts to teach Spanish at this period may have been largely seen as unnecessary by the vast majority and at odds with the original concept underlying the Welsh colony, but later, Powel's lessons in Spanish from the 1870s were reprinted on a weekly basis in *Y Drafod*, the local Welsh language weekly (1891–) in the 1890s, at a time when a knowledge of Spanish began to be viewed increasingly as a necessity amongst the inhabitants of the Lower Chubut valley.[102] Another settler, John Coslett Thomas, who arrived from Trealaw in South Wales as a young teenager with the rest of his family in 1875, also attended T. Dalar Evans's school. In his autobiography, he gives an interesting view of language and culture for a Trealaw boy recently arrived in Patagonia:

"In reading, writing and speaking the language of the school, which was Welsh, I was as backward as any of my age, and more so than some of my classmates. Except for Sunday school, this was the first and only Welsh school I was ever in. So little I knew of the Welsh language when I entered this school, and so Southwalian was my tongue, that I could not read nor recite Welsh correctly. I tried to recite a piece in an Eisteddfod that was held in a tent near this school house soon after we got there, but did not win because my pronunciation was incorrect. A Northwalian lad of my age, a son of one of the old settlers, took the prize with colours because of his diction."[103]

The fact was that even by the period 1890–95, there were 15 chapels in existence in Patagonia but only six schools.[104] William Meloch Hughes, came to Patagonia in 1881 and in the same year was employed as a teacher in the school associated with Moriah Chapel (Trelew). In his detailed volume of reminiscences he mentions the size of the class (25 pupils) and the fact that they had a wide range in age. Interestingly, he also points out that the local Committee for the colony stipulated that education was to be in Welsh. He was responsible for teaching geography, history and geometry in Welsh, despite a complete lack of textbooks apart from R. J. Berwyn's reading primer.[105] Inevitably, the generations of Welsh-Argentine children brought up in Patagonia during the 1870s and 1880s and a good deal of the 1890s were unilingual in Welsh (probably less so in Trelew), although many of their parents would have been, to a certain extent, bilingual in Welsh and English. During this period it was possible for non-Welsh speakers to become integrated linguistically into the Welsh community. There are numerous instances of how members of the native population also became proficient in Welsh, especially if they were brought up in the community.[106] The same was true of other individuals of various origins, especially if they lived in the non-urban districts of the Lower Chubut valley or Cwm Hyfryd. This process of integration was to be seriously jeopardized by the early years of the 1890s when the town of Rawson, and later the town of Trelew began to attract largely non-Welsh in-migration and immigration, largely as a result of the economic success of the colony. Likewise, the period of the 1890s represents very much a watershed for this period of generalized unilingualism. The Welsh colony had, by 1893, created five Welsh-medium schools in the valley and the government, as part of its growing policy to take over schools throughout the Republic, also had five. The state schools (or national schools) were expected to teach through the medium of Spanish. Clearly, the education question becomes a subject of paramount importance in considering how the Welsh community defined itself. The obvious independent-mindedness of the Welsh colony represented a threat to the centralist Argentine authorities and their desire to create national unity on the basis of a (fictitious) unilingual state. The Welsh colony had been conceived in the beginning as a semi-independent entity within the Republic, which would conserve its own religious and linguistic heritage with control over its local economy and governance, but the Welsh had not been able to assume sufficient control over the fate of the colony in political and demographic terms to ensure the continued predominance of the Welsh language. After the first two decades, the lack of available farming land within easy access of the irrigation system tended to slow down immigration from Wales. Opportunities had been seen primarily in terms of agriculture rather than in urban pursuits, and led slowly to the loss of Trelew as a Welsh town.[107]

As the Republic grew in stature, and the colony grew in prosperity, some clash of ideals was inevitable. The colony, for all its isolation in the first decade, was soon keen to build on links with the federal capital, Buenos Aires. Business links with the capital had been cultivated in the early years

Figure 3.1
Argentina with the Welsh Chubut region marked

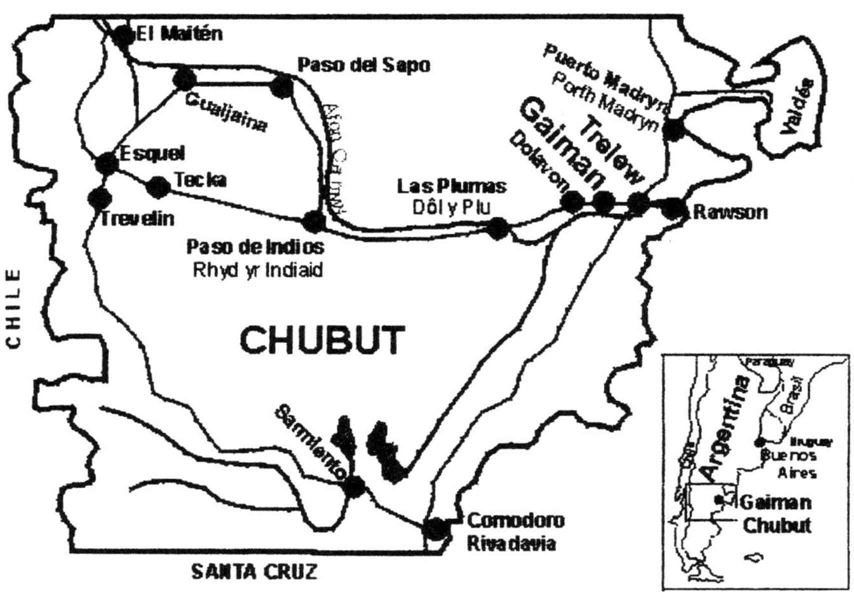

Source: *The Welsh in Argentina*, 2001, Sarah Stevenson

by such colonists as John Murray Thomas, who also forged links with the powerful English and Scottish business lobby in the capital. John Murray Thomas's trilingualism and ability to facilitate interaction between the Welsh-speaking colonists, the Spanish-speaking government officials in Rawson and Buenos Aires and the English-speaking business class in the capital was a precedent for the increasingly affluent members of the colony where, amongst the Welsh, trilingualism was common amongst the colony's elite. The central authorities were also increasingly suspicious of the Welsh colony because they interpreted the lack of enthusiasm for Spanish and Argentine culture as a form of inherent isolationism that suggested they were covertly pro-British and could seek to develop themselves into a British Protectorate. This may have been exacerbated by the continuing British influence in the financial affairs of the capital.[108]

During this period, there were 10 day schools each with approximately 50 pupils attending. The emphasis was on the employment of Welsh-speaking teachers, although Spanish was not excluded as such, given that the same schools were open to inspection by the Argentinian authorities. The colony had its own School Board chaired by Alejandro Conesa and, as committee members, such as John Murray Thomas, and Richard Jones Berwyn, Gregorio Mayo, and David Lloyd Jones.[109] A series of damning reports were sent to the central authorities from the Governor's office during the 1890s expressing anger at the colony's insistence on teaching through the medium of Welsh and thereby creating a new generation that knew next to nothing about Argentinian history and nationhood, despite the fact that a book on Argentine history had recently been produced in Welsh expressly for these pupils. Obviously, a situation was brewing, with the insistence that subjects were taught through Spanish, which would place children in Patagonia at the same disadvantage as those children in Wales who had been taught in a language they barely understood. The new state policy of the introduction of Spanish as the medium of instruction in schools was announced in the valley in 1895. The schools were officially expected to become Spanish-medium by 1896, notably by replacing untrained Welsh-speaking teachers who did not know Spanish sufficiently, with college-trained teachers who would teach only through the medium of Spanish. Clearly, the basic education of the children began to suffer, since so much time was now spent teaching Spanish. There was clearly resistance as well from the parents:

"Even though the government had built a grand school in Trelew, and had put into it a professor as headmaster, the majority of the children of Welsh families of Trelew still continued to attend with me at the Pont (Hendre) school, at least while I was teaching there. No doubt that I was teaching them things that their parents were far more ready to accept from me, than what was being taught at the Spanish school. Naturally, the Argentines did not look kindly on this situation, as they thought that what I, and others, were doing was to keep the children, even though they were born in Argentina, British and Welsh."[110]

The introduction of some education in the English language also, rather surprisingly, seems to have become a feature of a few schools in the valley in the 1890s. John Coslett Thomas refers to the need for teachers to use three languages in the classroom and this probably refers to what was the contemporary situation in Trelew, rather than further afield. An early educationalist, Robert Owen Jones, opened a small, independent school in 1889 in which the instruction was given in both Welsh and English. This probably reflects an influx into the town of non-Welsh speakers of British and Irish origin at the time of the railway construction, rather than a deliberate policy. Secondary education was made available in Lewis Jones's town house in Trelew for young ladies, from 1890, under the direction of Eluned Morgan, his daughter, aided by her cousin Mair Griffith; however this venture only lasted two years, caused by the ill-health of Mair Griffiths. Eluned's view of education was probably heavily influenced by her own experiences at Dr Williams's boarding school for young ladies in Dolgellau where she was sent from the colony to be educated. It is difficult to ascertain today in which languages the instruction was provided in the Trelew school. No doubt Welsh, English and Spanish had their place but comments by John Coslett Thomas suggest that English was certainly taught there, to the point that he calls the school an "English" school, which may be a slight exaggeration.[111]

After an absence of some four years, Eluned Morgan again returned to Gaiman where she concentrated her energies on the building of an Intermediate School (Ysgol Ganolraddol), sharing, as she did, the belief of parents in the Lower Valley that a complete education could not be provided by the state elementary schools. An Education Association (Cymdeithas Addysg) was created and she tirelessly campaigned for funding from the local population, in the belief that the school was necessary to ensure the future of the colony. Land was provided by the local municipality and the school was opened in 1906. Both from the architectural and educative perspective, the school was visibly based on similar secondary schools in Wales. The school became one of the best known secondary schools in the province over the following decades for the quality of the education provided. The classes were taught through the medium of Welsh, Spanish and English, with a clear emphasis on Welsh. Not surprisingly, a strong command of Welsh grammar and composition as well as English was stressed. Mathematics was taught mainly in Welsh but geometry in English. The records for the school dating from 1911 do not make it clear to what extent Spanish was used as a medium of instruction.[112] Eventually, and this was no doubt evidenced in the elementary sector in Trelew before the schools were taken over by the authorities, the common language between pupils of different ethnic backgrounds became Spanish and, without doubt, was perpetuated in later life. In fact, well after this period, when all the schools had become Spanish-medium, it became increasingly the norm for pupils from Welsh-speaking homes to communicate with each other in Spanish, since this had long since become the common language of the peer group in the urban sector. Since this school was, until 1925, the only secondary school and one whose reputation was very high, children of non-Welsh origin also attended. This was pre-empted largely by the creation of an all-Spanish secondary school in Trelew which also provided certificates that had official recognition. By 1927, there were 57 primary schools in the territory, all of which taught through the medium of Spanish.[113] The status of the Welsh Intermediate School was further eroded by the fact that daily transportation from the valley to Trelew became available.[114] Under pressure, in a period of hostility from the authorities, the Welsh secondary school eventually closed in 1947, but later reopened in a new form with the name Coleg Camwy and functions to this day.

The linguistic balance of the Lower Valley area in the areas close to Trelew and Rawson was changing in the first decade of the twentieth century. The growing Italian, Spanish, and indeed Anglo-British communities, became the defining force in the town of Trelew for the next few decades. Although difficult to quantify exactly in terms of ethnic origin, there were clearly families and individuals for whom English was the family language in the urban area.[115] Some prominent families in the colony had been English-speaking, for example the family of John Murray Thomas (who had arrived on the *Mimosa*), explorer, businessman and municipal politician, who had married into the Anglo-Argentine community of Buenos Aires and whose family settled in Rawson in the late 1870s in the outskirts of the town. The family was clearly bilingual in English and Spanish, although Thomas himself was trilingual. This apparent exception became less obvious by the early twentieth century when the opportunities offered by a prosperous colony attracted other English speakers. The Anglican Church, which had originally been established for Welsh-speaking members of the Church in Wales by Edwyn Cynrig Roberts,[116] soon became a focal point for the English-speaking minority. Their influence, in a period when the British were still an important force in the Anglo-Argentine community of Buenos Aires and the estancias of the north, later led to the foundation of an English-language college, which opened in 1914 and was run by Mary H. Gilbee.[117] Although called a college, it was in fact an elementary school, from which some of the pupils went on to the Welsh secondary school in Gaiman, or, more frequently after 1924, to the National College of Trelew, which taught only in Spanish. The Welsh community of Trelew had, it seems, been sympathetic to this new initiative and the fact that the vast majority of the names of the first generation of pupils at the English college were Welsh, seems to bear this out.[118] Inevitably, this college promoted an ideology based on sympathy with, if not allegiance to, the British Empire. Later, this institution eventually evolved into St David's College where both English and Spanish were taught (but not, apparently, Welsh!). The college was open to girls, and boys of younger age, although it became entirely a boys' school in 1927, and eventually closed in 1947.[119]

Welsh institutions

Various initiatives developed in the early years of the Welsh colony which would permit the strengthening and development of the economic infrastructure and, as a spin-off, would ensure that the Welsh language had a status beyond that of home, chapel and *chacra*. Probably the most influential of these initiatives was the creation of the CMC (Cwmni Masnachol Camwy), or the Chubut Cooperative Society. This organization made it possible for farmers to sell their produce via an organization that was created for the interests of the colony and one in which all the employees were Welsh-speaking. The Society was formed in 1885 during the period when it was still possible for such ventures to be entirely under Welsh control. This was an important step because previously farmers had to depend on middlemen who represented the interests of the mercantile class in Buenos Aires. In some cases, there was a language barrier between the farmers and these middlemen. A dispute at the end of 1884, between one of the farmers and a merchant in Rawson over the sale of timber in exchange for wheat, seems to have been the catalyst that led to discussions about the establishment of the cooperative society.[120] The fledgling organization sent one of their number to Buenos Aires to negotiate the sending of ships to collect produce from the colony and to bring merchandise for sale in the outlets of the cooperative society. The Cooperative Society was run, in the beginning, entirely through the medium of Welsh.[121] The branches of the Society acted as banks in the area before other financial institutions made any impact. Such an organization operated on the basis of shares owned by almost all the farmers of the region to create a working capital. Those who worked for the organization, especially those in administrative roles, did often reach these positions partly because of their ability to speak Spanish and English and thus were able to represent the interests of the community in their dealings with the Argentine authorities.[122] A branch was initially opened in 1886 in Gaiman under the management of William Meloch Hughes.[123] With the completion of the railway line, the main branch was transferred to Trelew in 1888, with another branch in Rawson. Eventually branches opened over the whole of Patagonia including Puerto Madryn, Dolavon, Nant y Pysgod, Tecka and in the southernmost enclave of Welsh colonization, Comodoro Rivadavia. The retail prices of goods brought in from Buenos Aires and the UK were set in order not to exceed a profit margin of 10 per cent which eventually caused the organization financial problems. The company was eventually liquidated in 1933,[124] having had only four directors in its near fifty-year existence, an indication perhaps of the stability of the company during the years of maximum prosperity in the valley. Following the devastating flooding of the valley in 1899, the Argentine President agreed to make Patagonia a duty-free zone as part of a recovery package.[125] This allowed the import of large numbers of British goods into the colony. Wheat imports from Chubut to Liverpool had started in the late 1880s and now continued; in fact discussion in the colony suggested that it was now more profitable to export to the UK than to Buenos Aires.[126] Several ships were employed almost exclusively for the import–export trade between

Chubut and Liverpool. The renewed links with Britain in economic terms also had cultural repercussions and may well have tended to suggest, in some minds, that Chubut was part of a larger economic and cultural network centred on the United Kingdom. At the same time, the Cooperative Society, whose working language was Welsh, and with control of the marketing of all agricultural produce, was able to help finance important cultural initiatives in the valley.

An important development in the valley was the appearance of the Welsh-language weekly newspaper *Y Drafod* in 1891, owned, edited and typeset in the first instance by Lewis Jones.[127] He had already produced an occasional newspaper called *Y Beirniad* in 1878, which had campaigned for the recognition of the rights of the colonists. *Y Drafod* was a four-page publication, which according to Lewis Jones in the first edition would, hopefully, provoke debate, cultivate ideas, and help educate the Welsh-speaking population of the valley about events in the rest of the world and about the Argentine Republic. Already, in 1892, financial considerations were endangering the continuation of the paper which led eventually to the paper being offered to the Cooperative Society in 1893. In the first place, the paper was run by a new company created in order to ensure its continuing publication. The Cooperative Society took over the printing of the paper finally and, were it not for this, the paper would almost certainly not have survived at the time, given that, although it had a relatively wide readership, the number of subscriptions in 1907 did not exceed 300.[128] The printing press was finally moved from Lewis Jones's mansion, Plas Hedd, to the premises of the Cooperative Society in Trelew where it remained until 1940, to be moved again to Gaiman where it is still published (2002) in a bilingual format now more reminiscent of the *papurau bro* found today in Wales and which act as regional and community monthlies. The survival of *Y Drafod* is also a tribute to the high level of Welsh-language literacy in the colony. Although to some extent the paper became the mouthpiece of the Cooperative Society, the quality of the editors ensured a high standard in Welsh journalism comparable, during the last decade of the nineteenth century and the first two decades of the twentieth, with similar publications in Wales. The Welsh-language newspaper was the only publication in the valley for many years, until in fact *El Pueblo* began to appear in Spanish in 1917.[129] As well as providing coverage of all aspects of the political scene in the valley, much of the column space in *Y Drafod* gave room to reminiscences of the early life of the colony and especially to literary endeavours, often the result of Eisteddfod competitions. The Welsh-language newspaper continued a tradition of campaigning Welsh journalism already in existence in Wales in the late nineteenth century, but also allowed the valley population to extend regularly their reading skills in areas not associated with the more familiar religious contexts of chapel and Sunday school. However, even at this early stage there were occasional articles in Spanish or English; perhaps not surprisingly the Spanish content grew in the mid-twentieth century but was very much an editorial prerogative. The inclusions of Spanish and English articles were probably more a matter of convenience, since they were often articles that had already appeared in other papers.

The Eisteddfod, a competitive festival of music and poetry familiar in Wales over the last two centuries in particular as a popular cultural event, also took root in the Welsh colony of Patagonia, as it had done in other concentrations of Welsh settlement. An attempt was made to emulate some of the high cultural aspirations of the National Eisteddfod in Wales. The awarding of a bardic chair was the traditional prize given to a poet at the annual Eisteddfod, normally for a poem in strict metre, or *cynghanedd*. In Patagonia, the first example of this tradition was in 1880 in the Frondeg district of Treorky, not far from Gaiman.[130] However important poetry was in the Eisteddfod, it seems likely that the late-Victorian love of choral music in the Eisteddfod made it especially popular and the competitive spirit between the choirs from various localities was the dynamic force which ensured the popularity of the festival from year to year. The influence of the late-Victorian Eisteddfod may have made itself felt through the numbers of settlers who arrived in the 1880s and 1890s. The first "Universal" Eisteddfod in Patagonia was held in 1891 with the participation of the whole valley area. Although all the competitions were in Welsh, some of the speeches from the stage were in Spanish, given by representatives of the local and central Argentine administration.[131] The competing choirs, rather than representing single chapels, were divided into the upper, central and lower valley areas, again underlining the cooperative spirit of the colony in general.[132]

The period 1890–91 saw an increasing number of new enterprises designed to promote the Welsh fact in Patagonia. Already, in 1890, the albeit short-lived organization Camwy Fydd (based as the name suggests upon the Cymru Fydd/Young Wales movement in Wales in 1886) had been formed to advance Welsh literature in the colony and to be a forum for discussion about the future of the colony. It does not appear to have espoused any particular political point of view, other than to support the Welsh character of the valley. This organization gave way to the St David's Association (Cymdeithas Dewi Sant) founded on St David's Day 1891 which is today the oldest of Trelew's cultural organizations. The St David's Association, having taken over the mandate of the defunct Camwy Fydd, as well as responsibility for the Agricultural Show in the valley, became the organizer and sponsor of Welsh cultural events. Its first major and long-term undertaking was the building of the Salón San David/Neuadd Dewi Sant in Trelew as a monument to the first Welsh settlers. The idea of a large spacious hall was seen as necessary as the main venue for the Eisteddfod, which was growing in stature, as well as concerts, and as the main venue for the St David's Day celebrations on 1 March. The use of the hall was always seen as being for the whole community of Trelew, regardless of ethnic origin, which in itself was a way of admitting the ethnic plurality of the town. The construction of the building and discussions about the building continued for many years until 1913 when it was used for the first time for the Eisteddfod. The official inauguration had to wait until the fiftieth anniversary of the First Landing of the *Mimosa* in 1915. The building remains to this day as a testimony to the Welsh contribution to the valley, although almost from the beginning it was used for a variety of functions not necessarily associated with Welsh culture, yet even in a later period when the language was declining in use in Patagonia, the records of the Association were kept in Welsh until 1940.[133] Yet, as an inspection of the certificates for shares issued by the Association as a limited company during the period *c.*1920 demonstrates, the use of Spanish was already taking hold.[134]

The importance of the Welsh chapel system

The importance of the socio-religious organization of the Welsh colonies of Lower Chubut and the Andes would be difficult to overemphasize.[135] During the whole period of Welsh immigration (1865–1911), almost all of those who arrived had been brought up in the Welsh nonconformist tradition. Nonconformity had its roots in seventeenth-century Wales and became the major form of religion for a very large proportion of the Welsh people by the end of the second decade of the nineteenth century. With the translation of the Bible into Welsh in 1588 and the development of a rich tradition of Welsh hymnology and theological discussion in eighteenth-century Wales, nonconformity became the most important bastion of the literary language and gave the literary language and those who were ministers and deacons, a high social status. Several of the early leaders of the Patagonian movement and those who came and worked in the colony, were ministers;[136] the chapel exerted an influence over the minds and behaviour of almost all in the Welsh colony until the advent of secularization during the 1930s and 1940s. The chapels also had a determining role in the field of education, first in the context of the Sunday schools which were attended by adults and children alike, and then the school houses which were built close to the chapels and eventually became the official state-run elementary schools after the end of the nineteenth century. In all, 32 Welsh-medium chapels in the Lower Valley were built between 1868 and 1925.[137] Two Anglican churches were also built, one in Trelew and the other in the upper valley village of Dolavon. Two chapels were built in the Andean Colony. The expansion of the chapels westwards along the north and south banks of the lower Chubut river and then in the Andean colony of Cwm Hyfryd (also known as Cwm Hydref or Colonia 16 de Octubre), makes it possible to track the growth of the Welsh colony. As in Wales, the chapels were built for the various denominations: Methodist, Congregationalist and Baptist, although, in time, the differences between them became blurred. Several of the buildings were lost during the serious flooding of the valley in 1899, but rebuilding largely ended during the beginning of the twentieth century.

Even given the retraction of the Welsh language from a range of external domains during the period 1920–50, the Welsh chapels managed to maintain themselves as the only undisputed bastion of the language outside the home. This does not imply, of course, that there was not a gradual and finally dramatic loss of religious practice towards the end of that period. The language had, by the 1950s, entered a period where its status had probably reached its lowest ebb, with parents widely becoming convinced that they should use Spanish in their everyday interaction with their children. This increasingly meant that the chapels alone could be responsible for any Welsh-language instruction for children who were increasingly becoming hostile to the language through peer pressure to identify entirely with Spanish. The chapels were caught in a paradox in which, in order to keep the children, they would have to reject the language that had been the vehicle and sustaining power of Welsh nonconformity for two centuries. Glyn Williams reports on the conflict that came to a head during the early 1960s[138] where conflict arose regarding the introduction of Spanish into the activities of the Welsh chapels, which was in danger of splitting the Welsh community into two factions. The conflict continued well into the centenary celebrations of the Welsh colony in 1965 with a heightened tension apparent during the organization of the 1965 Eisteddfod.[139] Other Protestant churches, mainly Episcopalian, which functioned in Spanish, established themselves in the valley. According to the same author, by the 1970s only seven of the original Welsh chapels remained open with a membership below one hundred.[140] In 2002, chapels in Trelew, Gaiman, Bryn Crwn, Bethesda, Drofa Dulog and Esquel (Andes) still held services in the Welsh language.

The Welsh Language in the urban sector: the loss of Trelew

Although the Welsh settlers created a range of institutions and companies that were designed to ensure the economic survival and prosperity of the colony, and created the conditions by which cultural survival in language and custom would be ensured through a social network based on chapel, kinship and other cultural bonds, there seems to have been no strong will to maintain a predominant presence in the expanding urban areas of Rawson and Trelew in either commerce, professional life or local politics. This, of course, eventually impacted the use of the Welsh language in the urban context relatively early in the twentieth century. Rawson (or as the Welsh originally called it Trerawson) was and remains (with a short interruption at the time of the flooding in 1899) the seat of provincial government; and in the first decades of the colony, was the focal point of the government-appointed officials. Based on the membership of the town council, the council debates in Rawson would most probably have been in Welsh until 1898 (excepting 1888 and 1889) when non-Welsh speakers joined the ranks of the councillors. This marks the date when the use of Welsh in the governance of the town came to an end. In Trelew (founded in 1886, and whose first municipal council was elected in 1904), Welsh as the language of municipal deliberations may have remained in sporadic use during the first few years of its existence but by 1907 and afterwards, the ethnically mixed nature of the council must have warranted the almost exclusive use of Spanish. Even if the Welsh language was not feasible in council meetings, judging by the names of the councillors, there was a considerable Welsh presence until about 1923. After this date, the Welsh members were in a minority.[141] The ownership of small businesses in Trelew for the year 1923[142] gives a clear indication of the relatively small number of shops and businesses owned by members of the Welsh community in that city. Of the approximately 455 businesses, professions and organizations listed, only 15 were recognisably Welsh in ownership. Although this does not take into account the relative importance of specific businesses, as for instance the grain mill owned by Evan Coslett Thomas, it does suggest a very reduced Welsh influence in Trelew in the field of commerce and local politics. This must also have been reflected in the language of the town. It is difficult to ascertain to what extent it was possible to use Welsh in shops and stores in Trelew in the 1920s. Although Welsh must have been heard frequently at this time from those who came into town from the Lower Valley region, both Spanish and Italian would also have been noticeable.

The influx of new immigrants into the towns of Trelew and Rawson was already reflected in the 1891 census, of which the results were published in *Y Drafod*.[143] The data are not easy to use, since all those born in Argentina, regardless of ethnic origin, are referred to as Argentines. Those described as British would be largely of Welsh origin, but must have included some Irish, Scottish and English individuals who may have come as part of the growth of the railway construction in the valley. Certainly, during the last decade and the first decade of the twentieth century, Trelew became increasingly a town that thought of itself as being divided in equal part between the Welsh, Spanish and Italian communities. The Italian community first created a mutual aid society in Rawson in 1891. A new Italian organization was created the following year in Trelew and a social centre was inaugurated in 1903. An influx of non-Welsh speakers arrived in Trelew from Rawson during 1899 and afterwards, partly because of the critical situation caused by the flooding of the valley when the Chubut broke its banks, a particular problem posed by the river at the time before the building of a reservoir. An additional influx was caused by the establishment of regimental barracks in Trelew, following the clash between the Welsh community and the authorities regarding Sunday drill, which all men below a certain age were required to perform. This conflict brought into clear profile the beginnings of widely differing lifestyles, cultural habits and behavioural expectations in the main town, if not the valley. The Welsh had lost their independent status as the predominant founding people of the Chubut valley:

"The Welsh were certainly not against the boys drilling on any other day, but drilling on a Sunday was very much against their beliefs. They wanted everybody to be able, if they wished, to go to the Sunday services. The Spanish, of course, thought otherwise. They thought that the Welsh were against the army as a whole, and against any kind of drilling whatsoever, and that the Sunday excuse was just an excuse... The Welsh made an application to the authorities to try and change the day of the drill, but this was protested strongly by the Spanish and the Italians because Sunday was for them a feast day, and to have the drill on any other day, even a Saturday, meant that they would have to lose work. The application was refused by the authorities for the same reason, saying that it would not be proper for them to listen to the complaints of one of the peoples over and above the others. They went on to say that it was, indeed, the obligation of every Argentine who was there, to follow the rules of the country."[144]

The non-Welsh population of Chubut Province was destined to grow exponentially between 1895 and 1915.[145] The Welsh and the Welsh language had become minoritized during the same period in the urban sector of the valley. Rawson in particular, excluding those born in Argentina, had over 1,500 people from Spain (many of whom were in fact Basques), nearly 700 from Italy, whilst native-born Welsh people represented only 355. Gaiman, which remained a bastion of Welsh language and culture, still had a majority of Welsh speakers although, in a total population of 3,660, there were at least 900 non-Welsh speakers of Spanish, Italian and Chilean origin; unfortunately, the linguistic origins of the Argentine-born population cannot be deduced from the basic data. However, it has been suggested that at this time (1915) the Welsh community of the Lower Valley was in the region of 4,000, of whom almost all would have been Welsh-speaking.[146] The Welsh population of the Cwm Hyfryd colony in the Andes,[147] grew considerably in size after about 1895 with its population of about 300, based on school attendance. Presuming a Welsh population of nearly a thousand, we have a rough calculation of 5,000 as the number of Welsh speakers in Patagonia during the second decade of the twentieth century.

Decline of the language

By the 1930s the Welsh population of the rural lower Chubut valley and Colonia 16 de Octubre was still largely Welsh-speaking, although the end of any sizeable immigration from Wales after the arrival of the *Orissa* in 1911 and the fact that demographically the Welsh were a minority in Trelew and Rawson meant that linguistic shift was predictable. The strength of the chapels remained a cohesive force in the Welsh-speaking rural districts along the valley but intergenerational language transmission will not take place if the language and ethnic origin of its speakers lack status in that society. Identity issues become noticeable in this period and became magnified in the following three decades.

The loss of the Welsh education provision gradually had the effect of making the children of the rural sectors bilingual from an early age, and many had opportunities to become trilingual, especially those who moved on to the private secondary sector or who lived in Trelew; but, as happens frequently in such situations, functional bilingualism or trilingualism is only a process towards unilingualism. Cultural events such as the Eisteddfod, the St David's Day celebrations and the Welsh-Patagonian festival of 28 July – Gŵyl y Glaniad – that celebrated the arrival of the *Mimosa* in 1865, were all indicators of the intensity of Welsh identity in the colony. The local Welsh newspaper *Y Drafod* gives full coverage to these events from the early 1890s and some idea of their decline can be gauged for the years 1930–1950. The years after the First World War also saw a decline in British influence in Argentina as a whole and this seems to be reflected in the decline of specifically British cultural and religious interests in Trelew. Also, links between Wales and Patagonia become more and more infrequent.[148] This may have effected the apparent decline in interest in St David's Day (1 March) which had been promoted by the St David's Association in Trelew, since both the Italian and Spanish communities of Trelew promoted their national days. The rapid growth of the non-Welsh communities in the urban sectors seems to have eventually shaken the confidence of the Welsh as a separate ethnic entity. There had been serious losses in the past, with the severe flooding of the valley in 1899, the Welsh-speaking heartland, and the loss of Welsh-medium schooling, the militia crisis, and discussions in the press about leaving Argentina altogether.[149] A significant contingent had left for Canada in 1902, and research was conducted by Llwyd ap Iwan (the son of Michael D. Jones) into the feasibility of relocating the whole colony to South Africa. His visit to South Africa and his glowing reports of the farming possibilities might well have led to considerable relocation, had it not been for his sudden death soon afterwards. The Welsh community had also associated itself to some extent with British interests in that last decade of the century and the gradual reduction of British involvement in Argentina may also have caused uncertainty about identity issues and the future of the Welsh community.

The Eisteddfod remained a popular event and, when held in Trelew in 1920, attracted a large attendance.[150] In the same year, St David's Day was well celebrated in Gaiman (but not in Trelew); and, interestingly, Gŵyl y Glaniad was celebrated in several of the chapels in the valley but not separately in Trelew. In 1925, both Trelew and several of the chapels celebrated St David's Day and, in Seion Chapel in Bryn Gwyn, a Youth Eisteddfod was instigated that attracted considerable attention.[151] Both the 28th July and the Eisteddfod were still considered of importance to the Welsh communities. This situation, based on reports in *Y Drafod*, continued until about 1932, which also saw a serious economic crisis in the country. In 1934, it was reported that St David's Day had not been celebrated in the valley and Gŵyl y Glaniad, which was for many Welsh-Argentines the more important of the two festivals, went almost unnoticed in Trelew, "for the first time in our history", as *Y Drafod* ruefully reported it.[152] Matthew Henry Jones notes that this evidenced the beginning of the unravelling of the tripartite unity in Trelew. The inhabitants of the town of Trelew had co-operated during the first two decades of the twentieth century in each other's festivities, the Welsh on 28 July, the Italians on 20 September and the Spanish on 12 October. The 28 July was now almost the only Welsh festival celebrated primarily in the rural districts. The Eisteddfod, which had been held annually from 1908 (and sporadically before that), was held only three times in the 1930s, and only eight times between 1937 and 1965.[153] St David's Day, to all outward appearances, was no longer celebrated by the early 1940s. No mention is made in *Y Drafod* for 1941 or 1942 and, by 1943, the St David's Association had, for the time, become inactive. During that year, Seion Chapel in Bryn Gwyn held a celebration, the only recorded celebration of St David's Day. This apathy was noticed in the community and mainly attributed to the inactivity of the St David's Association. Gŵyl y Glaniad was also almost ignored. It had been the custom for shops and offices to close in Trelew on 28 July but increasingly this too had stopped.[154] The Eisteddfod was being held, although after 1943 it was in decline until it was energetically revived in 1965. Some idea of the growing tendency to introduce Spanish into the proceedings can be found in the lists of competitions published in *Y Drafod* during this period.[155] Attitudes towards the Welsh language, especially amongst young people, until the mid-60s were largely that of a generation looking at an outmoded heritage, associated with older chapel-going relatives. This was to change gradually.

Survival and revival strategies

The centenary of the Welsh colony in 1965 was a turning-point in the decline of Welsh cultural activity and identity. It brought a renewal of direct contacts between Wales and Patagonia and heralded the beginning of visits by groups from Wales and a greater realization in Wales that the Welsh language had survived in Argentina and that many of the Welsh-Argentinians were again keen to promote their language and culture. One outcome of the celebrations was the renewal of the Eisteddfod, albeit in a bilingual form, and to celebrate their Welshness, albeit in a separate Argentine version. In the following years Chubut increasingly became a tourist venue for Argentines from the capital, and the Welsh renewal of its cultural roots led to the now familiar outcrop of *casas de te* where a traditional Welsh tea could be experienced in the beautifully decorated older houses in Gaiman and other Welsh centres, to the sound of recorded Welsh choir music. Welsh culture in Patagonia was in some senses in danger of becoming folklorized as a tiny bastion of non-hispanic Argentina, where the architecture, names and cultural events like the Eisteddfod were reminiscent of other ethnic *colonías* in the country whose roots went back to the early years of the Argentine state. This was not the whole picture, however, since the Welsh language, although long-since banished as a living language on the streets of Rawson and Trelew, was still the natural means of communication in many of the *chacras* in the valley and in the Andes. The Eisteddfod, although now thoroughly bilingual, aimed to involve both Welsh and Spanish speakers in choral and literature competitions that reflected their linguistic traditions.[156] The contribution of the Welsh to the early history of Chubut was also given greater prominence in street names, statues and commemorative plaques, one of the most outstanding being the statue celebrating the contribution of *la galesa* or the

Welsh woman to the early evolution of the colony, and erected in Puerto Madryn in 1965.

It had become clear that by the early 1990s, the language was mainly restricted to those born before *c.*1950, and indeed the attitude towards the language was of paramount importance in its actual use. A younger speaker of the language would now generally only use the language with older members of the family and community, if at all, but hardly ever with his or her contemporaries. Experience at school was also a defining factor, given that by now friendships and romantic bonds would be almost always undertaken through the medium of Spanish. Even the generation whose education goes back to the 1960s and who were in some measure able to speak Welsh, tended to reject that language when involved in peer-group activities. The language was tending to be associated with backwardness, the older generation and chapels. Yet, another very dynamic cultural initiative has taken place since the 1990s within the context of changing attitudes.

Given that the Welsh language is still spoken in many homesteads in the Valley (especially the town of Gaiman, and the rural districts along the Valley) as well as Trevelin in the Andes, including the *chacras* of Cwm Hyfryd, a survey was conducted by Dr Robert Owen Jones in these areas to quantify the vitality of Welsh and the interest and feasibility of setting in place, in those still traditionally Welsh districts, opportunities to teach Welsh as a second language. The survey, published in 1996, led to the first teachers of Welsh being sent from Wales to Patagonia the following year. The present author was privileged to be able to attend the meeting to welcome the first teacher who had been appointed to teach Welsh in the Andean regions of Esquel and Trevelin in 1997 and witnessed the clear enthusiasm of the local people, most of whom present did not speak Welsh. Three or more teachers are now sent on an annual or bi-annual basis to the three centres of Trelew, Gaiman and the Andes (Cwm Hyfryd).

Their purpose is not only to provide Welsh-language classes to adults and young people but also in some measure to stimulate interest and participation in other traditional aspects of Welsh culture that are associated with the language, including the choirs, modern Welsh youth culture, and occasionally chapel activities. Another paramount objective is the training of local tutors who can take over the work of teaching the language. A spin-off from this project has been the creation of Ysgolion Meithrin (Welsh-medium nursery schools) for those of pre-school age, closely based on the model that has been very successfully developed in Wales. This allows very young children to learn Welsh in a natural educative setting, although usually their parents are non-Welsh speaking. Funding for the scheme to send Welsh teachers came originally from The Welsh Office and was taken over subsequently by The National Assembly for Wales and has been encouraged and supported by the First Minister of the Welsh Assembly, Mr Rhodri Morgan. The scheme has attempted to provide classes to people of all ages. Recently, it has emerged that there is an increase in the numbers of classes for young children but that the adult classes have tended to stabilize. During 2001, 700 people attended classes in Welsh in Patagonia, with 149 hours of teaching per week.

It is probably too early, still, to come to any clear conclusions about the future of Welsh-language teaching in Patagonia on the basis of the work achieved since the launching of this scheme. Other ethnic language schemes exist in Argentina, including Basque, Catalan, Yiddish and German. Apart from such languages as German and Italian, they do not represent clearly defined communities in the country. Italian was a major language in Argentina in the early twentieth century, and German, and Swiss-German continue to be spoken, and in some cases taught, in areas of their settlement. What sets Welsh apart from these, is that it has a presence in clearly specific areas along the eastern Chubut valley and the Andean area around Esquel and Trevelin where it enjoyed majority status in rural settings until *c.*1950. Welsh has now become minoritized in all these areas and the survival of the language in Patagonia now depends on a wide range of conditions.

The introduction of the Welsh teaching scheme reflects a clear desire on the part of Welsh-Argentines to see their linguistic heritage as part of their identity as Argentines and that the language should be taught as part of the education of those who live in settlements that were founded by the Welsh. This, of course, should eventually lead to a debate about the place of heritage languages in post-colonial contexts. It is unlikely that many of those who are promoting the teaching of Welsh in Patagonia expect or even desire a utopian return to a (largely mythic) Welsh-speaking Patagonia. Spanish is accepted as the national state language. At the present moment, there are still appreciable numbers of adult Welsh speakers in Chubut; a considerable number of these, for varying reasons, have not transmitted the language to their children but have welcomed the scheme to teach Welsh as a second language for their grandchildren, now that attitudes have changed again towards the Welsh language. In the meantime, several hundred children are being introduced to the Welsh language through classes. At this point, it is unclear to what extent some of these children will become fully proficient and thereby ensure a continuum of Welsh-speaking during the twenty-first century. Many of the students have reached a high level of proficiency, one of them won the Learner of the Year competition at the National Eisteddfod of Wales in 2001. Will a situation be created whereby each succeeding generation will (as a matter of parental choice) learn the language in a school setting rather than from the parents? This is probably the least attractive option as a language maintenance strategy, but may be the most probable.

During the past few years, contacts between Wales and the Welsh communities in Chubut have grown rapidly. Greater travel possibilities have made Patagonia a tourist venue for some Welsh speakers. This has meant that some of the Welsh communities, especially Gaiman, have become visually very Welsh and, in this sense, the tourist attraction is not only aimed at the smaller Welsh market but at the many tourists from Buenos Aires who come to Chubut. The Welsh language is sometimes used for hotel names, businesses and bilingual (and trilingual!) menus are available in some of the teashops and hotels of Gaiman, Trevelin, and Esquel. Less superficially, the interaction between Wales and Chubut works on a variety of levels, apart from the British Council-run project to bring Welsh language teachers to Patagonia. Organizations such as Cymdeithas Cymru-Ariannin (the Wales-Argentina Association) have for many years been instrumental in promoting links between Welsh speakers in Wales and Patagonia. With the arrival of new technologies, other channels have been successfully explored. One of the most exciting is Dolen Ysgolion (School Link) which seeks to foster links between Welsh-medium schools in Wales and schools in Chubut where there is a sense of Welsh heritage. This allows children to communicate by electronic mail between the two countries, and it is hoped it will lead to the exchange of teachers in the future. The Eisteddfod in Chubut has gone from strength to strength and, although no longer predominantly Welsh in language, it has become adopted by people of all origins in the region and is recognized as the oldest cultural festival in Chubut Province. Thus, an essential part of Welsh culture has become an integral part of the culture of Chubut. In Welsh-speaking Wales, the existence of the Welsh in Patagonia has become more familiar in recent years owing to various television and radio programmes that have been devoted to life in modern-day Patagonia. In Chubut as well, local radio stations in both Trelew and Esquel have broadcast programmes of Welsh music and interviews. Live webcasts of the Chubut Eisteddfod have been made. A wide range of web material exists devoted to the Welsh in Patagonia.

Conclusions

In a period when centralized states may be beginning to be transformed in a way we cannot, for the moment, imagine clearly, and reorganizing themselves into new communities, it might be the right time to reappraise how regions will function as part of such new realignments. The discussion of such matters has a long history in western Europe and may now be reaching a point where, at last, the integral elements of the linguistic mosaic that are a feature of many European countries will not be seen as retrograde and threatening to central powers. Such debates have yet to be formulated in many of the constituent countries of the Americas, including Argentina. Ultimately, despite the healthy rediscovery of links between Wales and Patagonia, it must be a question for those in Chubut how they wish to promote Welsh and secure its survival. The danger is that Welshness will become folklorized in a centralized state that sees linguistic diversity within its borders as either a threat or, more frequently now, as a harmless relic of an earlier stage in the state's history. A Welsh-Argentinian is no less Argentine when he or she speaks Welsh (and Spanish); thus, let us hope that this enclave of Celtic speech in the Southern Hemisphere will thrive as Argentina recreates itself. The major danger to the newfound status of the Welsh language and culture in Chubut is the perhaps inevitable, yet not imminent, loss of the mother-tongue Welsh-Argentine speakers. If the provincial authorities in Chubut ever decide on a policy of promoting the living Celtic language first introduced there in 1865, then perhaps part of the research work in the policy construction would be to examine the experiences of other post-colonial societies like Australia, New Zealand and Canada. Clearly, such a policy could hardly ignore other heritage languages in the region, especially those of the indigenous peoples. Much depends, finally, on the attitude of speakers of Welsh in Patagonia and those of Welsh origin who may not have been brought up in the language. The links with Wales are also of paramount importance but, rather than depend upon a mindset that sees a reversal of language shift in a historical linguistic territory, it might be better to think in terms of a language acquisition development programme that respects the unity and diversity of the region and the country.[157]

Other *Colonías* in Argentina

It might be thought that the Welsh colonies in Argentina were a unique experience in the history of that country but it is sometimes forgotten that during the nineteenth century and early twentieth century, Argentina had a string of relatively small ethnic or multi-ethnic *colonías* throughout the republic. These settlements were encouraged by the Argentine authorities in order to populate areas outside of the Buenos Aires region. Between 1856 and 1875, 34 colonies were established between Santa Fe and Entre Rios.[158] A close inspection of the nationality of the settlers in each shows that several displayed an ethnic mixture, as for example the Esperanza colony of 1856, which was mainly made up of Swiss and German families. Several Italian and Swiss colonies are also listed, as well as a colony of Californian Protestants, New California. In addition to the Welsh colony founded in 1865, mention is made of another Welsh colony in Santa Fe, made up of 44 people who had left Chubut. Another secondary Welsh colony was set up in Sauce Corto (now Coronel Suarez), approximately 300 kilometres southwest of Buenos Aires.[159] However, few if any of the other colonies in nineteenth-century Argentina organized themselves quite like the Welsh into an ethnic and largely *separate* society with institutions that were designed with a clear intent to ensure their linguistic, cultural and economic survival. Nevertheless, a handful of these other *colonías* have survived until the present day and, in some ways, their present situation and that of the Welsh colony demonstrate some similarities.

A parallel can be drawn between the Swiss-German Colonía de San Jerónimo in Santa Fe and the Welsh Colony of Chubut. San Jerónimo was populated by members of the farming community from the Swiss-German part of Valais canton in Switzerland in 1858.[160] By 1864, the colony had a population of 485, of which 422 were Swiss,[161] and by the end of the following year the number had reached 800. The numbers arriving declined during the last period of immigration from Valais to San Jerónimo during the period 1871–78. Unlike many of the first Welsh colonists in the early years, the Valais Swiss were directly from an agricultural background and developed similar types of produce that had been familiar to them in

Switzerland, mainly in the field of dairy produce. They introduced into the area the typical cultural features of their homeland, especially those of instrumental music and dance. Unlike the Welsh, who were able to develop sophisticated social networks within the chapel system which acted as meeting places for social interaction as well as providing spiritual direction, the Valais Swiss lacked cultural networks, except the local church and the general stores. The local municipal council, established in 1873, was entirely run by Swiss members from the settlement. All the documentation associated with the council was kept for many years in High German. With a population of nearly 1,000 in 1872, the urban sector of the colony was still largely undeveloped but this changed radically in the mid-1880s when the town of San Jerónimo reached the equivalent level of the rural sector. By the early 1900s the population had reached 2,579,[162] and, unlike the town of Trelew for instance, by the 1920s a large range of small businesses in San Jerónimo were still in the hands of the descendants of the original colonists. Similar in-migration patterns that affected the Welsh colony during the twentieth century can be seen at work in the Swiss colony. The latter part of the nineteenth century, possibly with the beginnings of non-Swiss migration into the area, saw the creation of a Swiss Society in 1897 which parallels the functions of the St David's Association in the Lower Chubut Valley. This organization brings together the various cultural aspects of the Swiss community, especially dance and music, as well as attempting to foster the use of the Swiss-German dialect brought to Argentina by the original settlers from Valais and still used by certain families. These cultural manifestations were given a remarkable boost in 1991 at the time of the seven-hundredth anniversary of the founding of the Swiss confederation. This led to a series of visits by members of the Swiss Colony to the home region of their ancestors in Switzerland and vice versa. The fact that the Swiss-German dialect had survived in San Jerónimo for more than a century, enhanced the possibilities of creating new links between the colony and Valais canton. The rediscovery of the Argentinian Valais population created a wave of interest in the media and academic circles, since the dialect, dances and music preserved elements that had disappeared in Europe. The largely folkloric aspects of the remaining culture should be a lesson for those managing the present-day evolution of Welsh culture in Patagonia.

The reversal of language shift in Welsh communities in Patagonia is not usually referred to as such and, indeed, is more of a reflection of the historically recent rediscovery of the Chubut Welsh by Welsh people in Wales, rather than a planned strategy between local agencies and local people. It operates on the basis of experience in Wales itself (especially the successful Wlpan or intensive courses in Wales). As Joshua Fishman remarked,[163] a policy of no policy, such as we find in several countries, is technically permissive. Although demonstrating extreme hostility to Welsh in the early twentieth century, the Argentine state has a benign attitude of non-involvement in the efforts to bolster the use of Welsh in Chubut. In fact, it would be misleading to imagine the efforts that are taking place in Patagonia as being in the same category as the kind of attempts that are currently taking place in a number of forms in the home countries of lesser-used languages. The stages described by Joshua Fishman for Reversing Language Shift are unlikely to be applied to Welsh in Patagonia.[164] The attempts, not only in Patagonia but in a multitude of contexts in the Americas and elsewhere (outside of the homeland context), have more to do with the kind of identity issues that the same author refers to as ethnolinguistic saliency, whereby awareness and implementation of ethnic identity (or identities) varies and changes from one occasion to another.[165] Hyphenated ethnicity is a common feature in those countries that have seen multiethnic immigration and, for those who choose to emphasize their specific ethnic origin within a "non-ethnic" state, there will be a desire to learn the ethnic language and seek cultural events in order to expose that ethnic participation. It seems most likely that the growth in interest in Welsh in Chubut, especially amongst young people, has its origins in this newfound, multilayered identity which functions as much in Argentina, with its multiethnic origins, as it does in, say, Canada or the United States. Learning Welsh in Patagonia is not an attempt at reversing language shift but rather, enabling participation in Welsh-language cultural events such as the Eisteddfod, choirs and Welsh youth culture, and to access the cultural and ethnic interaction between Patagonia and Wales. This exercise reveals, at the very least, that within a Latin American ethnolinguistic identity, other identities, apart from the polarization between *hispanidad* and Anglo-America, are possible and that Latin American identification can also be valid on the basis of a range of languages, including those of non-Spanish immigration, as well as Welsh whose speakers ultimately contributed to the development of a local form of *Argentinidad*.

References

Bennett, Carol (1985) *In Search of the Red Dragon: The Welsh in Canada*, Renfrew, Ontario.

Birt, Paul W. (ed.) (2004) *Bywyd a Gwaith John Daniel Evans, El Baqueano*, Llanrwst.

Birt, Paul W. (ed.) (forthcoming) John Coslett Thomas, *Hunangofiant*.

Chamberlain, M. E. (ed.) (1986) *The Welsh in Canada*, Cardiff.

Coronato, Fernando (1999)(translation of Thomas Jones Glan Camwy) *Historia de los Comienzos de la Colonia en la Patagonia*, Trelew.

Davis, Evan E. (ed.) (1979) *Our Heritage: Early History of Tyn Rhos Welsh Congregational Church and Its Neighborhood*, Ohio.

Davies, Gareth Alban (1976) "Iaith y Bobl" pp.62–85, in *Tan Tro Nesaf*, Llandysul.

El Regional (Edición especial) (1975) "La Colonia 16 de Octubre", Gaiman, July.

Escuela No 39 de Bryn Crwn: Un recuerdo, Rawson, (n.d.).

Evans, Clery A. (1994) *John Daniel Evans, El Molinero*, Buenos Aires, (second edition).

Ferns, H.S. (1960) *Britain and Argentina in the Nineteenth Century*, Oxford.

Fiori, Jorge and De Vera, Gustavo (2002) 1902: *El Protagonismo de los Colonos Galeses en la Frontera Argentino-Chilena*, Trevelin.

Fishman, Joshua (ed.) (1999) "Sociolinguistics", in *Handbook of Language and Ethnic Identity*, New York.

Fishman, Joshua (1991) *Reversing Language Shift*, Clevedon, Multilingual Matters.

González, Virgilio (1998) *El Valle 16 de Octubre y su Plebiscito*, Trelew.

Graham-Yooll, Andrew (2000) *La Colonia Olvidada: Tres Siglos de Presencia Británica en la Argentina*, Buenos Aires.

Graham-Yooll, Andrew (1981) *The Forgotten Colony: A History of the English-Speaking Communities in Argentina*, London.

Gutierrez, Ramón, (ed. et al) (1998) *Habitat e Immigración: Nordeste y Patagonia*, "San Jerónimo. Enclave suizo en territorio santafesina", Buenos Aires.

Hall, Ruth (ed.) (1993) *The Welsh Way: Oral History in the Long Creek Welsh Community in Iowa*, Iowa.

Hughes, Osian, (1995) *Los Poetas del Eisteddfod*, Rawson, Chubut.

Hughes, William Meloch (1927) *Ar Lannau'r Gamwy Ym Mhatagonia*, Liverpool.

Humphreys, Lewis (1910) diary in *Y Drafod*, 15 April.

Ifans, Dafydd (ed.) (1977) *Tyred Drosodd: Gohebiaeth Eluned Morgan a Nantlais*, Pen y Bont ar Ogwr.

Jenkins, Geraint (1987) *The Foundations of Modern Wales 1642–1780*, Cardiff.

Jones, Lewis (1993) *La Colonia Galesa*, Rawson.

Jones, Aled and Jones, Bill (2001) *Y Drych and American Welsh Identities 1851–1951*, Cardiff, University of Wales Press.

Jones, Edi Dorian (1999) *Fotografías: Capillas Galesas en Chubut*, "Contacto Gales-Aborigen en las Capillas", Trelew.

Jones, Lewis (1898) *Hanes y Wladfa Gymreig*, Caernarfon.

Jones, Matthew Henry (1997) *El Desafío Patagónico*, volume 1 (1886–1903), volume 2 (1904–1913), volume 3 (1914–1923), volume 4 (1924–1933), volume 5 (1934–1943), Trelew.

Jones, R. Tudur (1975) *Yr Undeb: Hanes Undeb yr Annibynwyr Cymraeg 1872–1972*, Abertawe, Gwasg John Penry.

Jones, Robert Owen (1992) "From Wales to Saskatchewan via Patagonia" in *Celtic Languages and Celtic Peoples*, Halifax, Nova Scotia, pp.619–643.

Jones, Robert Owen (1988) "Language variation and social stratification: Linguistic change in progress", in Martin J. Ball (ed.), *The Use of Welsh*, Clevedon, Multilingual Matters.

Jones, Robert Owen (1998) "Yr Iaith Gymraeg yn y Wladfa", in Geraint J. Jenkins (ed.), *Iaith Carreg Fy Aelwyd*, Caerdydd, Gwasg Prifysgol Cymru.

Jones, Robert Owen (1997) *Hir Oes I'r Iaith: Agweddau ar Hanes y Gymraeg a'r Gymdeithas*, Llandysul, Gomer, p.310–311.

Jones, Thomas (1926) Glan Camwy, articles in *Y Drafod*.

Jones, William D. (1998) "Y Gymraeg a Hunaniaeth Gymreig mewn Cymuned ym Mhensylvania" in Geraint H. Jenkins (ed.) *Iaith Carreg Fy Aelwyd: Iaith a Chymuned yn y Bedwaredd Ganrif ar Bymtheg*, Caerdydd, Gwasg Prifysgol Cymru.

Jones, William D. (1993) *Wales in America, Scranton and the Welsh, 1860–1920*, Cardiff, Gwasg Prifysgol Cymru.

Jones, William Lloyd, Glyn "Ysbeithio neu Archwilio Patagonia", *Y Drafod*, October–December (1930).

Knowles, Anne Kelly (1997) *Calvinists Incorporated: Welsh Immigrants in Ohio's Industrial Frontier*, Chicago.

MacDonald, Elvey (1999) *Yr Hirdaith*, Llandysul, Gomer.

Matthews, Abraham (1995) *Crónica de la Colonia Galesa de la Patagonia*, Buenos Aires.

Matthews, Abraham (1984) *Hanes y Wladfa Gymreig yn Patagonia*, Aberdâr.

Morgan, Eluned (1918) article in *Y Drafod*, 18 January.

Mulhall, M.G. (1875) *Handbook of the River Plate for 1875*, Buenos Aires.

Musters, George Chaworth (1871) *At Home with the Patagonians*, London.

Rhys, William Casnodyn (2000) *La Patagonia que Canta*, Buenos Aires. Roberts, Guto and Roberts, Marian Elias (eds.) (1993) *Byw ym Mhatagonia*, Caernarfon.

Thomas, John Coslett (1994) *Autobiography*, Winnipeg, Manitoba.

Thomas, John Murray (1985) *John Murray Thomas's Diary of the Expedition to the Andes*, Camwy, Gaiman, November.

Thomas, Lewis H. (1971) "From The Pampas to the Prairies: The Welsh Migration of 1902", in *Saskatchewan History*, Winter, vol. XXIV.

Williams, Glyn B. (1969) "The Welsh in Patagonia: A Demographic Note", in *Norsk Tidsskrift for Sprogvidenskap*, p.238, Supplementary Volume.

Williams, Glyn (1968) "Incidence and Nature of Acculturation within the Welsh colony of Chubut: A Historical Perspective", *Kroeber Anthropological Society Papers*, Spring.

Williams, Glyn (1975) *The Desert and the Dream* (A Study of Welsh Colonization in Chubut 1865-1915), Cardiff, University of Wales Press.

Williams, Glyn (1991) *The Welsh in Patagonia* (The State and the Ethnic Community), Cardiff, University of Wales Press.

Williams, Myfi (1983) *Cymry Awstralia*, Llandybie, Christopher Davies.

Williams, R. Bryn (1962) *Y Wladfa*, Caerdydd, Gwasg Prifysgol Cymru.

Williams, R. Bryn (1960) *Awen Ariannin*, Llandybie, Christopher Davies.

Williams, R. Bryn (1960) *Crwydro Patagonia*, Llandybie, Christopher Davies.

Y Drafod, (census figures), 28 July 1892.

Y Drafod, "A Adawn ni y Wladfa?" (Shall We Leave Patagonia?), 22 September 1913.

iii.) The case of Breton/*Brezhoneg*

The International Committee for the Defence of the Breton Language
Kuzul Etrevroadel Evit Kendalc'h ar Brezhoneg
Comité International pour la Sauvegarde de la Langue Bretonne

The International Committee for the Defence of the Breton Language was established in Brussels in 1975 by non-Bretons as a lobby group on behalf of the Breton language. It has representatives and members in countries as diverse as the United States, Canada, Australia, Israel, the Netherlands, Wales, the Czech Republic, Costa Rica, Slovenia, Latvia and Lithuania. Estonia is the newest member.

The ICDBL is a non-political body which has always worked in cooperation with cultural groups in Brittany in order to raise international awareness of the need for greater recognition of the Breton language in the various fields of public life in Brittany, such as the education system, government administration, the media and all other areas which are vital to the survival and future life of the Breton language. The United States is by far the most influential member, with a membership of over a hundred. Over the years it has focused on fundraising for Breton schools, attempting to keep the US public informed, transmitting news releases from Brittany to the United States press and providing information to people seeking knowledge about Breton language lessons, music and other cultural endeavours. It publishes a quarterly newsletter – *Bro Nevez*.

The Canadian ICDBL, with a far more modest membership hovering around twenty, has nevertheless been successful in bringing the Breton case before the public. In 1998 it collaborated with the *Montréal Gazette*, the largest English language newspaper in eastern Canada, in producing an excellent article about Brittany by Jim Withers, who was dispatched by the *Gazette* to Brittany. News releases from Brittany are transmitted to the Canadian press. More recently, in the spring of 2002, the Canadian ICDBL was succesful in getting Canadian members of parliament to condemn France's refusal to grant public funds to the Diwan school system in Brittany. The Right Honourable Mr Joe Clark, former Canadian Prime Minister, now an opposition leader in the Canadian parliament speaking for himself and others, dispatched a letter of complaint to the French Embassy in Ottawa reflecting the traditional Canadian sense of fair play. Also, enquiries by Canadians about learning Breton or other Breton cultural endeavours are answered.

The European ICDBL representatives have tended over the years to focus on letter-writing to such bodies as the European Parliament, press, as well as European governments such as the Belgian Government, the Government of the Netherlands and others (not to mention the French Government itself). Welsh ties with Brittany are particularly close and have focused on logistical support, not only in the ICDBL, but also through cultural exchanges and the many Welsh staff in Breton schools. It is hard to measure the cumulative success of all these efforts but probably the ICDBL has contributed to changing the climate in favour of Breton. France can no longer ignore international opinion as it could in the first part of the twentieth century when repression of the Breton language was extremely severe.

Within Brittany itself today there is both optimism and frustration at the barriers which have been placed in the path of the Breton language. The decision by the French Council of State on 29 November 2002 against public funding for Diwan was a blow. In addition, France's continuing refusal to ratify the European Charter of Minority Languages and many other patently anti-Breton policies pose a great challenge to the Breton people. There are no easy answers to these questions but the general Breton answer seems to be to quietly keep working for change in spite of the unfriendly political atmosphere. A bilingual Breton/French private television channel, TV BREIZH, has been established by a Breton, Patrick Le Lay, who is the PDG of TF1, the main French channel. The Breton part (about two hours a day, some news and cartoons first of all) is much more important than it was before on the public television, but it is dispatched on the sattelite, and you must pay to get it. An Office of the Breton Language/Ofis ar Brezhoneg has been established to coordinate language efforts such as adult classes in Breton, daycare in Breton, guidance for municipalities in producing Breton signage and in general status and corpus planning for the Breton language, reflecting a new professionalism and better grasp of the problems facing Breton in ordinary society. Perhaps most importantly, enrolment in the Breton-medium schools of Diwan (associative), Div Yezh (public) and Dihun (Catholic) continues to expand robustly by 15 per cent to 20 per cent per annum, so that in parts of western Brittany 5 per cent and more of school children are now being educated through Breton at least half of their school time. Over all, no more than 3 per cent of the primary and secondary students of Brittany as a whole are in such schools but the trend is now clear. Finally, this book dealing with the six Celtic languages could not have been produced without a joint effort by the ICDBL in Europe and Canada.

Diarmuid Ó Néill
ICDBL Canada

The International Committee for the Defense of the Breton Language
Kuzul Etrevroadel Evit Kendalc'h ar Brezhoneg
Comité International Pour la Sauvegarde de la Langue Bretonne

Ar C'Huzul Etrevroadel evit Kendalc'h Ar Brezhoneg (KECKB) a zo bet savet e Brusel e 1975, gant nann-bretoned, evit bezañ un nerzh pouezañ evit difenn ar brezhoneg. Dileuridi hag izili anezhañ a zo e broioù ken lies hag ar Stadoù Unanet, Kanada, Aostralia, Israël, An Izel-Vroioù, Kembre, ar Republik Tchek, Kosta Rika, Slovenia, Latvia ha Lituania. Estonia eo ar vro ziwezhañ emezelet.

Ur stroll nann-politikel eo ICDBL hag en deus kenlabouret bepred gant kevredigezhioù sevenadurel Breizh evit lakaat anavezout war an dachenn etrevroadel an ezhomm da lakaat degemer ar brezhoneg da vat war zachennoù liesseurt ar vuhez foran e Breizh, evel an deskadurezh, ar mediaoù hag an holl zachennoù a zo ret evit ma zreistvevo ar brezhoneg ha ma vo un dazont gantañ. Kuzul ar Stadoù Unanet eo a-bell an hini pouezusañ gant ouzhpenn kant ezel. Abaoe bloavezhioù en deus lakaet da bal kas arc'hant evit ar skolioù brezhoneg, o klask kelaouiñ ingal kedveno ar Stadoù Unanet, o reiñ un diverrañ eus neventioù Breizh d'ar c'hazetennoù amerikan, hag o kinnig titouroù d'an dud a glask gouzout hiroc'h diwar-benn kentelioù brezhoneg, sonerezh, ha darvoudoù sevenadurel all. Embann a ra ur gelaouen drimiziek "Bro Nevez".

Kuzul Bro Ganada, gant un niver a dud un tamm mat bihanoc'h, endro da ugent ezel, a zo deut a-benn memestra da lakaat anavezout kudenn Vreizh gant an dud. E 1998 en deus kenlabouret gant Montréal Gazette, ar gelaouenn saozneg vrasañ e reter Kanada oc'h embann ur pennad mattre diwar-benn Breizh gant Jim Withers a zo bet skignet da Vreizh gant ar Gazette. Keleier eus Breizh a vez kaset d'ar c'hazetennoù kanadian. Nevez zo e nevez amzer 2002 eo deut a-benn ar c'huzul kanadian da lakaat izili parlamant Kanada da gondaoniñ Bro C'Hall evit bezañ miret da reiñ arc'hant publik d'ar skolioù Diwan e Breizh. E Enor an Aotrou Joe Clark, bet Kentañ Ministr Kanada araok, bremañ e penn an tu enep e Parlamant Kanada, en e anv e-unan hag en anv ar re all, en deus kaset ul lizher klemm da gannadti Bro C'Hall en Ottawa o lakaat war wel fair play boaz tud bro Ganada. a-hend-all e vez respontet da c'houlennoù Kanadaiz diwar-benn an deskiñ brezhoneg pe goulennoù all war ar sevenadur.

Dileuridi ar C'huzul en Europa, a vloaz da vloazh, o deus bet skrivet lizhiri da aozadurioù evel Parlamant Europa, ar c'hazetennoù, gouarnamantoù Europa, Gouarnamant Belgia, Gouarnamant an Izel-Vroioù, ha reoù all (hep menegiñ gouarnamant Bro C'Hall e-unan). Bras-tre eo liammoù Kembre gant Breizh hag ur skoazell a zo bet degaset n'eo ket hepken dre ar C'Huzul, met ivez dre eskemmoù sevenadurel ha dre Gembreiz a labour e skolioù Breizh. Diaes eo muzuliañ efedusted an holl strivoù-se, met moarvat en deus servijet ar C'Huzul Etrevroadel da wellaat an endro evit ar brezhoneg. Bro-C'Hall ne c'hell ket ober fae ken war ar c'hedveno etrevroadel evel m'he deus graet e lodenn gentañ an 20vet kantved pa oa en e washañ ar stourm enep ar brezhoneg.

E Breizh hiriv an deiz e kaver war-un-dro spi hag enkrez abalamour d'ar skoilhoù a vez lakaet war hent ar brezhoneg. Diviz Kuzul Stad Bro-C'Hall a-enep statud publik Diwan a zo bet ur stroñsadenn. Ouzhpenn-se, nac'hadenn Vro-C'Hall da gadarnaat Karta Europa ar yezhoù rannvroel ha minorel ha kalz divizoù all enep breizhat a zo un diaester bras evit ar vretoned. N'eus respont aes ebet d'ar c'hudennoù-se, met ar respont hol-lek a seblant bezañ kenderc'hel sioul da labourat evit ar cheñchamantoù en desped d'an aergelc'h politikel enebet. Ur chadenn skinwel brevez, TV BREIZH, zo bet savet gant ur breizhad, Patrick Le Lay hag a zo Penn rener TF1, ar chadennn c'hall kentañ. Lodenn ar brezhoneg (war-dro div eurvezh bemdez, gant un tamm keleier ha tresadennoù bew dreist-holl) a zo kalz brasoc'h eget war ar skinwel publik, met ne vez skignet nemet war ar satelit ha rankout a reer paeañ evit-se. Ofis Ar Brezhoneg zo bet savet da genurzhiañ an oberiantiz evel ar c'hentelioù brezhoneg evit an dud deut, skoazellañ an tiez kêr da sevel panellerezh e brezhoneg ha dre vras steuŷvekaat statud ha geriaoueg ar yezh dre ober ul labour a vicher nevez ha tapout krog gwelloc'h er c'hudennoù a zo da dalañ outo evit ar brezhoneg er gevredigezh voutin. Moarvat ez eus muioc'h a dud o tarempredañ ar skolioù brezhoneg Diwan (kevredigezhel), Div Yezh (publik) ha Dihun (katolik). Kenderc'hel a reont da greskiñ ingal etre 15 hag 20 per cent ar bloaz, hag e kornog Breizh, ouzhpenn 5 per cent eus ar vugale a vez skoliataet bremañ, evit an hanter eus an amzer da vihanañ, e brezhoneg. Barzh ar fin n'eus ket ouzhpenn 3 per cent eus an deskarded er c'hentañ hag eil derez e Breizh dre vras hag a zo e seurt skolioù, met digoret eo bet an hent bremañ. Erfin, al levr-mañ o plediñ gant ar c'hwec'h yezh keltiek, ne vije ket deut da vat hep ar c'henlabour etre kuzulioù an ICDBL en Europa hag e Kanada.

Diarmuid Ó Néill
(translation by Tangi Louarn)
Dileuriad Kanada an ICDBL

The case of Breton/*Brezhoneg*

Diarmuid Ó Néill and Marcel Texier

Breton Language Preface
Trugarezioù

Anaoudek-tre omp e-kenver ar C'helenner Joshua Fishman evit soursial ouzh ar brezhoneg hag evit aliañ ac'hanomp en hor strivoù da wellaat he stad. Ar brezhoneg a zo ar yezh keltiek nemetañ hag a zo bev c'hoazh war ar c'hevandir europat, un darn dreistpriz eus an hêrez europat, ha me gred, eus an hêrez denel a-bezh.

Distrujadenn fallakr an delwennoù e Bamian gant an talibanoù afganiz a voe un taol euzhus-meurbet evit an holl bed. Ken euzhus eo an distrujadenn kendalc'het ar vrezhoneg, hag eñ bev c'hoazh. En amzer tremenet, se a zo bet kaoz da poanioù-spered dreist-penn. An enkadenn-se a bad en deiz a hiziv. Ar Vretoned n'int ket evit gouzañv an dra-se ken. Abaoe war-dro tregont bloaz, strivadennoù divent o deus graet evit advuhezekaat o yezh. Souezhus-eston eo an disoc'hioù. Al lanv a zo o tont bremañ, se zo sur. Ned eo ket an dazont ken teñval eget un remziad zo. Hep mar ebet, ar brezhoneg a c'hell chom bev. Yac'h-kenañ e c'hell bezañ adarre zoken gant ma vo gwelloc'h he endro.

« A ! amañ emañ an dalc'h », evel ma lavarfe Hamlet. Bro-C'hall a chom ur vro kreizennet-spontus. En desped da kemmadurioù war-c'horre en he napoleonek frammadurioù politikel, bez ez eus netra cheñchet da vat en he donderioù. An holl framm stadel a zo ragaozet evit diskar pep danvez-kevezer ar galleg e pep korn eus ar vro. Bez ez eus hini pe hini eus ar politikerien gall hag a zo gouzañvusoc'h ha digoroc'h e spered eget hor talibanoù jakobin, anat eo, met sur awalc'h, biskoaz ne vint ar re-se e penn ar vro. Da heul, en hor stourm a-enep seurt nerzhioù didrec'hus, hervez ar wel, ar skoazell ar C'helenner Fishman a c'hell reiñ dimp evit urzhiañ hor luioù gant ampartiz hag implijout anezho gant ar brasañ efeduster a zo div wech deuet-mat.

En ur heuliañ e alioù, fizius omp ma c'hellomp derc'hel penn d'hor talibanoù betek ma ra un Europa liezeg a-gevret gant ar mennozh etrevroadel tuañ ar pouezerez en hor keñver. Dispar evit an deltu eo ar soñj-se. Mil bennozh Doue evidoc'h, Kelenner Fishman!

Preface

We are very thankful to Professor Joshua Fishman for taking an interest in the Breton language and suggesting ways and means to improve its plight. Breton is the only Celtic language still alive on the European continent, an invaluable part of the European heritage and, I dare say, of all mankind.

World opinion was rightly outraged at the vicious destruction of the Bamian statues by the Afghan Taliban. The continued destruction of the still living Breton language is similarly outrageous. It has, in the past, caused and still causes untold psychological suffering. The Bretons are no longer willing to accept this. For about thirty years, incredible efforts have been devoted to the rehabilitation of the language. The results are quite impressive. The tide has clearly turned. The prospects are certainly less gloomy than a generation ago. The Breton language can undoubtedly survive and even thrive should a more favourable environment prevail.

"Aye, there's the rub," as Hamlet would say. France remains a hypercentralized country. In spite of superficial moves away from its Napoleonic political structures, nothing has really changed in depth. The whole State machinery is geared to the wiping out of any potential rival to the French language, on any portion of the national territory. True, some French politicians are more tolerant and open-minded than our jacobinistic Taliban, but they are very unlikely ever to hold sway over the country. Consequently, against such seemingly insuperable odds, the help Professor Fishman can give us in intelligently marshalling our forces and using them in the most effective way, is doubly welcome.

By following his advice, we are confident that we can keep our Taliban at bay until a pluralistic Europe combined with international opinion tip the scales in our favour. It is a highly morale-boosting thought. A thousand thanks, Professor Fishman!

Marcel Texier

Rising to the difficult challenge that faces us

MANY PEOPLE may question the feasibility of these 15 proposals* and suggestions concerning Breton, or even the point of discussing them, considering the present financial and political limitations which face Breton and the language agencies such as Diwan and Ofis ar Brezhoneg which are labouring on its behalf.

However, such obstacles must not prevent open and frank discussion – in the present – of just what it will take to restore Breton to a healthy and vibrant role in the everyday family and community life of Brittany. Yes, of course there are limited funds for projects such as a daily newspaper in Breton which would have to be subsidized, for more branches of Dudi, for more Skol an Emsav classes. Yes, there are political obstacles to official status for Breton, to the expanded use of Breton in the civil service and to the mounting of new social programmes whose aim is to strengthen Breton in young families and build new, authentic Breton-speaking communities. Yes, of course 2002 may seem an arbitrary date for the beginning of more concerted efforts at a policy of Bretonization. However, whether Bretonization begins in 2002 or 2005 is not the point. The point is that it has to begin sooner rather than later because in 2020 the 300,000 native Breton speakers of Breizh Izel will be gone and can no longer be utilized for new social policies.

The key to solving problems of such magnitude lies in coming to understand them first and bringing about frank and serious debate among Bretons about just what is required to turn the tide for Breton. That is not the least objective of these 15 proposals.

The changing political face of Western Europe in 2003 and its implications for Breton sociolinguistic planning

One sensitive topic which haunts not only Bretons but other small ethnolinguistic groups in the world today is the question of to what extent political agitation is necessary to achieve the successful implementation of their particular socio-linguistic programmes? Firstly, it must be stated that *language is a political question* in the vast majority of cases, unless you are perhaps a university student trying to decide on whether German or Spanish would be a better subject for you to pursue. Brittany is unique in western Europe in that no significantly powerful regional political party has emerged which could lobby on behalf of the Breton language in an effective manner, as Plaid Cymru does for Welsh, or the Parti Québecois does for French in Quebec or the Basque and Catalan nationalist political parties do for their respective languages. (The existing Breton Nationalists do not exeed more than 5 per cent of the vote in Brittany itself.)

Clearly, without a strong political party and platform to agitate on behalf of greater state support for Breton language agencies and the policies they seek to implement, it is highly questionable whether such policies can ever really be implemented. At the time of writing, a Welsh Assembly is in existence, a Scottish Parliament is in existence, an independent Irish Government is in existence, even a Manx Government is in existence. An at least nominally autonomous Corsican Assembly is also in existence. Since 1979 Basque, Catalan and Galician autonomous governments have also been in existence to vote budgets for policies to safeguard their regional languages. It is hard to say how the Regional Council in Brittany can apply itself more effectively to this issue, or if a Welsh-style devolved assembly in Brittany is the answer.

The background to Reversing Language Shift

Theories of Joshua Fishman

The background to this study is the 1991 work of Joshua Fishman, *Reversing Language Shift*. This work attempted to put forth a more methodical manner in which endangered languages could be strengthened, as opposed to the often haphazard and not well-planned and often emotionally laden efforts of many language movements which more often than not fell short of success in tackling this very difficult and challenging problem.

Joshua Fishman is regarded as one of the more pre-eminent authorities in this field. The book included case studies of Irish-Gaelic, Basque, Frisian, Catalan, Yiddish (both secular and religious), Hebrew, Quebec French, Maori, Navajo, Spanish in the United States, as well as the Aboriginal languages of Australia. These case studies are revisited by the same author in a new book which was released in January of 2001, *Can Threatened Languages Be Saved?*, published by Multilingual Matters of England. In his latest work, Joshua Fishman adds several new languages – Otomi (Mexico), Quechua (Peru, Bolivia and Ecuador), Oko (Nigeria), Andamanese (India) and Ainu (Japan).

The central theme of the original work was that the most important facet of language renewal or restoration was the role of the family and the community in maintaining the critically important element of intergenerational mother tongue transmission of the language in question. Whatever other factors went into the equation, this was the one that would make or break the success of the language movement in question. In his work, Joshua Fishman outlines an eight-stage process which must be tackled by any language movement or agency concerned with this process, in order to achieve lasting success.

The eight-stage process is used in this analysis into the state of Breton in the year 2003. The year 2003 is an appropriate milestone to undertake such a study of the Breton language, marking as it does the beginning of the seventeenth century of the history of the language. Breton itself was introduced into Brittany by British immigrants and refugees in the 400s during the tumultuous period of the Anglo-Saxon invasion of Britain (from Denmark and Germany). It is to be hoped that efforts to rejuvenate this language, which is an important part of the cultural heritage of European civilization in the new millennium, will bear fruit.

*Proposals made in February 2000 in consultation with Joshua Fishman, Per Denez, Marcel Texier, Diwan and Ofis ar Brezhoneg at the time of the field research for the Nominoe Study of the Breton Language

The Nominoë Study of the Breton Language

This is an independent study of the Breton language today and the recommendations and proposals it makes do not necessarily reflect the opinion of Breton cultural bodies such as the Cultural Council of Brittany, Diwan, Ofis ar Brezhoneg or others.

Historical background

The language is, like Irish and Welsh, a Celtic language and also, like Irish, Frisian, Basque and others, an endangered language. Breton, with its 300,000 or so speakers on the edge of the Armorican peninsula, is also a rather obscure language to many North Americans and Europeans. Suffice to say that this "language of Arthur", as it is sometimes known, does indeed have its roots in the distant mists of Celtic Britain, as we shall see. Among other things, the Arthurian legends of old promise a return by Arthur himself and a restoration of the British Celts of Wales, Cornwall and Brittany to their rightful patrimony and presumably an improvement in the fortunes of their much-maligned culture and British Celtic speech. Breton RLS partisans might do well to ask themselves: failing a return by Arthur, is there anything they can be doing in the here and now to strengthen the Breton tongue and to better grasp the nature of the problems facing Breton today? To help answer these questions let us take a closer look at Brittany and Breton.

The official Region of Brittany consists of the four departments of Finistère, Morbihan, Côtes d'Armor and Ille et Villaine with a total population of 2,885,349 as of 1 January, 1996. The administrative capital of Brittany is the eastern Breton city of Rennes. A more inclusive and traditional definition of Brittany also includes a fifth department, Loire Atlantique which contains the historic city of Nantes or Naoned in Breton. The population of the five departments of Brittany was 3,945,249 as of 1 January, 1996. A more recent count in 1999 revealed 4,040,690 inhabitants in the five Breton departments.[166]

Loire Atlantique was partitioned from the rest of Brittany in 1941 by the

Vichy régime of Marshal Pétain, partly in retaliation for the large numbers of Bretons who were supporting the Free French National Council of Charles de Gaulle in London and partly also as a reproach to mainstream Breton nationalists, who had long been advocating a separate Breton state. This administrative designation is still being contested, however, by Bretons, both in the four official Breton departments and those living in the department of Loire Atlantique itself, who continue to regard themselves as Breton (71 per cent in a recent poll). This is hardly surprising, since for a thousand years the city of Nantes in Loire Atlantique was one of the seats of the Breton parliament and *de facto* capital of the independent Duchy of Brittany. There are, today, probably about 304,000 Breton speakers in western Brittany, with another 50,000 or so in eastern Brittany.[167] They constitute roughly a quarter of the population of western Brittany and about 15 per cent of the official region's population.

As virtually all Breton speakers are bilingual in both Breton and French, with the exception of elderly monoglots, in Brittany we have arrived at a state where Bretons living via Breton are still very much a part of the scene but where virtually all Bretons are also Bretons via French. In addition, the spread of English is creating a new class of Bretons via English. One trait which Breton does not share with Frisian, Basque, Catalan and certain other threatened languages is heavy net immigration from the dominant ethno-cultural group. Relatively few French migrants have been attracted to historically under-industrialized Brittany, rather the reverse; Paris and the centre have in the past drawn and continue to draw Bretons away from the rural regions of Brittany. Hence, the threat in Brittany is Bretons who have relinguified and gone over to French, not intrusive Frenchmen in search of employment. Frenchmen have, however, for long been on the scene in Brittany, of course. Since the union of Brittany and France in 1532, a significant stream of French-speaking outsiders arrived to serve as administrators, teachers, merchants, clergymen who, although not great in numbers, were clearly the vanguard of the first real challenge to Bretons by French on its home territory. Their impact would only grow over the next four centuries.

The efforts on behalf of Breton RLS are both similar and dissimilar to the other case studies examined in this volume. As one might expect in a highly centralized state such as France, up until very recently virtually all efforts, both organizational and financial, being expounded on behalf of the Breton language came from voluntary and not State sources. As we shall see, this situation has changed somewhat over the past quarter-century as local municipalities and departments, not to mention the Regional Council of Brittany itself, have increasingly played a role in funding Breton-medium schooling, as well as more Breton in administrative matters and other initiatives such as the new Ofis ar Brezhoneg/Office of the Breton Language which presently has branches in both Rennes and Carhaix and which will soon have an office in Nantes and yet another office in the Morbihan area by the end of 2001. Increasingly, the French Government itself has begun to match rhetoric with action and has begun to provide funding for Diwan, the main Breton-medium school organization, by agreeing to pay the salaries of the majority of Diwan teachers. In addition, on 7 May 1999 the French Government signed the European Charter of Minority Languages in Budapest.[168] Whether or not ratification will inevitably follow is a matter of debate at present among Bretons. While many language activists (on behalf of other minority languages in France such as Corsican, Occitan, Basque, Catalan, Alsatian and Flemish, not merely Breton) would argue correctly that there is still a long way to go, France's accession to the Charter is of great symbolic value and hopefully heralds a new era of better relations between Paris and the regional languages.

The majority of Reversing Language Shift initiatives today have their origins in local voluntary agencies, increased public funding notwithstanding. However, the increased role of the Cultural Council of Brittany and the agencies it has created, such as Ofis ar Brezhoneg, indicate that Breton RLS efforts are no longer on the fringes and are backed not only by Breton public opinion but also the official institutions of the region, not to mention the obvious implication that Paris itself has given a type of *de facto* recognition to RLS efforts in the region. As we shall also see, while no one would deny the obvious limitations which still come to bear on Breton language agencies and organizations, this has not necessarily prevented their effectiveness to a great degree and the Breton RLS scene is a particularly dynamic one in the first year of the third millennium, despite the hurdles and obstacles it has had to face. So many new undertakings, from Télé Breizh the Breton language television network, to the Dudi (after-school activity in Breton) association, are being and have been launched that it is difficult to say which ones are working and which ones are not, and if they are working how far-reaching is their effect. Perhaps most promising is Ofis ar Brezhoneg/the Office of the Breton Language itself, which is a body that can at last provide the necessary status and corpus planning that the Breton RLS movement can no longer do without. To some extent, these tasks were carried out in the past by Skol Uhel ar Vro/The Cultural Institute of Brittany but there is no question that Ofis ar Brezhoneg represents a new departure and a greater sense of professionalism on the part of language planners in the Breton RLS movement.

Breton is also the only Celtic language still spoken on the European continent. It is not, however, a derivative of ancient Gaulish, the Celtic tongue of ancient France and much of central Europe (it is clear, though, that Gaulish Celtic had a formative influence on Breton during the period 400 AD to 700 AD, as it remained widely spoken in northern France, including Brittany). Breton is rather, as its name implies, an import from Britain, having been brought to what is now Brittany by various waves of refugees and immigrants from Britain in the fifth and sixth centuries who were dislocated by the Anglo-Saxon conquest of Britain during this period. Breton remains closely related to Welsh and Cornish and more distantly related to Scottish-Gaelic, Irish and Manx.

The French census does not record linguistic minorities such as Breton, so those agencies working for the language must rely on surveys such as that carried out by the French language daily *Le Télégramme* of Brest on the number of Breton speakers in western Brittany in March–April 1997 which revealed some 240,000 speakers in western Brittany. A recent estimate by Ofis ar Brezhoneg estimates 304,000 speakers in all Brittany. Breton also does not have official status in Brittany or in France. Nor do the other minority languages of the state. Again, this is also unlike the other Celtic languages which either enjoy official status, as with Irish, or quasi-official status, such as Manx, Welsh and Scottish-Gaelic, and now also Cornish, as the UK Government recognized it in November 2002. The legal basis for this is Article 2 of the French constitution which declares explicitly that French is the language of the Republic. The continuing triumphal march of English as the world language has done nothing to assuage French fears that the French language must be safeguarded in France itself from encroachments by English. In Brittany too, knowledge of English is now widespread, further complicating the linguistic situation. Henceforth, in Brittany we must also take into account the growing numbers of Bretons conversant in English. The policy of centralization and assimilation of linguistic minorities in France which has been both policy and practice for the past two centuries ironically has its roots, to a great extent, in the era of the French Revolution which began in 1789. This was, to a certain extent, inevitable as it is estimated that at the time of the French Revolution only 40 per cent of the population of France understood French.

However, long before the French Revolution, and even before the annexation of Brittany by France in 1532, there were forces at work in Brittany and France which were bound to lead to the weakening of Breton and the strengthening of the role of French in the very heartland of Brittany itself. During the Middle Ages, even when Brittany was entirely independent, much of the Breton nobility and clergy adopted French because of its greater currency in Europe at this time. From this period also, many of the towns became largely French in speech, though not exclusively, because Breton retained its hold on the agricultural hinterland and urban merchants and tradesmen could not ignore this.

In addition, it must be remembered that a significant part of eastern Brittany had never been Breton-speaking.[169] The early British immigrants established political control over what would become the Duchy of Brittany but the Gallo-Roman population in eastern Brittany (particularly in the two very important cities of Rennes/Roazhon and Nantes/Naoned) retained its Latin speech which eventually evolved into Gallo, a language which should be regarded as a parallel development with French and not a dialect of French. Like standard French, it would appear that Gallo is a derivative of late Latin which has been heavily influenced by Gaulish. Gallo, like the dialect which eventually evolved into Parisian French, is one of the Langues d'Oil of northern France which include Picard, Normand, Angevin, Manceau and Poitevin.

From about the year 1100 onwards, Breton slowly yielded ground to Gallo and retreated westwards. It is estimated that by 1881 about 2,000,000 people out of 3.2 million in Brittany spoke Breton. By 1914 it is estimated that out of 3.1 million inhabitants of Brittany, at least 1,300,000 were still Breton-speaking. In addition, several hundred thousand Breton-speaking emigrants were to be found in Paris, northern France, Belgium, Canada and the United States, so that the Breton-speaking world at this time probably encompassed some two million souls and it is clear that Breton was the most widely spoken Celtic language in 1900.

Few would have predicted in 1900 that the twentieth century would witness the most massive erosion ever experienced in the sixteen-centuries-long history of the language. It is estimated that 90 per cent of the population of Basse Bretagne or western Brittany (Breizh-Izel in the Breton language) was Breton-speaking in 1900. In 1945 it is estimated that 75 per cent of the population of western Brittany was Breton-speaking. In 1997 a survey, considered to be reliable, carried out by *Le Télégramme*, the French language daily of Brest determined that only 25 per cent of the population of western Brittany, or some 240,000 persons, virtually all above the age of fifty, were still Breton-speaking. The same survey determined that a further 125,000 persons in western Brittany had a more limited command of the Breton language for a total of 365,000 persons with varying degrees of fluency in the language, not including the thousands of Breton speakers in eastern Brittany and Paris.

What could have wrought such thorough-going sociolinguistic dislocation in such a relatively short period of time? In the case of Breton, many theories abound but several facts can be deduced with relative certainty. Firstly, the critical period in question lies during the post-war era, broadly speaking from about 1945 to about 1960, when Breton parents virtually ceased raising their children in Breton and the critical cycle of intergenerational mother-tongue transmission broke down. The suddenness of Breton language collapse in and around 1960, while long in the making, was somewhat of a surprise to many. Despite the continued encroachments of French, Breton had maintained its hold over family and community life among all age groups into the post-war era, just as Welsh, Basque and others had, in spite of the adversities in question.

It would appear there are two main reasons for the accelerated shift from Breton to French during this period. One reason was economic; the drift from the land to jobs in the towns and the cities as mechanization reduced the need for farm labour during the 1950s clearly weakened Breton, particularly in south-western Brittany, where industrialization and urbanization were more marked and where the tourist industry attracted a steady stream of monoglot French-speaking outsiders.

The second reason the position of Breton was sharply undermined in this period was a political and ideological one. Post-war France was forced to come to terms with the phenomenon of widespread collaboration with the Nazi régime. Some Breton nationalists had worked with the Germans in the hope of establishing a separate Breton state. Little came of this. What in fact happened was an incredibly severe post-war suppression of virtually all forms of cultural expression of the Breton language, from journals to newspapers, to lessons in Breton, to use of Breton in the schools, limited as that had been.

The negative impact on the morale of the Breton people and their attitude towards their language caused by post-war rhetoric which often labelled Breton as a patois and, even worse, as a language championed by the enemies of France (such as those right-wing Breton nationalists who had sought to reach an accommodation with the Nazi administration between 1940 and 1944) cannot be overstated. In fact, a very high percentage of the Breton population seems to have sided with the Allies from an early point in the war. In addition, it should be noted that a position of neutrality was taken by mainstream Breton nationalism, particularly the BNP (Breton Nationalist Party). Suffice to say that the divisions caused by the Second World War still haunt Breton, as they do French society as a whole.

The situation began to ease somewhat in the 1950s, as Breton was re-introduced into the schools by a new socialist government. Breton had been officially barred from the schools in 1947. The Loi Deixoine of 1951, however, specifically permitted Breton at all levels of education, including university level but the goal of this legislation was really to permit use of Breton in order to make acquisition of French that much easier for children, not to strengthen the position of Breton and other minority languages in the schools. Ironically, through the 1950s and 1960s it was increasingly the parties of the left, including both the French socialists and communists, who now began to speak up for regional languages and greater decentralization, as opposed to the parties of the French right who were now more opposed to any concessions than ever. Within Brittany itself, in the immediate post-war years it is important to note that much of the opposition to Breton in the schools, or anywhere else in society, came from Bretons, even native speakers who viewed French as the language of the future and a tool to better the lives of the people. It was precisely during these years that Breton began to lose its hold on community life. Breton/French bilingualism was a necessary milestone on the road to a unilingual French-speaking society. By the 1940s at the latest, bilingualism was well advanced in Brittany and the stage was set for the showdown between Breton and French. Now, during the 1950s, the critical break began to occur. Succumbing to the various pressures of modernization and even French government rhetoric against the use of Breton, parents began to exclude Breton from their homes and use only French with their children. Breton, however, continued in use more strongly in certain areas, such as the north-west and central Brittany and hence the advance of French was an uneven one which, in the end, did not succeed in eradicating spoken Breton.

By the 1960s, in addition, a new activism began to take hold which often expressed itself through music such as that of Alan Stivell and proved effective in rejuvenating pride in the language, stimulating new literature and other activities which expressed themselves through Breton. It was this new activism which led to various protests carried out in the 1970s and to the establishment of Diwan in 1977. A further important outcome of the activism and lobbying of the 1960s and 1970s was the Cultural Charter for Brittany, signed in 1978 between central government and local representatives. The articles of the Charter, while somewhat ambiguous, did expound on the need for the greater teaching of Breton culture. While not exactly an endorsement of greater Bretonization of society, the Charter was clearly a watershed, in that both central and regional officials were acknowledging that the Breton language and culture could no longer be ignored, even if different parties read different interpretations into the nature of the agreement.

The state of Breton today

As with all minority languages, Breton has some factors working in its favour and others working against it. A recent survey carried out by *Le Télégramme* in Brest in March to April of 1997, covering western Brittany, the traditional Breton-speaking region, helps to give us a clear picture of the real state of the spoken language today.

It is estimated that in 1881 about 2,000,000 people or 64 per cent of the population spoke Breton. As mentioned previously, in 1914 about 1.3 million people out of 3.1 million in Brittany as a whole were estimated as Breton-speaking. Of these, about 500,000 are estimated to have been monoglot Breton speakers. This drops to about one million Breton speakers in 1945, out of a population of three million. Today, all the evidence points to a catastrophic fall to about 240,000 fluent speakers and another 125,000 semi-speakers for a total of 304,000 in Brittany as a whole.

The survey (which is considered reliable) of March to April 1997 in Basse Bretagne or Breizh Izel, the traditional Breton-speaking region of western Brittany, indicates a sharp drop over previous surveys. This region had been 90 per cent Breton-speaking in 1900 and 75 per cent Breton-speaking in 1945 and appears to have dropped to about 25 per cent in 1997. A survey carried out in 1987 determined that there were about 550,000 Breton speakers in this area. Of these, those over 65 were 73 per cent Breton-speaking, while of those over 35, all age categories exceeded the 50 per cent mark. This can reasonably be construed as evidence that up until about 1960, intergenerational transmission of the language continued in most households but soon began to decrease very sharply.

The survey of March to April 1997 indicated a sharp deterioration in the situation with only 240,000 Breton speakers in the same region of western Brittany, with an additional 125,000 classified as able to understand Breton but with a diminished ability to speak Breton for a total of 365,000 speakers and semi-speakers in western Brittany. Of these, 18 per cent speak it occasionally, but only 5.5 per cent daily. Those who can speak it well, range from 45 per cent of those over 75, 42 per cent of those in the 60–74 age group, 20.5 per cent of those aged 40-59, 5 per cent of those aged 20–39 with less than 1 per cent of those under 20. Another survey in 1991 had corresponding figures of 35.5, 39, 30, 8 per cent, (and omitted the under-twenty group). The 1997 survey revealed some geographic patterns also. Due to more intense economic and industrial development in the south-western coastal region of Morbihan, 14 per cent of the population at present speaks Breton. In the western department of Finistère/Penn ar Bed 22.5 per cent of the population is now Breton-speaking, while in the north-west in Côtes-d'Armor/Aodoù an Arvor (in its western half) 30.5 per cent of the population is at present Breton-speaking.

Clearly, the Breton language possesses an unhealthy age pyramid in its demographic composition and the annual attrition rate of lost speakers, as the elderly pass away, is not being matched by comparable numbers of new learners in the younger age groups.[170] On the other hand, the expansion of enrolment in the Breton-medium school networks has proceeded to the point that, in parts of western Brittany, 3 per cent and more of primary students are now being educated in Breton and appear to be acquiring a fair fluency, not to mention literacy, in the language. Further than that, the present annual growth rate of enrolment in the Breton-medium schools is about 23 per cent, indicating that the percentage of Breton-speaking children will shortly be in the 5 to 10 per cent range. Already, the 1997 survey is out of date regarding the under-20 age group, so fluid is the situation. As we have learned in Ireland and elsewhere, however, Irish-speaking youths do not add up to Irish-speaking communities, a fact that Breton RLSers must bear in mind.

Despite the massive erosion which has taken place over the past 120 years and which is still ongoing as older native speakers are lost every year, in the past quarter-century RLS efforts on behalf of Breton have overcome some Herculean obstacles and are clearly making a difference in the battle to save this Brythonic Celtic tongue.

Breton language activists have established a network of Breton-medium schools across Brittany which are expanding rapidly. They have launched a Breton-language television service. They have launched several Breton-language radio stations; numerous new periodicals and books in Breton are now being published to serve a clearly increasing market. Plans are proceeding to launch a Breton-language university within the next five years. A concerted effort to strengthen both youth and adult literacy in the language has been mounted. Municipality after municipality in Brittany has adopted a policy of Breton/French bilingualism. A region-wide agency, Ofis ar Brezhoneg/the Office of the Breton Language, has been established to carry out and monitor both status and corpus planning for the language in the future.

Ofis ar Brezhoneg is only a year old at the time of writing and the exact limits of its jurisdiction and just how far its mandate permits it to go in pursuit of greater Bretonization are still a matter of debate among both Bretons and the central administration in Paris.

What remains to be seen is whether or not Breton RLS efforts can reach a large enough segment of the population to achieve the critical mass that is necessary. What also remains to be seen is whether Breton can regain its hold on family and community life – something which it had retained until very recently, in sharp contrast with most other Celtic languages. The battle is not yet lost because, when all is said and done, a quarter of the population of Lower Brittany, the traditional stronghold of the Breton tongue, is still Breton-speaking. However, time is running out as the Breton-speaking population ages and nothing less than a continuation of the present massive efforts on the part of language activists – and a simultaneous realization (followed by action) by Breton RLSers that some less dramatic areas of endeavour such as family life and community life must be conquered as well – can in fact turn the tide for Breton. It is in this last area mentioned that the Achilles heel of the Breton movement may lie, for efforts at rebuilding home, family and community life in Breton are few and far between indeed, as we shall see. The realization that such efforts are a necessity, not a luxury, and their incorporation into the Breton RLS agenda, will come not a moment too soon.

Breizh-Izel, the traditional Breton-speaking region

Any discussion of the linguistic state of affairs in Brittany has had, for centuries, to take into account two linguistic realities in Brittany – Lower Brittany or western Brittany and Upper Brittany or eastern Brittany. Breizh Izel, which means Lower Brittany in the Breton language, lies west of an invisible demarcation line traditionally used to differentiate between the Breton-speaking west and the Gallo-speaking eastern parts of Brittany. It includes all of the department of Finistère and the western parts of the departments of Morbihan and Côtes D'Armor. Upper Brittany, or Haute Bretagne in French, includes the departments of Loire Atlantique, Ille et Vilaine and the eastern parts of the departments of Morbihan and Côtes D'Armor.

Despite the undeniable setbacks already mentioned, it is clear that Breizh Izel remains the stronghold of the Breton language. About a quarter of its inhabitants can still speak the language. More understand it. Many rural farming regions and small fishing villages still contain Breton-speaking networks that contain members of most generations and where the language is still in daily use. Here, Breton can still be heard in use by the fishermen, by farmers at work in the fields and on market day. It is also in Breizh Izel that enrolment in the Breton-medium schools is highest, enthusiasm for the language greatest.

As alluded to earlier, these same rustic traits are also what have traditionally led to past and present out-migration from the region to the industrial areas of northern France, as well as to Canada and the United States. Such out-migration has both sapped the strength of the language in its heartland.[171] and also led to accelerated Francization as returning emigrants (and soldiers in the cases of both the First and the Second World Wars) brought a greater fluency in French with them which they were not about to relinquish. The annual tourism along the south-west coast and greater industrialization in the same area have clearly weakened Breton in this region in a more severe manner than other districts of Breton-speaking Brittany. Nevertheless, there is also growth in the region, not only among the growing numbers of youth in Breton-medium schools but also among older individuals who are undertaking to learn or relearn the language.

While Breton today could no longer be called the dominant language in Breizh Izel, it could not be called a thing of the past either, as it is still a presence in that it is spoken and understood by between 25 per cent and 35 per cent of the population and, in addition, about 75 per cent of the new Breton-medium schools are to be found here. In addition, most adult classes in Breton, such as those run by Skol an Emsav and, in truth, the bulk of other cultural endeavours in Breton, are to be found here, while it is also in Breizh Izel that the ongoing policy of Bretonization is most visible in the increased public signage being posted in Breton. Whatever technocrats in Paris may think on the subject, the locals – and that includes local officials – have clearly adopted a policy of Breton/French bilingualism, as far as social policy is concerned and also at the municipal and departmental levels of administration, as far as circumstance allows.

Eastern Brittany

Eastern Brittany, known as Upper Brittany or Haute Bretagne in French, is the section of the country with the weakest Breton speaking tradition. Although most of eastern Brittany was at one time Breton speaking (until about the twelfth century), the two cities of Nantes and Rennes lie in a strip of territory which never became Breton-speaking. The two centres were, however, incorporated into the Duchy of Brittany but remained Latin-speaking, as did their hinterland. The local dialect of Latin speech, which was not far removed from the other northern French dialects, evolved into what became known as Gallo. It was during the Middle Ages that Gallo began to advance westwards at the expense of Breton, at a time when Brittany was still independent. This situation bears an ironic similarity to the relationship between Scottish-Gaelic and the local variant of Anglo-Saxon – Scots or Lallans – which began to advance to the west and north at the expense of Gaelic during the fourteennth century. With the advent of more generally available public education in the late nineteenth century, Gallo began to yield ground to standard French, just as did Breton. The Breton language, however, has come to be regarded as the national possession of all Bretons, whether in Lower or Upper Brittany. This attitude has undoubtedly contributed to the spread of Breton-medium schools in the towns of eastern Brittany and even the introduction of bilingual Breton/French signage in many municipalities in eastern Brittany – usually the harbinger of more bilingualism in the future.

Geographically, Upper Brittany encompasses just over half the land area of Brittany. It contains the entire departments of Ille et Vilaine, Loire Atlantique and the eastern parts of the departments of Morbihan and Côtes d'Armor. Although the Breton-medium schools of Diwan, Div Yezh and Dihun remain most strongly represented in the west, enrolment in the east is presently expanding by about 30 per cent per annum and is clearly catching up with rates in western Brittany.

While it may not at once be apparent, eastern Brittany is in many ways just as important for the future of the Breton language as is western Brittany. Due to its greater urbanization in centres such as Nantes and Rennes, about 2.5 million of Brittany's 4.1 million people are now to be found in eastern Brittany, as opposed to the 1.6 million inhabitants of western Brittany today. This is in contrast to the situation a century ago, when about 60 per cent of the population lived in the Breton-speaking west. In the long run, Breton must establish a foothold for itself in such places as Rennes and Nantes if it is really to put itself on an equal footing with French in the everyday life of Brittany. Just as Irish cannot ignore urban centres such as Dublin or Belfast and Basque cannot afford to ignore Bilbao or San Sebastian in its ongoing RLS efforts, neither can Breton afford to ignore the two largest cities in its midst. The importance of Montréal for the French language in Québec or of Barcelona for Catalan, can hardly be overstated and language policy for both cities is given careful reflection by the respective language agencies in question (L'Office de la Langue Française in Québec and the Directorate General of Language Policy in Catalonia). That said, the time may have come to acknowledge that different strategies are required for RLS in western and eastern Brittany. In western Brittany, clearly, there still exists the option (long since lost in most of Scotland and Ireland and Navarre) of strengthening Breton among younger sectors of the population, as Breton is still a presence among older segments of the population. Eastern Brittany, clearly, is another story altogether, as spoken Breton died out here in the Middle Ages and, in the farthest reaches of eastern Brittany, was never spoken at all. Breton RLS in the east will be a matter of eventually trying to reach all age groups without the benefit of an existing Breton-speaking population in place. Hence the expansion of family and community life in Breton here is all the more critical. It could be said that the challenge facing RLSers in eastern Brittany more closely approximates those that once were faced by activists on behalf of Hebrew in Palestine, or those facing activists on behalf of Cornish and Manx today – how to build family and community life in Breton when Breton has been dead for many generations in the very environment in which it cannot afford to lose out.

The future of Gallo

It is appropriate at this point to say a few words about Gallo, the Latin-based speech of eastern Brittany. Debate continues about whether or not Gallo constitutes a language in its own right or should be regarded as a dialect of French. The truth probably lies somewhere in between because Gallo clearly is something apart from standard French, which is based on the dialect of the vicinity of the Paris region and hence was less influenced by Gaulish Celtic than the other dialects of northern France, Gallo among them.

Like Breton, Gallo has suffered reverses in this century as standard French has gradually displaced Gallo from family and community life in eastern Brittany. In 1900 the number of Gallo speakers clearly exceeded 1,000,000. Public education, which was exclusively in standard French, did not become widespread until the late 1800s. As with Breton, this posed a severe challenge to the position of Gallo in society. Today, Gallo is probably not spoken by more than 250,000 or so persons, mainly of the older generations, with those under 50 having gone over almost entirely to standard French. The situation resembles that of Occitan.

In the future, it is clear that a policy of promoting both Breton and Gallo is the correct approach for eastern Brittany. Breton is regarded as an important symbol for all of Brittany and the success of Breton language efforts depend heavily on the promotion of Breton in eastern cities, such as Rennes and Nantes, not just western Brittany, but there is also no doubt that Gallo is something which is important to Bretons and is rightly regarded as part of the cultural heritage of Brittany. As of yet, no Gallo equivalents of Diwan or Ofis ar Brezhoneg have arisen; however, that does not mean that none can be formed in the future. Clearly, the same issues which Breton must face must also be faced by activists on behalf of Gallo. Gallo as a medium in the schools, more Gallo in the media such as radio, television, and printed matter. These are questions best addressed by the Cultural Council of Brittany and the existing Gallo cultural organizations. While the circumstances of Breton and Gallo are not identical today, it is probably fair to say that they face similar challenges. Hence, enthusiasts of Breton and Gallo probably can learn a lot from each other in their common endeavour to retain their cultural heritage.

The eight-stage GIDS scale for Breton

A stage-by-stage analysis of current RLS efforts on behalf of Breton and their prospects for the future

Stages 8 and 7: Reassembling the language and bringing it to adults, some of whom once learned it and still remember it marginally and others who never acquired it before

The fact that Breton is still today a living language in Brittany, with roughly 304,000 speakers and semi-speakers in both Lower Brittany and Upper Brittany, makes Breton a more widely spoken language than many other endangered languages in Europe. The apparent strength of numbers nevertheless cannot mask the perilous situation of the language today. Breton speakers are, in addition, concentrated overwhelmingly in western or Lower Brittany and also among the over-40 age groups. Today, however, many opportunities exist for adults to acquire Breton either for the first time or polish up a rusty knowledge of it.

Since the vast majority of native speakers of Breton are illiterate in the language and also usually only conversant in their own local dialect, efforts to teach adults to read and write the language also are an exercise in standardization, since the universally accepted standard KLTG is almost always the dialect employed. As early as 1932, the OBER correspondence school was set up free of charge to teach literacy in the language to adults. OBER is still in existence and demand is as strong as ever. Many other correspondence courses are now in existence with plenty of textbooks, cassettes and other teaching aids such as Minitel and the internet now available to isolated learners. Since the war, KEAV or Kamp Etrekeltiek ar Vrezhonegerien has brought people together for several weeks in July to practise their knowledge of Breton in a near-holiday environment. Other organizations offering courses in Breton to adults include Skol an Emsav, Ar Falz, An Oaled, Spered ar Yezh, Roudour, Stumdi and many others. In addition, on a local district level, several cultural organizations have formed which also offer evening courses in Breton for both youth and adults, such as Mervent in south-western Brittany, Sked in Brest and Emglev Bro An Oriant (Lorient).

Clearly, what is required in Brittany is greater scale. Many thousands of both native and non-native speakers have acquired both greater fluency and literacy through the various courses and organizations already in existence. Such organizations have already proved their worth. They also may have served their purpose in the sense that what is required now are greater numbers of literate adults to supplement the increasing numbers of young people who are emerging from the schools literate in Breton, and hence buy time for the language in the short run and build a more solid foundation for the language in the long run.

Stage 6: Establishing the vital linkage with youth, family, neighbourhood and community

It may be tempting for Breton RLSers to sense victory due to the impressive and, beyond a doubt, important achievements in Breton-language schools, publishing, radio and television. However, the danger is as great as ever that the need to rebuild stage 6 in Breton may be overlooked and that RLS advocates in Brittany may become complacent with the string of eye-catching successes being achieved. Indeed, it is here at the stage-6 level of the RLS scale that the weaknesses of the Breton language movement are most glaring. Whatever may be achieved in improving the image and status of Breton by launching new television and radio services in Breton, by increasing the number of Breton-medium schools and by securing official status for the Breton language, none of this can substitute for the creation, or rather recreation, of young Breton-speaking families and authentic Breton-speaking communities where Breton is an everyday medium of communication for all generations. The higher-order functions mentioned above all rest solidly on the foundation of family and community life and, if that foundation is solidly French-speaking, then what is being built on top of it in Brittany is a house of cards. True, languages can be strengthened in a secondary role. This is already the case in Canada where over a million Anglophones have acquired French as a second language, in Ireland where several hundred thousand people have acquired Irish-Gaelic as their second language, in the Netherlands where over 80 per cent of the population have acquired English as a second language. But Bretons must ask themselves: do they want a French-speaking society where Breton is reserved for schools and road signs, or do they want a Breton-speaking society where Breton is a living language used as an everyday vehicle for speech, whether buying milk or cashing a cheque at the bank? It may seem hard to believe, but a mother insisting on raising her children in Breton or the inhabitants of a small hamlet or town insisting on employing their rusty Breton can be as devastating to the further encroachment of French as any activity undertaken on the part of language activists or militants!

As we shall see, Breton language activists seem to be tackling every field but this one, although there are some isolated cases where Breton at the stage-6 level has been addressed in Brittany but with very limited results. There is no avoiding the crux of the issue: family and community life are the cornerstone of any language restoration efforts. Belated recognition of this fact is taking place in Scotland and Ireland (where new Irish-speaking communities are in fact becoming a reality in Dublin, Belfast and Cork) – not to mention the social programmes instituted by the Basque Government geared towards young families and the younger sectors of the population.

Media, education, and administration are important, but more important is the family-home-neighbourhood context. The question that must be asked is: Where are children growing up with Breton at home and in the child-and-adult community?, before school?, out of school and after school? If there are no such communities, then Breton is an icon, not a naturally living and breathing language-in-culture. Twenty Breton-speaking families living and raising their children in proximity to one another are worth more than twenty poets, politicians, musicians and school principals "advocating". Who wants to build stage 6? Who is doing it? Who is helping them? How can more young adult speakers of Breton as a second language be prepared to raise their soon-to-be-born children with Breton as a first language? These are the questions that Breton status planners and language activists should be asking themselves.

One positive development in the arena of building community use of Breton has been pointed out by Lois Kuter and that is the growing number of bars and clubs which are holding Breton evenings or where Breton use is encouraged all the time and patrons are encouraged to feel comfortable using Breton, even if they are not very proficient in it. It is just such developments as this which must be encouraged.

Young adults have to be taught "Parenting skills in Breton: poems, games, routines, prayers, riddles, songs, reading-readiness, etc." Grandparenting in Breton is another crucial course that needs to be offered without charge everywhere. It is also one that could utilize the large number of over-40 Breton speakers who still have a solid command of the language. Linking kindergartens to grandparents, linking parents to grandparents, linking elementary and secondary schools to out-of-school clubs (sports, choirs, hobbies), old-age homes, theatre groups in Breton, etc. Community organization and community building in Breton: these are key. Breton language agencies, such as Ofis ar Brezhoneg and Skol Uhel ar Vro, must focus on exemplary instances of such linkages so that they can be nurtured and financial support planned for them.

Dudi

Dudi is an after-school centre where children in the 6–12 age bracket are immersed in Breton and engage in sports, crafts, arts and music and go on field trips together. It was founded in 1985 by Lena Louarn as a branch of Skol an Emsav. Lena Louarn is presently the editor of the Breton-language magazine *Bremañ* and the President of Ofis ar Brezhoneg. The initial branch was opened in Sant Brieg/Saint Brieuc but several others are now in operation in Rennes, Lannion and Vannes. Riwall Le Menn is the present director. Dudi is an excellent example of the kind of backup support which must be provided to the Breton-medium schools but, in order to be effective as far as Brittany as a whole is concerned, Dudi or something very similar to it must be available in all communities in both Lower and Upper Brittany. Dudi must be held up as an example of what is needed and planning carried out to increase its availability on a larger scale.

KEAV – Kamp Etrekeltiek ar Vrezhonegerien

KEAV was founded shortly after the war and is, as its name implies, a summer camp where Breton speakers gather annually. Initially it took place for only one week but now operates throughout most of the summer. One of the conditions is that only Breton be spoken and that French be avoided as much as possible. The present director is Anna ar Beg. We examine it here because, although it does so only on a temporary basis, KEAV does in fact recreate a Breton-speaking society even if only for an annual summer period. Hundreds of people are brought together every year in a near-holiday environment to practise their use of Breton at the six KEAV centres, all located in western Brittany. While such an undertaking is useful in reinforcing the Breton of those who already have a knowledge of the language, KEAV and other existing summer camps where Breton is spoken are essentially only episodal backups which buy time for the language.

The fact of the matter is that at present there are no efforts underway in Brittany to launch new and authentic Breton-speaking communities or even Breton-speaking networks. Such new Breton-speaking communities and networks are a necessity in both Lower and Upper Brittany if Breton is to be strengthened at its foundational level. The already established Irish-speaking community in Belfast and the planned Irish-speaking communities in Dublin and Galway are pertinent examples here. Also extremely relevant are efforts underway since 1979 by the Basque and Catalan Governments to strengthen Basque and Catalan in areas where Xish is still spoken but has lost ground among younger age groups. This is because Breton is still widely spoken throughout western Brittany among the older generations, hence Breton-language agencies do have the Basque option of targeting younger age groups, particularly new families, for Bretonization through social planning. Such a two-tiered strategy may be what is required in Brittany; that is, both new Breton-speaking communities in areas where the language has been lost (eastern Brittany) and the strengthening of the language in communities where the language is still spoken but has been weakened among younger age groups (western Brittany). The key word here is "community" in some shape or form. Whether or not such efforts are geared specifically towards such community life in Breton will prove crucial to the success or failure of the survival of Breton as a spoken language.

Stage 5: The attainment of literacy, independent of the public education system

In Brittany, as elsewhere in western Europe, literacy began with Latin. Writing in Breton began in the late fifth century. Although the Church favoured Latin, it was in fact the clergy who nurtured literacy in Breton through the centuries, not only translating most of the significant religious works into Breton but also in ensuring that the language was taught to those seeking an education, usually aspiring clergy or the children of the nobility who could afford an education. As French became more widespread in the Middle Ages among the upper classes and mercantile classes, it was again the clergy, eager to ensure that the peasantry received a proper catechism and could understand the mass, who saw to it that priests in Lower Brittany were fluent – and literate – in Breton. (The catechism was published in the four main Breton dialects). This remained the case even after French had become the dominant language of the Breton parliament and polite Breton society. In the period following the annexation of Brittany by France in 1532 and even following the French Revolution in 1789, it was again the Breton clergy, ever concerned to protect their flock from the supposedly decadent concepts of Paris, who continued to favour Breton and continued to preach the mass in it, dispense catechism in it and keep church records in it. The great conflict between church and state in France in the early 1900s did little to change this pattern and the Breton clergy, like the French clergy at large, used the pulpit to criticise the socialist governments of the day. They didn't plan to, but they became guardians of Breton literacy. It is a little-known fact today that, because children in western Brittany were to taught to read and write the catechism in Breton until well into this century, there were in fact several hundred thousand people at one time who were literate in Breton. Today the figure probably does not exceed 40,000.

For the greater part of recent history, literacy in Breton had to be acquired outside of the school system. The various courses for adults such as OBER, KEAV, Mervent, Skol an Emsav, etc. have been mentioned. Despite the fact that Brittany is a part of France, virtually all of her schools are and always have been staffed by Breton-born teachers. Nevertheless, they almost exclusively use and have used French as their language of instruction. Even though Frenchmen were thin on the ground in Brittany, the schools were controlled by Bretons utilizing French. With the advent of Diwan in 1977, for the first time a divide now existed between type 4a and type 4b schools. Diwan and the subsequently organized Breton-medium schools of the public and Catholic systems are, in effect, schools of the type 4a model, Bretons instructing through Breton. The remaining French-medium schools are, in effect, type 4b schools with Bretons instructing through French (*see also Table 2.6, p.78*) They may be staffed by Bretons but they are run under the auspices of Frenchmen.

The various organizations in place are sufficiently well distributed so that anyone who wishes to learn to read and write Breton, in addition to speaking it, can do so. Those thousands of adults who have already acquired literacy in Breton could not have done so without these organizations. The time may have come, however, to recognize that adult literacy in Breton, and the social and language planning necessary to achieve this on a wider scale, is a necessity if Breton is to survive on a viable scale in the twenty-first century.

Stage 4: Education in Breton and learning Breton at school

Education in Brittany underwent a revolutionary change in 1977 with the establishment of Diwan, the first Breton-medium school network. Diwan is of great symbolic importance to Bretons. It represents the embodiment of their hopes that their language can somehow be saved. Inspired by both the Basque-medium Ikastolak schools of the Franco era and the Welsh-medium Ysgolion Meithrin of the 1960s, Diwan was the first concrete example of a type 4a school to appear on the Breton scene. Breton is the only language of instruction for the nursery and primary students until the age of seven, when French is gradually introduced as a medium of instruction. Beginning at age ten, English is also introduced as a language of instruction and a fourth language, usually either Spanish or German is introduced as a subject. Diwan students not only match the academic performance of students in type 4b schools, they quite often exceed it.

Diwan has continued to expand to this day in all five departments of Brittany. It provides Breton-medium education at the nursery, primary and secondary levels. One of its most important goals for the future is to establish a Diwan school in every canton in Brittany and thereby make access to Breton-medium education available to all who desire it. Presently, the organization is involved in negotiations with the French Department of

Fig. 4.1
General reference map of Brittany

Source: *The Celtic Languages*, Martin Ball, 1993

Education to secure a public statute recognizing Diwan as a public service. This would entitle the organization to full public funding. At present, the status of Diwan is that of a private organization. Its greatest difficulty is lack of proper public funding, particularly in regard to secondary schools. Its annual budget as of the school year 1999/2000 was about 13,000,000 French francs. Of this, about 4.75 million francs was provided by regional, departmental and municipal governments. In addition, the French Department of Education pays the salaries of the majority of Diwan teachers, both primary and secondary. Although the annual contribution to Diwan's budget from these various sources is rising by about 1,000,000 francs per annum, at least 5 million francs every year must be raised through private fundraising.

A training centre for new Diwan teachers has been established in Kemper/Quimper. In addition, another training centre for Breton language teachers for both Diwan and Div Yezh exists in Sant Brieg/Saint Brieuc. Dihun, the Catholic Breton-medium organization, has its own training courses for Breton language teachers. Owing to the various financial difficulties, recruiting of secondary teachers is more difficult due to the fact that only short-term contracts with Breton language teachers can be signed. In its negotiations with the French Government, Diwan has often joined forces with other minority educational groups such as SEASKA, the Union of Basque-language teachers in France, (the counterpart of Unvaniezh ar Gelennerien Brezhoneg – the Union of Breton language teachers). Further expansion is planned in the future at university level, with plans for a Breton-language university at Karaez/Carhaix. In general, Diwan takes an optimistic viewpoint of future developments, although it has a realistic view of the struggles that still lie ahead. Increasing European integration and federalism are seen as a good thing by Diwan.

The Diwan Crisis – Autumn 2001

In the summer of 2001 an agreement was signed between Diwan President Andrew Lincoln and the French Education Minister Jack Lang, providing for the integration of Diwan into the public system of education. This would have allowed greater government funds for the training of teachers, the establishment of new schools (particularly secondary ones which are always more difficult to maintain for minority-language education advocates than primary ones, even in Ireland), greater access to public funds for other Diwan projects and, in other words, full recognition of Diwan as a public service. The Breton negotiators had asked for an expansion of teachers to accommodate an annual growth of 12 per cent in enrolment, or for an additional 445 teachers in the school year 2002/2003. The French side would only agree to a 5 per cent growth rate, or 120 teachers for 2002/03. However, the agreement was attacked by the French teachers' union as well as other influential establishment voices in Paris, leading to the action by the French Council of State in September of 2001, vetoing the agreement between Diwan and the French Education Minister. Finally, in November 2002 the French Council of State ruled against public integration – and public funds for Diwan. At the time of writing, the Cultural Council of Brittany and Diwan have filed a formal complaint against France in the European Court of Human Rights in Strasbourg. It may take three years before the case is resolved. The future of minority-language education in France hangs in the balance.

Due to parental demand, both the National Education (public) system and the Catholic schools in Brittany introduced bilingual Breton/French streams in the 1980s, Div Yezh and Dihun respectively. Although the intensity of exposure to Breton is not quite as intense as with Diwan, Dihun and Div Yezh are essentially type 4a schools. While absolute numbers are at present still modest – some 8,877 students out of some 797,000 primary and secondary students in Brittany (or at the primary level 2.3 per cent of all Breton students as of September 2003) – it is clear from the annual growth rate of over 12 per cent, that Breton-medium schools are likely to continue their expansion to a point where they account for a far higher percentage of Breton students, perhaps in the range of a quarter to a third of Breton students, some time within the next two decades.

Also on the scene in Brittany are type 4b schools where Breton is offered as a subject but the language of instruction is French. At present, an indeterminate number of students are taking Breton as a subject (roughly between 15,000 and 20,000). However, the exposure of students in the National Education System, with the exception of the Div Yezh bilingual streams, can be at best described as fleeting and certainly not intense enough to impart a good knowledge of Breton, let alone fluency in the language.

Breton-medium students themselves seem to recognize the importance of the role they are playing in the survival of Breton culture and have even formed their own union – Dazont – which means "future" in English. Those Bretons who are committed to ensuring their children acquire a solid fluency and literacy in Breton put little faith in the non-Breton-medium schools and usually strive to have their children enrolled in Diwan, Div Yezh or Dihun classes. Nevertheless, the increased availability of Breton, even as a subject in the National Education System, is also widely seen as an improvement over the previous state of affairs prevailing until the 1970s where Breton was almost entirely absent from schools and was present only as a tool with which to aid children in acquiring a knowledge of French more rapidly.

The percentage of Breton students who are now taking Breton as a subject is, as mentioned, difficult to determine. The proportion of Breton students who are in schools where Breton is present neither as a subject nor as a medium of instruction is probably still well over 90 per cent. Clearly, Breton-medium education must achieve greater mass to have a significant impact on Breton society in the long run. It would appear that this is beginning to come to pass, as in parts of western Brittany over 3 per cent of primary students are already enrolled in Breton-medium schools and it would appear that in Brittany as a whole probably between 5 per cent and 10 per cent of Breton students will, within the next decade, be enrolled in such schools.

Stage 3: Breton in the work sphere

Many trades still function in Breton, but this depends on how prevalent Breton is in the area. Fishermen often prefer Breton off the coast of the Bigouden country, but this isn't the case everywhere in the fishing industry. Breton fishermen operating off the coasts of Britain, Ireland and Spain often make use of Breton in radio communications which cannot be understood by anyone listening in. In central Brittany, in Braspars and Gourin, the farmers use Breton both at work and at home. Breton is also still widely used at the markets on market-day. With so many bilingual Bretons, the use of one language or the other is largely dictated by circumstances. Breton may also, it turns out, be spoken in the workplace outside of Brittany. In Paris, one of the subway terminals was manned mostly by Bretons from Lower Brittany in the 1970s, and as a result, the messages, the communications, the conversations were all in Breton.

At the turn of the century many commercial enterprises in Lower

Fig. 4.2
Percentage of Breton speakers, 1962

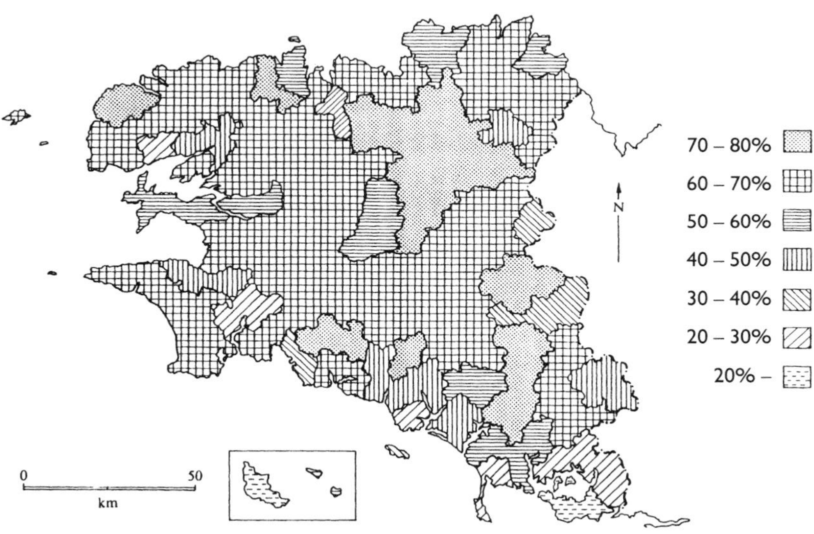

Fig. 4.3
The decline in the use of Breton in church by 1927

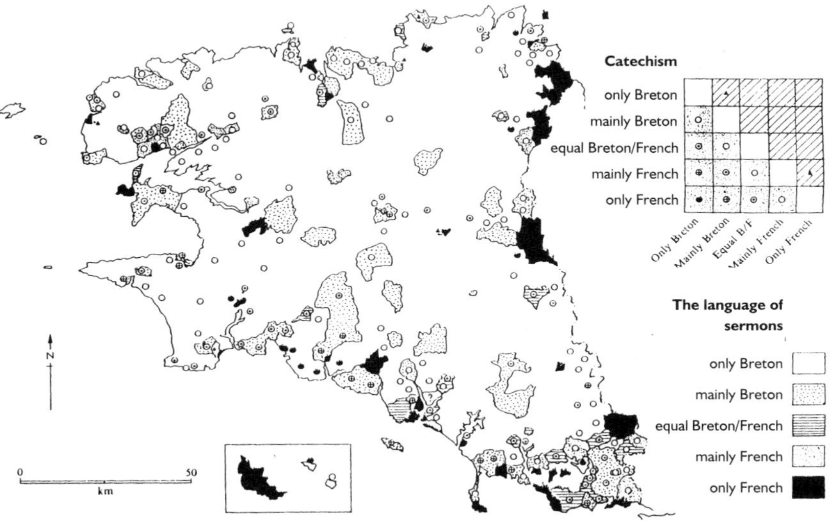

Brittany posted their signs and literature in Breton as well as French. This was a tacit admission, not only of the dominant role still played by Breton as a spoken language in society, but of the existence of Breton literacy among sectors of the Breton population. But, by the 1930s and 1940s French became much more dominant in this area, and by the 1960s French was close to being almost the only language in the commercial field. This situation has changed today with local enterprises in particular employing Breton on signage as well as for advertizing purposes. To a lesser extent, this is also true of larger national and even multinational companies such as Volkswagen and Intermarché.

In general, however, it is accurate to say that the dominant, almost exclusive language of the workplace is now French more than ever. As the Breton-speaking population ages and leaves the workforce the previous situation of an essentially bilingual workforce is being replaced by an even more exclusively French-speaking one. At one time, while middle and upper management avoided use of Breton, even though many such people could speak it, the language continued to perform a function among the lower order members of the workforce itself. Clearly, the workplace is one important arena where RLS efforts in Brittany have to be focused, as no language can afford to allow itself to be ousted from this area which is so critical in shaping a people's assessment of the actual importance of Breton in society. As we shall see below, plans are afoot to strengthen Breton among small businesses and, by definition, in the workplace – but again, the question of critical mass arises, and whether or not Breton RLSers can make an impact in this important field in the next generation will be part of the equation of whether or not Breton can retain a place for itself in society and then build on that.

Stage 2: Local government services and media

At the local level, the Regional Council of Brittany has played, over the last twenty years, an increasing role in supporting both media in Breton and local governmental services in Breton. In 1999, the Ofis ar Brezhoneg/Office of the Breton Language was established, with branches in both Rennes and Carhaix, to be followed by future branches in Nantes and Morbihan. This new institution, an offshoot of Skol Uhel ar Vro/The Cultural Institute of Brittany, is intended to be a means of promotion, development, observation, and development of new terminology in the Breton language. It also

Table 4.2
Breton-medium education for the school year 2004/2005

2004/2005 Tot: 9,668		Penn-ar-Bed	Aodoù-an-Arvor	Mor-Bihan	Il-ha-Gwilhen	Liger Atlantel
Diwan	Prim+Sec.	1,662	465	465	100	191
Tot. (2,834)						
Div Yezh	Prim+Sec.	1,264	840	854	461	130
Tot.(3,549)						
Dihun	Prim+Sec.	1,111	334	1,667	125	48
Tot. (3,285)						

Table 4.3
The absolute numbers of students in Brittany, 2001/2002

2001/2002	Aodoù-an-Arvor/Côtes d'Armor	Penn ar Bed Finistère	Il ha Gwilhen Ille et Vilaine	Mor-Bihan Morbihan	Liger Atlantel Loire Atlantique
Primary	52,285	85,660	90,643	65,448	117,841
Secondary	47,880	75,550	80,190	58,268	105,302

Table 4.4
Bilingual Breton/French education in Brittany
Differing levels of enrolment in the 5 departments of Brittany (2000/2001)

A. Primary
B. Secondary

Finistère	Côtes d'Armor	Morbihan	Ille et Vilaine	Loire Atlantique
A)2,368 (2.709%)	A)1,001 (1.87%)	A)1,679 (2.51%)	A)374 (0.404%)	A)275 (0.22%)
B)428 (0.876%)	B)223 (0.45%)	B)153 (0.25%)	B)53 (0.06%)	B)0

Table 4.5
Differing levels of enrolment in the official region of Brittany (4 departments) versus historic Brittany (5 departments in 2000/2001y

2001/2002	PRIMARY	SECONDARY	TOTAL
4 dept's. – total num.	294,148 students	261,860 students	556,008 students
Breton medium total	6,366(2.16%)	997 (0.3%)	7,050 (1.24%)
5 dept's. –total num.	411,975 students	367,166 students	779,141 students
Breton medium total	6,693 (1.7%)	997 (0.22%)	7,377 (0.9%)

carries out public opinion polls and collects data on developments concerning the Breton language. It is the chief body in Brittany with regards both to status planning and corpus planning for the Breton language. It operates in close liaison with the Regional Council and receives its entire budget from the Council.

National and even local administration are carried out almost exclusively in French. While, increasingly, Breton municipalities are posting signage in both Breton and French (and in so doing they are receiving guidance from Skol Uhel ar Vro, Servij ar Brezhoneg and Ofis ar Brezhoneg), actual provision of services to the public in Breton is not guaranteed by law. Hence, while Breton is, in reality, used with the public by local officials, this is a strictly off-the-record undertaking.

There has been a great deal of activism since the 1960s and 70s to get Breton officially recognized by the French administration. As a result, Breton is now legally admissible in court, but since there is little funding for Breton interpreters, and since only activists have tried thus far to enforce use of the language in court (and often been told by the judge to speak French), it is hard to tell what would happen today if a monolingual Breton elder appeared in court. The same activist struggle also covered the ability to write cheques in Breton, which has been found admissible by the French courts. In practice, if a Breton speaker shows up at a government office and cannot be understood by the clerk, it is not unusual for the clerk to go and find someone who knows Breton. However, such accommodation is by no means guaranteed by law.

In the towns, particularly in Finistère, a phenomenon common to all minority-language regions can be encountered; government workers, doctors, nurses, shopkeepers, lawyers, etc. actually often either know Breton or know some of it. If they are dealing with a Breton speaker, who is not really fluent in French, the language they will speak is a mixture of both. The main words will be Breton, the grammar mostly French, the order of the words very close to Breton. Unfortunately this is also a trait of languages in their later stages of decay, where the speech of the endangered language is being corrupted by more and more intrusions, both grammatically and vocabulary-wise, from the dominant language.

The media story is somewhat more successful than other areas. At present there are three government-run television stations operating in Brittany. Only one of these, however, FR3, broadcasts in Breton and only for four hours a week. However, on 1 September 2000 Télé Breizh, the first mainly Breton-language television service, began broadcasts (a significant amount of French language and other Celtic languages are also part of the programming). This project was launched at the instigation of the Cultural Council of Brittany. One of the goals of Télé Breizh is to coordinate its programming so as to assist the Diwan schools. Such broadcasts will try to serve as a link between Breton-speaking children and non-Breton-speaking parents. This strategy attempts to draw on the experience of S4C, the Welsh-language television service with which Rozenn Milin, the new director of Télé Breizh, worked for several years. About 50 per cent of this new service will be funded by the Agricultural Credit Union of Brittany with the remainder of the funding coming from private sources. The success of both Sianel Pedwar Cymru (S4C) and Telefís na Gaeilge, television services in Welsh and Irish-Gaelic respectively, augur well for Télé Breizh but, as with other minority-language television services, it must be remembered that Télé Breizh will always be surrounded by an ocean of French-language television programming and that while a television service is an invaluable and important tool in the rehabilitation of the image and status of Breton, RLSers must not rely on it as a substitute for parenting and pre-school infant care in Breton.

The Breton language is present on 13 different radio stations broadcasting in Brittany. These include two public service radios, Radio Bretagne Ouest /Radio Breizh Izel (12 hours a week in western Brittany) and Radio France Armorique/Radio Arvorig (two hours a week in the Rennes area) as well as two associative radios; Radio Kreiz Breizh and Radio Bro Gwened (both for 18 hours a week) and Radio Kerne (Quimper), etc. This expansion in the use of Breton over the airwaves is a revolutionary success story in itself, as the language was not heard on radio until the 1940s and remained virtually absent from this area throughout the 1950s and 60s. Breton-language radio, however, at least in the initial stages of RLS, cannot hope to compete with the volume of French-language broadcasting available to the public in every part of Brittany.

The two daily newspapers of Brittany are *Le Télégramme* of Brest and *France Ouest*. An attempt several years back to launch a Breton-language daily, failed. Both existing dailies are in French but carry weekly columns in Breton, mostly about learning the language rather than actual news coverage. Publishing activity in the Breton language today is intense, despite the obstacles of a limited readership (about 30,000 to 40,000 estimated Breton readers) and little State support. While there is as yet no daily newspaper in the Breton language, weekly, monthly and quarterly newsletters, newspapers and magazines are numerous. These include *An Here*, *Al Liamm*, *Bremañ* (circulation 1,000), *Mouladurioù Hor Yezh*, *Brud Nevez*, *Hor Yezh*, *Al Lañv*, *Imbourc'h*, *Sterenn* and others. At the same time, publications in Gallo are on the rise with, for example, the literary review *Le Lian*. Several publishers have entered the professional and commercial field. These include Coopérative Breizh, Keltia, Skol Vreizh, and Al Liamm. The bulk of publishing they handle, be it magazines or books, is in French but the percentage of output in the Breton language and also in Gallo has clearly expanded in recent years. With annual sales of 4.5 million euros and 60 per cent of the Breton market, Coopérative Breizh is the leading publisher in Brittany, followed by Ouest France (which is really a French publisher rather than an exclusively Breton one such as Coopérative Breizh). About 10 per cent of the books it publishes are in Breton with the remainder being in French. Of those books published in Breton, about 60 per cent are related to learning the language and only about 40 per cent are novels or other titles in Breton. In addition, while the number of Breton dictionaries and learning aids being sold annually is rising both absolutely and proportionately, ordinary titles in Breton are remaining stable in sales, evidence that the number of Breton-language readers also, is apparently remaining stable.

Also worthy of mention is the great tradition of Breton-language theatre with its travelling troupes. As so often, political criticism and activism are expressed through the culture of Breton music and satire.

Stage 1: Breton in the higher areas of work, education and government

Here, at the higher order level functions, we can see most clearly how severely Breton has been dislocated in the higher echelons of society even in its very own traditional heartland. The four universities of Brittany, Brest, Rennes, Lorient and Nantes all use French as their administrative language and their main language of instruction. The one minor exception being that some courses are now taught through Breton at Rennes university. The Université de Haute Bretagne-Rennes II probably has the strongest programme of Breton-medium instruction. All classes in its Celtic department are taught through Breton and this includes not only such subjects as history, geography and linguistics but will soon extend to Breton-medium instruction of technical and engineering subjects. It had 335 students studying Breton (69 per cent) out of a total of 485 in the 1999/2000 academic year. The Université de Bretagne Occidentale in Brest had 53 students or 11 per cent, the Université de Bretagne Sud in Lorient also had 11 per cent or 34 students studying Breton as a subject and the Université de Nantes had 9 per cent or 30 students studying Breton.

At Brest University, Breton is taught only as a subject and is not used as a language of instruction at all. The University of Nantes in the department of Loire Atlantique, now supposedly no longer a part of Brittany, does at least offer Breton as a subject, if not a language of instruction. Perhaps the most promising development are the plans of Diwan to create a new Breton-language university at Carhaix/Karaez which is expected to begin operation in 2005. It is envisaged that the new facility will accommodate the rising number of Breton-speaking graduates from the secondary level schools of Diwan, Div Yezh and Dihun. Of course, many obstacles and hurdles remain to be overcome before a Breton-language university becomes a reality and it will likely be some time before the new university establishes its credentials academically but it is yet another sign that the Bretonization goals of the language movement for Breton society at large are, with every passing year, becoming a reality.

In the administrative arena, local civil servants often use Breton in their dealings with the public – as they always have – but this is entirely the prerogative of the individual official, although sometimes the attitude of local municipal authorities can have a bearing. In general, however, it is safe to say that Breton plays no significant role or function at the higher levels of government administration. Not only has Breton no official status in Brittany, it has no status in France or at a European level (for example in dealings with bodies representing the European Community, such as its parliament or various agencies). Not since the early 1700s (when the Breton parliament still sat) has Breton exercized or dispensed any of the higher-order functions of a language in government administration. True official status for Breton is a goal of all the agencies presently labouring on behalf of the Breton language, including Ofis ar Brezhoneg but it is a goal which seems as far off as ever.

In the economic sector, the present situation, while not what it should be, has changed slightly for the better. National and foreign companies operating in Brittany rarely, if ever, carry out operations in Breton, let alone publish literature or commercial advertizing in the language. Some notable exceptions are Volkswagen, Leclerc, Intermarché, Carrefour and some airline companies which have begun to use Breton in their advertizing (although Breton was recently banned on Air France). Local smaller enterprises, of course, do have recourse to Breton but only in a secondary role to French and usually only when absolutely necessary – as when dealing with the decreasing number of Breton monoglots. Nevertheless, here too the situation is changing as local businesses and shops have increasingly begun to post signs in Breton and are printing commercial advertizing and leaflets in Breton. Perhaps most promising is a project underway by André Lavannant to set up an association of businesses who use Breton in the workplace. As Mr Lavannant is one of the individuals who helped found Diwan and is one of those who launched Télé Breizh, there is reason to be optimistic about this project as well. It should be noted too that speaking Breton on public occasions, once taboo, whether for religious, cultural or civic occasions is also on the rise, another sign of the times.

In summary, it can at least be said that Bretons are aware of the need for Breton to make a breakthrough in all three of these areas, hence the ambitious and well thought-out plans to establish more Breton-speaking businesses, to establish a Breton-medium university, and to push for official status for the Breton language. Broadly speaking, however, at the time of writing, Breton has not secured a significant place for itself in any of these domains and it remains to be seen how successful Breton will be in establishing a foothold in the universities, the upper management levels of the economy, finance and the higher levels of government.

Concluding remarks

Breton has achieved a number of successes since the mid-1970s which are clearly of great importance for the future of the language; its introduction into the school system as a medium of instruction on an ever-increasing scale, (the annual rate of increase in children who are enrolled in Breton-medium schools is presently about 12 per cent per annum), the establishment of a Breton-language television network, increased publishing in the language, its increased use in other media, such as radio and the theatre, and by municipalities all over Brittany. A new generation of not only Breton-speaking children but Breton-literate children – something unprecedented in Brittany – is being turned out by the schools in ever-increasing numbers. A wide range of programmes from pre-school to school to workplace to media are being put into place at the time of writing. In order, however, to avoid the pitfall of "too little, too late" Bretons must achieve more critical mass in all these areas if their efforts are to be crowned with success. Pre-school in Breton, primary school in Breton, radio, books and TV in Breton are all necessary components of any RLS agenda and they are all present in Brittany but they must be present everywhere, not just in certain towns or areas. Judging by recent growth rates, it would appear that these trends and institutions will continue to grow. In addition, the Breton language movement is not without goals and direction. As articulated by Ofis ar Brezhoneg, official status for the Breton language in Brittany as well as its more widespread use at the administrative level in dealing with the public, whether regionally, departmentally or municipally, is envisaged. A public statute is being sought by Diwan to recognize the school system for what it is – a public service. Increased Bretonization of this society is also evident in the increasing amount of signage being posted bilingually in Breton/French, not only in western Brittany but also in eastern Brittany. This is an important development because such increased visibility of Breton does keep the language in the public eye and consciousness.

Nevertheless, the most critical question facing Breton today – its reestablishment at the stage-6 level, that of the intergenerational, demographically concentrated family-home-neighbourhood-community – is not being addressed in any significant way and, even worse, may not even be comprehended by most language activists on behalf of Breton today. It is clear that less than 1 per cent of Breton families are raising their children in Breton and, while this figure is tending to rise slightly as the parents of children in Breton-medium schools often make an effort to speak Breton around their children, these efforts cannot be equated by any means with the reestablishment of Breton-speaking communities. While KEAV, Skol an Emsav and the other summer camps are a useful instrument in constituting, even if only temporarily and seasonally, "new Breton-speaking" communities, the proficiency in Breton they impart to people cannot be maintained from year to year.

There is no dodging the main question. Unless Bretons focus squarely on the demographic concentration of Breton speakers at the home-family-neighbourhood-community level,[172] particularly in western Brittany where it is not too late to utilize the 300,000-strong reservoir of native speakers in the over-40 age group, whose Breton can still be reactivated and who could supplement and strengthen new Breton-speaking communities, the erosion of Breton as a community language will continue unabated, probably at the same disastrous rate as during the five post-war decades. Uncomprehending Breton language activists will be left scratching their heads (again, like the Irish before them) wondering aloud, "What went wrong? The schools are full of Breton, but nobody speaks it!" There is no need to labour the point – the schools are not enough. Diwan by itself is not enough. Language restoration is a complex sociolinguistic phenomenon which must encompass the involvement of all sectors of the community and all age groups and it is not only unjust to place the responsibility for language restoration solely on the shoulders of children, it is also a fatal error.

Community-wide social programmes in Breton and new Breton-speaking communities

The strengthening of existing Breton-speaking communities. A new Breton-speaking community in each canton?

One possibility in this respect would be for groups of Breton-speaking families to form in clusters around the Breton-medium schools, be they Diwan, Div Yezh or Dihun (Diwan being a more probable candidate, for ideological reasons). Communal and group activities for these Breton-speaking families could be organized. Despite the surrounding French-speaking milieu, such communal groups would allow for the establishment of Breton-speaking youth groups and also for the organization of Brittany-wide programmes for pre-school care in Breton (perhaps staffed by elderly native speakers on a volunteer basis), youth groups in Breton, grandparenting in Breton, instruction for young families on how to raise their children in Breton and the provision of instructors, as well as parenting aids such as games, riddles, songs, prayers, reading-readiness books in Breton for parents and other forms of guidance for these new Breton-speaking families and communities, as well as financial assistance for them. While financial resources and staff are limited, we have seen in Brittany how much can be achieved at the local voluntary level without large sums being expended. A realistic and attainable strategy might be the establishment of a new Breton-speaking community in each canton, both in western and eastern Brittany. Such a stratagem would not be out of step with the Diwan goal of establishing a Diwan school in every canton of Brittany. It is worth stating that Diwan might also be the most appropriate agency for ensuring pre-school infant care in all of Brittany, as well as the coordinator which, in the initial stages at least, could help in the formation of new Breton-speaking community life relying on its already widespread infrastructure, which will continue to open new schools in new cantons. The existing schools, and those established in the future, could become the nuclei of new Breton-speaking networks or communities. While some would probably regard such a task as operating beyond the mandate of Diwan, no other organization at present in Brittany possesses the infrastructure or trained personnel capable of instituting such a social programme on any significant scale. The Dudi organization and other youth groups are, at present, too localized and limited in their scope. One possible solution would be for a new organization to be established, working closely with Diwan (but separate from it), Ofis ar Brezhoneg and Skol an Emsav to attend to the task of organizing such new Breton-speaking networks and their support network in the vicinity of all Diwan schools. It might sound revolutionary and difficult to achieve but nothing short of this will halt the further erosion of Breton as a spoken community language – or begin to build up significant numbers of new speakers among the younger generations. The concept of Diwan, Skol an Emsav and Ofis ar Brezhoneg collaborating in the establishment of new Breton-speaking communities can, of course, only be food for thought for the present, as such a widescale undertaking would require a consensus among these bodies and others, such as the Cultural Council of Brittany and the Regional Council of Brittany – the democratically elected and representative bodies of Breton political and cultural life.

It should be recalled that, while any such proposed Bretonization goals like this, or any other, may or may not be practicable in the present due to financial, logistical and even political constraints, however, this does not mean that no thought should be given to just exactly what forms of status planning it will take to re-establish Breton on an equal footing with

French as one of the two major languages of Brittany, a goal which the Breton people have clearly and unequivocally adopted.

Another problem which must be addressed is the massive illiteracy in Breton among all age groups and sectors of the population, even among native speakers. Again, a Brittany-wide policy and stratagem would have to be formulated and then implemented among both Breton speakers and non-Breton speakers. The present practice of employing the long-established KLTG standard dialect should be continued with any new literacy initiatives. Again, it has to be recalled that present circumstances may or may not be expeditious for expanded programmes of adult literacy but this should not prevent such issues from being discussed openly and frankly.

While the agencies working for the Breton language, such as Ofis ar Brezhoneg, Servij ar Brezhoneg, and others, are only establishing themselves and are still at a very formative stage (as opposed to the somewhat older Skol Uhel ar Vro), the formulation and the eventual implementation of such programmes (free of charge and available to all) in the community at large and, indeed, throughout all of Brittany, will probably make or break the revival of the Breton language.

Western Brittany today, despite the massive erosion of the past century, still possesses a pool of about 300,000 native Breton speakers and semi-speakers who constitute about a quarter of the population. They are almost entirely confined to the over-40 age group, nevertheless, they still constitute a reservoir which could be utilized over the next two decades for the implementation of such social programmes. In effect, these native Breton speakers constitute ready-trained social workers who, because they are in the older age brackets, have more time on their hands for volunteer work than younger people; but their Breton-speaking abilities must be utilized rapidly, for, every passing year, more and more elderly native speakers pass away. In the Autonomous Basque Region in Spain, the policies of the Deputy Ministry For Language Policy have demonstrated since 1979 that it is possible to strengthen use of the weakened language (Basque) among younger sectors of the population through social programmes instituted specifically for this purpose. It is worth noting that by 1979, Basque (like Breton today) had largely retreated to the older sectors of the population. This is no longer the case today, as Basque has clearly made inroads among young families and other sectors of the under-40 population. As much of this progress was made by utilizing older native speakers, as well as overt government social programmes, there is little reason to suppose that the same principle does not apply to Breton. Ofis ar Brezhoneg, Skol Uhel ar Vro and other Breton-language agencies could establish direct liaison with the Deputy Ministry For Language Policy in the Basque country of Spain and the Directorate General of Language Policy in Catalonia in order to benefit from what Basques and Catalans have learned about what works and what does not work in regards to strengthening a weakened language among younger sectors of the population, because both Euzkadi and Catalonia are examples of where, as in Brittany, the challenge is to arrest language decline in very specific age groups. This is particularly true of western Brittany. Other bodies which could prove to be useful because of their similar role are Bwrdd Yr Iaith Gymraeg/The Welsh Language Board, Foras na Gaeilge/The Irish Language Board and Comhdháil Náisiunta na Gaeilge/The National Association of Irish.

With regards to eastern Brittany, the same broad principles apply, despite a somewhat different linguistic history. Here, no pool of native speakers has existed since the Middle Ages but, unless Breton-speaking communities are formed, particularly in urban centres such as Nantes/Naoned and Rennes/Roazhon and indeed on a canton-wide basis, then there can be no question of establishing Breton as a widespread vehicle of communication on a par with French. Here too, just as in western Brittany, programmes encompassing the wider community must be implemented among all age-groups, not merely school-age children. Breton-speaking families have to be encouraged to cluster together as much as is possible so as to facilitate joint social and communal activities coordinated for them. As Basque has proved during the 1980s and 1990s, it is possible to strengthen a weakened language among younger sectors of the population and indeed within the family, even after that language has been confined to older sectors of the population (as Breton now is in western Brittany).

During the past quarter-century, between 1975 and 2000, Breton has made phenomenal progress. Relying largely on local initiative and resources, though to a significant extent inspired by Welsh, Basque and even Canadian initiatives in bilingualism and bilingual education, Bretons have, in effect, reestablished the infrastructure of a Breton-speaking society. Breton-medium schools are a reality and it is clear that their growth will continue, very probably to the point where a quarter or more of Breton primary and secondary students are being educated primarily through Breton. Also, in media, Breton is already a modest success story: Télé Breizh the Breton language television network, Radio Kreizh Breizh and Radio Arvorig with their increasing influence, the large and increasing number of newspapers and magazines in Breton.

In addition, the climate has changed favourably on behalf of Breton. Breton public opinion solidly supports the hard-won gains by Breton in the schools, municipal administration and elsewhere. France too, has changed, to some extent for the better, in its position on minority languages and signed the European Charter for Regional or Minority Languages in Budapest on 7 May 1999. Ratification of the treaty by the French Government will – hopefully – follow (many Bretons are sceptical). French public opinion has also grown somewhat more tolerant on this issue as 67 per cent recently stated in a poll that they supported the use of regional languages in schools. Clearly, France too, not just Brittany, is changing.

The new proactive attitude towards the Breton language by the Breton people themselves, however, is probably more important than any change in state policy. The old stigma of Breton as a language for farmers, fishermen and old people is gone, replaced by a new pride in Breton as a modern language, a Celtic language and a desirable element of the Breton heritage. Without this change of heart on the part of the Breton people towards their language, none of the very considerable achievements which have been attained in the past quarter-century could have taken place. Nevertheless, it is difficult not to see the strong parallel between Breton and her sister Celtic language, Irish. Much has been achieved, yet the main problem facing Breton has not been addressed – the reestablishment of the language at the family-home-neighbourhood-community level on any scale whatsoever. Time will tell – probably within the next generation – whether Bretons can recognize this fact and successfully meet the challenge. In addition, those who are working for the Breton language have to bear in mind the complexities of the Breton identity itself. Many Bretons regard themselves as only Breton, others as only French, while the majority appears to fall somewhere in between. This strong attachment to the French language, to French culture and indeed to France itself was demonstrated during two world wars by an almost fanatical devotion to France, as evidenced by the fact that in both world wars the Breton level of enrolment in the French armed forces was higher than for other sectors of the French population. The fact that 95 per cent of the Free French naval forces during the War

Table 4.6
Breton-language students: the growth of enrollment, 1977–2002

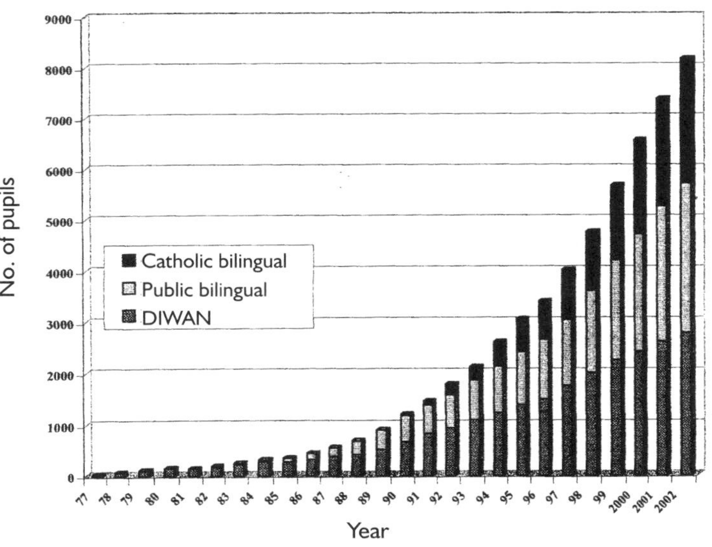

were Breton is only one example of this. Nationalism has long been on the scene in Brittany but thus far the majority of Bretons have rejected independence and even autonomy, hence it would appear that Bretons are still pursuing a more pluralistic and federal France which they can call home, while at the same time desiring cultural autonomy for their region. True, the more robust Celtic nationalism of Ireland, Scotland and Wales has not gone unnoticed in Brittany and, despite the relatively mild aspirations of Bretons today, Breton nationalism has yet to take on the stronger dimensions that nationalism has assumed in Scotland and Québec, for example.

So, clearly, while Bretons are stubbornly determined to keep their ancient Celtic tongue, they are also equally keen to retain French as a valuable tool in the modern world. Hence it is clear that what Bretons are really pursuing is bilingualism, unlike those activists who have laboured on behalf of Québec French in the present (in pursuit of French only) or Hebrew in Palestine during the 1920s (in pursuit of Hebrew only) and made no secret of their aspirations towards a unilingual French- or Hebrew-speaking society. Regionalism and nationalism have affected Brittany, just as the other smaller nationalities of Europe, but the future result will be one tailored to suit Breton needs and desires – not those dictated by others.

It is clear to anyone who has spent time in Brittany that there is a vast undercurrent among the people to see their language live. The reverses suffered by the language in this century are deeply regretted by the people and they truly wish to see it survive, even if they are sometimes at a loss to say how this may be done. Just how the various challenges – of formulating and implementing policies geared towards greater Bretonization of the schools, the family, the community, the various media, the civil service, effectively mobilizing public support and participation in such programmes, not to mention the need to work with and sometimes around a largely centralized French bureaucracy – are met, will determine what the future holds for Breton.

Proposals and recommendations for future language planning with Breton

Proposals and suggestions of the Nominoë study

Proposals and suggestions of the study and how they fit into the different stages of Reversing Language Shift

Aims and goals

Primarily to restore Breton as the chief language of the community in western Brittany and to strengthen its use in eastern Brittany also. Another aim is hopefully to illustrate how Gallo, the other traditional vernacular of Brittany, may be strengthened in eastern Brittany.

The main thrust of the proposals:

i) A Two-Stage Policy or Approach to Bretonization For Brittany

ii) Aid for Gallo.

A two-stage policy of Bretonization. The first stage is a policy of Bretonization in Breizh Izel or western Brittany beginning in 2004 or thereabouts, so as not to overextend the limited financial resources of the Breton-language bodies such as Ofis ar Brezhoneg, Diwan, Skol Uhel ar Vro, the Cultural Council of Brittany etc. and also in order to immediately address the issue of the declining Breton-speaking population in Breizh Izel whose Breton-speaking ability must be used as soon as possible. The second stage would be the extension of a policy of Bretonization to eastern Brittany beginning about 2010. In eastern Brittany, however, the position of Gallo must also be taken into account and, while Breton speakers and new Breton-speaking communities in eastern Brittany must be aided, so must Gallo speakers and cultural organizations. Just what form of aid to Gallo is most effective and appropriate is a matter for the Gallo cultural organizations and the Regional and Cultural Councils of Brittany. Likely, this would entail greater media in Gallo and even schools where Gallo is the medium of instruction.

Bretonization incorporating the principles of Reversing Language Shift

This policy of Bretonization should ultimately entail:

I.) Community

I.i) The establishment of new Breton-speaking communities in each canton (initially the cantons of western Brittany but later to be followed by the cantons and towns of eastern Brittany). New Breton-speaking communities are the central tenet of stage 6.

I.ii) The establishment of a new organization to assist young families who wish to raise their children in Breton. Existing language agencies are already overtaxed and such a new body, whose mandate is the establishment of new Breton-speaking communities, would signify an unequivocal commitment and link to stage-6 efforts.

I.iii) The mounting of a publicity campaign aimed at young parents to raise their children in Breton and to use Breton at home. This would be much like Welsh Language Board advertizing. Again, priority should initially be given to western Brittany. (Also stage 6)

I.iv) Learning aids and counselling must be provided to young families who opt to raise their children in Breton. Booklets on parenting skills in Breton, poems, games for children in Breton, prayers, riddles, songs, reading-readiness in Breton, etc. Such services and supplies, so necessary in any serious attempt to rebuild family and community life in Breton, could best be provided by the new organization recommended above to coordinate the rebuilding of Breton language use at stage 6.

I.v) Grandparenting and babysitting in Breton free of charge is another crucial course which must be made available all over western Brittany while there is still time to utilize the large numbers of older Breton speakers. Such a service might be coordinated by Skol an Emsav because of its links with adult learners, or even Ofis ar Brezhoneg but, however linkages are established with older native Breton speakers, they provide valuable backup for stage-6 efforts in general.

I.vi) The expansion of the Dudi Breton-speaking youth groups to every community. Youth groups in Breton are not merely backup for stage 6 but are an actual part of the process of providing a Breton-speaking environment for youth outside of school.

I.vii) A publicity campaign to attract Breton speakers in Paris, northern France and Belgium back to the new Breton-speaking communities in Brittany. Financial and political constraints are a consideration here, it is true, but the present and past efforts by the Irish Government to attract Gaelic speakers back to western Ireland did in fact have some success in increasing the Irish-speaking population. Hence, such a stratagem may also secure some success for Breton. (Stage 6)

II.) Education

II.i) The continued establishment of new Breton-medium schools in each canton by the Diwan, Div Yezh and Dihun organizations with priority being given to Breizh Izel during the next decade. This corresponds to the stage 4 level but is necessary for stage 6 to take root.

II.ii) The establishment of a Breton-medium university. Diwan aspires to establish one at Carhaix/Karaez in 2005 but it cannot be overstressed how important it is to have such an institution, whether at Carhaix or anywhere else. Efforts to expand Breton at university level fall within the range of stage 1 and hence are greatly dependent on the success of earlier efforts at the stage-4 and stage-6 levels.

II.iii) The planned establishment of more classes for adults in more Breton communities to help expand adult literacy in Breton. At present, about 9,000 adults across Brittany are enrolled in Breton language classes. (In Wales there are about 23,000) The organizations which are presently offering lessons in Breton to adults are: Skol an Emsav, Ar Falz, An Oaled, Spered ar Yezh, Roudour, Stumdi and many others. A more coordinated and united effort by these organizations to bring Breton to a greater segment of the adult population in Brittany could be mounted. (Stages 8 & 5)

III.) Media

III.i) The establishment of a daily newspaper in the Breton language, perhaps subsidized by the Cultural Council of Brittany. (Stage 2)

III.ii) The continued expansion of Breton on radio and television. Télé

Breizh, which began broadcasts on 1 September, 2000, mainly in Breton for 17 hours a day (although with a fair amount of French-language broadcasts and also programmes from other Celtic countries), was a major victory in the battle to save the Breton language. An increase in Breton-language broadcasts on other television and radio stations should continue and can help reinforce the position of the language in the media. (Stage 2)

IV.) The Work Sphere

IV.i) A policy of Bretonization must be extended to the workplace. Ofis ar Brezhoneg is already assisting organizations, municipalities and private companies which ask for guidance regarding terminology in the Breton language. The project by André Lavanant to launch new Breton-speaking business enterprises is a good example of what must be undertaken. (Stage 3)

V.) Political Status

V.i) The campaign to secure official status for the Breton language in all five departments of Brittany must be increased and intensified. Only then can Breton language use be extended within the civil service at all levels of administration whether on a municipal or a departmental or a regional level. Indeed, all of the efforts and recommendations mentioned above will be fortified when official status for Breton becomes a reality. Unfortunately, language is a political issue and long-term efforts to strengthen Breton cannot, in reality, ignore the legal status of the language (or lack thereof).

Notes

1. The GIDS Scale and the Celtic Languages

The general tenor of the conclusion continues to lay emphasis on the theories of Joshua Fishman that efforts to re-establish the threatened languages in question (the Celtic languages) at the home-family-community level are absolutely critical. Perhaps even more critical is the realization of and implementation of this theory and its conversion into reality in the Celtic countries. While Celtic speaking communities have formed in all six countries, usually in proximity to a Celtic-medium school, they are nowhere near the critical mass that is required to turn the tide. (See in general *Reversing Language Shift* and also *Can Threatened Languages Be Saved?* by Joshua Fishman, published in 1991 and 2000 respectively by Multilingual Matters of England.)

2. The Diwan Crisis and rejection of public integration by the French Council of State
This crisis, closely followed by the Breton press as well as publications in other Celtic countries, between the Autumn of 2001 and the final disappointing climax in July 2002 with the final refusal by the French Council of State of public integration (and hence public funds), was one of the most disturbing and divisive in the history of Diwan. At the time of writing, the former Diwan administrative council has been dissolved and a new one will take its place. While Bretons are clearly shaken by these developments, there is also a recognition that the Breton educational organizations must regroup and form a united front in the face of this setback. On the positive side, demand by the Breton public for a Breton-language education for their children remains as robust as ever. (For a detailed understanding of the evolution of this crisis, see the issues of *Kannadig*, the French language quarterly published by the Union of Breton Language Teachers throughout 2001 and 2002. English speakers can get an accurate picture of the turn of events by looking at either *Carn* (published by the Celtic League) throughout 2001 and 2002 or *Bro Nevez*, the quarterly of the US ICDBL, throughout 2001 and 2002).

3. For a generalized look at the recent political and linguistic changes in the Celtic countries see *Celtic Dawn*, by Peter Berresford Ellis and published by Y Lolfa in 2002. It goes far towards explaining both the historical background of Celtic nationalism, as well as its present state of evolution.

4. See also *The Celtic Revolution* by Peter Berresford Ellis (Y Lolfa, 1985) for an account of the historical background of each of the six Celtic nations.

References

Ar C'hozh, Armelle, President of Kannadig (UGB or the Union of Breton Language Teachers): Kannadig 72, February 2001, "Objet de circulaires"; a summary of issues in a letter to the French Minister of Education, p.45.

Baker, C. (1993) *Foundations of Bilingual Education and Bilingualism*, Clevedon, Avon, Multilingual Matters.

Broderick, G. (1991) *Language Contact in the British Isles: Proceedings of the Eighth International Symposium on Language Contact in Europe*, Douglas, Isle of Man.

Casson, M. (1993) "Cultural determinants of economic performance", Journal of Comparative Economics, Vol. 17, pp.418–42.

Castells, M. and Hall, P. (1994) *Technopoles of the World: The Making of 21st Century Industrial Complexes*, London, Routledge.

Cooke, P. (1989) "Ethnicity, Economy and Civil Society: Three Theories of Political Regionalism", in C. H. Williams and E. Kofman (eds.), *Community Conflict, Partition and Nationalism*, London, Routledge, pp.194–224.

Cooke. P. (1993b) "Globalization, economic organization and the emergence of regional interstate partnerships", in C. H. Williams, (ed.), *The Political Geography of the New World Order*, London, Wiley, pp.46–58.

Council of Europe (1992) *European Charter for Regional or Minority Languages*, Strasbourg, Council of Europe.

Dorian, Nancy C. (1988) "*The Celtic Languages In The British Isles*".

Durkacz, V. E. (1983) *The Decline of The Celtic Languages*, Edinburgh, John Donald.

Delaporte, Raymonde (1990), *Elementary English–Breton Dictionary*, Cork University Press.

Denez, Per (1998) *Brittany, a Language in Search of a Future*, The European Bureau For Lesser Used Languages.

Durkacz, V. E. (1983) *The Decline of The Celtic Languages*, Edinburgh, John Donald.

Ellis, Peter Berresford (1985) *The Celtic Revolution*, Talybont, Y Lolfa.

Fishman, Joshua (1991) *Reversing Language Shift*, Clevedon, Multilingual Matters.

Fishman, Joshua (2001) *Can Threatened Languages Be Saved*?, Clevedon, Multilingual Matters.

Gardner, N., Puigdevall i Serralvo, M. and Williams, C. H. (2000) "Language Revitalization in Comparative Context: Ireland, the Basque Country and Catalonia", in C. H. Williams, (ed.), *Language Revitalization: Policy and Planning in Wales*, Cardiff, University of Wales Press, pp.311–61.

Grin, F. (1996) "Economic Approaches to Language and Language Planning", *International Journal of the Sociology of Language*, Vol. 121, pp.1–16.

Grin, F. (1999) "Minority Languages and Regional Economic Activity", mimeo, Flensburg. ECMI.

Grin, F. and Vaillancourt, F. (1997) "The Economics of Multilingualism", *Annual Review of Applied Linguistics*, Vol. XVII, pp.43–65.

Harris, John (1988) "Spoken Irish In The Primary School System", *International Journal of the Sociology of Language*.

Hechter, M. (1975) *Internal Colonialism: The Celtic Fringe in British National Development*, London, Routledge.

Hemon, Roparz (1975) *A Historical Morphology and Syntax of Breton*, Dublin, The Dublin Institute For Advanced Studies.

Heusaff, Alan, *Carn* 105, The Celtic League, Dublin, Ireland

Huggins, R. and Morgan, K. (1999) "Matching a National Strategy with European Intervention", *Agenda*, Summer, pp.15–18.

James, Simon (1998) *The Atlantic Celts – Ancient People or Modern Invention,* London, British Museum Press, pp.44–46.

Jones, R. M. and P. A. Singh Ghuman (eds.) (1995) *Bilingualism, Education and Identity*, Cardiff, University of Wales Press.

Kuter, Lois; *Bro Nevez* #77, February 2001, U.S. ICDBL

Kuter, Lois, "France Says No!: Diwan Schools and Integration into the French Public School System", *Bro Nevez* August 2002, ICDBL United States.

Kuter, Lois, "The School Year In Brittany", *Bro Nevez*, November 2002, ICDBL United States.

Mac Donnacha, Seosamh, *Carn* 116, "The Status of Irish In The Irish Education System", p.9.

Minority Rights Group, (1991) *Minorities and Autonomy in Western Europe*, London, Minority Rights Group.

Mlinar, Z. (ed.), (1992) *Globalization and Territorial Identities*, Aldershot, Avebury Press.

Morris Jones, R. and Ghuman Singh, P. A. (eds.) (1995) *Bilingualism, Education and Identity*, Cardiff, University of Wales Press.

Morris, John (1973) *The Age of Arthur*, Weidenfeld and Nicholson.

Morris, John (1982) *Londinium: London in the Roman Empire*, Weidenfeld and Nicholson.

O'Driscoll, Robert (1981) *The Celtic Consciousness*, Celtic Arts of Canada.

O'Riagain, D. (1989) "The EBLUL: its Role in Creating a Europe United in Diversity", in T. Veiter (ed.), *Fédéralisme, Régionalisme et Droit des Groupes Ethniques en Europe*, Vienna, Braümuller.

O'Riagain, P. (1992) *Language Planning and Language Shift as Strategies of Social*

Reproduction, Dublin, Instituid Teangeolaiochta Eireann.

Osborne, D. and Gaebler, E. (1992) *Reinventing Government: How the Entrepreneurial Spirit is Transforming the Public Sector*, London, Addison Wesley.

Puigdevall i Serralvo, M. (1999) "Politica Linguistica al Pais de Galles", in *Politiques Linguistiques a Paisos Plurilingues*, Barcelona, Institut de Sociolinguistica Catalana. pp.97–111.

Rayfield, J. R. (1970) *The Languages of a Bilingual Community*, The Hague, Mouton.

Saunders, G. *Bilingual Children: Guidance For The Family*, Clevedon, Multilingual Matters.

Vaillancourt, F. (1996) "Language and Socioeconomic Status in Québec: measurement, findings, determinants and policy costs", *International Journal of the Sociology of Language*,121, pp.69–2.

Van Langevelde, A. P. (1993) "Migration and Language in Friesland", *Journal of Multilingual and Multicultural Development*, Vol. 14, No. 5, pp.393–411.

Williams, C. H. (1993a) "Towards a New World Order: European and American Perspectives", in C. H. Williams (ed.), *The Political Geography of the New World Order*, London, Wiley, pp.1–19.

Williams, C. H. (1994) *Called Unto Liberty: On Language and Nationalism*, Clevedon, Multilingual Matters.

iv.) Cornish/*Kernewek*

Samples of the three main Cornish dialects and a newly-advocated dialect on the scene – Unified Cornish Revised

i) Modern Cornish

An Vulvoran

Me ath clowaz en eglos euh an vylgy, Conna mar wheag, ma meppig teag, Pell thur an plassow salez ve, Tho ve devethez theze, ma meppig teag. Theze me vedn rei ma vertew gwerthias, Theze ma lowenez gwethias rei. Cusk agoy thom gwily moar, Cusk gen ve, ma meppig teag, ha trig gen ve, Pell thur cavow kesadow an beaz, Pell thur cavow kesadow an beaz. Nag eze mernaz whecca vel ma bownaz, Nag eze mernaz veeth en gwlascor ve, Pell athor an beaz a deez merwal. Deez eker gen ve, ma meppig teag, Che a veath pednzhivik pednzhivigian, Che a veath pednzhivik euhall, brauz, Rowlia teez covaithack luck, Rowlia mawe ha moze keffreze oll leb ew teag. Deez eker gen ve en dadn an moar, Deez eker gen ve en dadn an moar. Gwear ma lagadgow vel dowrow an vylgy, Rooz ma bleaw, ma meppig teag, Gwidn war an todn an devran ve. Oll me a rei tha ge, ma meppig teag. Medall ma deffreh veath gurrez oll adro theze, Ha ma gwessiow theze leb vadnam rei, Down et agon gwily moar, Agoy down, ma meppig wheag, gon honen oll, Pell thur cavow kesadow an beaz, Pell thur cavow kesadow an beaz.

Richard Gendall

ii) Common Cornish/*Kernewek Kemmyn*

Raglavar

"Tus Kernow, prag a's tevia dyski Kernewek?" Hemm o govynn Henry Jenner, Tas an Dasseghynas dell y'n hynwir. Hag ev y honan a worthebis dhe'n keth govynn na yn unn leverel, "Drefenn i dhe vos Kernowyon." Wosa Jenner dhe dhyllo y *Handbook of the Cornish Language* y'n vlydhen 1908 yndella ow kul may tassaffa an yeth, Kernewek re devis, megys dell re beu hi gans lies hag a gar aga thaves. Ytho oll an re hag a gar an yeth a vydh pes da ow kweles an studhyans a hol. Rann yw a'n derivas a veu gwrys gans Professor Ken McKinnon a-barth an Governens Predennek (yma gwir pryntyans Derivas EKOS/SGRUD gans an keth governans na) An hwithrans gwrys gans Professor McKinnon yw an ledenna ha'n skiansekka re beu gwrys bys y'n eur ma. Ha my ow skrifa an geryow ma, nyns yw an kas ervirys hwath an kas dredho may kemmerer Kernewek a-ji an Chartour Europek mes tus Kernow a vynn pup-prys gorthebi dhe wovynn Henry Jenner. "Ni a gews Kernewek drefenn ni drefenn ni dhe vos Kernowyon."

Wella Brown

iii) Unified Cornish

Rak henna, a vreder aban usy genen ny dre wos Jesu an fydhyans dhe entra y'n sentry, der an hens noweth ha bew, a wruk ef ygery dhyn der an vayl (hen yw der an kyk), hag aban a'gan bus ughel pronter mur a-ugh an chy a Dhew, geseugh ny dhe nessa gans colon lel ha gans lunfydhyans a fyth ha'gan colonnow purjys a dhrok-gowsys ha'gan corfow golghys yn dowr pur. Geseugh ny dhe synsy fast an confessyon a'gan govenek heb hokkya, rak ef nep re bromysyas yu lel. Geseugh ny kefrys dhe bredery fatel yllyn ny exortya an yl y gyla the vos kerenjedhek ha dhe wul oberow da. Na esyn ny ankevy dhe guntell warbarth kepar del yu certan re usys dhe wul, mes ow confortya an yl y gyla, the voy ha the voy, pan welough why an jeth ow nessa.

Nicholas Williams

iv) Unified Cornish Revised

Rag henna, a vreder aban usy genen ny dre wos Jesu an fydhyans dhe entra y'n sentry, der an hens noweth ha bew, a wrug ef egery dhyn der an vayl (hen yw der an kyg), hag aban a'gan bues uhel pronter muer a-ugh an chy a Dhew, geseugh ny dhe nessa gans colon lel ha gans luenfydhyans a fedh ha'gan colonnow purjys a dhrog-gowsys ha'gan corfow golhys yn dowr pur. Geseugh ny dhe sensy fast an confessyon a'gan govenek heb hockya, rag ef neb re bromysyas yw lel. Geseugh ny kefrys dhe bredery fatel yllyn ny exortya an eyl y gela dhe vos kerenjedhek ha dhe wul oberow da. Na esyn ny ankevy dhe guntell warbarth kepar del yw certan re usys dhe wul, mes ow confortya an eyl y gela, dhe voy ha dhe voy, pan welough why an jedh ow nessa.

Nicholas Williams

Development of Cornish Language and Literature

Kenneth MacKinnon
University of Edinburgh and Bòrd na Gàidhlig

Origins of the language

The Cornish language is one of six surviving related "Insular Celtic" languages and is most closely related to Welsh and Breton. Its relatedness to these languages stems historically from the victory of the West Saxons at the Battle of Dyrham in AD 577 (some 10 miles north of Bath) which effectively split the southern Britons into two peoples, the ancestors of the present-day Welsh and Cornish.

The subsequent advance of the Anglo-Saxon Kingdom of Wessex into the south-western peninsula of Great Britain, the territory of Dumnonia, resulted in population movements from the Dorset and Devon areas overseas into Brittany and Galicia (north-western Spain). In Brittany, British speech survives as Breton to the present day. Trading links and exchange of population of related speech continued between Cornwall and Brittany from the sixth century until the sixteenth – and in some form even up to our own times.

Subsequent defeats of the south-western Britons brought early English influence as far as the River Ottery in north Cornwall in 682, and to south-eastern Cornwall between the Tamar and Lynher rivers in 710. In 722 a Cornish victory regained territory and stemmed English advances, subsequently reversed in defeats in 753, 815 and 838. This period probably represents a period when a Cornish rather than a Dumnonian or British identity was in the course of formation. In 936, Athelstan's decisive defeat of the Cornish resulted in their final expulsion from Exeter and elsewhere in Devon, fixing the boundary at the Tamar, where it has remained ever since.

The absorption of Cornwall within the Kingdom of England was not immediate. Cornwall was regarded as a separately named province, with its own subordinated status and title under the English crown, with separate ecclesiastical provision in the earliest phase. There were subsequent constitutional provisions under the Stannary Parliament, which had its origins in provisions of 1198 and 1201 separating the Cornish and Devon tin interests and developing into a separate parliament for Cornwall, maintaining Cornish customary law. From 1337 Cornwall was further administered as a "quasi-sovereign" royal Duchy in the later medieval period.[172]

The implication of these processes for the Cornish language was to ensure its integrity throughout this period. It was, throughout most of the Middle Ages, the general speech of essentially the whole population and all social classes. Over the greater part of the first millennium and a half of its separate and distinctive existence, the Cornish language functioned as the majority speech for all economic and social purposes in the life and society of Cornwall. This was certainly the case throughout its early and middle periods up to the end of the Middle Ages. It had, of course, begun to weaken in eastern Cornwall by the end of this period – but throughout this period it was renewed and strengthened by trade and commerce with Brittany, and the settlement in Cornwall of Bretons speaking a closely related language and assimilating into the speech-community.

The situation changed rapidly with the far-reaching political and economic changes from the end of the medieval period onwards, and language-shift from Cornish to English progressed through Cornwall from east to west from this period onwards. The numbers of Cornish speakers during this period have been estimated by Dr Ken George from various sources.[173] He regards the numbers of speakers as coincident with total population more or less between the Domesday enumeration of 1086 and the early thirteenth century, with numbers estimated between 15,000 and 20,000. Growth continued with some divergence from a total population to a likely peak of 38,000 in 1300 (some 73 per cent of the total population of Cornwall at that time), before the demographic reversal of the Black Death in the 1340s. Thereafter, numbers of Cornish speakers were maintained at around 33,000 between mid-fourteenth to mid-sixteenth centuries against a background of substantial increase of the total Cornish population.

From this position, the language then inexorably declined until its cessation as community speech in its last local areas at the end of the eighteenth century.

Three popular risings within a century and a half of the Tudor Accession and attendant loss of life – both from battle and in subsequent reprisals – accelerated this process, especially amongst Cornish speakers of child-bearing age. There was considerable disruption of the accustomed way of life. The Reformation considerably reduced traditional ties with Brittany.

During its middle period, Cornish underwent changes in its phonology and morphology. An Old Cornish vocabulary survives from 1100, and manumissions in the Bodmin Gospels from even earlier: *c.*900. Place-name elements from this early period have been "fossilized" in eastern Cornwall as the language changed to English, as likewise did Middle Cornish forms in Mid Cornwall, and Late Cornish forms in the west. These changes can be used to date the changeover from Cornish to English in local speech, which, together with later documentary evidence, enables the areas within which Cornish successively survived to be identified.

Middle Cornish is best represented by the Ordinalia, which comprise a cycle of mystery plays written in Cornish, it is believed at Glasney College in Mid Cornwall, between 1350 and 1450. They were performed throughout areas where the language was still extant, in open-air amphitheatres (playing-places or "rounds" – plenys-an-gware, y in Cornish) which still exist in many places.

There is also a surviving religious poem *Pascon agan Arluth* (The Passion of our Lord). These texts enable a corpus of Middle Cornish to be ascertained. Later miracle play compositions include *Beunans Meriasek* (the Life of St Meriadoc) datable to 1504 and William Jordan of Helston's *Gwreans an Bys* (The Creation of the World) dated 1611. These may hark back to older forms of the language, for other writings in the sixteenth century show the language to have been undergoing substantial changes which brought it into its latest surviving form (Late or Modern Cornish). These writings include Tregear's translation of Bishop Bonner's "Homilies" *c.*1556–8.

The decline of Cornish

The period between the Tudor Accession and the Civil War was one of considerable political and economic change. During this period the Cornish – as a people – rose three times in conflict with the highly centralizing English state of which Cornwall now formed a very definite part. In the preceding later Middle Ages, under the Normans and their successors, the Cornish economy developed on its three staples of fish, tin and copper – tin especially.

This last was regulated by the Stannary Parliament which had a far-reaching and independent legislative role in Cornwall. This engendered some stability for Cornwall – and for its language. There may even be some evidence that the language re-established itself to some extent eastwards once again.[175] However, there was a major rising in 1497 on the issues of central control of the tin trade, confiscation of the Stannary charters and suspension of Stannary government – this against a general background of Tudor centralization at home and expansion abroad.

The sense of identity of the Tudor monarch with the Arthurian heritage was thus shattered by a popular uprising against additional taxation for war with Scotland. The rising, led by Thomas Flamank, lawyer of Bodmin, and Micheal Joseph "An Gof", blacksmith of St Keverne, ended in failure. It was however commemorated five hundred years later in 1997 by Kerskerdh Kernow ("Cornwall marches on"), a mass march from St Keverne to Blackheath.

The "Prayer-Book" rising of 1549 had an explicit language dimension. The Reformation and the concomitant changes in the newly independent Church of England led to the removal of images from parish churches and the imposition of an English-language prayer-book in place of the accustomed liturgy in Latin.

The petition to the king was explicit that: "we the Cornyshemen, whereof certain of us understande no Englyshe, utterly refuse thys new service", (Article 13). The rising was suppressed with some ferocity and summary execution of prisoners: several thousands perished, and the aftermath was particularly severe.[176]

These risings have been likened to the 1715 and 1745 Jacobite Rebellions in Scotland – with similar implications for the language.[177] Cornwall's efforts during the Civil War may have won some degree of temporary local autonomy but were, on the whole, a period of destabilization for the Cornish language. The later outcome of the imprisonment and acquittal of Bishop Trelawny (1687) provided Cornwall with a national icon who, with popular support, won over adversity.

During this period of unrest and rising the language was unrecognized by any official translation of liturgy or scripture. From 1560 catechisms and sermons were allowed in Cornish – albeit instrumentally – where English was not understood, but these measures were insufficient to give a literary and religious base for the language, as was the case in Wales. Cornish versions of the Lord's Prayer, the Ten Commandments and the Apostles' Creed date from these provisions. However, without the mainstays of a Cornish Bible and Prayer Book, standardization of the language did not occur and thus a full literary corpus of Cornish of this period was not transmitted. Without a stabilizing or conserving standard, the language in its latter phases continued to develop increasing disparity from its pre-Reformation manifestations in miracle play and religious literature.

The gathering pace of change in the seventeenth century brought further unrest and civil war. In this, there was much military activity in Cornwall, and these disturbances further destabilized the Cornish-language speech community. However, writers in the seventeenth and eighteenth centuries continued to develop the language as a literary medium, even though by this period it was in substantial decline demographically. The genres within which the language was developed extended to encompass biblical translation, technical writing, transcriptions of traditional oral lore, letters, verse, epitaphs, topography and history. These writings of the "Newlyn School'" and in particular the Boson family, comprise much of the corpus of Late Cornish literature.[178]

Despite there having been no translations into Cornish of the Prayer Book and the Bible with the sixteenth century Reformation, Cornish was used in church services for the Lord's Prayer, Creed and sermon. In the late seventeenth century these uses ceased. The last places using Cornish were at Landewednack on the Lizard until 1667, and at Towednack in West Penwith until 1678.[179] In the seventeenth century George estimates the numbers of Cornish speakers as dropping to 14,000 by mid-century and to about 5,000 by its end.[180]

In 1700 Edward Lhuyd (1666–1709), Welsh speaker, antiquary, philologist and Keeper of the Ashmolean Museum in Oxford, visited Cornwall as part of his researches into the six "Celtic" countries, and published these in 1707 as *Archaeologia Britannica*. To this four-month visit we owe much of our knowledge of the pronunciation of Cornish in its last vernacular form, the preservation of much Late Cornish literature (which would have been greater, save for a destructive fire at his printers), and indeed the earliest identification of the Celtic languages as such.[181]

By Lhuyd's time, Cornish was spoken only in the utter extremities of

Cornwall. In these last areas it persisted tenaciously into the last decades of the eighteenth century. Its last reputed speaker, the celebrated Dolly Pentreath, died in 1777 – although examples of Cornish speakers are attested later. (see below)

In his *Archaeologia Cornu-Britannica* of 1790 Dr William Price of Redruth provided a review of the language in its last vernacular phase, its last traditional writers such as Tonkin and Gwavas, and its last everyday users who outlived Dolly Pentreath. These included Thomson the composer of her epitaph in 1789 – and others too.[182] However, by the turn of the century, Cornish had almost certainly ceased both as vernacular and community speech. It may well, however, have survived longer in family transmission.

With the advent of Methodism in Cornwall from Wesley's first visit in 1743 reaching St Ives and St Just (in which areas the language still lingered) and also as far as Scilly, a new popular religious movement was engendered which soon became the predominant religious identity in Cornwall. Methodism remained overwhelmingly strong in Cornwall from the mid-eighteenth to well beyond the mid-twentieth centuries. It had a vigorous lay ministry and adult class movement, but with the weakness of Cornish at this time, there was little prospect of a demotic Cornish-language local preaching tradition – as occurred through Manx in the Isle of Man, and which considerably enhanced and maintained the language there. There is no record of tradition of use of the language for worship in Cornish Methodism. By the mid-eighteenth century, Cornish was evidently no longer seen by its last speakers as appropriate to the religious "high domain" – even in Methodism. In the following century, however, Jacob George, Methodist class leader of Mousehole, made a collection of surviving Cornish words and expressions in his area.[183]

Cornwall had traditionally been one of the more industrialized areas of Britain, with its metalliferous industries, both extractive and smelting – especially of tin, which had been commercially important since antiquity. The exhaustion of streamed tin and the change over to deep hard-rock mining, which started to be extensively developed during this period, occurred while the language was still generally extant in west Cornwall. By the end of the century, steam power was being developed in Cornwall, especially for pumping and other mining applications. The Cornish language thus came to contribute greatly to the terminology of metalliferous and hard rock mining, as this was the leading world area for their development.[184]

The main corpus of written Late Cornish derives from this period. Its writers were educated men, and included skilled tradesmen, clergy, men of affairs, the successive generations of the Boson family of Newlyn, lesser gentry, and professionals. They spanned the period of the later seventeenth to the mid-eighteenth centuries, and have provided not only original writings, collections of the writings of others and of oral Cornish lore, but also accounts of the state of the language and its areas of use in their day.

By the last years of the eighteenth century, Cornish speakers were only still to be found in the remote western coastal parishes between St Ives and Penzance. Even here, the majority of the population had probably ceased to use the language, and it is remarkable that knowledge of the language persisted in family tradition throughout the nineteenth century. The domains in which Cornish was used during this period included reciting the Creed and the Lord's Prayer, and for counting – especially for fish in places like Mousehole, Newlyn and St Ives – with examples even being attested well into the twentieth century.

Sociologically, the language can be seen as retaining significance in spiritual life – and instrumentally in keeping control of a transaction within the indigenous sphere. The early collectors and revivalists have communicated the names and locations of persons who were able to produce examples of traditionally communicated Cornish – some may even have been "semi-speakers" who had been able to understand the language in their youth at the turn of the eighteenth and nineteenth centuries.

Economic change from the later eighteenth century brought about a process of emigration, especially as the fortunes of fishing, mining and agriculture fluctuated. The opening up of new mining areas abroad provided a strong pull factor.[185] Cornish people were migrating to North America by the mid-eighteenth century and there is evidence that these included Cornish speakers. William Gwavas (1676–1741) corresponded to North America in Cornish.[186] Today there is a worldwide diaspora of "Cousin Jacks and Jennys". In Australia, especially, this has developed particular links with the homeland in places like Moonta and Broken Hill. This diaspora has even more recently developed an interest in acquisition of Cornish language.

"Apostolic Succession": Cornish in the nineteenth century

Knowledge of Cornish did not cease with the passing of the last native speakers. Its knowledge and cultivation were, however, maintained for over a century by other means. Cornish words, phrases and formularies were passed on orally by ordinary Cornish working folk, and Cornish-language studies were progressed by a number of academic scholars.

There are numerous reports of Cornish being used for counting – especially of fish in west Cornwall. These numeral sets required the name for the fish in question to stand for the numeral "one", and "two" was generally rendered by the Cornish word for "next". Collections of Cornish words still in use in fishing, children's pastimes, and more generally were made by a number of scholars throughout the nineteenth century and even into the twentieth.

Berresford Ellis reports scholars such as Edwin Norris, who collected the Cornish Creed in 1860, W. D. Watson in 1925 with reports of numerals and the Lord's Prayer, J. H. Nankivell in 1865 on traditional numerals, Rev W. S. Lach-Szyrma in 1864 reporting the word collections of Couch and Thomas Garland, as well as researches of his own. Lach-Szyrma introduced Henry Jenner (1848–1934), a Cornishman working in the British Museum, to informants at Mousehole. Further contacts, including sources amongst Jenner's relations by marriage, led to his further work in collection of vernacular Cornish from amongst its last tradition-bearers, and laid the basis for his pioneering work in language-revival.

J. Hobson Matthews, librarian of St Ives reported John Davey, schoolmaster of St Just and Boswednack, near Zennor (1812–1891), as the last person with sufficient traditional knowledge of Cornish to be able to speak some, and recorded a short piece of original verse.[187]

Tradition has it that Davey kept his Cornish alive by speaking to his cat. From within the speech-community of the last semi-speakers came a *Memoranda of Old Cornish Words* still current in Mousehole and Newlyn in 1868 collected by Jacob George, Methodist class-leader of Mousehole.[188]

Cornish scholarship developed in this period with the publication of Cornish texts and dictionaries. In 1859 Edwin Norris published his edition of the Ordinalia as *The Ancient Cornish Drama*. Davies Gilbert published John Keigwin's version of *Pascon agan Arluth* in 1826, and the latter's translation of Jordan's *Gwreans an Bys* in 1828. The discovery of *Buenans Meriasek* in Wales led to its editing and publication in 1872 by Whitley

Stokes. The discovery of the "Charter Fragment" by Jenner on the verso of estate charters from Mid Cornwall led to publication in 1877.[189]

In 1880 Miss M. A. Courtney and T. Quiller Couch published a *Glossary of Words in Use in Cornwall*. Frederick Jago's *Ancient Language and Dialect of Cornwall* appeared in 1882 and his *English-Cornish Dictionary* in 1887. This built upon earlier lexicographical work: Charles Rogers's *Vocabulary of the Cornish Language* of 1861; and Rev Robert Williams's *Lexicon Cornu-Britannicum* of 1863. Collections and meanings of Cornish names were published by R. S. Charnock in 1870, and by Rev John Bannister in 1871. These efforts were followed by Lach-Szyrma's *The Last Lost Languages of Europe* in 1890. This even contained some elementary lessons in Cornish.

References to, and knowledge of, the existence of the language were kept in public consciousness by popular folk literature such as the collections of folk tales by Hunt and Botterell.[190] Use could even be made of the language in other fiction such as children's stories.[191] Likewise, local scholarship in parish histories and the like communicated further knowledge of the language.[192] Recollection of the language had been perpetuated amongst ordinary Cornish working people, and the educated public had been reminded of the presence of the language around them. The grounds were thus fairly well set for revival. The "apostolic succession" had been secured – the phrase is Nance's (see below) – and recovery of the language was a possibility.

The early revival

Jenner's work in restoring the Cornish language was published in 1904 as *A Handbook of the Cornish Language*. It formed an effective basis for language revival and learning. The back cover observed: "...There has never been a time when there has been no person in Cornwall without a knowledge of the Cornish Language".[193] Jenner approached this work from the background of a previous study of Manx.[194] He had become a bard of the Welsh Gorsedd in 1899 and of the Breton in 1903. He took the Bardic name of Gwas Myghal.

In these encounters there had been some resistance to the acceptance of Cornwall as a Celtic nation with the loss of the language as a living everyday speech. This was to be reversed at the Caernarfon Celtic Congress in 1904 when Jenner spoke to the theme of "Cornwall – a Celtic Nation", produced his *Handbook*, and arranged to receive a congratulatory telegram in Cornish. He successfully vindicated his point.

Undoubtedly Cornwall today owes its sense of Celtic identity to this initiative. In 1907 he formulated a Cornish Gorsedd ceremony but the inauguration of Gorseth Kernow, at Boscawen-Un stone circle, did not follow until 1928. It has been held annually since and has become an important institution in Cornwall's cultural and civic life. It has stimulated a great deal of artistic production, including much in Cornish, promoting literary competitions from 1940 onwards. From 1932 it has acknowledged fluent Cornish speakers by receiving them as language bards.

Associated with Jenner in the earliest phase of the revival was L. C. Duncombe-Jewell who inaugurated the Kowethas Kelto-Kernuak (or Celtic-Cornish Society) on the pattern of revivalist organizations in other Celtic countries. It was short-lived but influential. In its two or three years of active existence it initiated much that was taken on board by later organizations and it secured the publication of Jenner's *Handbook*. It thus cemented in place the foundation of the revival.[195]

Henry Jenner is widely acknowledged as "the father of the Cornish revival", but Robert Morton Nance (Morden) was undoubtedly the leading figure in the first half of the twentieth century. He was born in Wales of Cornish stock in 1873, settling in the St Ives area in 1906. Jenner had based his revival of Cornish on "where it had left off", i.e. Late or Modern Cornish. His ideas on spelling and pronunciation had been influenced by Lhuyd and the tradition of speaking Cornish of its last semi-speakers.

Together with Jenner, who had settled at Hayle, Nance founded the first Old Cornwall Society at St Ives in 1920. By 1925 the society had grown into a federation throughout Cornwall, and the first issues of its journal *Old Cornwall*, which continues today, spelt out a radical "gathering of the fragments of the past" in order to initiate a forward-looking agenda whereby Cornwall's national identity, culture and language could be secured in the context of what really amounted to a political agenda and an appeal to youth and the coming generation.

A youth movement was in fact established: Tyr ha Tavas (Land and Language). The movement also produced a literary magazine *Kernow* (Cornwall) between 1934 and 1936, which was the vehicle for a lively, revived Cornish-language literature, featuring stories, articles and verse of some literary quality, together with re-publication of the classic texts, and articles on language revival. This provided an additional incentive for learning Cornish: there was something worthwhile to read.

The reasons why Nance broke with Jenner's ideas on taking Cornish forward from where it left off deserve to be better researched and understood. Surviving colleagues of Nance and Jenner were unable to shed much light,[196] but it seems fair to say that Nance wanted a sense of connectedness to Cornwall's classic literature, and an idiom and spelling system which would enable the religious drama and verse of the late medieval period to be accessed.

Modern scholars such as Richard Gendall draw attention to a greater corpus of material in Late or Modern Cornish. However, its literary merit may be parlous and its spelling system much different from the Ordinalia and Pascon agan Arluth. Nance's ideas on the medieval basis for the revived language were assisted by Henry Lewis's *Llawlyfr Cernyweg Canol* (Handbook of Middle Cornish, published 1923, second edition 1946) despite its appearance in Welsh.[197] There does not seem to have been a personal rift between Nance and Jenner – they continued to correspond – but whereas earlier correspondence was in Jennerian Cornish, later correspondence was in English.

A. S. D. Smith, a Welshman who took the bardic name of Caradar, was the third of the leading early revivalists, acquiring his Cornish from Nance's Cornish for All.[198] Caradar's publication, *Lessons in Spoken Cornish* (1931) was influential in promoting the first generation of Cornish revivalists who acquired the language in order to speak it. His Cornish course *Cornish Simplified* first appeared in 1939 and is still available.

Other phrasebooks were published by W. D. Watson, *First Steps in Cornish* (1931) and by Edwin Chirgwin, *Say it in Cornish* (1937). By the outbreak of war there were Cornish-language classes in both Cornwall and London which had formed the basis of a small group of people who were able to speak and write to each other in Cornish.[199] The language was being used in public ceremony at the annual Gorseth meeting, and from 1933 in an annual church service. In the words of Morton Nance: "One generation has set Cornish on its feet. It is now for another to make it walk".

The revival seemed set fair to continue on these lines. In the words of A. S. D. Smith after the vicissitudes of war: "The decline of Cornish ... need not be regretted... We have a compact medieval language, whose idiom is Celtic and little likely to undergo further change... Cornish will be as fully intelligible 1,000 years hence as it is in the present year of grace, 1947".[200] Forty years on, things were to be very different.

Language use in the revival

Overview

The earliest revivalists, such as Lach-Szyrma, Jenner and Nance had probably little initial speaking ability in Cornish – but they certainly wrote in it; surviving publications and letters attest to this. However, Jenner and Nance seem to have acquired speaking ability before the First World War. The inter-war period witnessed a substantial development, in that this early phase of revival took speaking ability seriously. The establishment of Gorseth Kernow in 1928, and the commencement of church services in 1933 were spurs to spoken Cornish in public use – even if at first only in ritual and ceremony. Plays by Nance (*An Balores*, 1932), and Peggy Pollard (*Bewnans Alysaran*, 1940, *Synt Avaldor*, 1941, and *Synt Tanbellen* shortly after) assisted the process of familiarization with spoken Cornish.

So too did the production of verse – as several of the first circle of Cornish speakers were active composers of verse. By the 1930s a circle of at least twelve people were able effectively to speak and use the language, including Nance's daughter, who had been brought up to speak the language, arguably the twentieth-century revival's first "native Cornish speaker".[201]

After the dislocations of war, the Cornish language movement made slow but steady progress. *Old Cornwall* regularly continued to appear, with frequent Cornish-language items. From 1952 a new periodical, *New Cornwall*, was started by Richard Gendall. It was subsequently edited by Helena Charles, and from 1956 by Richard Gendall and M. Jenkin of Leedstown. The magazine carried items of contemporary interest and current issues, again with frequent contributions in Cornish. It ran until 1973.

With the re-establishment of a Cornish-language periodical *An Lef Kernewek* in 1952, also under the initial editorship of Richard Gendall, contemporary written Cornish again found an outlet. The editorship subsequently passed to E. G. Retallack Hooper who continued the magazine until 1983. By this time, a further Cornish-language magazine, *An Gannas* (The Ambassador), had been established from 1976. Spoken Cornish was assisted by the availability of Nance's recordings of 1954 on gramophone records.

Music has been an important domain for Cornish-language use. The first broadcast of Revived Cornish was in a programme of choral music in 1935. It was well received and a series followed in which six Cornish choirs took part. In the post-war period, this beginning was slow to be built upon. However, music came to play an important part in the later revival. Folksong and traditional music, from the seventies onwards, became an important introduction to the Cornish language for many. Cornish language was featured by the folksinger Brenda Wootton, the folk group Bucca (Hobgoblin), and the dance side Cam Kernewek (Cornish Step). Choral singing, which has been a longstanding feature on the Cornish cultural scene, renewed its interest in Cornish-language singing, and today many choirs include Cornish-language items in their repertoire – notably Celtic Chorale which formed to support Methodist services, especially in the Cornish language.

In the 1970s new uses for Cornish began to spread from the revival circle into wider Cornish society. The folk music revival stimulated interest in Cornish folksong. A song collection, *Canow Kernow – Songs and Dances from Cornwall*, was published in 1966.[202] The folk music revival which got under way at this time produced folksingers in Cornwall such as Brenda Wootton who sang in Cornish – chiefly Richard Gendall's compositions – and the folk music group Bucca singing in Cornish, playing and performing Cornish dance.

These performers were popular in Cornwall, and internationally. Their recordings, originally on LP, are still currently available on cassette and CD. They brought a knowledge of Cornish to a wider and more popular audience. This extended use of Cornish brought the language into new domains and was an important factor in incentivizing more people to learn it. The popularity of Cornish in song led to the re-publication of *Canow Kernow* – it is still available – and to a further collection of Cornish song and dance music, *Hengan* in 1983.[203]

The 1970s also witnessed the establishment of extended opportunities to use spoken Cornish. From 1975 there has been a language weekend in residential accommodation. This has expanded into holiday camp accommodation and has grown to more of a week than a weekend. Other day events, such as Cornish-language walks, commenced at this time. At this time a number of young families began to use Cornish as a home language, and an organization Dalleth (Beginning) was formed in 1979 to support bilingualism in the home and linked issues. In 1981 a children's periodical Len ha Lyw (Read and Colour) commenced in support of early language acquisition.

Publishing of Cornish-language material was taken forward by the establishment of a specialist press. An Lef Kernewek in Camborne undertook some publication of Cornish language texts, and its efforts were subsequently joined by Lodenek Press of Padstow. More recently, the output of Dyllansow Truran, managed until his death in 1998 by Leonard Truran of Redruth, published an impressive book list for a one-person enterprise of books in Cornish and about Cornish. Since his death, the book stock has been managed by Tor Mark Press, a division of D. Bradford Barton of Truro, an imprimatur specializing in popular handbooks on Cornish subjects.

Public worship has become an increasingly important field of use for Cornish. There have been annual services since 1933, and formal services have now increased to eleven annually, together with Christmas carol and harvest services. There has been an increasing development of aids to worship: translation of liturgy, scripture, hymns and psalms. Landmark publications include: vespers in Cornish 1935, hymnary and psalter 1962, Book of Common Prayer 1980, editions of Mark and John 1976, and a lectionary in 1978. More recently the translation of scripture has been taken very seriously.

In 1983 the Language Board recognized a body concerned with Bible translation: Kescoweth Treloryon Scryptor Sans (Fellowship of Translators of Holy Scripture). This has now been superseded by the work of Keith Syed of Charlton Kings, a scholar of Hebrew, Greek and Aramaic who has a complete translation in hand of the whole biblical canon from the original languages. It is hoped to publish the whole Bible in Cornish in the near future.

Estimates of numbers of speakers

Estimates of numbers able to speak Cornish effectively during the twentieth century are difficult to assess. The criterion adopted in this study is “the ability to hold a general conversation at ordinary speed on everyday topics”. The best indication is in the numbers of language bards admitted to the Gorseth, and from 1967 numbers successfully passing the examinations of the Language Board at the then highest grade. In the first year of its operation, 1967/68 there were 20 successful presentations to its examinations, rising to a peak of 93 in 1981, of whom nine passed at the highest grade. However, in both earlier and later years there were more passes at the highest grade.[204] In 1983, seven language bards were received into the Gorseth. By 1984 there were 18 learners' classes operating throughout Cornwall, and five elsewhere.

These indications might suggest growth of an effective speaking community to about one hundred – but a more cautious contemporary estimate places numbers around forty.[205] In the period immediately prior to the language reforms and controversies of the later 1980s, numbers of effective Cornish speakers probably increased from about 50 to 100.

Since this period, there has been a very definite increase in the pace of language development. Many of the organizations and individuals consulted during this study felt that there had been positive effects of the tripartite split. Research into the language in its various forms was seen as having been very greatly stimulated. Literary production greatly expanded, as the use and range of the language-varieties were demonstrated by their users. The associations of the three main language-varieties established classes and Cornish-language events, and began more actively to campaign on behalf of their own causes. The spirit of competition had stimulating effects. Public debate brought about a greater public awareness of the language and its communities of speakers.

The more recent revival and the language controversy

The post-war period was one of consolidation and gradual growth for the language movement. The revived language began to engage in a process of language development, with neologisms being coined and gaining parlance. It was a period also of development of the written literature, encompassing publication of newly-discovered texts from the classic period, short stories, translations of scripture, and from other languages such as Welsh, drama and verse. An anthology of literary Cornish of all periods *Kemysk Kernewek* (A Cornish Miscellany) was published in 1964.[206] New textbooks for this new phase of the revival appeared by P.A.S. Pool, *Cornish for Beginners* in 1961, and by Richard Gendall, *Kernewek Bew* (Living Cornish) in 1972.

In 1951 a group of language bards and former members of the pre-war Tyr ha Tavas and Young Cornwall organizations formed Mebyon Kernow (Sons of Cornwall) as a pressure group seeking further self-government for Cornwall. This has later turned into a political party, Mebyon Kernow

– the Party for Cornwall. It has a strong political and economic agenda, but has always placed linguistic and cultural matters to the forefront in its public appeal. In 1969 a Cornish National Party was formed.

In 1967 the Gorseth and the Federation of Old Cornwall Societies set up Kesva an Tavas Kernewek (The Cornish Language Board). This was intended as an examining authority and language academy. In its original composition it lacked academic representatives – at least such as would be recognized by university Celtic scholarship. Such may have been desirable, in view of Charles Thomas's earlier reservations and his later call for an authoritative historical dictionary covering all periods of the language, together with diplomatic editions of the classic Cornish texts.[207]

Growing criticism of the Nancean Synthesis was beginning to be felt. There had been criticism of the deficiencies in Middle Cornish being supplied by Welsh and Breton cognates in "Unified" Cornish. These, and the lack of a "down-to-earth literature", were criticisms made by Tim Saunders in 1972.[208] The academic world had always been cautious of the revived language. Academic study of Cornish – perforce in institutions outwith Cornwall – had concentrated upon the medieval language. In 1972 Cornwall gained its own research institution, the Institute for Cornish Studies. Its first director, Charles Thomas, regarded Nance's "Unified" as never having been sufficiently explained, neologisms as insufficiently using place-name and dialect resources, and the pronunciation based upon shaky models.[209]

Dissatisfaction with the spelling and pronunciation of revived "Unified" Cornish motivated Ken George to propose a reform on phonetic lines to regularise the pronunciation as it may have been *c.* 1500, and to bring spelling into line with a series of proposed pronunciation changes. His work was computer-assisted and was published in 1986.[210] George placed his ideas before the Language Board, and a general meeting of all interested parties and individuals within and outwith Cornwall was convened in St Austell. It recommended that the Language Board examine the case for reform and feasibility of the proposals.

In July 1987 the Language Board accepted George's proposals on a vote of 14 to 1(Richard Jenkin dissenting). This decision could be said to reflect the wishes of the community of speakers and users of Cornish, as the Board had been restructured in 1985 with a majority (14 out of 20) of its members being elected by Cowethas an Yeth Kernewek, the speakers' organization established in 1979.

The language-variety which resulted from these moves was named "Common Cornish" or Kernewek Kemmyn – now generally referred to as "Kemmyn" for short. George's reaction to the language debate and his later ideas were presented in 1995 as "Which base for Revised Cornish?" as well as in grammars and dictionaries.[211]

These far-reaching changes in the sound system and written appearance of the language were not universally accepted. Those who preferred to remain within the Nancean "Unified" system, such as Peter Pool, Richard Jenkin, Ray and Denise Chubb, used an existing association to institutionalize their preferred language-variety: Agan Tavas (Our Language). Its membership was originally for fluent speakers and by invitation only. It was reformed in 1990 and made open to all who supported the continuity of Nance's "Unified" variety (Unys, in Cornish).

This was not the only fallout from these events. Richard Gendall had been a longstanding figure in the movement: as a teacher of the language and author of an innovative and effective textbook, songwriter and scholar. His reaction to this language-reform was to return to Jenner's original basis of Modern or Late Cornish and to develop the revived language from its last traditionally spoken form.

Although not going back to Lhuyd's spelling conventions (which were, after all, merely a phonetic system to indicate the pronunciations which he heard), he took the corpus of language of its last writers as the basis of spelling, and claimed that the corpus of Modern or Late Cornish was greater and lexically richer than that of the medieval texts. This was also capable of being supplemented by survivals in dialect and place-names. So far as neologisms were needed, these could be supplied by loanwords from English, reflecting the international currency of such terms. His ideas have been expressed in articles and books[212] and his extensive researches have been published as dictionaries and grammars.[213]

The Late/Modern Cornish movement established a language council, Cussel an Tavaz Kernuack, in 1988 which comprizes founder members and representatives chosen by Late/Modern Cornish speakers and learners in formal classes and informal groups.

The early stages of this controversy were at times heated and acrimonious. There was considerable cultural investment of those who had effectively learned the language and campaigned for it, and who had studied the language, thought carefully about it and its problems, had engaged in substantial research on these problems, and framed systems to address them. This undoubtedly produced strongly held views on the language, which were, in many cases, incompatible and led to protracted debate.

This was against a background of general progress in the language and previously growing numbers of learners and effective speakers. In 1981 Wella Brown, a leading figure in the movement and author of a standard grammar of Unified Cornish, estimated the number of effective speakers at around 40.[214] The situation may well have stimulated more people to learn the language – although numbers presenting at examinations and attending language weekends seemed to slump during the period 1987-91.[215]

On the positive side, the controversy has been seen as stimulating research which might otherwise not have been attempted, and the production of publications and learning materials on an unprecedented scale. Ways forward have been seen in the joint statement of representatives of the three language-varieties in 1991 who concluded that "... this document proves that these groups can put aside their differences as and when necessary," and that "... the main differences are in the spelling and pronunciation".[216]

The Cornish Sub-Committee of the UK Committee of the European Bureau for Lesser-Used Languages was formed in 1995. All the three main language organizations are represented upon it, together with representatives of authorities and organizations having business with the language. It has played a key integrating role.[217]

The Gorseth has played an important part in the reconciliation of the language-variety controversy. It has continued to recognize Nance's Unified Cornish alongside Kemmyn. From 1999 it has also accepted entries to its literary competitions in Modern or Late Cornish, and it has also published a Book of Prayers for Cornwall using all three varieties.

The Language Board has also continued to recognize "Unified" in its examinations, alongside Kemmyn, as long as there is demand. If there is, and if the Board were also to recognize Modern or Late Cornish, as does the Gorseth, further resolution of this situation might be assisted.

The spirit of mutual recognition which has ensued is viewed by Deacon as something of a truce. The controversies have, on the whole, died down. Organizations and individuals have, in the main, got on with the task of language development. The output of publications and materials has been quite impressive, bearing in mind the slender resources with which they have been funded – generally self-funded. Deacon also draws attention to the legitimacy of reasons for language choice often not being scientific: different varieties may appeal to different social sectors. He also points out that the language debate had not been joined and debated by academic linguists and language specialists, and there is need for a scholarly debate on the linguistic issues involved.[218]

In recent years though, these issues have begun to interest academic linguists. Glanville Price at Aberystwyth has taken an interest in the Modern or Late Revived variety and feels that this overcomes many of his objections to the invented status of "Unified" or Kemmyn, which he had dubbed "Cornish". There was reaction to this term, and Price has emphasized that he did not intend it as pejorative.[219]

A similar critical view of the Kemmyn revision has been taken by Jon Mills at Luton, who feels it to be "linguistically naive" and not a suitable basis for language revival. He makes critical points too regarding the re-spelling of place-names whose Cornish language forms are being altered in order to conform with Kemmyn spelling conventions, producing forms which never existed within the traditional language.[220] Nicholas Williams at Dublin is also highly critical both of Kemmyn and Late/Modern revived Cornish. Concerning Kemmyn, he comes to different conclusions concerning the relationships of Traditional Medieval and Late Cornish.

He feels that it would have been more prudent to have based the pronunciation and spelling on the latest period when the language was a full vernacular. This, for Williams, was the period *c.*1505–1611 which is represented by at least three major texts. His ideas were presented in *Cornish Today* in 1995 and have subsequently developed further.[221] Williams has proposed the revision of Unified Cornish on these lines as "Unified Cornish Revised". His advice is accepted by the continuing "Unified" Cornish movement, Agan Tavas, as a way forward. Some of the leading proponents of Late/Modern Cornish have also conversationally observed that their and his Late Cornish models may, in practice, be drawing together.[222] It is fair to state that the academic views of these language specialists are firmly held and robustly argued. Deacon's call for a scholarly debate might, if it were implemented, indeed spark off further contention.

It would seem now to be a matter of fact that there are at least three varieties of the revived language in existence. The largest in numerical terms appears to be Kemmyn, and it is certainly the most productive in publications and language resources. It may, in a Darwinian sense, yet win the day pragmatically in terms of numbers. It may, nevertheless, yet have to argue further if Cornish progresses further in public life. There will be a problem over the spelling of place-names if public signage in Cornish is further implemented.

This may well involve the consultation of onomastic and linguistic specialists and the accommodation of the different varieties over mutually agreeable spellings. This may not be an easy process. Over three-quarters of Cornwall's place-names are Cornish and, in western Cornwall, their present spellings derive from the Late or Modern Cornish period. In the east, place-name spellings testify to earlier periods of the language's historical development. If public authorities and public services use Cornish more extensively, the form in which the language is used will require consideration.

There is currently no single standardized form of the language which is accepted by the generality of speakers and users of Cornish. At present, a number of Cornishes legitimately exist. It should be remembered that this is in fact the case with English, domestically (with Standard Southern English, and Standard Scottish English as well as Scots itself) featuring in their respective education systems, and worldwide (with British, Indian, American and Australian Standard Englishes). Each of these is a Standard English capable of being readily understood (albeit with some distinctive features) by speakers and readers of the other.

In the case of the other Celtic languages, these too have their dialects. Substantial differences exist between North Welsh and South Welsh. There is a standard learners' form, Cymraeg Byw (Living Welsh) and the development of a common broadcast standard, neither of which are intended as prejudicial to local dialects. In the case of Irish, there are three major regional dialects. The need for a non-territorial standard form became evident on independence in the early twenties. This was accomplished by spelling and other reforms implemented officially in the later forties. Nevertheless, local dialect is still used in public education in the Gaeltacht areas.

The situation in Brittany is even more fraught than in Cornwall. There are some seven competing forms or dialects of the language and these are often associated with specific political ideologies. The varieties of present-day revived Cornish may be likened to dialects, interestingly formed, not

Figure 5.1
Cornish speakers compared with the total population

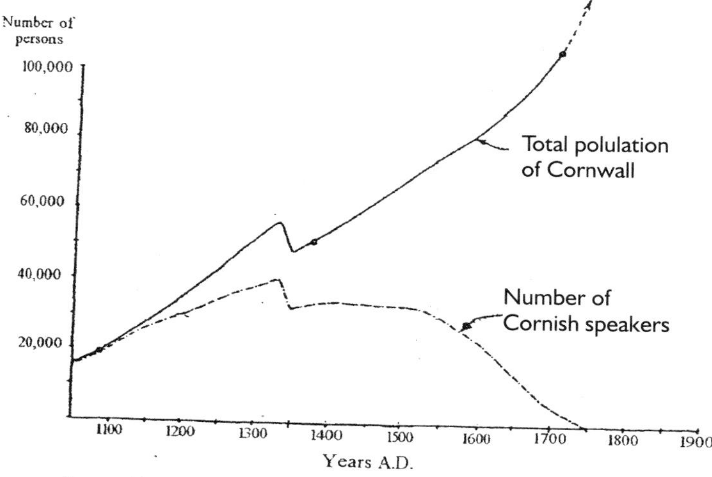

Source: Ken George (1936), *How many people spoke Cornish traditionally?* in Cornish Studies, pp. 67–70

Figure 5.2
The retreat of Cornish through the centuries

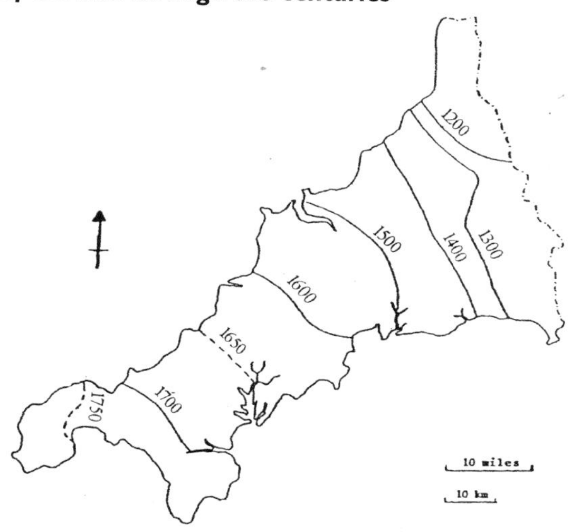

Figure 5.3
Schools with Cornish-language classes or clubs, 1983–1984

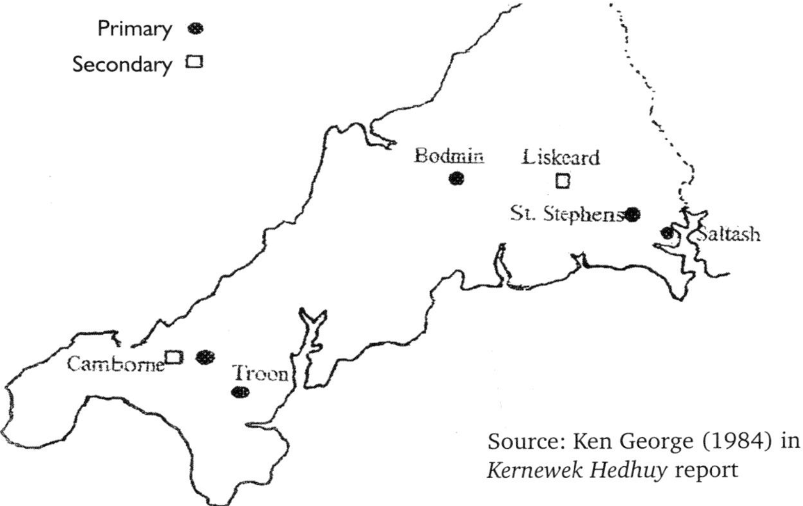

Source: Ken George (1984) in *Kernewek Hedhuy* report

Figure 5.4
Schools with Cornish-language classes or clubs, 1999–2000

Source: Geoff Griggs (2000), Modern Languges Advisor, Cornwall Education Authority

Figure 5.5
Adult Education evening classes in the Cornish language, 1983–1984

Source: *Kernewek Hedhuy* report (1984), Appendix 7

Figure 5.6
Adult Education evening classes in the Cornish language, 1999–2000

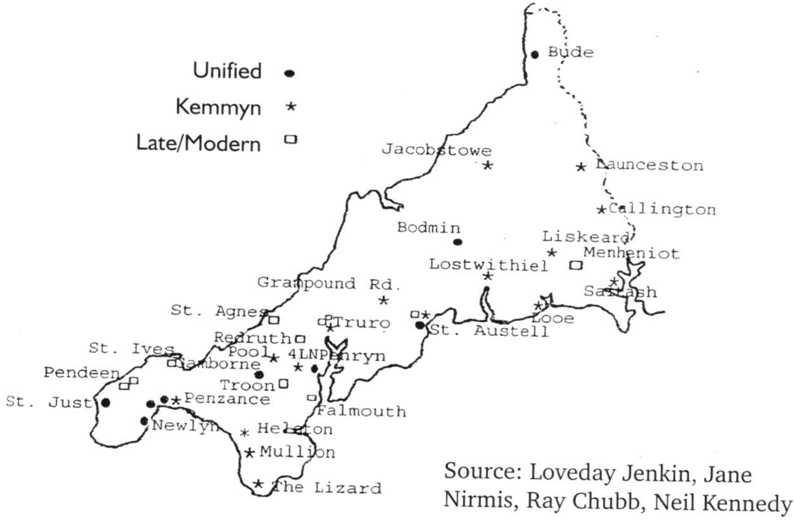

Source: Loveday Jenkin, Jane Nirmis, Ray Chubb, Neil Kennedy

on geographical or social bases, but upon learners' preferences, needs and loyalties.

The way forward lies with the speakers, learners and users of Cornish themselves. There seems to have been progress in this respect as the community of speakers develops. The different forms of Cornish become more familiar to each other and a process of accommodation commences. Some institutions use all three. For example, the Cornish subcommittee of EBLUL enables all three forms to be used. This did not produce any particular problems at the meeting attended as part of this particular research. A simultaneous translation into English for non-Cornish-speaking members was also provided.

Kemmyn and Unified Cornishes have developed neologisms from root forms within the language itself, or use similar constructions, as do Welsh or Breton. These are reviewed and approved by a sub-committee of the Language Board. These forms would be very largely intelligible to a Late or Modern Cornish speaker – even though this latter form tends to take over new vocabulary as a borrowing from English or common international usage. Although spelling conventions between the various forms of the language give a markedly different look to the written forms, the pronunciation is not so markedly divergent as to make them mutually unintelligible. Even the spelling conventions can become familiar with practice and use.

Cornish literature: from its origins to the present day

In its earliest known phase we have very few literary examples. In Old Cornish there is a very small corpus comprizing little more than a vocabulary, manumissions and glosses on the margins of the Bodmin Gospels. Texts in Middle Cornish are more replete – and the foregoing account of the development of the language fairly well notes them all. The more recent literature is also outlined. In the words of Henry Jenner: "Why should Cornishmen learn Cornish? There is no money in it, it serves no practical purpose, and the literature is scanty and of no great originality or value. The question is a fair one, the answer is simple. Because they are Cornish".[223]

Jenner's nineteenth-century Utilitarian concern with money, practical purpose and value were of his day. They may now be challenged, not only in terms of the economic and political functions of language, but also in terms of the quality of literature that was to be produced in the revived language.

Good general guides to the literature are provided by Berresford Ellis 1974,[224] and Murdoch 1993.[226] The classic and the traditional literature is well summarized by Gendall 1994.[227] His purpose is the notation of vocabulary – not literary criticism – and his estimates of word count are: 1,000 in the corpus of Old Cornish, 67,320 for Middle Cornish, and 89,639 for the Modern Period. This represents the lexical basis on which Cornish was revived.

From the outset, the revival actively produced a lively written literature. Early scholars such as George Sauerwein, Henry Jenner and Duncombe-Jewell produced verse, and this genre was further developed by the succeeding revivalists: Morton Nance, Allan-Collins, W. C. D. Watson, A. S. D. Smith, Edwin Chirgwin, Peggy Pollard, Retallack Hooper and quite a few others. Their productions and those of many others of the more recent revival have recently become more easily accessible with the publication of an anthology, *The Wheel*, edited by Tim Saunders.[227]

From its inception in 1925, Old Cornwall regularly carried items in Cornish, and together with the specifically Cornish-language periodical press (noted earlier) an increasing output of verse, short stories and prose articles has continued with increasing momentum. Allan-Collins (Halwyn) published many short stories in Cornish through these media, and in the local press (such as *The St Ives Times & Echo*), and a collection *An Den ha'y Dheu Wreg* (The Man and his Two Wives) in 1927. Both Nance and Peggy Pollard wrote several plays in Cornish. The inception of services in Cornish from 1933 led to translation of hymns, liturgy and scripture. The Gospel of Mark was the first complete book of the Bible to be translated in full, by A. S. D. Smith, which appeared in 1960. Nance published a collection of folk tales in Cornish in 1939, *Lyver an Pymp Marthus Seleven* (Book of the Five Miracles of St Selevan).

Further literary production followed after the war: A. S. D. Smith's *Nebes Whythiow Ber* (A Few Short Stories), 1947, and *An Seyth Den Fur a Rom* (The Seven Sages of Rome), 1948, and, posthumously, *Trystan hag Ysolt* (Tristan and Iseult a verse saga), in 1951, completed by D. H. Watkins and appearing in 1973. A. S. D. Smith also left an unpublished translation of the Welsh *Mabinogion*.

Following on from this period, the work of Richard Gendall as short story writer and songwriter must be mentioned. His Cornish language songs were featured by the late Cornish folksinger Brenda Wootton and were popular at events and festivals and in recordings throughout Cornwall and beyond. Spoken Cornish had only previously been available on disc of Nance reading traditional Cornish material.

The increase in literary production which has taken place since, deserves a critical study of its own. Berresford Ellis takes the account as far as 1974, and Tim Saunders to 1980. His poem collection, *The High Tide 1974–1999*, spans this period[228] – and it epitomizes a period of considerable literary growth, and a fivefold increase in numbers able to speak and read Cornish. Much of the literature of this period remains available. It is written in "Unified" Cornish, which makes it a little unfamiliar to Kemmyn and Modern/Late Cornish readers.

The bulk of literary output over recent years has been in Kemmyn. Specialist outlets have been established retailing this material at high–street bookshops: An Lyverli Kernewek (The Cornish Bookshop – Helston, from 1997), Gwynn ha Du (Black and White – Liskeard, from July 1998), and Just Cornish (St Just, from May 1999). These enterprises are all essentially committed to Kemmyn, so it is difficult for production in the other language-varieties to find a specialist outlet. However, An Lyverli holds the book stock for the Cornish Language Board – and hence has the Unified backstock, which it can supply. It currently carries a book list of 110 titles in Cornish. These range over such genres as learners' materials, novels, short stories, verse and song, children's books, classic texts, and religious literature.

Cornish literary magazines have greatly stimulated literary production. Although these have been "little magazines", their effect has been considerable. In the thirties there was *Kernow* (Cornwall), which developed after the war into *An Lef Kernewek*. More recently there has been *Delyow Derow* (Oak Leaves), taking this tradition of letters in "Unified" Cornish up to 1996. Each of the three varieties of revived Cornish has developed its own periodical. These focus on information, general and language issues rather than literary Cornish. More recently, however, a North American publication, *An Balores* (The Chough) provides a literary medium for all three revived Cornishes.

Mode of use

From a Written Record to a Spoken Language

The nineteenth-century Cornish scholars were concerned with the transmission of the written language and the collection of what still remained in oral lore and transmission. The early twentieth-century revivalists were concerned with developing these remains into the basis for a revived spoken language. This chapter attempts to evaluate their success a century later at the turn of the twentieth and twenty-first centuries. The main criterion for everyday language fluency explored in face-to-face interviews and in the three focus groups of this study with representatives of the three main language-varieties, was the ability to "hold a general conversation at ordinary speed on everyday topics". This has been taken in this study as the definition of effective speaking ability, as used below. The results are noted below together with the various ways in which the language is used by its speakers today in everyday life.

Of the original revivalists a century ago, Smith identified five as having speaking ability. Berresford Ellis names twelve who were able to do so by the 1930s. From Gorseth records of reception of language bards it can be shown that this number had grown to some 38 by the outbreak of war.[229] From records of Language Board examination passes, the number passing at the then highest level (Grade Three) had increased to 10 per annum by 1976, and to 22 by 1983. From 1989 a Grade Four was introduced as the highest ability level, with two candidates passing in that year, and rising to 15 by 1999.

Wella Brown estimated around 40 effective speakers in 1981, although a larger number had by this date passed the Language Board's examinations at highest level: 131 having done so between 1962 and 1981.[230] Between 1962 and 1987 there had been a total of 213 passing at Grade Three, and between 1989 and 1999 a total of 58 passing at Grade Four, making a total of 271 altogether (and a total of 309 passing at Grade Three).

The estimates of general language ability in Cornish, as reported by face-to-face informants and at focus group meetings, varied quite widely in individual instances. In some cases a personal estimate might be a wild guess – and in other cases quite a considered evaluation of evidence and experience. Bearing in mind the methodology of eliciting this information from identified language-activists, who varied widely in their personal estimations, the results must be read with caution. The levels of ability elicited extended from the minimalist position of "a few words and phrases" (e.g. knowing that "Kernow" means "Cornwall", etc.) to speaking on complex or special topics. The principal criterion is, however, fluent everyday conversation.

The results from the focus groups were inclined to be even more divergent in the cases of the first individuals offering an opinion. Subsequent respondents tended to be very influenced by the earlier speakers. These results are reported in Tables 5.1 and 5.2.

It should be very strongly cautioned that in terms of reliability these results are merely the aggregation of personal opinions and impressions. They cannot be taken as representative statistics of the present-day language situation. This information could only be reliably elicited by a properly targeted and representative language-use survey, or by questions on the Government's own Opportunity Survey and Population Census.

It must also be emphasized that the data in Table 5.1 represent mean values. The apparent precision of these average values should not be regarded as actual or real.

More realistic results were obtained from those specifically representing the three main organizations in reporting the language abilities of their known membership. Table 5.2 below summarizes the opinions of leading members of the language organizations concerning the language abilities of their members. Greater confidence can thus be placed on these findings. Cornish may, however, also be acquired quite independently of these means. Some effective learners may not have taken any examinations or been received as language bards.

Today, estimates of numbers of speakers can run into several hundred, but speakers of Kemmyn fairly consensually estimated around 200 effective speakers. Unified Cornish (Revised) claims about 20. Late/Modern Cornish speakers claimed around 25.

Numbers in other areas where the language is known to be studied (including those outside the United Kingdom) can only be conjectural.

Questions on numbers learning Cornish and using it within the family amongst the 17 language activists interviewed, produced mean estimates of 459 adults learning the language, 126 learners under 16, 171 persons using the language in family life, 20 children acquiring the language as "native speakers", and 85 acquiring knowledge of the language otherwise

Table 5.1
Impressions of numbers speaking Cornish at different ability legels. The data represent mean values only.

Cornish language Ability levels	Impressions of members of focus groups			All forms of Cornish
	Kemmyn	Unified	Modern	
On complex special topics	200	150	100	445
Fluent conversation	200	585	363	840
Simple conversations	3,000	1,000	500	2,900
Simple sentences	5,000	1,500	4,000	5,437
A few words and phrases	300,000	175,000	55,000	2,275
Number in the group	26	14	20	17

Table 5.2
Estimates of members' ability by representatives of language groups

Cornish language ability levels	Kemmyn	Unified	Modern	Total
On complex topics	100	10	10	120
Fluent everyday conversation	200	20	25	245
Simple conversations	150	15	30	195
Simple sentences	35	15	30	80
A few words and phrases	10	20	60	90
Learners in classes	285	80	80	445
Learners by correspondence	297	25	3	325
Learners by language magazines	300	50	100	450

within their families. Again, it must be stressed that without a representative and targeted language-use survey these results are a matter for individual conjecture.

The results of this study suggest that there may be about 300 effective speakers of Cornish (with about 30 reported for the London area). This estimate is based upon numbers passing the Language Board examinations at highest grades in recent years, together with language bards received previously. If this estimate is realistic, this study, in contacting some 84 Cornish speakers, encountered between a quarter and one third of the speech community.

Present-day language use

Introduction

This study was able to sample a variety of situations of everyday use of the language. This process included 46 face-to-face interviews with representatives of language organizations and organizations having business with the language, language activists and scholars. Of these, 34 were Cornish speakers. There were also four interviews by telephone, of whom two were Cornish speakers.

There were three focus groups of Cornish speakers from each of the three main language networks. The numbers in these groups totalled 60 persons. This number included 12 Cornish speakers who were also individually interviewed, and 48 other Cornish speakers. Thus, the study sample comprized 98 persons, of whom 84 were Cornish-speaking, representing between a quarter and one third of the estimated speech-community total. From all these sources, respondents reported a wide variety of language uses from their experience. The principal researcher also visited events and participated in meetings at which Cornish was spoken.

A questionnaire was used in the face-to-face and telephone interviews. It should be appreciated that not all respondents were able to provide answers to all of the questions contained in these questionnaires, nor was it anticipated at the outset that they would be able to do so.

Ability to respond to particular questions was constrained by respondents' own knowledge of particular issues, reflecting the wide range of organizations and individuals that were consulted during the research, and amount of time that respondents were able to devote to the interview. Accordingly, this chapter reports the data that are available to us from the questionnaire survey, supplemented by evidence from the focus groups, reflecting these constraints, which any similar exercise faces.

Home and family life

Some 10 named families resident in Cornwall were reported or reported themselves as using Cornish as the family language within the home, and as the language in which they raised their children. A further two cases reported specifically communicating knowledge of Cornish to their children, although only one parent spoke it. These cases were distributed across west, mid- and south-east Cornwall. This factor has hindered face-to-face contacts and the establishment of playgroups. Nevertheless, this study can report meetings with children who were heard unprompted to speak the language with their parents, and vice versa. Although the number of these cases is not large, this achievement, without any large measure of official impetus to do so (as in the Republic of Ireland), and in the context of a small-scale and largely self-resourced language movement, is noteworthy. Impressions communicated in focus groups of numbers of homes where some Cornish might be used at some time during the typical day ranged from "very few" to "maybe 250". Participants also frequently commented on their own early experiences in having had some Cornish phrases taught to them at home.

Social life outwith the home

Opportunities to use the language in general social life often have to be specifically made. Respondents often mentioned the nearby presence of other Cornish speakers in their local areas, and reported using Cornish for normal everyday encounters in streets, shops, etc. One small network meets for a drink on the way home – this study can report a natural meeting of companions who used the language socially in this way. Otherwise the language organizations arrange activities such as "fun days", rambles in the country, day events, Yeth an Werin (Language of the People – social meetings in pubs, etc.), language weekends and language festivals.

Entertainment will often provide a focus for language users to meet for "the crack" and to use the language conversationally. During the study period, a Breton dance night at St Agnes took place, Can Rak Kernow (A Song for Cornwall) at Truro, and Racca Day at Bodmin. Cornish language users were involved in these performances, and others formed part of the audience. In autumn a major folk festival, Lowender Peran, takes place at Perranporth and this features Cornish as a platform and performance language, along with special language days and activities.

Respondents and focus groups provided many instances of use of Cornish in everyday life. Some examples include a Cornish-speaking electrician and a bricklayer, each of whom encountered a workmate who knew the language, and they each used the language "on the job". Shops and pubs were most frequently reported as places where local Cornish speakers encountered one another and used the language in daily social exchanges. One woman said, "We should use the language more, even to people we don't know. They might be a Cornish speaker."

Cornish in the workplace

Interviewees reported using Cornish at work – as the electrician and bricklayer noted above. Two persons at least were identified as learning the language because they needed to know it in their work (in library and research services). Two other Cornish speakers reported the presence of other Cornish speakers where they worked (in a local government department and a technical institution), and that they regularly spoke in the language to their work colleagues.

Public ritual, ceremony and services

From the beginnings of the revival, such uses as the Gorseth ceremonies and religious services have provided a "high domain" of everyday language use. Cornish-language services now take place at least once a month. Some coordination of this activity is effected by the Bishop of Truro's Ecumenical Advisory Group on Services in Cornish, set up in 1974.

The main providers are Anglican, Methodist and Catholic – but all services are ecumenical. Services are conducted by Cornish-speaking ordained clergy, lay readers and local preachers. There is an increasing demand for use of Cornish at weddings, christenings, funerals, and other personal and public ceremonies, which takes the language well beyond the actual effective Cornish-speaking community.

Just before the study period, millennium commemorations occurred – some of which were reported as featuring the language in various ways. Towards the end of the study period, the annual St Piran's Day commemorations (5–6 March) included Cornish-language plays as well as ceremonial, and the opportunity for language users to congregate together in a more secular context.

Progress in language restoration

The revival of Cornish as a living, spoken language is nearing its centenary.[231] As is evident above, the language is being used by its speakers across a range of everyday purposes. Families use Cornish as a home language and raise their children to speak it. There is a lively scene of cultural events which Cornish speakers attend to enjoy – and to meet other Cornish speakers. There are leisure activities – both formally organized and entirely informal – noted above. Some informants noted that once they knew everyone who spoke Cornish, but now they often meet complete strangers who speak Cornish to them. There are now shops which will sell to you in Cornish – and others which sign, label and brand their goods in Cornish. Thus, Cornish is starting to have business uses.

The GIDS scale and Cornish today

A network of Cornish speakers is using the language once again for everyday purposes. It would be possible to evaluate the success of the language revival to date in terms of Joshua Fishman's ideas in his study *Reversing Language Shift*.[232] His study is particularly concerned with small language communities which are approaching, or which have suffered, "language-death". Fishman discusses the circumstances of cases of successful language restoration and provides a theoretical structure which numerically small language-groups may pass through to successful language regeneration.

Fishman details a typology of language restoration: the Graded Intergenerational Disruption Scale (GIDS) from a near-extinction phase (GIDS 8), to a fully restored language functioning fully in all domains (GIDS 1). It must be emphasized that this scale is concerned with levels of actual use, irrespective of the actual numbers of the minority and majority speech communities involved – or of the proportions of the minority within the majority speech communities. It is therefore a qualitative rather than a quantitative scale. The present study has identified the language from its lowest point in the nineteenth century and described developments in the twentieth. In Fishman's terms, this study reports the progress of revival through the following stages:

GIDS Stage 8: "Most vestigial users are socially isolated old folks and (the language) needs to be reassembled from their mouths and memories and taught to demographically unconcentrated adults." This stage corresponds with the late nineteenth century when collectors were noting oral transmission from semi-speakers, and revivalists were attempting to codify the results into dictionaries, grammars and language courses.

GIDS Stage 7: "Most users... are a socially integrated and ethnolinguistically active population but they are beyond childbearing age." Probably most of the early revivalists in the early twentieth century were, but one at least was teaching his child Cornish.

GIDS Stage 6: "... the attainment of intergenerational informal oracy and its demographic concentration and institutional reinforcement." By 1939 there was an active group of young people and students who had learned the language. After the war, marriage and family formation began to produce another generation who knew the language from their infancy. The group comprized a network in touch through informal contacts, the creation of Cornish language organizations and regular events.

GIDS Stage 5: "... literacy in home, school and community, but without taking on extra-communal reinforcement of such literacy." This is where the language movement very largely stands today. The language is being used as a home language, children are taught to read and write, as well as speak it. A developing Cornish-language press produces learning and resource materials for children. Without exception, respondents did not distinguish between speaking, reading and writing abilities in Cornish. These were all felt to be pretty much the same, which is understandably the case, since Cornish is predominantly acquired through classes, books and written materials. There has been some development of the language in school education, which is described further in The Cornish Language in Schools (below). Cornish is seen above as getting into community use in various ways – even beyond the network of speakers, and it is being institutionalized in Cornish life in entertainment, language events, public signage and official uses.

The further stages of the GIDS outline the progress of a reviving language through the stages of lower grade education, the lower work sphere, lower governmental services and mass media, and to higher level educational, occupational, governmental and media domains. These stages represent the agenda before Cornish today.

Representatives of the three main language-varieties all reported uptake of Cornish amongst learners of all age groups. A "gaping hole" was reported amongst the 18–24 age group for Kemmyn, and the other language groups also reported low uptake, about 10 per cent, of their members in this age group. Largest uptake was reported amongst the middle-aged (e.g. for "Unified" 50 per cent in the 45–59 age group and for Late/Modern 80 per cent in the 25–44 age group). Although these are only impressionistic estimates, they point to concern with appeal to young people. However, there were under-25s at each of the focus groups and they contributed to discussion.

Respondents reported Cornish as having great value in naming ordinary things: roads, houses, boats, children, and domestic animals. In this way the language is being used again across a wide sector of Cornish people. The rituals of everyday life, and public ritual and ceremony too, are becoming domains in which an increasing proportion of the public wishes its ethnic identity and heritage language to be used. The commercial applications in branding and language display in advertizing are seen as ways in which assurance can be signalled of Cornish quality and authenticity. The focus groups generated strongly argued points concerning the symbolic function of the language in securing specific recognition for Cornwall at regional level.

The Cornish language thus has its challenges today – as it had in the past. Respondents reported increasing emphasis on what the three main language-varieties have in common: mutual intelligibility and understandable spelling conventions. The language movement increasingly sees these forms as akin to dialects, as indeed modern English has both regional dialects and different official forms, which pose few problems today. The language institutions are developing mutual recognition and ways of working together. Kemmyn and Unified users frequently testified that only spelling really distinguishes them. Users of "Unified" and Modern/Late Cornishes speak of the ways in which their speech-varieties are becoming closer together.

Above all, the observations of learners and users of Cornish today emphasized the importance of the language for Cornish identity – not necessarily in a political sense – but in terms of regional development and cultural heritage. For many, it was an important source of self-identity. One family woman struggling to make ends meet and without educational qualifications said, "I really feel somebody, now that I can speak Cornish!"

New domains of everyday use: the Arts and the Media

The Arts

The arts continue to be an important domain for Cornish-language use. They operate as opportunities for Cornish speakers and learners to come together and use the language either as performers or audiences. As is the case with other Celtic languages, they form an important overall part of the language "scene".

The dance movement has expanded as Cam Kernewek developed new shoots, and new groups formed. These include Ros Keltek (Celtic Rose), Tan ha Dowr (Fire and Water), Otta ny Moaz (Look at us go!) and Astever yn (Replenishment). Bucca was the seedbed for other groups using Cornish in public performance: Dalla (Origin, Dazzling), Sowena (Good health – Prosperity), The Bolingey Troyl Band, Zabuloe, and others. Cornish Music Projects and Hubbadillia are two groups which bring Cornish language and music activities to schools.

More recently, Cornish language has been celebrated in pop and rock music. There are several groups using Cornish, including Skwardya (Ripping) and Mamvro (Mother Land), and an annual Can Rak Kernow (Song for Cornwall) event in which Cornwall's nomination for the Pan-Celtic Song Festival is chosen. Today's lively Cornish music scene comes together at events like the now week-long Lowender Peran (Joy of Perran) at Perranporth which since 1978 has extended its tourist season to mid-October, and Racca Day at Bodmin in February.

The Gorseth has, since 1928, been the principal patron of the Cornish-language arts. Its annual meeting in early September is the means of encouraging literary and artistic composition in a wide variety of genres for both young people and adults. The associated Esethvos Kernow (Cornwall's Eisteddfod) is an important platform for performance.

In the spoken word media, Verbal Arts Cornwall has been active since 1993. It has organized and promoted events and co-operated with other organizations in featuring Cornish language as well as Cornish dialect in its work. It is very conscious both of inter-Celtic links and the Cornish diaspora. It has organized events at Lowender Peran and the Wadebridge Folk Festivals, and at Goel an Yeth, the Cornish Language Festival. It has organized school events and school clubs, seminars, new writing projects, theatre projects with Cornwall Theatre Company and Knee-High Theatre, local poetry and verse competitions – and much else. It is in the course of reformulation as Awen (Inspiration) – with proposals for future projects in public local arts, radio writing, poetry performance and a website.

Cornish-language theatre and poetry have the capacity to reach widespread and local audiences. Pol Hodge, for example, as a Cornish-language poet, has undertaken over 120 poetry readings since October 1994 (with a mean attendance of 50), has published a collection of verse and has made a feature film on his work. Cornish-language interest has also been reported in connection with the A39 Theatre Company.

Wild West Films have made *An Dewetha Geryow a Dolly Pentreath* (The Last Words of Dolly Pentreath), Linynnau Safron (Saffron Threads), *Ledyans Leven Dhe Gernow Garow* (A Smooth Guide to a Rough Cornishman) and *Splatt Dhe Wertha* (Plot for Sale). This last, a short surrealistic comedy, won the festival Golden Torque award at the 18th Celtic Film and Television Festival held in St Ives in April 1997. The programme was broadcast by West Country Television at the close of the festival. West Country Television (now Carlton) produced *Kernow Palooza* for the 1999 Festival. Other companies are also involved in this genre, such as A38 Films and West Country Films. The availability of these productions on video, as well as the broadcast media, represents a significant advance in the uses and genres of the language.

The Media

Cornish has only recently begun to be used again in broadcasting media. There is a half-hour Cornish-language programme on Sundays on BBC Radio Cornwall. Pirate FM had carried two one-minute Cornish-language news broadcasts in a contemporary news format. However, a recent management change has withdrawn them, reportedly in case Devon listeners are put off the station. However, Pirate FM does sponsor Can Rak Kernow (A Song for Cornwall).

Cornish-language television has been developed under West Country TV and some half-hour Cornish-language features and films have been broadcast. The Regional Film Archive, covering both BBC and ITV in the south-west region, has traced the use of Cornish language in regional programming back to 1962. Use in films can be traced back at least to the 1940s.

There is a weekly Cornish-language column (on Tuesdays) in the regional daily, *Western Morning News*. This aims at a popular audience, handles popular issues and has a partly bilingual format. Otherwise press features in Cornish are sporadic.

Public signage and language display

This represents a domain of particular importance for the "visibility" of Cornish. Many towns now display or incorporate a Cornish welcome in their name boards. Outside Penzance station is a granite block stating "Pensans a'gas Dynargh – Penzance welcomes you". The controversies over this issue were featured on the Dolly Pentreath film noted above.

The naming of new streets and public buildings also constitutes a contemporary domain for Cornish language. District Councils are the authorities for road and street naming. Carrick District Council, for example, has a supportive policy on designating Cornish-language names for new streets and public buildings. That such uses are now to be found, is an indication of the progress made by the language revival in making a wider public aware of the language and in developing goodwill towards it.

Parish and town councils have the opportunity to put up Cornish-language and bilingual name-boards. In the St Ives and Penwith area, this was done prior to the Inter-Celtic Film Festival in 1997. One of the problems here is which form of the language will be chosen. In this last case it was Kemmyn – leading to controversy over the form in which the Cornish name of Camborne was used. The Cornish Sub-Committee of the UK Bureau for Lesser-Used Languages was consulted and is reported as having an advisory panel on this issue. The Language Board also has a working party on place-names and other Cornish name requirements. The Board has contacts with The Welsh Language Board and academic place-name specialists in Wales for reference and guidance.

Educational provision

Introduction

Respondents in this study frequently raised the issue of educational provision for Cornish as a "problem area". The future prospects for the language were seen as very much bound up with opportunities to learn it in both adult and school-level education. The development of pre-school and primary education through the medium of the language has been a means of Welsh regaining demographic normality, and of encouraging demographic development for both Gaelic and Irish.

Adult education classes

The Situation Pre-1980

There had been adult education classes in Cornish in both Cornwall and London before the war. These were conducted by Morton Nance at St Ives and elsewhere by A. S. D. Smith. In 1933 Smith noted classes in seven Cornish towns, involving 60 adult learners A correspondence circle was started by Smith at this time, and continued by F. B. Cargeeg. In some form, this continued throughout the war years.[233] In London in the post-war years classes were conducted by A. V. Allan-Collins and Trelawney Roberts.[234] In the post-war period, classes resumed in Cornwall, and in London at the City Lit.

In 1967 the Cornish Language Board was set up by the Gorseth and the Old Cornwall Federation. This took over the business of running examinations in Cornish which the Gorseth had previously itself undertaken. These examinations were in three grades, with proficiency being marked by being received by the Gorseth as a language bard. Initially the examinations were at three grades, with a language proficiency test, taking students to a little beyond GCE O-Level equivalent.

Adult education over the past twenty years

The 1984 Report on the State of the Language notes that by 1983/84 the numbers of adult education classes in Cornwall had increased to 18, in: Falmouth, Bodmin, Camborne, Saltash, Hayle, Helston, Launceston, St Just, Padstow, Lostwithiel, Liskeard, Penzance, Torpoint, Perranporth, St Austell, Newlyn East, Truro, and Newquay. Outwith Cornwall, classes were being held in Taunton, Bristol, London, Rennes (Brittany) and in South Australia.[235]

The Language Board was producing grammars and learning materials for its then three grades of language proficiency and was conducting examinations. These provided some incentive and a yardstick for students' progress. The 1984 Report also provided details of the successes at these grades between 1968–1983. Overall, these indicate increasing numbers and proficiency. Total passes at the respective grades rose from 20, 25 and

26 in 1968–1970 to 93, 61 and 59 in 1981–83.[236]

The examinations are now organized across four grades, with additional focus on culture and history (these highest grades are taken as "equivalent to everyday fluency").

More recently a fifth grade has been introduced under the aegis of the Institute of Linguists. This equates to first-year degree-level proficiency.

The present study was able to identify 36 formally organized classes in Cornwall. Sixteen classes taught Kemmyn, at: Callington, Four Lanes, Grampound Road, Helston, Jacobstowe, Launceston, Liskeard, The Lizard, Looe, Lostwithiel, Mullion, Penzance, Pool, Saltash, St Austell, and Truro. Nine classes were organized in Unified, at: Bodmin, Bude, Camborne, Newlyn, Penryn, Penzance (two classes), St Austell and St Just. There were eleven classes in Late/Modern Cornish, at: Falmouth, Menheniot, Pendeen (two classes), Redruth, St Agnes, St Austell, St Ives, Troon, and Truro (two classes). Membership figures for 28 of these groups totalled 284, suggesting an estimated 365 total enrolment in all classes.[237] (See also: Table 5.2.)

Other learners may be attending Goel an Yeth (the language week organized for Kemmyn), Penseythun Kernewek (the language weekend in Unified), and the Late/Modern Cornish language days. Other informal classes and self-help groups were also reported, which altogether would almost certainly bring the total to the estimates of 445 learners provided by the three main language groups (see Mode of Use section). Outwith Cornwall there are classes in London at three levels at the City Lit (in Kemmyn), at Bristol (in Unified) and in Australia. Tutors are generally well experienced, often as longstanding language bards, with Language Board qualifications at the highest grades. Otherwise, teachers are professionally qualified or, in at least one case, hold the City & Guilds Further Education Teachers Certificate C&G 730.

The classes are generally small groups which do not muster the minimum numbers for a college or other adult education class. Most meet in pubs, people's homes, village halls and the like. In the cases above of two class groups, some separate provision for beginners and more advanced students has been possible, although classes are generally mixed in ability. Classes are meeting in college premises at Falmouth, Pool, Penryn, St Austell and Truro.

For Kemmyn and "Unified" Cornish, the Language Board provides an examination scheme, which extended to a fourth grade from 1989, which takes account of Cornish literature and culture, and more recently an advanced Level Five, in conjunction with The Institute of Linguists and which can function as the first part of a degree course. Moderation and validation are provided by the Modern Languages Advisor of the Cornwall Education Authority, and there are active links with the Welsh Language Board and examinations authority. In recent years, total passes at Grades 1–4 at the Cornish Language Board's examinations have totalled 90 in 1997, 76 in 1998 and 61 in 1999.[238]

The adult education classes in Late/Modern Cornish are not on the whole geared towards examinations as such. Classes at Truro have utilized an NVQ-type of attainment testing, validated by CENTRA, a Lancashire-based organization. This body has now merged with several others, including the South West Association for Education and Training, into the Awarding Body Consortium through which the scheme is now operated. This involves about half the class enrolment. Otherwise, with Late/Modern Cornish, the examination scheme is not so well developed. However, the Cornish Language Council is considering a scheme on similar lines to the "GCE-equivalent" attainment scheme of the Welsh Joint Education Committee. Age-profiles of learners are generally reported as predominantly middle-aged (65 per cent in 30s and 40s, with perhaps 10 per cent aged under 30, and 25 per cent aged 50 and over).

Kernewek dine Lyther (Cornish by Correspondence) was established in 1982/83 and has been organized to date by Ray Edwards of Sutton Coldfield. After its first year of operation, it had 19 enrolments, of whom only four were resident in Cornwall, and the remainder elsewhere in the UK and world-wide. By 1989 enrolments had increased to 130, and by 1999 to 297 – the 1990s showing particularly steady growth of interest year on year.[239] Correspondence tuition is also organized by Agan Tavas in Unified Cornish, and by Teer ha Tavaz for Late/Modern Cornish. In the cases of Kemmyn and Unified Cornish, these schemes are linked to the Language Board examinations, as with their adult classes generally.

The Cornish language in schools

Earlier developments

In the early revival, Cornish was introduced into local authority schools by revivalists like Edwin Chirgwin who were also teachers. In the post-war period, Cornish language was taught at E. G. Retallack Hooper's private Mount Pleasant House School in Camborne. In the course of time, it became possible to take Cornish at secondary level through a GCSE Mode 3 scheme which was operated by the Welsh Board. Cornish began to feature in the local authority system where there were teachers able and interested to teach it – as at Helston where Richard Gendall taught languages for many years.

Before the 1980s the number of schools teaching Cornish was very small, involving only a handful of pupils.

The 1984 State of the Language Report noted seven schools where Cornish had been taught up to that time. Five were at primary level: Saltash, St Stephen's by Saltash, Bodmin, Troon and Camborne. There were only two secondary schools reported as teaching the language: at Camborne and Liskeard.

With the increasing economies in education and local government, and subsequently the introduction of the National Curriculum and local management of schools, the subject teaching of Cornish was reported as increasingly difficult to organize – or to find a place for Cornish Studies within an increasingly crowded curriculum. The language continued in some places as a lunch-break or after-school activity or club.

Cornish in schools today

For the purposes of the present study, a survey was undertaken by the Modern Languages Advisor who circulated all local authority schools regarding their present (1999/2000) provision for Cornish language. This varied from school to school.

Although Cornish is taught in Cornwall's schools, those that do so are few in number, and involve a relatively small number of pupils. Current provision is generally extra-curricular in the form of lunchtime or after-school classes and clubs. With the devolution of resource management and policy to schools, provision for Cornish language is now a matter for individual schools rather than overall local authority direction. However, the education authority has a policy and resource document on Cornish Studies in schools, and the language features within this. Modern language policy is supportive of Cornish and assists initiatives in the language in various ways, such as validation and moderation. Teaching resources include the authority's own Cornish Studies pack, and a Cornish language pack.

In many cases, Cornish is taught by one of the school's own teachers, and sometimes as part of the Cornish Studies programme. In other cases, there is a visiting teacher who is paid from school funds or from charges made for extra-curricular activities. Funding difficulties can hinder these developments, as can the availability of suitably qualified teachers.

Primary schools

At primary level, some form of actual teaching of the language was reported at 12 schools, as follows:

- Wendron teaches years three and four topic-based classes for 20 minutes per week.
- At Roskear, the school has taught Cornish for three terms now, with a teacher remunerated by Verbal Arts Cornwall.
- At St Mawes, Cornish is taught as part of the curriculum in years three to six, and there is also a Cornish-language club.
- At St Michael's, Helston, Cornish is taught by a visiting teacher in a weekly after-school class also open to all Key Stage Two pupils, staff and parents – with accreditation available.
- There is also a weekly club with a visiting teacher at Ludgvan.
- At Heamoor, Cornish is taught at a lunchtime club to year six pupils.
- At Treyew, the language is taught as part of the Cornish Studies module in year five (summer term).
- Weeth organizes an activity club, weekly for two terms, based on Language Board Grade 1 examination to years three–six.
- Coads Green integrates the language with Cornish dancing at Key Stage Two, and teaches words, phrases and greetings.
- St Neot has introduced Cornish with years four, five and six.
- Godolphin has two half-hour lunchtime classes in Cornish, and

another in Cornish singing, open to years five and six.

- At Brunel (Saltash), Cornish is used in assemblies, and for registers with both Key Stage One and Two pupils. There has been a weekly after-school club which is to be restarted, with opportunities to take Language Board Grade 1 examinations. The school choir sings in Cornish.

Some primary schools (such as Foxhole, Penryn and Lanlivery) reported past activity and would like to re-introduce Cornish. At Boskenwyn, a Cornish grace is used at meals and pupils learn Cornish songs. The school has a Cornish motto. Suitable textbooks and a resource pack and video for teachers without specific language ability were identified as priorities for provision if the language is to expand in schools.

Secondary schools

At the secondary stage, four schools were identified as providing teaching in Cornish:

- At Liskeard Community College and Newquay Tretherras, there are lunchtime clubs preparing for the Language Board's new modular examinations, involving eight and four pupils, respectively.
- At Pool, up to 15 pupils are working towards the Language Board's Grade 1 exam.
- At Truro, there is an after-school club for Sixth Form pupils studying "Unified" Cornish.

Between 1985 and 1988 there was a GCE scheme for Cornish Language under the school's own scheme at Pool. There were two or three successful candidates each year. Between 1988 and 1996 this was superseded by a GCSE scheme. This was organized under the Southern Examining Board until 1991. It was then taken over by the Welsh Board and ran until 1996. Over this period there were 42 successful candidates – but this rate was insufficient to ensure its continuation. Pupils at the above four secondary schools now take the Language Board examinations (presentations and passes details were not communicated in survey returns). Examinations are moderated through the County Education Authority's Advisor for Modern Languages and validated by the QCA.

Cornish studies and Cornish language research in higher education

Cornish in primary and secondary school-level education does not provide a basis for Cornish as a subject area in its own right in Higher Education. There are no degree schemes in Cornish Language anywhere – let alone degree schemes taught through the medium of Cornish, as there are in Welsh, Irish and Gaelic contexts. Cornish has been taught as a subject in the University of Wales at Aberystwyth and Lampeter.

In 1972 the Institute of Cornish Studies was established by the University of Exeter and Cornwall County Council. It is located in Truro, with a permanent staff of director, secretary and full-time research fellows. It produces an academic journal, *Cornish Studies*, which reflects its work, encompassing not only archaeology and history (the specialities of the Institute's first and current directors) but also language and culture, natural history and the environment, social and economic fields. It has developed new perspectives in cultural history, the Cornish language and its revival, migration and social issues such as housing and health in Cornwall, Cornish literature and tourism. Research staff are currently involved in language, cultural studies, politics, mining and natural history research.

The University of Exeter has recently introduced two higher degree schemes through the Institute of Cornish Studies: an M.A. in Cornish Studies and an M.A. in Celtic Studies. These degrees may include Cornish language studies.

The Cornish Language Board has an active concern with linguistic research into Cornish language: its historic forms, lexicon, grammar, and onomastics. It has working parties in these fields and actively develops links with academic institutions and research initiatives. The Board has sponsored a new academic journal – one exclusively devoted to research into Cornish language: *Agan Yeth – Cornish Language Studies*. Its first issue appeared in October 1999 and carried high-quality articles reviewing Gendall's Practical Dictionary of Modern Cornish, Ute Himnem's dissertation on the sociolinguistics of Cornish and Welsh, an article by Rod Lyon in Cornish on Cornish playing-places, and the Cornish Bible Project by Keith Syed. A second number is currently in preparation.

The other language movements are also involved in research: "Unified" through Nicholas Williams at Dublin, and Late/Modern Cornish through the work of Richard Gendall.

Issues

There have been attempts to start a Cornish-language playgroup for pre-school infants. These efforts have been frustrated by the territorial distribution of the parents themselves. It has meant that there has never been sufficient critical mass in any one area to sustain a viable group. To overcome this, organizations such as Dalleth and Agan Tavas have developed support materials.

The presence of Cornish in the primary stage is heavily dependent upon the presence of a Cornish-speaking teacher, the sympathy of school staff, local management resource budgets, and especially head teachers. This study reports parental demand for Cornish as a second language in the school system but it is again distributed across many catchment areas, and a "critical mass" calling for provision has been diluted by distance – unlike the more concentrated demands experienced in the Northern Irish, Gaelic and Welsh contexts.

Where Cornish is taught as part of the integral school curriculum (as at Wendron, St Mawes, Treyew and St Neot), it is taught to whole-year and Key Stage groups – and hence to all pupils as they pass through these stages. Otherwise, where there is only a lunchtime or after-school class or club, the numbers involved are relatively small.

Without a developed playgroup stage, prospects for wider provision of Cornish in primary schooling are more difficult – let alone a Cornish-medium primary stage being established in the foreseeable future. However, Cornish as a second language should be a feasible proposition, as has long been the case for the other Celtic languages in their respective countries. These all make provisions for their languages within the Core Curriculum, in the cases of the National Curriculum in Wales generally, and Northern Ireland where Irish features in its schools, and the Curriculum and Assessment Working Paper Gaelic 5–14 in Scotland.

For the language to progress within the education system, it needs to be more clearly indicated within the schools curriculum, as the other Celtic languages are within their own systems. In order for it to be more widely taught, with some place for it within the school day as well as in extra-curricular classes and clubs, it would need the support of properly resourced and remunerated peripatetic teachers. Where teachers without Cornish-language proficiency wished to introduce the language, resource packages and videos would be required. To provide these would require funding and resourcing. A decision would also have to be made concerning the form of Cornish to be used in these classes.

The difficulties in restoring a state-recognized schools-level examination were also identified by our consultees as a problem for the advancement of Cornish as a school subject, especially at secondary level. Local management of schools was also frequently cited as a difficulty in making a place for Cornish within school life, and finding resources for it. However, in other Celtic countries greater local autonomy has often been seen as the means whereby enhanced provision for the language has been secured.

Organizations promoting Cornish

Introduction

There is a wide range of organizations involved in, or connected with, the language. Our research has identified a total of over 40 such bodies. These can be broadly categorized as follows: language organizations, dedicated to the promotion of the language; cultural organizations; organizations in political and public life; communication media organizations; private sector enterprises, and organizations active in religious life.

Language organizations

Gorseth Kernow: The Gorsedd of Cornwall

The Gorseth was founded in 1928 on the model of those already established in Wales and Brittany. It acted originally as the chief centre for language revival and came to produce examinations for language learners until this function was taken on by a specially constituted Language Board. It conducts an annual ceremony at which bards are received for proficiency in the language and conspicuous services to Cornish language, culture and life. There is only one order of admission, quite deliberately to avoid distinctions of grade and hierarchy. Proclamations are also celebrated at other major cultural events. The Grand Bard is generally a distinguished figure in the language movement and is appointed for three years.

The Gorseth has promoted language and literary activities through both Unified and, more recently, Kemmyn varieties. Since last year, it has admitted Late/Modern Cornish for its competition entries. It has also recently issued a book of prayers for Cornwall produced in all three language varieties. It has thus become an important institution, which gives recognition to each form of the revived language. Its principal sources of income are the bards' annual subscriptions.

Kesva An Taves Kernewek: The Cornish Language Board

In 1967 the Gorseth and the Federation of Old Cornwall Societies set up the Board to be an independent language-planning and examining authority. A revised constitution in 1982 now constitutes 21 members, 15 of whom are elected from the body of speakers (Kowethas), two each from the Gorseth and Old Cornwall Federation, and one member each from the County Council and University of Plymouth.

Its turnover in the mostly recently completed financial year was in excess of £15,000. Its principal income has been a grant of £5,000 over five years from the County Council, augmented by a grant this year of £3,000 from the Council's new language fund. There have also been grants from: Heritage Lottery Fund; the Duke of Cornwall's Fund, for a dictionary; the European Commission, for a grammar, and from Caradon and Carrick District Councils, for purchase of computers. In 1987 the Board adopted the Kemmyn form as its standard. It has, however, pledged to provide its services, and to make its examinations available, in the continuing Unified/Unys language-variety.

Kowethas An Yeth Kernewek: The Cornish Language Fellowship

This is the members' organization for the Kemmyn language-variety. Established in 1979, it aims to promote Cornish in everyday life. It organizes the annual Goel an Yeth. This has grown out of the original weekends, Penseythun Kernewek, and for some years has been attracting between 200 and 300 users and learners of Cornish. The organization promoted Dythyow Lowender (Fun Days), and Yeth an Werin (Language of the People) – social meetings in pubs, etc. These events are now largely autonomous and self-organizing.

There are also links with other Celtic-speaking organizations. Kowethas acts as publisher for books printed in Kemmyn, apart from grammars, dictionaries and other language-resource material, and books in English about the language. It has a current list of some 124 titles. The organization works on an annual turnover of approximately £10,000.

Dalleth: Beginning

With the use of Cornish as a family language, Dalleth was established in 1979 to provide support, develop language materials for children learning the language, and to press for bilingual education and nursery provision. There were about six families at that time who were using the language in the home and raising children bilingually. It has been reported to us that there are approximately 12 such children who have become "native speakers" in this way.

Agan Tavas: Our Language

This body was formed in 1986 to organize speakers using Nance's Unified Cornish. Originally it was by invitation of fluent speakers only. With the tripartite split, it continued in the form of an existing organization staying with the original revived form of the language. In 1990 it was reformed on an open membership basis. Its aims are to ensure continued support for "Unified" Cornish and it organizes events, supports classes and campaigns for language use. It has an organizing council, Consel Agan Tavas, and aims at "including Kemmyn and Nowedja users in an inclusive and open way". Postal tuition is provided, together with a website with interactive learning. Since 1992 Agan Tavas has published a magazine, *An Gowsva* (The Talking Shop) on a twice-yearly basis in Unified Cornish, with some English content. There has also been a literary magazine, *Delyow Derow* (Oak Leaves), which was published between 1988 and 1996.

Cussel An Tavas Kernuack: The Cornish Language Council

This is the authority for the Late or Modern Cornish language-variety. It bases this on the writings dated between 1558–1776, and aims at standardization within the middle of that period. It has five members representing language specialists, teachers and users. It undertakes research, publishes grammars, dictionaries and language resources. It is funded by its members and voluntary donations. It has recently been assisted by a grant from the County Council's language fund for the production of a language course.

Teer Ha Tavaz: Land And Language

This is the members' organization for the Modern or Late form of the language. It acts as an imprimatur for publications and as a centre for language-related activities. Cornish language classes are currently organ-

Figure 5.7
The revival of Cornish in the 20th century

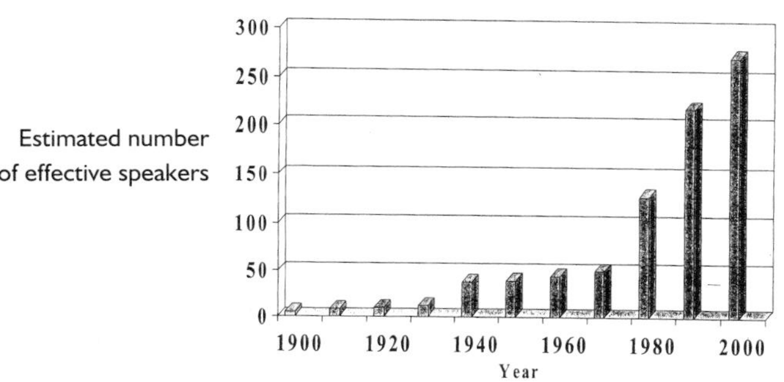

Sources: A.S.D. Smith (1947), *The Story of the Cornish Language*, Camborne, pp.12–14; P. Berresford Ellis (1974), *Cornish Language and Literature*, London, pp.152–170; Treeve Crago, Gorseth Archives; Jane Ninnis, State of Language Statistics.

Figure 5.8
Cornish language classes, 1999/2000: estimated numbers of students by language-variety

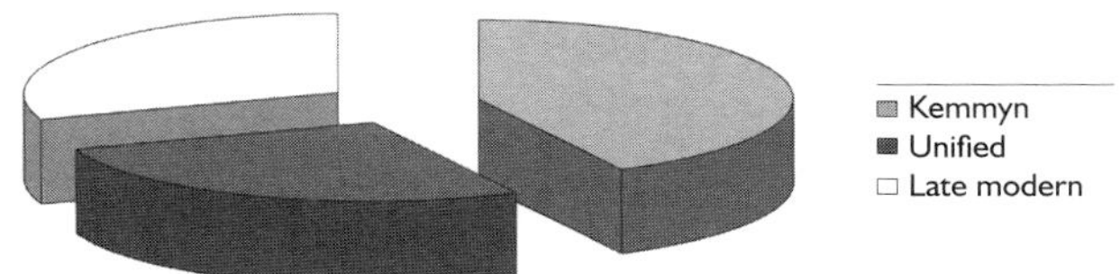

Kemmyn: 161, Unified: 103, Late/modern: 114; total students: 378

Figure 5.9
Cornish language classes, 1999/2000: numbers of classes by language-variety

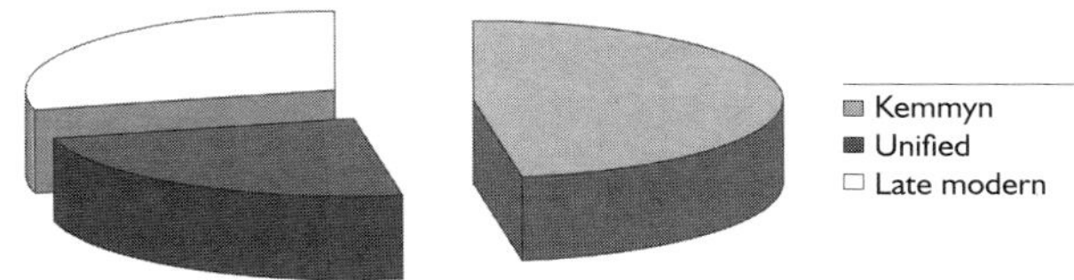

Kemmyn: 18, Unified: 9, Late/modern: 11; total classes: 38

Source: *State of Language Statistics*, 1999 (Jane Ninnis)

ized at Truro and St Austell Colleges. Postal tuition is also undertaken. It was formed in 1986, and has recently been assisted by a £1,000 grant for evening classes' needs.

Cornish Sub-Committee of the UK Bureau for Lesser-Used Languages

This body reports to the UK Committee of the European Bureau for Lesser-Used Languages. The sub-committee was set up in 1995, and its 20 or so members represent all branches of the language movement, together with other organizations having an interest in the language, such as the County and District Councils, the Gorseth and Old Cornwall movements. Prior to the inception of the sub-committee, the UK Committee had supported the applications for EU grant funding from DGXXII for the publication of Ken George's dictionary and Wella Brown's grammar (£3,000 each). The sub-committee is an important institution as it provides a forum for all aspects of the language movement – and is one of the very few institutions to do so.

Cultural organizations featuring the Cornish language

Esethvos Kernow: The Eisteddfod of Cornwall

This is a triennial festival of Cornish language literature, music and culture. Formed on a similar basis to the Welsh Eisteddfod, it is held in various centres throughout Cornwall and involves many Cornish organizations across and beyond the language scene.

The Celtic Congress

This longstanding organization, whose roots go back to the early days of the language revival, is represented by a Cornish Branch. The annual congress of the whole organization is to meet in Bude in April 2000.

Celtic Film and Television Festival

This organization was formed in Scotland in the late 1970s. It is still headquartered there, although it has active branches in each of the Celtic countries. It has greatly stimulated the production of Cornish-language films and video. The 18th annual festival was held in Cornwall for the first time in 1997. The Golden Torque award was won by a Cornish-language production: *Splatt dhe Wertha* (Plot for Sale) which was produced by Wild West Films. These efforts have been assisted by EU DGXXII, West Cornwall Film Fund and Lottery sources. Video and film production has been stimulated by these activities, and there are two other organizations involved in Cornish-language film production: A38 Films and West Country Films.

Lowender Peran: The Joy of Perran

This now week-long folk festival at Perranporth has been organized since 1978. Featuring Cornish language and traditional culture, it also has a strongly international dimension. Cornish is used as a platform language at all events and there is a Cornish language day. Four out of its six directors are Cornish speakers. The events include visiting performers and groups from the other Celtic countries.

The festival is a showcase for Cornish traditional music and dance, and a major opportunity for Cornish speakers to get together socially and culturally. Organized around it is voluntary work in schools, and the festival has led to the production of a Cornish dance video and book. It attracts about 3,000 visitors and is viewed as an important means of extending the tourist season in Perranporth into mid-October.

The organization is constituted as a limited company with charitable status. It has attracted funding of approximately £2,000 in recent years (£200 from the parish council, £1,600 from Carrick District and £250 from Cornwall County Council).

Cornish Music Projects

This is a small business partnership which has operated since 1998 on a commercial basis. It is involved with Cornish language and music activities in schools, networking with other organizations to promote music workshops and performance events. These activities are supported by a research programme into Cornish traditional music material, and the production of books and recordings. The organization has obtained grants from a range of sources (e.g. from Directory of Social Change) and has received funding from the County Council, Regional Arts Lottery Fund (with Cornish Music Guild) and the Elm Grant Trust. The two partners are involved in other performing groups and bands.

Federation of Old Cornwall Societies

This movement was founded by Robert Morton Nance between 1922 and 24, and still has active branches throughout Cornwall, and a regular journal, Old Cornwall.

Verbal Arts Cornwall – Awen (Inspiration)

This was formed in 1993. It is active in support for Cornish language and dialect in schools; and in wider community activities at Cornish-language events, writing projects, theatre events, poetry and verse. It has developed active links with the Cornish diaspora and other Celtic countries. Assisted by South West Arts, it aims to become a self-financing business.

Cornish Dance Society

This was formed in the 1990s to promote Cornish dance and customs. It organizes events and workshops, publishes a newsletter and hires costume. It acts as an umbrella organization for Cornish dance sides – which include those with a Cornish-language persona (e.g. Asteveryn, Otta ny Moaz, Tan ha Dowr). Although not specifically a language organization, it nevertheless supports the language and culture in various ways.

Cornish Music Guild

As a parallel to the Dance Society, the Music Guild has an important coordinating function and supports various traditional music groups which have a more specifically language-oriented performance policy (e.g. Dalla, Sowena, Bolingey Troyl Band, etc). Formed in 1987, it has charitable status and operates on an annual budget of approximately £2,000. It aims to promote Cornish music and composers and a greater use of Cornish material – especially in Cornish music and dance. Cornish language has been used for calling at traditional dance and Cornish-language events.

Organizations in political and public life

Mebyon Kernow

This organization was formed as a political lobby for Cornwall in 1951. It attracted support from across the political spectrum and beyond. Most of Cornwall's MPs were members. When it became a political party it lost these affiliations. It has always given a place to the language in its programmes, as it was originally formed by language bards and others prominent in the language movement. It has a quarterly magazine and branches throughout Cornwall.

The Celtic League

This Inter-Celtic political forum is represented by a Cornwall branch. The League and its Cornish Branch were both formed in 1961. The objectives of the organization are self-rule for the Celtic nations, the promotion of their languages and cultural and political self-determination. Lobbies and language campaigns have been undertaken. There is an Inter-Celtic quarterly magazine (*Carn*) which has regularly featured Cornish language articles since its inception in the early 1970s. These articles have, in recent years, been accepted in any recognized form of Cornish. The League has very slender resources and receives no third-party funding.

Cornwall County Council

The Council has an arts officer who is a Cornish speaker and who undertakes a coordinating function for the Cornish language. She maintains an information source on Cornish-language organizations. The Council has recently adopted a framework policy of support for the language and it has circulated all the District Councils seeking its joint adoption. This has been forthcoming for Carrick, Kerrier, Penwith and North Cornwall Councils, although Caradon and Isles of Scilly have not yet followed suit.

District Councils

The four Councils that have adopted the County framework policy for Cornish language will be invited to send representatives to the Cornish Sub-Committee of the European Bureau. Two (Penwith and Carrick) have produced supportive action for Cornish signage. Although it has not yet ratified the County policy, Caradon has funded a Cornish-language class for its employees, while Carrick has produced a newsletter in Cornish.

Cornish Bureau For European Relations (COBER)

COBER exists to make available to Cornish organizations information relating to Europe. It has been involved in a variety of initiatives including the designation of long-distance paths and waymarking, with European assistance (e.g. The Saints' Way). It has a Cornish-language profile and is represented on the Cornish Sub-Committee of EBLUL.

Organizations using Cornish in communications media

Cornish Language Films

As noted above, these are chiefly represented by Wild West Films, A38 Films and West Country Films. The first of these has been assisted with funding from European sources, West Cornwall Film Fund and Lottery sources. In recent years it has produced four specifically Cornish-language productions and another which also features the language.

Radio

Cornish language has been used in broadcasting by two stations in Cornwall: BBC Radio Cornwall and Pirate FM. Radio Cornwall currently carries a short magazine programme and news in Cornish on Sundays.

Organizations Promoting Cornish in Enterprise

An Lyverji Kernewek: The Cornish Bookshop

Located in Helston, this was established in 1997. Start-up capital was a combination of a small-business loan, mortgage, and overdraft facility. It is now virtually financially self-supporting. There are facilities for workshops, publishing and meetings on the premises. The enterprise holds the book stock of the Cornish Language Board and Kowethas. It retails these together with Cornish-interest books and promotional material.

Gwynn ha Du: White and Black

This shop is located in Liskeard. It aims to promote the Cornish language, show Cornish books to the public and act as a focus and shop-window for the language. Its start-up capital was very small (chiefly donated as gifts) and it relied initially on voluntary work in its initial phase since 1998. It now has a full-time manager and New Deal funding. All accounts and records are kept in Cornish and telephones answered in the language. The initiative has been developed through Kowethas an Yeth.

Just Cornish

This is a one-person enterprise, located on one of St Just's main streets. It sells Cornish-language and language-interest books in English, together with crafts with a specifically "all made in Cornwall" sales policy. It was established in May 1999 with self-found start-up capital.

Kernow Designs

This one-person enterprise supplies the three Cornish bookshops and others with Cornish-language materials.

Organizations promoting and using Cornish in religious life

Bishop of Truro's Ecumenical Advisory Group on Services in Cornish

This body was set up in 1974. Although an Anglican initiative, Methodist and Catholic interests are specifically included as the chief denominations providing worship in Cornish. It has a very slender working budget. There are now at least 11 formally organized services in Cornish held annually – with other services such as Carol and Harvest Services. It has also been involved in the development of Catholic liturgy.

Bredereth Sen Jago: The Brotherhood of Saint James

This fellowship was established in 1988 and is principally concerned with organizing pilgrimages on an open denominational basis. Its aims and activities encompass concern with Cornish history, saints and place-names and its membership includes speakers and teachers of the language. Its finances are minimal.

Funding sources

Funding Awarded to Cornish Language Groups

From our consultations with organizations and individuals involved in the promotion and development of the Cornish language, it appears that there has been little history of funding activity over the last 20 years. Our consultations indicate that this probably reflects the generally small-scale nature of these organizations over this time. Many of the organizations are run by small groups of individuals, who may not necessarily have the expertise or knowledge to make applications for funding to national/European organizations.

We have identified third-party funding of approximately £50,000.

Cornish-language organizations have generally received small amounts of funding for their activities over the period. One of the main sources of funding has been local authority. Verbal Arts Cornwall is unique, in that it has been supported entirely by South West Arts which provides £21,000 annual funding. This funding is used for the promotion of the Cornish language and dialect in arts events. It has also been used for the past three terms to remunerate a post at Roskear primary school for teaching the Cornish language (as mentioned in "Cornish in Schools Today" above).

There have been a small number of successful applications to the European Commission DGXXII. Two of these were grants awarded (via European Bureau for Lesser Used Languages) under the Minority Languages programme, for the publication of two books (a Cornish dictionary and a book on the grammar of modern Cornish). In both cases, £3,000 was awarded. The Minority Languages programme then required 50 per cent matched funding (it is now 55 per cent).

Of those organizations that disclosed the amount of funding awarded, just over half received £1,000 or over, with the funding mainly ranging between £1,000 and £3,000. Just under half of successful applicants received under £1,000.

Over the last 12–18 months, there has been a general move towards helping organizations involved in the promotion and development of the Cornish-language and assistance to these groups appears to be growing. In the current financial year, Cornwall County Council has allocated £5,000 to Cornish-language organizations, primarily for assistance towards publications. This money has been distributed between the three Cornish language movements (£3,000 to Kemmyn; £1,000 to Unified; and £1,000 to Late/Modern). The £5,000 Cornwall County Council fund will continue on an annual basis from the present financial year onwards.

Also, The Celtic Congress is holding its annual inter-Celtic gathering in Cornwall in April 2000. North Cornwall District Council has contributed £500 towards this event.

Funding and Support Potentially Available to Cornish Language Groups

Local authorities within Cornwall tend to operate generic programmes for their areas and generally do not run any schemes specifically related to Cornish-language activities.

Our consultations suggest that Cornish-language organizations would have been able to source very little European funding over the period. However, Cornish-language organizations were able to source at least one European fund over the period. This was the Minority Languages Programme. It provides support for: developing language skills (teaching aids, training, publications, etc); information, such as publication of magazines; language description and standardization; and economic and social protection of the language, such as using the language on signs.

References

Historical

Dalriada Heritage Trust (1999) *An Introduction to the History of the Cornish Language*, Brodick, Taigh Arainn.

Ellis, Berresford P. (1971) *The Story of the Cornish Language*, Truro, Tor Mark Press.

Ellis, Berresford P. (1974) *The Cornish Language and its Literature*, London, Routledge.

Gendall, R. M. M. (1994) *1000 Years of Cornish*, Liskeard, Teere ha Tavaz.

George. K. (1986) "How Many People Spoke Cornish Traditionally?" in *Cornish Studies*, first series No. 14, Redruth, Institute of Cornish Studies, pp.67–70.

Murdoch, B. (1993) *Cornish Literature*, Cambridge, Brewer.

Payton, P. (1996) *Cornwall*, Fowey, Alexander Associates.

Payton, P. (1999) *The Cornish Overseas*, Fowey, Alexander Associates.

Smith, A. S. D. (1947) *The Story of the Cornish Language – its Extinction and Revival*, Camborne, Camborne Printing and Stationery Company Limited.

Smith, A. S. D. (1969) *The Story of the Cornish Language* (revised by Hooper, E. G. R.), Camborne, An Lef Kernewek.

Wakelin, M. (1975) *Language and History in Cornwall*, Leicester, Leicester University Press.

Contemporary

Brown W. et al (1991) *The Cornish Language*, Cornish Language Board and others.

Brown, W. & Sandercock, G. (1994) *The Cornish Language Board: A Policy Statement*, Saltash, Cornish Language Board.

Brown, W. (1988) *The Cornish Language in Primary Education*, Leeuwarden, Fryske Akademy I EMU-projekt No. 27.

Cowethas an Yeth Kernewek (1984) *Kernewek Hedhyu – Report on the State of the Language*, Truro, Cowethas an Yeth.

Deacon, B, (1996) "Language Revival and Language Debate – Modernity and Postmodernity", in Payton, P. (ed.) (1996) *Cornish Studies*, Second Series No. 4, Exeter, University of Exeter Press, pp.88–106.

Deacon, B. et al (1988) *Cornwall at the Crossroads?*, Redruth, Cornish Social and Economic Research Group.

George, K. (1988) *Aspects of the Cornish Revival*, Maddrell memorial lecture, Douglas, Manx Language Society.

George, K. (1993) "The Revived Languages: Revived Cornish", in Ball, M. J. with

Fife J. (eds) (1993) *The Celtic Languages*, London, Routledge. pp.644–654.

George, K. (1995) "Which Base for Revived Cornish?" in Payton, P. (ed.) (1995) *Cornish Studies*, Second Series No. 3, (1995), Exeter, Exeter University Press, pp.104–124.

George. K. (1986) "Appendix – Cornish", in *Commission of European Communities (1986) Linguistic Minorities in Countries Belonging to the European Community*, Luxembourg, Office for Official Publications of EC., pp. 194–195.

Hale, A. (1997) "Genesis of the Celto-Cornish Revival?; L. C. Duncombe-Jewell and the Cowethas Kelto-Kernuak", in Payton, P. (ed.) (1997) *Cornish Studies*, Second Series No. 5, Exeter, Exeter University Press, pp.100–111.

Hirner, U. (1997) "Language Death and Revival: a Sociolinguistic Comparison between Cornish and Welsh", unpub. M.A. Thesis, Department of Language Development, University of Graz.

Payton, P. (1997) "Identity, Ideology and Language in Modern Cornwall", in Tristram, H. L. C. (ed.) (1997) *The Celtic Englishes*, Heidelberg, Universitätsverlag C. Winter.

Payton, P. (ed.) (1993) *Cornwall Since the War*, Truro, Institute of Cornish Studies and Redruth, Dyllansow Truran.

Payton, P. "The Ideology of Language Revival in Modern Cornwall", in Black R. et al, (eds.) *Celtic Connections – proceedings of the 10th International Congress of Celtic Studies* Vol. 1, East Linton, Tuckwell, pp.395–424.

Penglase, C, (1994) "Authenticity in the Revival of Cornish", in Payton, P. (ed.) *Cornish Studies*, Second Series No. 2 (1994), Exeter, University of Exeter Press, pp.96–107.

Tregidga, G. (1995) *The Politics of the Celto-Cornish Revival 1886–1936*, in Payton, P. *Cornish Studies*, Second Series No. 5, Exeter, Exeter University Press, pp.125–150.

Westland, A, (ed.) (1987) *Cornwall – the Cultural Construction of Place*, Penzance, Parten Press.

Williams, G. (1994) *Report on Cornish: Barcelona*, Instituta Sociolinguistica de Catalunya, EU Euromosaic Project.

Williams, N. J. A, (1995) *Cornish Today: an Examination of the Revived Language*, Sutton Coldfield, Kernewek dre Lyther.

Linguistic

Brown, W. (1992) *A Grammar of Modern Cornish*, Callington, Cornish Language Board.

Coileain, S, "The Pronunciation of Cornish", unpub. B. Phil thesis, University of East London.

Dunbar, P. and George, K. (1997) *Kernewek Kemmyn: Cornish for the Twenty–First Century*, Saltash, Cornish Language Board.

Gendall, R. M. M. (1991) *A Student's Grammar of Modern Cornish*, Liskeard, The Cornish Language Council.

Gendall, R. M. M. (1997) *A Practical Dictionary of Modern Cornish*: Part One Cornish – English, Liskeard, Teere ha Tavaz.

George, K. (1991) *The New Standard Cornish Dictionary, An Gerlyver Kres Cornish – English/English – Cornish*, Saltash, Kesva an Tavas Kernewek.

George, K. (1993) "Cornish", in Ball, M. J. with Fife, J. (eds.) *The Celtic Languages*, London, Routledge, pp.410–468.

George, K. (1993) *An Gerlyver Meur – The Complete Cornish-English Dictionary*, Saltash, Cornish Language Board.

Grant, A. P. (1998) "Defending Kernewek Kemmyn" (review article of Dunbar, P. and George, K. (1997) q.v.), in Payton, P. (ed.) *Cornish Studies*, Second Series No. 6, Exeter, Exeter University Press, pp.194–199.

Jago, F. W. (1882) *The Ancient Language and Dialect of Cornwall* (Reprint 1984), Truro, Netherton & Worth.

Jago, F. W. (1887) *An English – Cornish Dictionary* (Reprint 1980), London, Simpkin Marshall.

Jenner, H. (1904) *Handbook of the Cornish Language*, London, Nutt.

Kennedy, N. (1996) "Cornish Today: A Modern Cornish Perspective" (review article of Williams, N. J. A. (1995) q.v.), in Payton, P. (ed.) *Cornish Studies*, Second Series No. 4. Exeter, Exeter University Press, pp.171–181.

Lewis, H. (1946) *Llawlyfr Cernyweg Canol*, Cardiff, University of Wales Press, (English translation by Glanville Price, *A Handbook of Middle Cornish*, in press for 2000).

Wakelin, N. A., Broderick, G. (1991) *Language Contact in the British Isles*, Tuebingen, Niemeyer, pp.199–226.

Nance, R. M. (1952) *An English–Cornish Dictionary*, Marazion, Worden, for Federation of Old Cornwall Societies.

Nance, R. M. (1955) *Cornish–English Dictionary*, Marazion, Worden, for Federation of Old Cornwall Societies.

Payton, P. "Cornish", in Price, G. (ed.) (forthcoming) *Language in Britain and Ireland*, Cambridge, Cambridge University Press.

Price, G. (1998) "Modern Cornish in Context" (review article of Gendall, R. M. M. (1997) q.v.), in Payton, P. (ed,) *Cornish Studies*, Second Series No. 6, Exeter, Exeter University Press.

Thomas, A. R. (1984) "Cornish", in Trudgill, P. (1984) *Language in the British Isles, Cambridge*, Cambridge University Press, pp.278–288.

Weatherhill, C. (1995) *Cornish Place Names and Language*, Wilmslow, Sigma Leisure.

Williams, N. J. A. (1996) "Linguistically Sound Principles: the Case Against Kernewek Kemmyn", in Payton. P. (ed.) (1996) *Cornish Studies*, Second Series No. 4, Exeter, Exeter University Press. pp.64–87.

III. The Goidelic/Gaelic languages

i.) The case of Irish/*An Ghaeilge* in the Irish Republic

Diarmuid Ó Néill

Irish Language Introduction

An Ghaeilge – Réamhrá (An Phoblacht)

Sé an phríomhfhadhb atá ag gluaiseacht na teanga ná nach bhfuil dearcadh soiléir acu ar ná dúshláin a bheidh ann amach anseo. Ceaptar gurb é an dúshlán is mó ná cad iad na céimeanna is gá chun an dúshlán sin a bhaint amach – sé sin labhairt na Gaeilge in Éirinn a chur i gcrích, in éineacht leis an mBéarla. I gcumarsáid le Gaelscoileanna, Foras na Gaeilge, Conradh na Gaeilge, an tIontaobhas Ultach agus eagraíochtaí dá leithéid, tá sé le feiscint nach bhfuil Rialtas na hÉireann i gcoinne na Gaeilge mar atá Rialtas na Fraince i gcoinne na Briotáinise agus na dteangacha Ceilteacha. Ceaptar go bhfuil Rialtas na hÉireann ar an taobhlíne – níl siad i gcoinne na Gaeilge ná níl siad ar thaobh na Gaeilge, ach ceapann daoine a bhfuil taighde déanta acu ar an gceist seo go bhfuil siad i gcoinne na Gaeilge. Braitheann suim an Rialtais sa Ghaeilge ar chúrsaí eacnamaíochta ach ní deirtear é seo go hoscailte.

Ach chun an fhírinne a rá, sin mar atá an scéal i measc phobal na hÉireann freisin, sé sin go nglacann siad leis an scéal go bhfuil an Béarla mar phríomhtheanga le 160 de bhlianta anuas, agus tá siad sásta leis sin. Sin é an fhadhb is mó atá ag Gaeilgeoirí – meon an phobail a athrú ó thaobh na teanga. Taispeánann leathnú na ngaelscoileanna go bhfuil suim éigin ag an bpobal sa Ghaeilge. Glacann daoine leis an smaoineamh go bhfuil an Ghaeilge ina mórchuid dá n-oidhreacht. Mar shampla, tá sí le feiceáil ar chomharthaí oifigiúla ach tá sé an-deacair í a bheith mar phríomhtheanga i ngnáthúsáid.

Braitheann aon straitéis i gcomhair an dá chuid den tír ar roinnt toscaí, mar atá: tacaíocht airgeadais, dlíthe, polaitíocht agus caidreamh poiblí. Cé nach bhfuil ach 6 per cent de dhaltaí na hÉireann i ngaelscoileanna, de réir taighde a rinne Gaelscoileanna d'úsáidfeadh 30 per cent de na tuismitheoirí múineadh trí Ghaeilge dá mbeadh an seans acu. Mar sin, seo seans tábhachtach. Tá an-chuid fadhbanna ag na gaelscoileanna ó thaobh easpa foirne, easpa airgid, easpa foirgneamh agus easpa scoileanna ag an dara leibhéal de bhrí go bhfuil na bunscoileanna lánGhaeilge an-scaipithe. B'fhéidir go réiteofar an scéal seo de réir mar a leathnaíonn líon na scoileanna lánGhaeilge ag an dara leibhéal.

Ceapann Comhdháil Náisiúnta na Gaeilge gur ábhar dóchais é an dream mór cainteoirí Gaeilge óga seo atá ins na gaelscoileanna faoi láthair agus tá an ceart acu. Tá tuairimí éagsúla ann ar conas é seo a shaothrú. Déanann Comhdháil Náisiúnta na Gaeilge an teanga a spreagadh i ngnéithe éagsúla i measc an phobail. I láthair na huaire, tá cláracha éagsúla ar siúl acu i nGaillimh, Corcaigh, Port Láirge, Ceatharlach an Muileann gCearr agus Baile Átha Cliath. Tugtar "Gaillimh le Gaeilge" ar an gclár sa Ghaillimh. Tá sé mar aidhm acu an Ghaeilge a chur chun cinn i ngach gné den phobal. Ceapaim Comhdháil Náisiúnta na Gaeilge nach leor an deontas a fhaigheann siad – €500,000 agus deichniúr foirne i gcomhair na dtionscnamh éagsúil atá ar siúl acu gan trácht ar scéimeanna nua.

Patrick Flavin

Introduction
(The Republic)

One of the most pressing issues facing the Irish language movement is gaining a clear and unequivocal picture of the challenges facing it in its efforts to rebuild an Irish-speaking Ireland. Perhaps the most pressing issue before the Irish language movement is the challenge of actually taking those steps then deemed necessary and following through on them until the goal is reached – until Ireland is Irish-speaking once again. When we say Irish-speaking we mean Irish-speaking in a bilingual manner with English, for no one would suggest that the world's most important language – English – be discarded. In speaking to individuals from the various language organizations such as Gaelscoileanna, Foras na Gaeilge, Conradh na Gaeilge, the Ultach Trust as well as Comhdháil Násiúnta na Gaeilge, one does not get the impression that the Irish Government is seen as an adversary by them in the manner that the French Government clearly is an adversary to the Breton language movement or that the British Government has traditionally been an adversary to the Celtic languages and, to a lesser extent, still is (though with a slightly better track record than the French or Spanish governments). However, the Irish Government is generally seen as being on the sidelines – not directly involved in the battle to save Irish – but yet, strangely, not really opposed to efforts on behalf of Irish. However, those who follow that government's behaviour can discern a real opposition to Irish in government circles. It would appear economic considerations are at the root of the Irish Government's somewhat intellectually dishonest position on the Irish language – of wanting to be seen as a supporter but not taking the necessary measures to actually promote the language.

To a certain extent, this ideological positioning of the Irish Government mirrors Irish public opinion and that Irish public being referred to has used English, not Irish, as its first language for 160 years now. Not since about 1830–1840, when some four million or so souls spoke and/or understood Irish, has that language really been a dominant force in the daily life of the nation as a whole. In short, part of the problem may be that the Irish people have simply become too accustomed to using English. Hence, part of the challenge for language activists may be in breaking down psychological barriers to the acceptance of Irish as a daily vehicle of speech. People do, on the surface, accept Irish as something desirable that their children learn in Gaelscoileanna or elsewhere. People do accept Irish as part of their heritage and consider it appropriate that Irish be the first official language, as well as visible everywhere in public signage. But it is not easy to accept a different language for daily usage when it was last spoken by one's great grandparents or others even further back in the family constellation.

Any serious effort to mount a more widespread and thoroughgoing strategy on behalf of Irish in both parts of Ireland must take into account various factors. These are: funding, legislative, public relations and political in nature. Firstly, greater funding and staffing for the organizations and their branches that promote Irish. Although only about 6 per cent of primary school children in the Irish Republic are presently educated in Irish-medium schools (the figure includes Gaeltacht children), opinion surveys carried out by the Gaelscoileanna organization itself indicate that something like 30 per cent or more of parents would enrol their children in an Irish-medium school if they had the opportunity. So, clearly, here is an opportunity which has yet to be addressed.

Patrick Flavin

Irish: "what can be done?"

Diarmuid Ó Néill

IN THE WORDS OF JOSHUA FISHMAN in his 1991 treatment of Irish, we may rightly ask just that. The implied answer by Mr Fishman seemed to be that, indeed, a lot more could be done. In Ireland today, the Ireland of 5.7 million souls, we have a situation where the Irish language is a factor to be reckoned with.

In the 2002 census in the Republic, some 339,541 people, or 8.65 per cent, declared daily usage of the language in the Republic with 75,125 in Northern Ireland in 2001 claiming more or less total fluency (with 167,490 claiming knowledge of the language). Some 1,570,894 persons, or 42 per cent of the Republic's 3,917,336 residents, declared themselves Irish-speaking to some degree. We must, however, treat this figure circumspectly and look at more specialized categories such as daily speakers, Gaeltacht speakers, Gaelscoileanna students etc. to gauge the real strength of the Irish language today.

Some 42,000 schoolchildren, or about 6 per cent in the Republic and 1.5 per cent in the north, are being educated primarily through the medium of the Irish language in the new Gaelscoileanna. In addition, the western Gaeltachtaí, while weakened, is still a reality with a 2002 population of 86,517, of whom 62,157, or 71.84 per cent, are Irish speakers. So, clearly, with about 414,000 functional, fluent and semi-fluent speakers in the Irish Republic and Northern Ireland, the Irish language, along with Welsh and Breton, is in fact one of the stronger European minority languages in terms of absolute speakers, native speakers, adult learners and school users. (Donncha Ó hÉallaithe estimates only 20,723 daily speakers above 19yrs in the Gaeltacht today and another 52,111 speaking Irish daily outside the Gaeltacht, giving a total of 72,834, or 2.6 per cent – the overall figure, inclusive of all ages, would be 9.05 per cent. However, the reader may note that this somewhat pessimistic figure does not take into account Gaelscoileanna students and competent non-daily speakers of Irish, as well as lapsed native speakers who are hardly ignorant of the language).

Nevertheless, as Fishman has pointed out, there is a feeling of malaise among those in the Irish language movement that things should have advanced much further by now. There is a sense, as Fishman put it, of "what went wrong?" with the post-independence revival effort which got under way in 1921. Much more was expected for the Irish language than has been achieved. By revival, the Irish truly did mean and do mean restoration, that is a return to daily usage by all sectors of the population in both family and community life.

That said, it should be noted that Irish has in fact made substantial advances since 1921. More than mere tokenism has been achieved. Official status came almost immediately and was proclaimed in 1922 in Article four of the new constitution. In the English-speaking east, Irish was indeed introduced much more extensively into the education system and also government administration.[240] The number of fluent Irish speakers began to grow at a moderate rate in eastern and long-Anglicized cities such as Dublin, Cork, Waterford, Dundalk etc. In the west an Irish-speaking Gaeltacht of about 150,000 residents was, for the first time, defined in 1926 and special measures implemented for it to preserve and foster Irish (as opposed to the English-speaking Gaeltacht, or about 93 per cent of Ireland at that time) and these measures were not ineffective.

Not only was the untrammeled advance of English slowed down in the west but a new eastern Gaeltacht was established in Meath by Irish-speaking families from Galway in the 1930s. As we shall see, however, what would transpire in Ireland on the language issue during the first 81 years of independence would be an uneven effort, with both voluntary and government language bodies caught between an incomplete knowledge of how to tackle the truly difficult and daunting task of salvaging the ravaged Irish language in Ireland as a whole and certain limitations or self-imposed restraints by the Irish themselves who, for psychological and economic reasons, were not prepared to jettison English to any great extent because of the economic traumas of the 1800s. In short, the Irish were, and still are, being pulled in two different directions on the language question.

Today, a debate still continues about the extent to which Irish RLS efforts should be carried out in Irish society and just how much bite should be given to Irish language legislation designed to safeguard the legal status of the language. At the time of writing, the new language bill just introduced by Éamon Ó Cuiv, Minister for the Gaeltacht and Culture, has finally been modified with several amendments which met with satisfaction from the Irish language bodies. The legislation had originally been assailed even by Foras na Gaeilge, the all-Ireland language body, as not giving the language enough protection in legal proceedings, the civil service, the media and other areas as well. As we shall see, this and other developments in modern Irish society are symptomatic of opposing pressures. On the one hand, the demand for language revival is still quite strong, while on the other, there are still pressures from the private sector and the traditional establishment not to jeopardise hard-won economic gains by tampering with the status of English in the workplace, the financial sector, higher education, and bureaucracy in almost all fields of Irish life where the predominance of English is almost exclusive.

We shall examine these factors and try to determine what might be done in the present and the future to restore Irish to a healthier status as a widespread vernacular in the daily life of the country on a much more significant scale.

Historical background

Archaeological evidence strongly suggests that around the year 300 BC iron-using Celtic-speaking people invaded eastern Ireland. It would appear that they were carriers of the well-known La Tène culture which developed in eastern France, superseding the older Halstatt Celtic culture of earlier centuries which is well documented in the Celtic territories of Bavaria, Austria, Bohemia, Hungary and elsewhere.

The Celts and other Indo-Europeans, such as the Italic peoples, seem to have been latecomers to western Europe. It is clear that older non-Indo-European languages preceded them in western Europe and indeed are well documented. The Basque language, spoken to this day by about 700,000 people in Spain and France, is the most notable example. This it should be noted, has a special relevance to Britain and Ireland, in that it is now clear that the Neolithic and Bronze Age population of the British Isles sprang from the ancient Basque population who colonized Britain and Ireland about the year 5000 BC, introducing agriculture, the first villages, the Megalithic tombs of Stonehenge, Newgrange and Carnac in Brittany and later, bronze metal working. The many dark-haired Irish and British people one still encounters today are testimony to the vibrant and still omnipresent contribution of these early colonists to the modern Irish and British gene pools. Elsewhere in western Europe, the older non-Indo-European Etruscan language remained in use and was written extensively in northern Italy from about 775 BC to 200 AD. Other clearly pre-Indo-European languages such as Iberian, Tartesian, Rhaetic, Camunic, Aquitanian and Pictish in Scotland persisted into the Roman era and beyond.[241] More specifically, in Ireland itself, it is likely that Gaelic jostled with older languages for several centuries before emerging as the dominant language in Ireland sometime in the Roman era.

With regards to insular Celtic, that is Goidelic and Brittonic, as opposed to the continental dialects of Celtic which were still spoken extensively in Europe at the start of the Roman era in northern Spain, France, Belgium, southern Germany, Bohemia, Austria, Switzerland, northern Italy, the Balkans and even in Turkey, little can be said with certainty about where and when or why Q-Celtic and P-Celtic diverged. P-Celtic, or Brittonic, seems to be closer to Gaulish than Gaelic and also it would appear that Gaelic represents a more archaic and conservative version of Celtic than Brittonic. Whatever the origin of their differences, Gaelic had come to be the dominant language in Ireland by the start of the Roman era, while Brittonic had come to dominate most of Britain by the time of the Roman occupation, with pre-Celtic speech apparently confined to northern Scotland and possibly Wales. (In general, academics accept 500 BC as the likely arrival date for the Celts in Britain).

One issue which should not be overlooked by linguists dealing with the Celtic languages is the extent to which they were influenced by the older Bronze Age languages they encountered in Britain and Ireland. There is no question that loan words, place-names and probably also grammar were affected by the speech patterns of the older inhabitants. No-one who has listened to English as spoken today in Ireland and Scotland could seriously argue that Gaelic has had no influence on modern speech patterns. Hence, the impact of pre-Celtic speech in those far off times must have been all the greater.

By the late Roman era, Gaelic was rapidly expanding in territory. The older pre-Celtic languages of Ireland (one possible example being Érainn) were now confined to western and southwestern Ireland while Gaelic was making inroads even in Britain, with Irish colonies being established in Wales, Man and Argyll. Although the Gaelic kingdoms established in Wales were eventually subdued and assimilated, the Gaelicization of Man was achieved no later than the fifth century, while Argyll was clearly Gaelic in speech by the late fourth century at the latest and indeed possibly earlier, although we should bear in mind the military prowess of the Pictish kingdoms does not suggest or support the idea of early unchallenged Gaelic colonization in Scotland.

By the late fourth century, Roman Britain, like the rest of the empire, was Christian. Intense efforts were now made to neutralise Barbarian raids by converting the Irish, Picts and other northern peoples to Christianity. Patrick, Palladius and others were extremely successful in Ireland where the Irish, who had been exposed to the wealth, prosperity and superior technology of Roman Britain, partly turned a blind eye to missionary efforts and indeed seem to have encouraged them, as well as trade contacts. By the mid-fifth century, Irish raids on western Britain had ceased as newly-installed Irish bishops and Christianized native rulers denounced warfare on fellow Christians in Britain.[242]

Efforts at converting the Picts met with only limited success and not until Colomba in the sixth century were the Picts and the other peoples of northern Scotland successfully converted. Indeed, it was Pictish raids on eastern Britain in the 420s which caused the British to import Anglo-Saxon mercenaries from Denmark and Germany and install them as a protective garrison on the east coast of Britain. In 442 they revolted, intent on seizing Britain for themselves. Although by 600 AD much of modern England was in Saxon hands, Wales, Dumnonia, Strathclyde and northern Britain remained in Celtic and Pictish hands.

The Christian culture of Britain was severely jolted by this development but Ireland and Gaelic culture generally entered a new golden age with the Latin alphabet being drafted to write the Irish language by the late fifth century. This was an important development, for it broke the monopoly of Latin on literacy in western Europe and soon the Britons, the Saxons and apparently even the Picts drafted the Latin alphabet to write their own languages. Irish monks carried the Christian religion and Latin learning to the Picts, the English, the Germans, the Magyars and the Slavs, establishing more than 3,000 new churches, monasteries, abbeys and other religious establishments in northern Europe between the sixth and the eleventh centuries. Highly valued Irish scribes, clerks and advisers came to be in demand at many a European court, including that of the great Charlemagne.

Towards the end of the late eighth century, Norse raids on Britain, Ireland and much of northern Europe began to pose a challenge to not only Irish society but the new civilized Christian order of northern Europe in general. Though England was almost conquered by the Danes, the Vikings eventually were absorbed and assimilated. In Ireland, they established many of modern Ireland's towns. Dublin, Cork, Limerick, Waterford and Wexford were all Norse foundations. The Vikings stimulated trade but cannot be said to have established it, for the great Atlantic maritime trade routes had been in use since Neolithic times. Many Norse loanwords did, however, come into Irish during this period. They usually concern warfare and urban life. It is possible that the Viking raids, and the attendant disruption they caused, did disrupt and prevent the emergence of a more solidly united Irish polity or state as happened in neighbouring Scotland despite Norse and English incursions.

Linguistically, it is likely that Norse speech survived only in the Dublin and Wexford areas at the time of the Norman invasion in the early twelfth century. However, the Normans, like the Norse who preceded them, could make little impress on the linguistic habits of the population at large, as they were not numerous enough and were essentially only a conquering élite. Norman French and English speech were confined to the Pale around Dublin and other pockets. The rapid assimilation of most Norman-era settlers into Irish culture and language led to the coining of the phrase "more Irish than the Irish" and indeed by the fourteenth century, speeches at the Anglo-Norman parliament in Dublin, on occasion had to be translated into Irish so that his majesty's Norman lords could understand them.

It was the Tudors, under Henry VIII, who launched the Reformation that truly set in motion forces which would almost lead to the destruction of the Irish language. The first attempt at large-scale English plantation came in 1556 in Offaly and Laois counties. This plantation and the Elizabethan plantation of Munster in 1586 were largely unsuccessful and met with violent Irish resistance which ultimately deterred further English colonists, who were now increasingly attracted to the free land, better climate and (somewhat) safer conditions of the American colonies. (French and Indian massacres and warfare in New England and elsewhere on the American frontier remained for several centuries, a deterrent to British and Irish colonists alike bound for the New World).

The chapter on Irish in Ulster summarizes the linguistic changes brought about by the Ulster plantations.

The nineteenth century and linguistic/cultural change

One mistake that Irish language enthusiasts still make to this day is the assumption that simplistic explanations, such as English-language schooling alone, or the famine, should be regarded as the explanation for the rapid contraction of the Irish language between 1800, when some 3.5 million persons, or 85 per cent, of the population spoke Irish and 1901, when only some 641,000 persons, or 14.4 per cent, still spoke Irish.

The truth is that the losses suffered by Irish in the 1800s stemmed from a combination of causes; the inferior political status of the language dating from the Williamite period, the *de facto* abandonment of the Irish language by the Catholic church during the 1800s (e.g. the establishment of Maynooth College for Catholic priests in 1795 with its English-only instruction), the increased importance of English for would-be emigrants to the United States and Canada after 1812, the need to know English for economic and employment reasons in Ireland itself, the increased desire of all classes to educate their children and ensure their literacy – something which could be done almost exclusively only through English (in 1893 only two Irish-language books were in print) and, finally, the famine indeed was the horrendous catalyst that many believe it to be, in convincing the last doubters that English was indispensable.

All of these factors began to bear more intensely after 1800. From its two main bridgeheads in eastern Ulster and southern Leinster, English began to spread first into north Leinster and the Catholic districts of Ulster in the early decades of the century and later into solidly Irish-speaking Munster and Connaught. It is important to remember that these developments predate the establishment of the English-only national schools in 1831. By this point, English language schooling was more of a consequence than a cause of language shift, as parents wanted English for their children, although there is no question that these English-only schools were tools of an Imperialist system.

In *Emigrants and Exiles*, Kerby Miller comments on changes taking place:

"Before 1750, probably the great majority of the rural Irish and many urban dwellers as well spoke little or no English. In all but a few eastern counties – Dublin, Kildare, Wicklow and Wexford – Catholics were predominantly, or almost exclusively, Irish-speaking; and even in these counties, pockets of Irish speakers endured. Evidence from the early eighteenth century is scanty but later travellers usually remarked on the widespread usage of Irish. In 1775 Richard Twiss reported that the language was "still understood and spoken by most of the common people", and in the same decade Arthur Young found Irish speakers everywhere but in two Wexford baronies and in Dublin city; as late as 1837 another observer discovered fluent Irish spoken in a glen only ten miles from College Green. In towns farther west, the lower classes, as well as merchants and shopkeepers engaged in rural trade, spoke Irish: in 1812 Edward Wakefield was astonished that in Cork city "the Irish language is so much spoken among the common people ... that an Englishman ... is apt to consider himself in a foreign city" and in Connaught and west Munster towns, magistrates had to employ translators to administer justice. In late eighteenth century Ulster, most Catholics clung to Irish in spite of their proximity to large numbers of Protestants." [243]

By the 1820s and 1830s the pace of emigration increased but not to anything like the massive famine and post-famine levels. Hence, we should not automatically assume that Irish was regarded as redundant in pre-famine society. Emigration was avoided, where possible, and English was valued but not necessarily to the exclusion of Irish which retained its hold on family and community life, if not the upper echelons of society. Irish census results for the 1800s do not approach credibility until about 1881. Hence, we must make educated estimates and guesses regarding this period. It would appear that of Ireland's 9 million people in 1845, about 4 million spoke Irish as their first language and at least another million were no more than a generation or two removed from it and would have spoken or understood some Irish. It is also worth noting that about half a million Irish speakers were also to be found in the United States, Canada and Britain even before the famine, so Irish was very much a lively part of Irish life and the Irish world, not only in Ireland but also in the diasporas in Britain and America during the mid-nineteenth century.

Pre-famine attitudes towards Irish

Without trying to downplay the importance of the upheaval of the famine, we might do well to remember some equal truths about Irish attitudes towards the Irish language, particularly in the pre-famine era. Firstly, pre-famine Ireland had not entirely given up on the Irish language, despite the advance of English. Emigration to North America was unpopular due to indentured labour and other coercive methods employed in the 1700s in order to recruit manpower for the British colonies. Hence, English did not have quite the same spell over Irish speakers in 1820 or 1830 as it would come to have by the 1890s as a necessary tool in the New World. Not only landless labourers and cottiers, but also well-to-do farmers were at home in Irish in this era. Munster and Connaught were predominantly Irish-speaking, however Irish was still widely spoken in north Leinster and among Ulster Catholics (though restricted to the older generations by the time of the famine, with some noteworthy strongholds such as the Strabane region in Tyrone, northeast Antrim, south Armagh and County Louth across the border in north Leinster; in all of which, Irish was still spoken into the 1950s). Only eastern Ulster, Dublin and South Leinster had entirely abandoned Irish by 1840. People in Waterford, Cork, Galway and elsewhere were not in the same rush to follow their lead and completely drop Irish, though English was spreading there also. In 1834 a Protestant parson in County Kilkenny observed;

"The English language rapidly advances for, so anxious are the people to speak it in the country, that the mountain farmers who cannot speak English, and who send their children to hedge schools, will scarcely allow them to speak Irish at home".

Even many towns remained solidly Irish-speaking very late. An English visitor to the town of Waterford in the early 1800s asked two women "why they were speaking in Irish when they could speak English". They replied that "they preferred to use Irish". Hence, we should be careful before making assumptions about pre-famine attitudes towards Irish as something perceived as redundant. English clearly had come to be seen as something to be valued by the 1830s but not necessarily to the exclusion of Irish.

In *Emigrants and Exiles*, Kerby Miller comments on the persistence of Irish in the pre-Famine era in spite of the pace of change:

"However, all these changes could not add up to the homogenized "west British" culture to which many upper- and middle-class Irishmen aspired. Anglicization was glaringly incomplete; the modernizers were too few, the traditionalists too many and poverty, parochialism and self-interest discouraged and prevented most rural dwellers from abandoning all the customs which had cushioned their ancestors against adversity. In short, at least half the Catholic population still clung to Irish and/or to many of the customs once inextricably associated with it."

It was the trauma of the famine that shook the faith of the Irish people, not only in the Irish language but in Ireland itself and mass emigration would continue long after the famine. In Ireland itself, the Irish-speaking lower classes were almost obliterated (farm holdings of less than 5 acres fell from 40 per cent in 1841 to 3–4 per cent in 1851) while more well-to-do farmers and town dwellers now turned their eyes towards America – and the English language. Some 2.5 million Irish speakers were still to be found in Ireland after the famine but attitudes had now changed. Social advancement, indeed physical survival, were now seen as dependent on ability to speak English whether in Ireland, Britain or North America. With an almost frantic urgency, the Irish people began dropping Irish as fast as possible and even going to great lengths to prevent their children from learning it, so that by 1891 (the first reasonably reliable Irish census) only 680,174 still spoke Irish, including only 3 per cent of Irish children.

The famine was the hammer blow which almost destroyed Irish. On the famine's eve, Irish was spoken by some four million souls as opposed to about 414,000 reasonably fluent speakers in 2002. That is, for every Irish speaker today there were ten 150 years ago. The famine was severest in the Irish-speaking districts of the west and southwest. About 1.5 million people died between 1845 and 1851 and some 3 million left Ireland for the United States, Canada and Britain between 1845 and 1855 (only 240,000 had emigrated between 1831–1841). Adjusted census figures indicated at least 2,134,000 Irish speakers remained after the famine, out of 6.5 million inhabitants (the traditional 1851 figure of 1.5 million has long since been discarded as an undercount), and even this 1851 figure of 2,134,000[244] should be regarded as somewhat of an undercount as many bilingual persons clearly declared themselves as English-speaking only. We can get a grasp of the demographic devastation emigration wrought on Irish in Kerby Miller's commentary;

"Most important, although in prior decades most Catholic emigrants had come from English-speaking or rapidly Anglicizing districts in eastern and central Ireland, the Famine exodus had a decidedly Gaelic character. Munster and Connaught where in 1841 over two thirds of the inhabitants spoke Irish, contributed at least 50 per cent of the Famine emigration. Hazarding the reasonable and conservative guess that half the emigrants from Munster and Connaught and 5 per cent of the remainder spoke Irish, it would appear that at least half a million of those who left between 1845 and 1851 were Irish speakers. Although these estimates are admittedly sketchy, the point is that in comparison with previous decades, a substantial proportion of those emigrating in 1845–1855 regarded Irish as their primary if not only language. North American sources substantiate this phenomenon as Canadian port officials in the 1840's frequently commented on 'the inability of entire shiploads of immigrants from Ireland to speak English'."

So, although Irish in post-famine Ireland was widespread – more widespread than we have in fact traditionally been inclined to believe – its position now rapidly eroded and, even more ominous, attitudes towards Irish and indeed Ireland itself took on an almost totally negative and hopeless tone. Mass emigration now took place on an unprecedented scale. Some 7 million Irish emigrants left Ireland for the United States alone between 1851 and 1921. The Catholic population of Ulster fell from 55 per cent in 1841 and 51 per cent in 1861 to 44 per cent in 1911, so there were also future political implications in this mass exodus to America.

[Note: The census of 1841 is considered an undercount of the population by several hundred thousand persons. The first language census of 1851 which recorded 1,524,000 Irish speakers is also regarded as a severe undercount, as one fourth of households did not receive the language questionnaire, with more recent estimates putting Irish speakers between 2.1 million and 2.5 million in 1851 – *after* the famine.]

Within Ireland itself the new fatalistic attitude towards Irish accelerated the shift to English by parents who realized that even in Ireland their children would have access to civil service positions only if they mastered English, hence many now excluded Irish from their homes.

Nevertheless, roughly a million Irish speakers, some 949,932 or 18.2 per cent of the population were enumerated in 1881. By 1891 this had fallen to 680,174 and only 3.5 per cent of Irish children were now Irish-speaking.

Table 6.1
Irish population change

Irish Population Change 1841 – 2001/2002		
Province	*1841 Census*	*2001/2002 Censuses*
Ulster (9 counties)	2,339,263	1,931,838
Leinster	1,982,169	2,105,449
Munster	2,404,460	1,101,266
Connaught	1,420,705	464,050
6 Ulster co. (N. Ireland)	1,649,000	1,685,267
3 Ulster co. (Don., Cav., Mon.)	740,263	246,571
26 co. (Irish Republic)	6,526,124	3,917,336
Total Ireland	8,175,124	5,620,603

Note: The census of 1841 is considered an undercount of the population by several hundred thousand persons. The first language census of 1851 which recorded 1,524,000 Irish speakers is also regarded as a severe undercount as one fourth of households did not receive the language questionnaire with more recent estimates putting Irish speakers between 2.1 million and 2.5 million in 1851 – *after* the famine.

Despite its relative numerical strength, Irish by the late nineteenth century had come to occupy the position that Breton occupied after 1965 – a widely spoken language but only by those over the age of 30 or 40.

However, organized efforts to salvage the Irish language now began in earnest. In 1876 the Society for the Preservation of the Irish Language was founded. In 1893 the Gaelic League was founded by Douglas Hyde to promote the Irish language. By the outbreak of the First World War, hundreds of branches of the Gaelic League had been established all over Ireland. Long Anglicized urban dwellers in Dublin, Belfast and elsewhere now began to reacquire a command of Irish and, for the first time in a century, the Irish language began to experience growth in both numbers and national prestige.

Irish since independence

By the time of independence in 1921 the number of fluent speakers had fallen to roughly 250,000. So it was indeed with the famine that a change – for the worse – set in among the Irish people and their view of the Irish language which we could label a "Victorian" attitude, as it was certainly a drastic change from previous centuries, indeed even from previous decades before the famine in the early 1800s when Irish remained the unquestioned national language, despite British rule and the consequent advance of English.

National independence clearly transformed the status of the Irish language. The new Free State Government set about redefining the place of Irish in the life of the nation. Irish was made an official language, Irish signage was universally posted, the new Irish coins, stamps and banknotes employed Irish, economic assistance was provided to the Gaeltacht (in the 1920s the population of the Gaeltacht was over 250,000 and assistance from the Irish Government unquestionably slowed down its decline and the advance of the English language in western Ireland), Irish was introduced into all primary schools throughout the Irish Free State. The Gaeltacht Commission Report of 1926 redefined the Gaeltacht and established a new ministry to attend to its needs.

The ideology of the new state aspired to the creation of a Catholic, rural, Gaelic-speaking society. Unfortunately, the feasibility of these goals was debatable. The Irish Free State was 10 per cent Protestant, while Northern Ireland, within its admittedly gerrymandered borders, was about 63 per cent Protestant at this time. Hence, no policy which preached the primacy of the Catholic church in an island where a quarter of the population was not Catholic, was realistic or just. The attempt to keep Ireland a rurally-oriented society as espoused by Éamon de Valera was equally unrealistic, as migration from the land to the cities and abroad had begun in the 1800s and sharply accelerated in the 1950s as increased farm mechanization left many farm labourers redundant. An ever-increasing proportion of the population was to be found in Irish cities which grew moderately in the 1960s and more rapidly thereafter. The stringent Catholic censorship of the new state was equally unrealistic in the modern world.

The goal of restoring the Irish language in Ireland ("Ireland not merely free, but Gaelic as well, not merely Gaelic, but free as well" so eloquently expressed by the Irish hero Patrick Pearse) on the other hand was a purely legitimate and more realistic one than early and more recent policy makers imagined. It was also a goal which historically and to this day has attracted both Protestants and Catholics, so it may be described as a largely positive and unifying factor in Ireland's cultural life.

In 1929 Irish was made a compulsory subject in secondary schools. Some rather bold initiatives for the time were successfully mounted by the government, e.g. the establishment of a new eastern Gaeltacht in Meath in the 1930s through the transplantation of Irish-speaking families from Galway and, to this day, Irish is still spoken there. Irish was introduced into the bureaucracy and the civil service. Teachers and civil servants were dispatched to the Gaeltacht to learn Irish or improve their command of it. Several Dublin police departments had become solidly Irish-speaking on their own initiative by 1936. Surely no other government and certainly not the British administration would have done more for the Irish language. (In Northern Ireland at this very time the Irish language had entered a difficult new era of suppression by the Unionist authorities).

While it was agreed initially that action had to be taken on behalf of Irish, there was some degree of confusion about how to tackle the problem which, with hindsight, we can see was underestimated. There was a concept that if Irish was introduced more universally into the schools, then the language would reinvigorate. Although by 1940 a fairly high percentage of school children were indeed being instructed mainly through Irish, INTO, the Irish teachers' organization, attempted to sound the alarm that the system in place was failing to produce competent and fluent Irish speakers.

It should also be mentioned that during this period a standard Irish dialect was established in 1948, based on both Connaught and Munster Irish, which was an important step in corpus planning, especially as there were three major dialects before the advance of English. The Roman alphabet was also adopted in the post-war period in place of the old Gaelic script and archaic spelling forms simplified, greatly facilitating publishing in the language.

During this time, the Gaeltacht areas remained underdeveloped and large-scale emigration from them continued. The people of the Gaeltacht were exhorted to continue to speak Irish to their children but politicians were not prepared to do this themselves.

A government department was established in 1956 whose mandate was both for the Gaeltacht and the Irish language. Today its title is the Department for Community, Rural & Gaeltacht Affairs. In 1959 Údarás na Gaeltachta was established. Later, in 1965, a Government White Paper on the Irish language was published.

In 1961 Telefís Éireann, Ireland's television service, began broadcasting. This contained some Irish language programming but was almost exclusively in English. Planning for Irish during the first 80 years of independence was not well thought out, although one should bear in mind the enormity of the task that faced state planners – how to resuscitate a language which over 90 per cent of the population had abandoned before national independence.

One occurrence during the late 1960s and early 1970s is indicative of official attitudes towards Irish. During this period, Joshua Fishman acted as adviser to the Irish Finance Minister, Charles Haughey. He was informed by Fr Colmán Ó Huallacháin of the Institiúid Teangeolaíochta Éireann/ the Linguistics Institute of Ireland that certain recommendations were being sidetracked and brushed aside by the Irish government. Joshua Fishman resigned in disgust in April 1971 but not before penning this note to the Irish Government: "... during the past decade I have been consultant on language matters to a dozen governments ... most of my recommendations have been accepted ... some rejected recommendations that were not to their liking ... what does disturb me is the now quite apparent delaying tactics whereby recommendations are neither rejected nor implemented but simply surrounded by administrative silence and inaction ... after four years, I have come to the conclusion that I have been used not as a consultant but as an unwitting participant in a master plan to do nothing...".

Recent past

Moving ahead to the recent past and the present, let us look at government and voluntary initiatives and attitudes towards the language. Relations between the voluntary language agencies and the government are mainly positive, with lack of sufficient funding being one of the few irritants; however, as stated above, in speaking with people from these agencies one does not get the impression that the Irish Government is perceived as an adversary. By and large it has provided funding and technical assistance to Gaelscoileanna, Telefís na Gaeilge, Raidió na Gaeltachta, Raidió na Life, Udaras na Gaeltachta, Conradh na Gaeilge, Comdháil Náisiúnta na Gaeilge, Foras na Gaeilge and other language bodies, both voluntary and government-controlled. Officially, the present policy is to build a bilingual Ireland through Irish by choice and not imposition.

However, it is when we come to the Irish Government's dealing with more ambitious and thoroughgoing initiatives such as the Official Language Act, official status for Irish in the European Union, the extension of Irish in the civil service and, most important of all, the establishment of new Irish-speaking communities, that we encounter real resistance to the Irish language to an astonishing degree. The scuttling of the Scéimeanna

Pobail project in the 1980s, advocated by Bord na Gaeilge, which would have established six new urban Irish-speaking communities (with two in Dublin) is only one example of the line Irish speakers are expected not to cross.

The establishment of Gaelscoileanna in 1973, however, led to the growth of a movement which has had considerable success. Its parent-driven approach led to a rapid increase in the number of Irish-medium schools in the eighties and nineties (see graphs and bar charts, p.314) with five or six primary schools opening in some years. In recent years, however, the Dept of Education has taken steps to curb this growth, introducing stringent rules for recognition and a lengthier process which have ensured that in recent years only one or two schools a year have opened. They have attempted to close some seven Gaelscoileanna founded in recent years (an attempt which was successfully resisted) and now, in 2004, have refused recognition to two schools which complied with all requirements and demonstrated an abundant demand.

The establishment of Raidió na Gaeltachta in 1972 came after years of pressure and the operation of a pirate radio in Connemara and it has developed into an excellent 24-hr service. It was only after over 20 years of campaigning that Telefís na Gaeltachta (now TG4) was established. TG4 broadcasts from 7a.m. to about 2a.m. and most of its output is in English. The majority of the core of 4 or 5 hours in Irish is subtitled, so it is essentially a bilingual service. They have stated that more programmes in Irish cannot be produced unless more funding is forthcoming from the Government and there is absolutely no sign of that happening.

Hence, despite the undeniable progress being made in the schools, media and elsewhere, it is difficult to avoid the conclusion that the Irish language is being held at arm's length. The Irish establishment – government, economic and religious – seem to view Irish as the proverbial friend whom one wants to see do well – but not too well.

This establishment resistance to Irish, which is interestingly not entirely shared by the general public, is not easy to explain but the answer may lie in economic considerations. Ireland's successful programme of industrialization since the 1950s is heavily bound up with foreign investment; British, European, American, Asian and other (as opposed to native Irish companies which are of increasing importance, nevertheless). English is the indispensable tool needed here. It would appear that the Irish Government is shutting out the Irish language for economic reasons. Their fears in this respect are not supported by the experience of countries such as Germany, the Netherlands and Denmark which have drafted English for economic reasons but have retained their national languages.

Without realizing it, and certainly not out of malice, the Irish Government has adopted an off-the-record Victorian policy of throwing table scraps to Irish but blocking real and thoroughgoing programmes to re-establish Irish solidly on a community basis, such as the Scéimeanna Pobail or Community Projects[245] undertaking proposed by Bord na Gaeilge in the 1980s which would have established six new urban Irish-speaking communities, as well as the proposals of Father Cólman of the Irish Language Institute in the 1970s, not to mention the consistent warnings over the past thirty years by Dr Fishman that unless Ireland focuses squarely on the demographic concentration of Irish speakers in new communities (as a first step), particularly in the urban east, then the re-vernacularization of Irish as an everyday vehicle of speech is doomed to failure. Precious time and resources continue to be wasted by both the government and the voluntary language bodies, in the old pattern of not addressing the real problem – while people tire of the failures of the present unsuccessful programmes.

Official attitudes towards Irish

One of the most widely held and flawed misconceptions held by the Irish Government and economic establishment is that, but for English, Ireland would still be inhabited by an impoverished barefoot Irish-speaking peasantry, possibly still subsisting on potatoes and water (which is pretty much what it had come to in much of Ireland by the mid-1800s).

In reality, it was political independence in 1921, not the English language, which empowered the Catholic middle class to take charge of the economy and eventually led to the economic reforms which were launched by the Irish Government in the 1950s (specifically the Lemass government) which are responsible for Ireland's subsequent economic and industrial expansion and population growth. If it had been knowledge of English which was the key to economic progress, then the Irish economy would have taken off in the 1700s which is when knowledge of English began to become widespread, at least in eastern Ireland.

Between 1971 and 2001 the population of Scotland declined from

5,228,000 to 5,040,000 while the population of the Irish Republic rose from 2,978,000 in 1971 to 3,917,000 in 2002 and is likely to continue its growth for at least the next two decades. Economic policies within the UK are still designed primarily for the benefit of the central London-based region. Clearly, Scottish and Welsh industries have suffered from a lack of local control to the point that out-migration is still a serious problem, whereas in Ireland it no longer is. Clearly, more than a knowledge of English is needed to prosper in the modern globalistic economy. Control over one's own economy, not mastery of English, is the key. Yet many language and economic planners in Ireland still are clearly continuing to act on this flawed assumption or fear. That fear being that a more Irish-speaking population and workforce will deter foreign investment and hinder the flow of goods and persons between Ireland on the one hand, and English-speaking Britain and the United States on the other.

Whether the Irish Government or Foras na Gaeilge admit to it or not, it is precisely these economic fears which most recently manifested themselves in the exclusion of the private sector from statutes in the recent Official Language Act enacted in 2003. Clearly, there is a fear that US, British, European and Asian investors will be scared off by Irish-language legislation in the private sector of the economy, with its close ties to the larger international economy.

The real question for language planners and activists in Ireland is "Can the Irish Government and Irish society accept Irish as a language on a par with English and other modern languages?". This is a very important ideological question which must first be spelled out clearly before any coherent attempt can be mounted to change the English-only ideology of the existing Irish establishment, be it economic, political or religious. None of the party policy papers on the Irish language by any of the major Nationalist political parties in Ireland, whether in the Republic or the north, even come close to addressing the issue of a real expansion of Irish in society. Put quite simply, Irish society at large, through its representative bodies, political, cultural economic and religious, must come to a collective decision that Irish really should be brought back into daily life on a par with English, much as Irish society collectively decided between 1820 and 1850 that English must be brought into all facets of daily life.

Then, and only then, can a real effort be mounted to restore Irish in the daily life of the nation and into habitual everyday use. Despite the significant gains by Irish in the educational, media and other sectors, Irish society has not yet crossed this rubicon which would allow for real expansion of the language in a manner similar to what is being mounted for Basque, Catalan, Welsh or Québec French.

The Eight-Stage GIDS Scale for Irish in the Republic

A stage-by-stage analysis of recent and current RLS efforts on behalf of Irish in the Republic and their future prospects.

Stages 7 and 8: Reconstructing Irish, adult acquisition of Irish as a second language, and cultural interaction in Irish involving adults

Although a significant amount of vocabulary and expressions must have been lost on the demise of Irish as a community language throughout much of Ireland, particularly Leinster, in the 1700s and 1800s, its position has never been quite as desperate as has sometimes been painted. Extensive written records of Irish in manuscript form from the 1600s, 1700s and 1800s, whether in southern dialects or the Ulster dialect of Irish, are in existence and there is no need to reconstruct missing pieces of the language (as with Cornish). Literature in Irish is now relatively easy to access, along with dictionaries and grammars.

Regarding interaction in Irish involving adults, there is a fairly strong tradition of revivalist Irish usage throughout the twenty-six counties, whether in the form of Irish-speaking "pub nights" or in the more formal setting of Conradh na Gaeilge classes which have operated since the foundation of the Gaelic League in 1893. While Irish still tends to be a language associated with the school years, there has been a moderate but steady growth of fluent adult Irish speakers outside the Gaeltacht in the post-independence period.

Stage 6: Establishing the vital linkage with family and community

This is a question for the Irish language movement which will just not go away. Until both the Irish Government and Foras na Gaeilge not only acknowledge the importance of establishing Irish-speaking communities and networks in the urban east but also elsewhere in the country – and act upon this conviction – there will be no real and substantial progress for the advancement of spoken Irish in society. At the time of writing, Foras na Gaeilge and the Irish Government have done neither. There has, of late, been some evidence that Foras na Gaeilge is coming around but seeing is believing. Let us look at some very relevant examples of existing urban Gaeltachtaí in Ireland.

The importance of the establishment of the Shaw's Road Gaeltacht in west Belfast in 1969 cannot be overstated, not only for Irish in Ulster but for Irish in Ireland and indeed for all endangered languages everywhere. It is the first urban Gaeltacht to be established in Ireland and attempts are presently being made to emulate it eventually in Dublin and Galway (a Cork urban Gaeltacht is already in existence which we will discuss below). Irish is the dominant language of the family and is now being intergenerationally transmitted (Irish is now in its third generation of transmission in the Shaw's Road Gaeltacht). An Irish-speaking church, Irish-speaking businesses and an Irish-medium school serve the community which numbers over 1,000. Irish language signage is everywhere visible and the Irish language is also audible everywhere. Another highly pertinent example is the small but important Gaeltacht established in the city of Cork by a small group of families numbering perhaps about 60 persons. Initiatives like this, which lift Irish off the floor from school use to real family community use and set the stage for the critical intergenerational transmission of Irish, are what needs to be promoted on a wide scale in Ireland.

Stages 5 and 4: The attainment of literacy in Irish, learning Irish at school and education in Irish

As mentioned above, classes to improve speaking ability in Irish, as well as literacy in the language for adults, date from 1893 and the establishment of the Gaelic League. By 1911 over 508 Gaelic League classes had been organized around Ireland in English-speaking areas and trips to the Gaeltacht for learners were already being organized even at this early date. With the establishment of the Irish Free State in 1921, Irish was introduced into all schools as a compulsory subject. Although Irish-medium schools have never formed a majority of Irish schools, they had become a sizable minority by 1950. However, by 1970 wholly Irish-medium schools outside the Gaeltacht had decreased drastically in number.

Also symptomatic of the increased enthusiasm for Irish has been the surge since 1974 of the Gaelscoileanna movement, or Irish-medium school system, so that today, in 2003, there are over 200 primary and secondary Irish-medium schools operating in Irish. There are close on 42,000 children outside the Gaeltacht, in both the Republic and in Northern Ireland, being educated through the medium of Irish, who represent about 6 per cent of children in the Republic and about 1.5 per cent of children in the north. It is a reassuring sign to see so many thousands of children in Irish-medium schools and, perhaps equally important, so much interest on the part of parents in seeing their children securing an education in Irish.

When we bear in mind that those children who graduate from Gaelscoileanna 4A schools, really are fluent Irish speakers, whereas those who graduate from 4B schools almost never are, this author is forced to the conclusion that Gaelscoileanna must become the norm for all school children eventually, in order to lay the foundations for greater Irish use in other areas which we are presently discussing.

Stage 3: Irish in the workplace

Effectively, Irish is not used as a full, living language in the workplace in most of Ireland, with the exception of the Gaeltacht and limited other capacities, such as some civil service posts, and in the administration of Irish-language organizations. As discussed below, the role of Irish in the workplace is much the same as the role of Irish in business. Outside the Gaeltacht and various work programmes co-ordinated there by Udaras na Gaeltachta, Irish does not occupy a significant position in the workforce, even by Irish speakers. In addition, this is a particularly touchy topic as the Irish government is very wary of programmes to impose Irish, particularly on foreign investors, for fears of causing a flight of foreign capital. These fears are not unfounded, so again it is a question of trying to find the happy medium and promote and accommodate Irish speakers in the workplace without antagonizing British and American investors.

Stages 2 and 1: Irish in the media, government and business

One area where the Irish language has made advances with the assistance of the government in recent years is in the realm of the media. Since the 1970s we have seen the establishment of radio and television services in the Irish language. Raidió na Gaeltachta and Teilifís na Gaeilge broadcasts can be seen and heard nationally, while Raidió na Life serves the Dublin area. Raidió na Gaeltachta was established in 1971 and broadcasts exclusively in Irish 24 hours per day and focuses on the Irish-speaking districts. Raidió na Life began broadcasts to the greater Dublin area in the late 1990s.

In 1996 Teilifís na Gaeilge, now TG4, the Irish-language TV channel, came on the air. The station broadcasts for over 19 hours per day, 7 days a week, with an average of 6 hours of Irish language programmes on the channel per day. Likewise, both the BBC's Ulster radio and TV services introduced more Irish language programming during the 1990s.

A new Irish-language weekly, *Foinse*, was established in recent years, with government assistance, to serve Galway and the other western Gaeltachtaí in particular, as well as Irish speakers on a greater national basis. The recent establishment of an Irish-language daily, *Lá*, in Belfast, however, indicates that there remains a need for an Irish-language daily in the Republic as well and hence a need to upgrade *Foinse* to the status of a daily.

In the realm of government, Irish is faring less well than in the media sector. Here the language truly retains a token position, although service in Irish can often enough be obtained from many government offices, even outside the Gaeltacht. However, it is clear that any future campaign to strengthen Irish in the community must be complemented by a greater Gaelicization of the bureaucracy, along the lines of greater Basquization and Catalanization of government services in Euzkadi and Catalonia. In those two regions, bilingualism with Spanish has replaced Spanish monoglotism in the government bureaucracy and it is clear that this is the moderate middle-of-the-road path that Ireland should be pursuing but has yet to take up.

When we look at the role of Irish in business, we come face to face with the reluctance of the Irish Government to push too aggressively when it comes to Irish in the workplace (recall the exclusion of mandatory use of Irish in the private sector in the recent Official Languages Act by the Minister for the Gaeltacht). As stated elsewhere, this is a question which really goes to the heart of whether or not the Government is really going to take solid action to strengthen Irish in society, period. In any case, promotion of the Irish language must begin in the family and the community before one can even begin to debate its role in the upper echelons of government and in the economic sector.

Proposals for Irish

Any serious effort to mount a more widespread and thorough-going strategy on behalf of Irish in both parts of Ireland must take into account various factors. These are funding, legislative, public relations and political in nature. Firstly, greater funding and staffing for the organizations and their branches that promote Irish. Problems facing the Gaelscoileanna organization are severe understaffing, under-funding, extreme difficulty in providing satisfactory accommodation and a problem with the transition from the primary to the secondary level of education (also experienced by Diwan, the Breton-medium education system) due to the fact that primary institutions are more widely distributed geographically than the less numerous secondary ones. This is a problem which clearly might recede with an expansion in the number of both primary and secondary Irish-medium schools, which is in fact continuing to occur. Gaelscoileanna, like others in the language movement, do not perceive the government as an adversary, although, clearly, some education ministers have been more supportive of the organization than others.

Comhdháil Náisiúnta na Gaeilge, which is the co-ordinating body for voluntary organizations, sees in the growth of a large new cohort of Irish-speaking children and adolescents a window of opportunity which must not be missed. In this they are entirely correct. Opinions diverge on how to carry Irish usage from the school to the community at large, but Comhdháil Náisiúnta na Gaeilge has for many years been trying to stimulate usage of Irish in the wider community, through sponsoring a programme of the use of Irish by various communities. These include Galway, Cork, Carlow, Waterford, Mullingar and soon Dublin. The programme for Galway, for example, is entitled Gallimhe le Gaeilge or Galway with Irish. It aims to promote Irish in the community, in both the private and the public sectors (more signage in Irish, more announcements in Irish, more Irish-speaking staff, etc.) and is on a voluntary basis. Comhdháil Náisiúnta na Gaeilge, however, regards its budget of only half a million pounds (800,000 euros) and staff of 10 as inadequate either for mounting more effective and efficient projects in the future, or for the more efficient administration of existing projects. So, clearly more funding and more staff are an issue on the agenda for the Irish language movement.

Also on the agenda of Comhdháil Náisiúnta na Gaeilge[246] are improvements to the legislative status of the Irish language. They are lobbying to have Irish recognized as an official working language of the European Union, albeit as a second-tier language such as Dutch or Portuguese (English and French having been long recognized as the two main working languages of the European Union). Within Ireland itself, Comhdháil Náisiúnta na Gaeilge lobbies for greater provision of services for Irish-speakers; sometimes unsuccessfully (as when it recently failed to persuade the government to guarantee the availability of Irish-speaking psychiatric workers for the mentally-ill in Irish-speaking areas). One recent success by Comhdháil Náisiúnta na Gaeilge has been its lobbying efforts to get the existing Official Languages Bill into legislation.

With Foras na Gaeilge, the new all-Ireland body to promote Irish throughout the island, there are some potential jurisdictional problems, such as how to enact new programmes in both the Irish Republic and Northern Ireland simultaneously, while the latter remains under a totally different national jurisdiction. There exists also the issue of quite simply standing up for the Irish language in Northern Ireland where, traditionally, the Irish language has been not only underpromoted but suppressed. Let us be optimistic and hope that a more affirmative approach to Irish-language reform in the north is taken perhaps through greater co-operation between the Dublin Government and Nationalist political parties and language bodies in the north. The well-known enthusiasm of the Nationalist community in Ulster for the Irish language is a resource which cannot afford to go untapped in the battle to save Irish. It should be stated that the same right of access to Irish and services in Irish must eventually become the norm in Ulster, as well as in the south. It is often forgotten that Irish remained widely spoken in Ulster well into the 1800s and as late as 1820 was probably a majority language among Ulster Catholics and was also spoken by a fair few Ulster Protestants.

Another subject which must be looked at, or rather revisited, is the question of proposals put forth on behalf of Irish in the recent past. Joshua Fishman was party to proposals from the Irish Language Institute which the Irish Government of the day rejected. Another serious proposal that was rejected was the Community Projects concept of the early 1980s – the Scéimanna Pobail. Put forward by Bord na Gaeilge, this included the

Figure 6.1
The Irish language in 1800

A Reconstruction

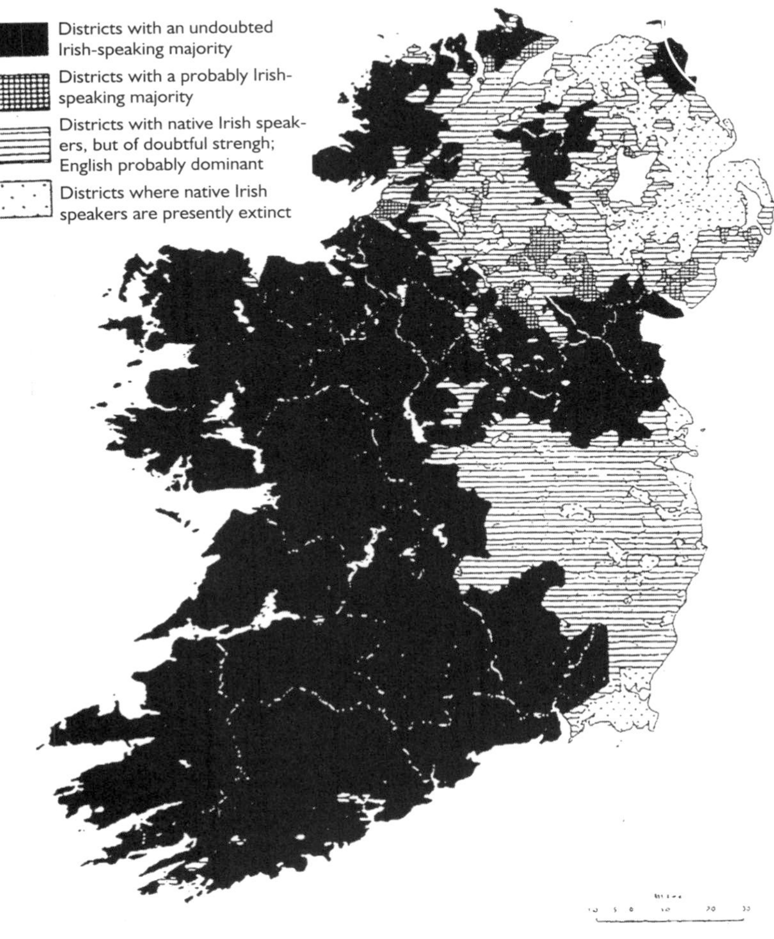

Source: projected figures based on Census 1851, produced by the Irish government. The Ministry of Culture in Dublin owns the copyright of figures 6.1 to 6.7.

Figure 6.2
The Irish language in 1851

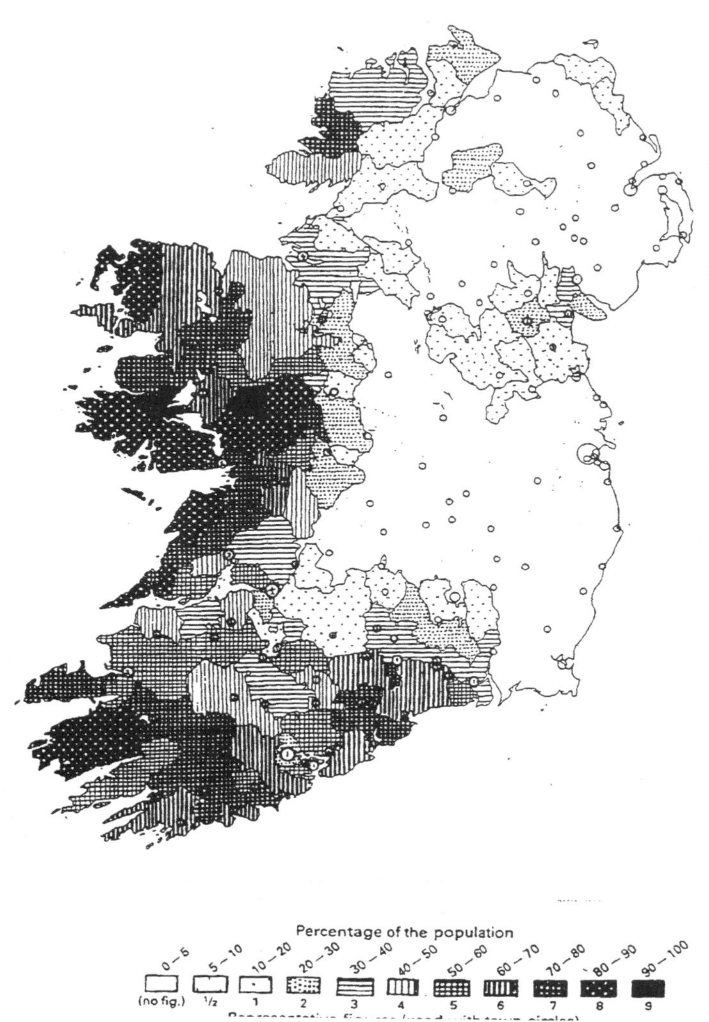

Source: Irish speakers by towns and baronies, Census 1851

Figure 6.3
The Irish language in 1891

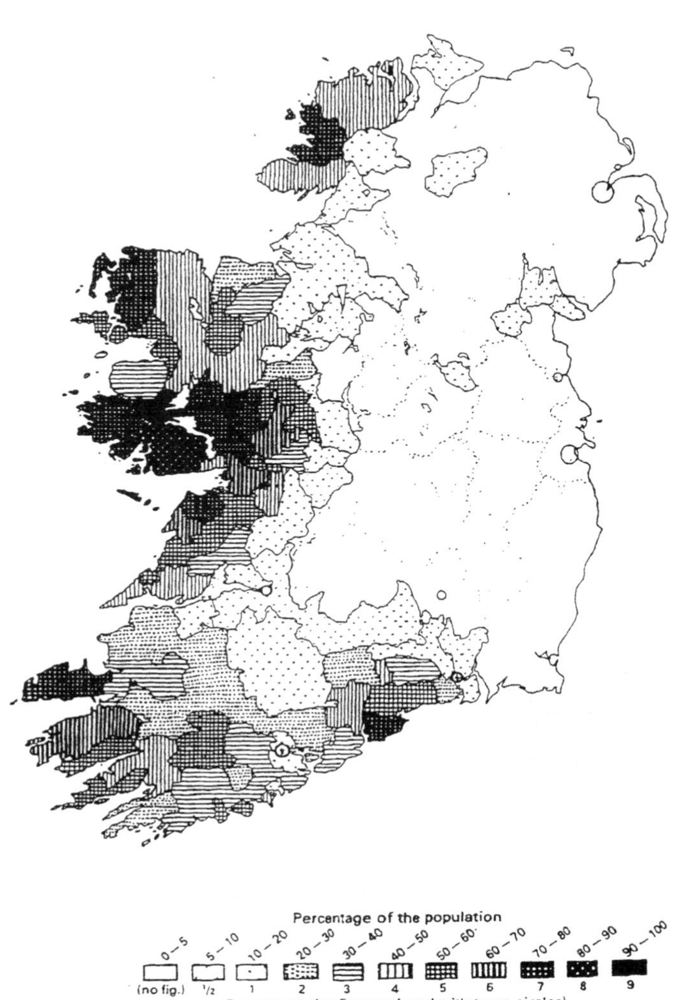

Source: Census 1891

Figure 6.4
The Irish language in 1911

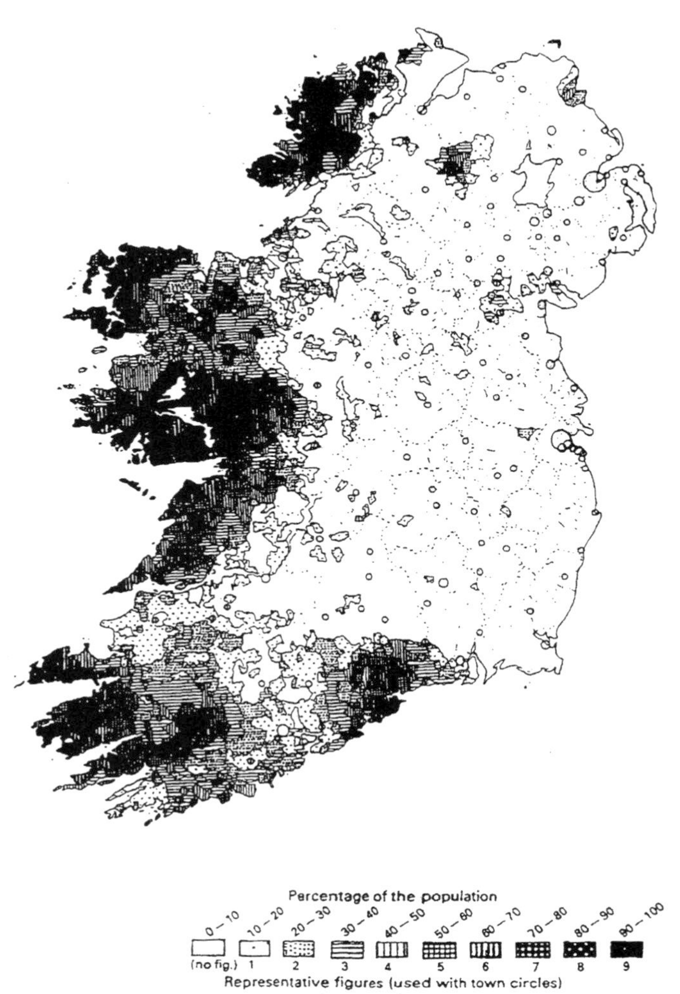

Source: Irish speakers by towns and district electoral divisions, Census 1911

Figure 6.5
The Irish language in 1926

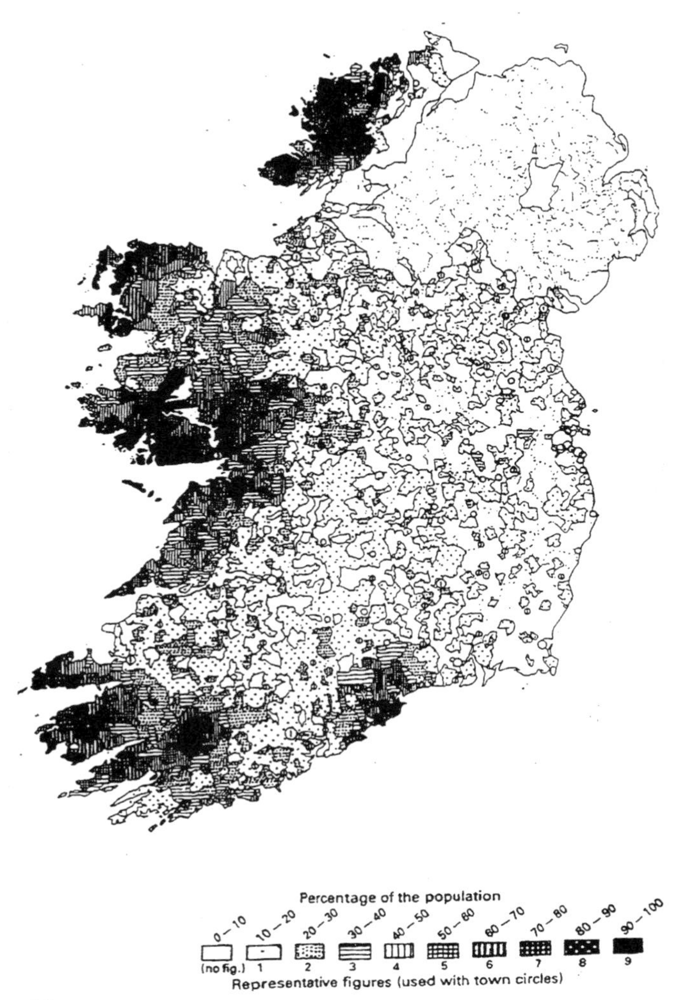

Source: Irish speakers by towns and district electoral divisions, Census 1926

Figure 6.6
The Irish language in 1956

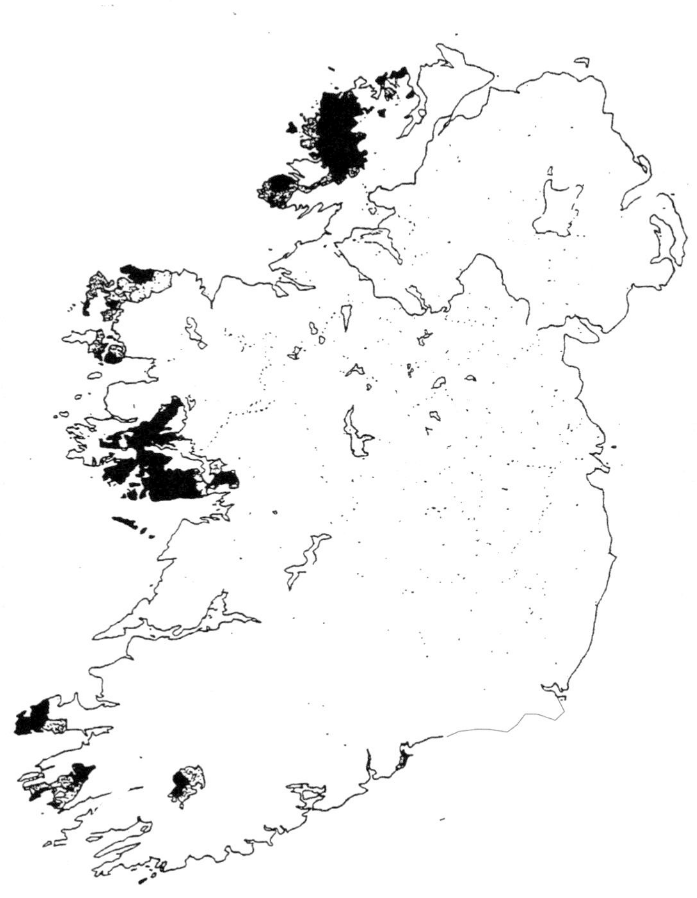

The dark and shaded areas reflect the density of Irish speakers. The Gaeltacht was redefined in 1956 as 'Nua-Ghaeltacht'. Sources: *Límistéirí Gaeltachta 1956* and the author's survey, 1957.

Figure 6.7
The Irish language in 1985

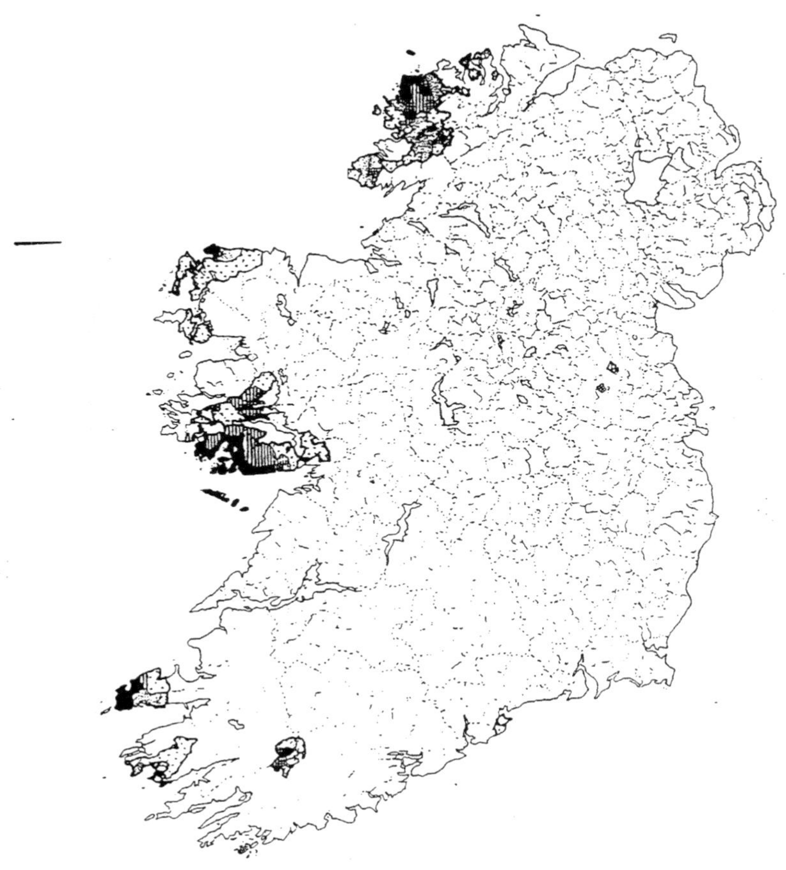

The Gaeltacht 1981–6: a tentative categorization of the real state of the language. The dark and shaded areas reflect the density of Irish speakers. Sources: Census 1981; *deontas* returns 1981–2, 1985–6.

establishment of new Irish-speaking communities in the Dublin area and elsewhere (initially two in the Dublin area). Although the official approach of the Irish Government and its representatives in the language movement remains Irish through choice and building Irish within the community, the consensus among most sociolinguists today is closer to the position taken by Joshua Fishman. That is, that the demographic concentration of speakers of the said language must take place at the home-family-neighbourhood-community level (stage 6 in the Fishman GIDS scale) before the language can advance to higher-order functions, such as greater use in the media, workplace and civil service, etc.

The goal of the vast majority of those working on behalf of the Irish language is to restore it to full health as one of the two main daily vernaculars of Ireland. It is acknowledged here that this goal has not been pursued vigorously enough in the past by the Irish Government and its main language body Foras na Gaeilge. It must be stated clearly that the past and present policy of the Irish Government of Irish by choice for those who wish it, is failing to make headway against the endless tide of Anglicization which is still ongoing in our new globalistic world.

There are encouraging signs that the new all-Ireland language body Foras na Gaeilge has learned from past mistakes and is preparing to embrace a more community-based approach to language renewal. What we do not really have, is a solid commitment to a living Irish language by the Irish Government. The Irish Language Bill was finally released in 2003 by the Minister of the Gaeltacht, Mr Ó Cuiv, retitled as the Official Languages Act but was met initially with opposition from the language movements as not doing enough to protect the language in the legal domain and elsewhere. After some negotiation, satisfactory amendments were reached which seem to have addressed the concerns of the language movement for now (the Government's legislation has been accepted by Comhdháil Náisiúnta na Gaeilge, the chief voluntary agency).

The role of Irish in the critically important private sector has, however, yet to be really buttressed by government legislation, in the opinion of many. The key ingredient will be effective implementation and we will have to wait to see how vigorously this is pursued. However, the Bill includes the establishment of an Irish Language Commissioner (now appointed and well received) and he seems to be going about his business in an effective manner.

Some hard questions must be asked. Looking at the role played by Irish governments past and present, Irish public opinion must ask; collectively speaking, are these actions the actions of a government and establishment which is really behind Irish? Watering down the Irish Language Bill to a great extent? Half-hearted commitment to Irish-medium education? It sounds like a harsh commentary but these are the hard questions which the Irish public must start asking.

We must be clear about the fact that the existing establishment in Dublin, government, economic and religious, while not opposed to Irish, is not in reality at present supportive of the steps which would be necessary to reestablish the language on any significant scale. This study is reluctantly forced to reject the traditional position of the Irish Government and the various language agencies, of damage control and what has amounted to a sometimes impatient deathbed vigil beside Irish; rather, it embraces a policy of growth and expansion for the Irish language. That means new Irish-speaking communities, expansion of Irish-medium education to far higher levels (at least 60 per cent), far more media in Irish, greater efforts to win hearts and minds back to the daily usage of Irish and perhaps an even greater sea change – a change of heart on the part of those working for the language, whether in the government or voluntary sector, not to mention a change of heart by society at large, even, perhaps, of the Dublin bureaucracy. All this does not mean that there is no hope of change. Foras na Gaeilge, a relatively new body, may yet prove to be a strong catalyst for Irish in the future, provided it adopts some major policy changes. In addition, circumstances for Irish are more favourable than in the past – more people literate in Irish than ever before, more fluent speakers (in the range of about 414,000 speakers in both the Irish Republic and Northern Ireland as of 2002), more media and publishing in Irish. In short, Irish is within striking distance of re-establishing itself as a widely spoken community language, if the opportunity is taken up.

The change of heart mentioned entails an acceptance of the Irish language again, back into Irish life. Back into Irish families, Irish communities, Irish businesses, Irish religious institutions and all other facets of Irish life on a daily basis. The Irish people want to see Irish as a living language again – spoken in banks, at sports matches, at work, in supermarkets, in the street and everywhere else.

It should be mentioned that these goals by and large apply also to the

Catholic and Nationalist population of Northern Ireland (820,000 or so persons) and one could not even begin to apply them there without strong backing from Dublin (from both government and voluntary agencies). More and more Protestants in the north have taken an interest in the Irish language but it must be understood that their primary loyalty is to the English language and culture as well as to Ulster Scots and these loyalties must be safeguarded legally, regardless of what the future political status of Northern Ireland may be.

Today, it is clear that Ireland is changing rapidly, both in demographic terms and in economic developments. These ongoing changes have implications for the Irish language and what might be done for the language in the future.

It is apparent from the census of 2002 in the Republic and that of 2001 in Northern Ireland that profound changes have taken place in Ireland as a whole since 1961. The successful programme of industrial and economic development (the "Celtic Tiger") pursued in the Republic since the late 1950s has proved to be an enormous success and has drastically reduced emigration and actually brought about immigration to Ireland, particularly in the last decade. Combined with a still relatively high birth rate by European standards, the population of the Irish Republic has thus climbed from 2.8 million in 1961 to 3.9 million in 2002. Due to political difficulties and consequent heavy emigration, the population of Northern Ireland has climbed only moderately from 1,536,000 in 1971 to 1,685,000 in 2001. In addition, the disturbances in Northern Ireland caused internal migration in the form of both Protestant and Catholic migration out of districts where they were a minority, or from formerly mixed districts, for greater security; e.g. the departure of Protestants from border districts and of Catholics from Protestant sections of Belfast and other towns. In both parts of Ireland it is clear that urbanization and a tendency for the population to shift from west to east has continued.

Both Dublin and Belfast now have over a million inhabitants in their larger conurbations and the growth of regional cities has now gathered momentum. In 2002 Dublin had 1,004,000 inhabitants, Belfast 910,000, Cork 186,000, Derry 105,000, Limerick 87,000, Galway 66,000 and Waterford 46,000. Over three-quarters of the island's population of 5.7 million is now urban, as opposed to only 52 per cent as recently as 1971 (in the Republic). Some three-quarters of the population is also to be found in the eastern half of the country. It goes without saying that the new demographic distribution of the Irish population has implications for future language planning, the most obvious being the need to focus RLS efforts on an increasingly urban eastern-centred population, if those efforts are to have any relevance.

Irish has survived not only in the western Gaeltachtaí but in new eastern Gaeltachtaí, such as those created in Meath, Belfast and Cork in the twentieth century and, significantly, it has experienced growth in the country at large, both north and south. Most important are the new cohort of persons in the Anglicized east who have acquired Irish as a fairly fluent second language. Native speakers, who numbered about 250,000 in 1926, now probably account for no more than about 80,000 of Ireland's 414,000 speakers.

Most observers concur that a new attitude[247] is evident towards the Irish language among younger generations. Whether this is due to increasing economic self-confidence, or is part of a wider trend among European minorities, is unclear. What we can say is that the younger generation clearly is more open to having its children educated in Gaelscoileanna and to using Irish with them at home and elsewhere. This new openness towards Irish on the part of the younger generation must be utilized, just as the enthusiasm of Ulster Nationalists for the language ought not to go untapped in any overall strategy for real promotion and growth for the Irish language in the new millennium.

Below are listed some very specific proposals which are geared, not towards artificial and half-hearted revival efforts, but real growth and expanded usage of the Irish language in everyday life.

Specific proposals and suggestions of the study and how they fit into the different stages of Reversing Language Shift for Irish

Aims and Goals

Primarily to restore Irish as the chief language of the community in a bilingual capacity with English (this study by no means advocates that English be dropped by any individual) among Ireland's 5.7 million

Figure 6.8
Numbers of primary and secondary schools, 1972–2003

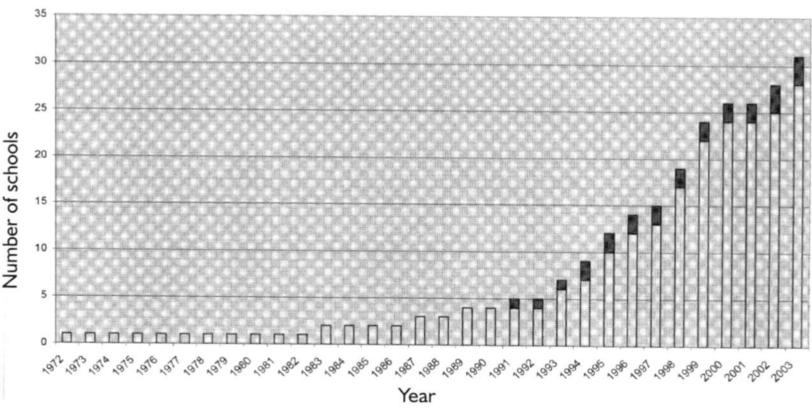

Figure 6.9
Growth of the number of children attending all-Irish schools outside the Gaeltacht, 1990–2003

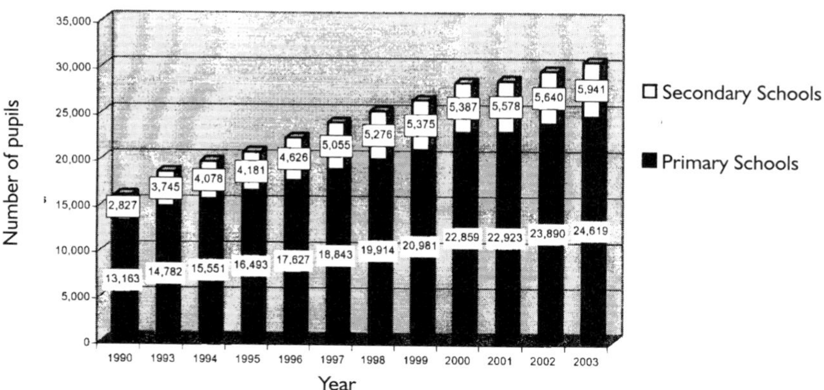

people, while at the same time respecting the position of English and the Ulster Scots dialect as the two main speeches of Ulster's 858,000-strong Unionist community.

The Main Thrust of the Proposals:

i) A two-stage policy or approach to the promotion of Irish for Ireland as a whole

ii) Legal and constitutional clarification of the status of Ulster Scots and English as the two chief speeches of Ulster Unionists, as well as speeches which must be given legal recognition in Irish society.

A two-stage policy of Gaelicization. The first stage is a policy of Gaelicization in the Gaeltacht and the larger cities and towns, beginning at some point in the near future, or thereabouts, so as not to overextend the limited financial resources of the Irish-language bodies such as Foras na Gaeilge, Gaelscoileanna, Udaras na Gaeltachta, Conradh na Gaeilge, the Ultach Trust, Comhdháil Náisiúnta na Gaeilge and also in order to immediately address the issue of the declining Irish-speaking population in the western Gaeltachtaí whose Irish-speaking ability must be utilized.

The second stage would be the extension of a policy of Gaelicization to the smaller towns and rural areas of Ireland at large, beginning about 2010. In Ulster, however, the position of both English and Ulster Scots must also be taken into account and, while Irish speakers and new Irish-speaking communities in Ulster must be aided, so must Ulster Scots and English speakers and cultural organizations. Just what form of aid to Ulster Scots is most effective and appropriate is a matter for the cultural organizations representing Ulster Scots.

The promotion of Irish, incorporating the principles of Reversing Language Shift

The critically needed policy of Gaelicization should ultimately entail the proposals below: (drawing on previous analyses)

I) Organizational

I.i) The establishment of a central research and evaluation unit to serve all programmes for teaching, utilizing or strengthening Irish, regardless of what government department might be in charge of them.

I.ii) The provision of resources for corpus planning and its implementation. Irish–French and Irish–German dictionaries are required, as are glossaries of new terminology.

I.iii) The immediate establishment of an organization, either with or without government support, to coordinate the establishment of new Irish-speaking communities in both urban and rural areas. It should be remembered that new Irish-speaking communities have already been established in Belfast and Cork, while several attempts have been made to establish a Dublin Gaeltacht. These ventures must be expanded upon and more critically serve as the model for other urban and rural Irish-speaking communities that would eventually serve as the foundation for a new Irish-speaking Ireland.

II) Community

II.i) Both government and voluntary language organizations must accept, once and for all, that the creation of communities with Irish as the first language has to become a clear priority and their new guiding ideology. The old, failed methodology of Irish by choice must finally be put aside.

II.ii) The establishment of new Irish-speaking communities in each urban and rural community in Ireland, both north and south (initially the larger towns but later to be followed by the rural communities and smaller towns of Ireland). New Irish-speaking communities are the central tenet of stage 6.

II.iii) The establishment of a new organization to assist young families who wish to raise their children in Irish. Existing language agencies are already overtaxed and such a new body, whose mandate is the establishment of new Irish-speaking communities, would signify an unequivocal commitment and link to stage-6 efforts.

II.iv) The mounting of a publicity campaign aimed at young parents to raise their children in Irish and to use Irish at home. Again, priority should initially be given to the larger urban centres such as Dublin, Belfast, Derry, Cork, Limerick, Galway, etc., (also stage 6).

II.v) Learning aids and counselling must be provided to young families who opt to raise their children in Irish. Booklets on parenting skills in

Irish, poems, games for children in Irish, prayers, riddles, songs, reading-readiness in Irish, etc. Such services and supplies – so necessary in any serious attempt to rebuild family and community life in Irish – could best be provided by the new organization recommended above – to coordinate the rebuilding of Irish language use at stage 6.

II.vi) Grandparenting and babysitting in Irish, free of charge, is another crucial course which must be made available all over Ireland, as the large numbers of middle-aged Irish speakers can be utilized. Such a service might be co-ordinated by organizations such as Foras na Gaeilge, the Ultach Trust or Comhdháil Náisiúnta na Gaeilge but, however linkages are established with older native and second-language Irish speakers, they provide valuable backup for stage-6 efforts in general.

II.vii) The expansion of Irish-speaking youth groups to every community. Youth groups in Irish are not merely backup for stage 6 but are an actual part of the process of providing an Irish-speaking environment for youth outside of school.

II.viii) A publicity campaign be mounted to attract native Irish speakers in Britain, the United States and elsewhere back to the new Irish-speaking communities in Ireland. Financial and political constraints are a consideration here, it is true, but efforts by the Irish Government to attract Gaelic speakers back to western Ireland might in fact have some success in increasing the Irish-speaking population, (stage 6).

III) Educational

III.i) There must be a review of the teaching of Irish with closer attention and scrutiny paid to what works and what does not work when it comes to creating new and fluent young Irish speakers.

III.ii) The continued establishment of new Irish schools in every community by the Gaelscoileanna organization, to the point where at least 50 per cent to 60 per cent (and eventually a much higher figure) of primary children are using Irish as their primary school language. This corresponds to the stage 4 level but is necessary for stage 6 to take root.

III.iii) The establishment of an Irish-medium university. Fairly extensive courses are already taught through Irish at Galway University and at others but the failure to establish an actual Irish-language university during the first 80 years of independence is symbolic of a hesitancy to make a real commitment to the language. Efforts to expand Irish at university level fall within the range of stage 1 and hence are greatly dependent on the success of earlier efforts at the stage 4 and stage 6 levels.

III.iv) The planned establishment of more classes for adults in more Irish communities to help expand adult literacy in Irish. The figure in Ireland is not insignificant but needs to grow in order to have greater impact. The organizations which are presently offering lessons in Irish to adults are affiliated with Foras na Gaeilge, Comhdháil Náisiúnta na Gaeilge, Conradh na Gaeilge and the Ultach Trust. A more coordinated and united effort by these organizations to bring Irish to a greater segment of the adult population in Ireland could be mounted, (stages 8 & 5).

IV) Media

IV.i) The establishment of a daily national newspaper in the Irish language, perhaps subsidized by Foras na Gaeilge. The most obvious path to pursue in this case would be to upgrade *Foinse* in the Republic to a daily in the same manner that *Lá* recently was in Belfast. Any such Irish-language daily should be offered free of charge to all organizations and families that request it, (stage 2)

IV.ii) The continued expansion of Irish on radio and television. Teilefís na Gaeilge, which began broadcasts two years ago, was a major victory in the battle to save the Irish language. An increase in Irish-language broadcasts on other television and radio stations should continue and can help reinforce the position of the language in the media, (stage 2).

V.) The Workplace

V.i) A policy of promoting Irish must be extended to the workplace. Sporadic initiatives have been launched in the workplace by government agencies but have lacked the permanent resolve that is a prerequisite for success, (stage 3).

VI.) Political Status

VI.i) The campaign to secure official status for the Irish language in the

European Union and in Northern Ireland must be increased and intensified. Only then can Irish-language use be extended within the civil service at all levels of administration, whether on a parish, municipal, county, regional or national level in both north and south. Indeed, all of the efforts and recommendations mentioned above will be fortified when official status for Irish becomes a reality in these sectors. Unfortunately, language is a political issue and long-term efforts to strengthen Irish cannot, in reality, ignore the legal status of the language (or lack thereof – recall the fate of the recent language bill for Irish).

References

Ball, Martin (2002) *The Celtic Languages*, London, Routledge Press.

Bell, G. (1976) *The Protestants of Ulster,* London, Pluto Press.

Bord na Gaeilge (1981) *Sceimeanna Pobail; Final Report of Coiste Comhairleach to Bord na Gaeilge*, Dublin.

Census Data:

Committee On Irish Language Attitudes Research (CLAR) (1975) Report (1975) Dublin Stationery Office.

De Freine, S. (1978) *The Great Silence*, Dublin, Mercier Press.

Department of Education For Northern Ireland (1974) *Primary Education, Teacher's Guide*, Belfast, HMSO.

Dorian, Nancy C. (1988) *The Celtic Languages In The British Isles,* Dublin Institute of Advanced Studies.

Durkacz, V. E. (1983) *The Decline of The Celtic Languages*, Edinburgh, John Donald.

Farrell, M. (1976) *Northern Ireland, The Orange State,* London, Pluto Press Ltd.

Fishman, J. (1991) *Reversing Language Shift*, Clevedon, Multilingual Matters.

Fishman, J. (1967) "Bilingualism with and without diglossia", *Journal of Social Issues* 23 (2) pp.29–37

Fishman, J. (2001) *Can Threatened Languages Be Saved?*, Clevedon, Multilingual Matters.

Freine, Seán de, (1965) *The Great Silence*, Foilseacháin Náisiúnta Teoranta.

Gaelscoileanna, Dublin (oifig@gaelscoileanna.iol.ie): information on schooling.

Harris, John (1988), "Spoken Irish In The Primary School System", *International Journal of the Sociology of Language*.

Hindley, Reg (1990) *The Death of The Irish Language*, London, Routledge Press.

Kermode, Mark, "Funding Refused For Irish Schools In The North", *Carn* 106, p.14.

Mac Donnacha, Seosamh, "The Status of Irish In The Irish Education System" *Carn* 116, p.9.

Miller, Kerby A. (1985) *Emigrants and Exiles*, Oxford University Press.

Ó Cuiv, Éamonn (1998) Speech, International Conference on Language Legislation, Killiney, County Dublin, 15 October 1998.

Ó Luain, Cathal, "Irish, Growth and Decline", *Carn* 100.

Ó Luain, Cathal, "Irish Language News" *Carn* 102.

Ó Luain, Cathal, "Irish Language News", *Carn* 114.

Ó Murchú, Helen and Máirtín, (1999), *The Irish Language*, Dublin, EBLUL.

Ó Rahilly, T. F. (1972) *Irish Dialects Past and Present*, Dublin, Institute For Advanced Studies.

Ó Snodaigh, P. (1973) *Hidden Ulster*, Dublin, Clodhanna Teo.

Rayfield, J. R. (1970) *The Languages of A Bilingual Community*, The Hague, Mouton.

Saunders, G. (1982) *Bilingual Children: Guidance For The Family*, Multilingual Matters.

Wagner, H. (1979) *Gaeilge Theilinn*. Dublin, Institiúid Ard Léin.

Weinrich, U. (1974) *Languages In Contact*, The Hague, Mouton.

ii) Irish in Northern Ireland

Diarmuid Ó Néill

In Northern Ireland, as we have seen, the circumstances surrounding the Irish language movement diverge dramatically after the partition of Ireland in 1920 from the circumstances pertaining to the language movement in the newly-created Irish Free State. While the language movement in Ireland as a whole before 1920 had not been earnestly assisted by the State, let alone promoted, it had by and large been allowed to function and even expand without a great deal of interference. In the early 1900s Irish was expanded in the school curriculum in the north as well as the south and new branches of the Gaelic League continued to open in Ulster communities. In short, the Dublin-based British administration tolerated Irish.

All this would change with partition. In 1920 about 45 per cent, or 750,000, Ulster inhabitants had been Roman Catholic as opposed to about 900,000, or 55 per cent, being Protestant. In addition to the fierce fighting which had broken out in the 1919–21 War of Independence between Irish and British forces all over the country, the north witnessed particularly savage anti-Catholic pogroms[248] which did not cease with the Anglo-Irish treaty in 1921. Over 50,000 Ulster Catholics fled to the south while about 80,000 Protestants were likewise more or less coerced into leaving the south, mainly for Britain but also for Northern Ireland and Canada. Needless to say, there was a massive disruption of life in Northern Ireland for both Protestant and Catholic in this period. By 1923 only one Gaelic League Branch was still functioning within Northern Ireland and many Gaelic League members were either in jail or had fled the north altogether.

The new Unionist-dominated northern state was determined to curtail any gains the Irish language had made in Ulster before 1920. Since 1878 Irish had been permitted in the school curriculum (as a subject) making various significant advances over the years. After 1922 the Unionists took control of the education system and funding for Irish language classes and the time allotted to them in the school curriculum were curtailed. Not only Irish in primary education but also Irish in secondary education came under increasing attack from the Unionist administration in the 1930s and 1940s. Only in the 1980s would some progress be made, as London took charge of more and more Ulster affairs from local Unionist hands. Irish was excluded utterly from official media and administration and, during the long winter of Unionist administration, retreated into the voluntary language bodies, Catholic social circles and the Nationalist-oriented curriculum of the Catholic schools. It would take the volcanic eruption of the Troubles in 1969 which brought down the Unionist administration to open some opportunities for reform in the field of Catholic civil rights but also in the status of the Irish language in Ulster.

Past Perspectives

The Ulster Plantation

In 1609, following the defeat of Ó Néill at Kinsale and the Flight of the Earls, the new circumstances made possible a joint English/Scottish exploitation of Irish resources and plantation of the lands confiscated from the departed Gaelic Ulster Lords. The union of the English and Scottish crowns by the Scottish king James VI (thence James I of the United Kingdom) further facilitated this collaboration. Traditionally, English settlers and tenants had been difficult to attract to Ireland because of its damper climate, poorer farming conditions and constant native revolts. Lowland Scots colonists were, however, attracted by the prospect of more affordable Ulster leases. It would appear that about two-thirds of the Ulster planters came from Scotland and about one third-from northern England, those from England being Anglican and those from Scotland being mainly Presbyterian but also, many of them, Anglican. It should be noted that while the politically suspect and Gaelic-speaking Highlanders were not invited, it is clear that many of the planters from Argyll and also Galloway were Gaelic-speaking. Both Ulster Scots and English now became important languages in Ulster.

However, the plantation was only partly successful, in that over half the Ulster population (likely closer to two-thirds until the famine) remained

Native Irish and Catholic. While Antrim, north Down, north Armagh and parts of Derry County came to be mainly Protestant and English in speech, much of Ulster – counties Donegal, Cavan, Monaghan, Tyrone, Fermanagh, south Armagh and south Down – remained not only mainly Catholic but Irish-speaking as the census of 1851 confirms (older Ulster Catholics were almost all enumerated as native Irish speakers in this first language census).

English and Scots colonists did not feel secure or safe in western, central and southern Ulster, far from the new market towns and forts established in eastern Ulster, and where they were an exposed minority among the dispossessed native Irish. These fears were indeed confirmed in the rebellion of 1641 when thousands of Scots and English planters were massacred by the Irish. Again, in 1689 the plantation town of Londonderry came under siege by native Irish forces with dreadful losses there and elsewhere in the province. The linguistic consequences of settlement in Ulster were that, while an English- and Scots-speaking element was introduced, the Irish language was not really dislodged anywhere in the province because Catholics continued to speak it almost to the exclusion of English well into the early 1800s.

Linguistically, however, it was the Williamite period of the early 1700s which did lead to the establishment of English on a large scale in two important regions. They were southern Leinster and eastern Ulster. More peaceful conditions in the early 1700s did attract new English and Scottish settlers to Ireland in general and these two areas in particular. The rich soil of south Leinster counties such as Carlow, Wexford, Offaly, and Laois, for the first time attracted not only English landlords but tenants and craftsmen and other more plebeian settlers. In fact, as recently as 1861, the population of south Leinster was about 25 per cent Protestant and of Planter stock. One of the consequences of this was that many Catholics in south Leinster (like those of Dublin before them) became bilingual English/Irish speakers during the 1700s. While Irish was rarely dropped entirely, the fact that Catholics were drawn into the English-speaking economic world of Dublin, Britain and the Empire at large, would have important implications for the future of Irish, later, in all parts of the country.

Eastern Ulster too attracted new Scottish and English settlers in the early 1700s, however the Catholic population (about two thirds of the population) remained almost exclusively Irish-speaking into the early 1800s, partly because of more limited social and economic intercourse with Protestants and apparently also a more nationalistic determination to hold on to Irish language use than permeated the inhabitants of Dublin, Wicklow, and other regions in this period.

Irish in twentieth-century Ulster

It is important to remember that native Irish-speaking pockets remained in Northern Ireland well after partition in 1921. Even though the census of 1911 was the last to record Irish in the Six Counties (until 1991) it is clear that, for many decades, Irish continued in native use in the Strabane region of Tyrone, the Glens of Antrim and south Armagh likely into the 1940s and 1950s. Indeed, use of Irish in the north clearly never ceased.

It is also worth noting the strength of the Irish language in Ulster in 1911, for even at this late date some 75,000 Irish speakers were enumerated in Ulster – some 10 per cent of the Nationalist population – as opposed to 66,000 in Leinster, a testimony to the sheer life force of Ulster Irish even 60 years after the famine. True Ulster Irish speakers in 1911, like most of the other 550,000 Irish speakers at this date, were overwhelmingly concentrated among the over-50 age bracket (indicating that Irish occupied the same position in 1911 that Breton occupies today) but the strength of Ulster Irish at this late date is a testimony to the enduring strength of the language in Ulster past and present. Of the 1.4 million Ulster Catholics before the famine, it is likely that at least 500,000 or so were Irish speakers, despite the advance of English after 1800.

The modern political context

Since the establishment of direct rule from London in 1973, official attitudes to Irish began to alter. The first funding for new projects was approved in the late 1980s. Limited financial assistance was now extended to Irish-medium schools in Belfast and elsewhere for the first time. Not until 1998, however, did the UK administration truly open the door to real long-term possibilities for thoroughgoing reform as part of the larger peace breakthrough which took place that year with the Good Friday Agreement.

The Good Friday peace agreement in 1998 and its impact

The pertinent section of the Good Friday Agreement towards the Irish language is as follows:

"Sec. 3 All participants recognize the importance of respect, understanding and tolerance in relation to linguistic diversity, including, in Northern Ireland, the Irish language, Ulster Scots and the languages of the various ethnic communities, all of which are part of the cultural wealth of the island of Ireland.

"Sec. 4 In the context of active consideration currently being given to the UK signing the Council of Europe Charter for Regional or Minority Languages, the British Government will, in particular in relation to the Irish language, where appropriate and where people so desire it:

- take resolute action to promote the language
- facilitate and encourage the use of the language in speech and writing in public and private life where there is appropriate demand
- seek to remove, where possible, restrictions which would discourage or work against the maintenance or development of the language
- make provision for liaising with the Irish language community, representing their views to public authorities and investigating complaints
- place a statutory duty on the Department of Education to encourage and facilitate Irish medium education in line with current provision for integrated education
- explore urgently with the relevant British authorities, and in co-operation with the Irish broadcasting authorities, the scope for achieving more widespread availability of Teilifis na Gaeilige in Northern Ireland
- seek more effective ways to encourage and provide financial support for Irish language film and television production in Northern Ireland
- encourage the parties to secure agreement that this commitment will be sustained by a new Assembly in a way which takes account of the desires and sensitivities of the community."

Foras Na Gaeilge: the new all-Ireland language body

One of the most important aspects of the Peace Agreement was the agreement to set up a statutory cross-border implementation body to promote the Irish language. For the first time since partition, an attempt has clearly been made to address the questions facing the Irish language in both parts of Ireland.

Issues which influenced the debate on the role of the new language body were the number of departments, their responsibilities and areas where co-operation between the Irish Republic and Northern Ireland could take place.

The Shaw's Road Gaeltacht: an important development for Irish in all parts of Ireland

Established in 1969 by 11 families in West Belfast, this dynamic and still-thriving language community is an important example of successful urban renewal for Irish and indeed all other threatened minority languages. It is particularly important for those working on behalf of the Celtic languages when one bears in mind how they are often marginalized in the urban arena.

While it is not entirely surprising that such an ambitious and successful undertaking was mounted by the Nationalist community in Belfast, it was and remains to this day a very considerable achievement which merits not only more study by sociolinguists in general but by Celtic language activists in particular, who increasingly must meet the challenge of how to activate and mobilise Celtic speakers in the increasingly urbanized population of the Celtic countries, particularly as the traditional rural Celtic-speaking heartlands contract.

For the increasingly urban population of both parts of Ireland, the importance of this example of successful urban RLS can hardly be overstated. No successful RLS programme can be mounted in Ireland without new urban Gaeltachtaí in Dublin, Belfast, and the other regional cities.[249]

New Gaeltacht proposed for County Tyrone

Another development which must be mentioned and which is coming to light at the time of writing, is the proposed new Gaeltacht in Altmore, County Tyrone. Anounced towards the end of 2003, it would house about

Figure 7.1
Growth of the Irish-medium schools in Northern Ireland
Source: Gaelscoileanna

Year/ Bliain	Primary Schools/ Bunscoileanna	Secondary Schools Iarbhunscoileanna
1972–1982	1	0
1983	2	0
1984	2	0
1985	2	0
1986	2	0
1987	3	0
1988	3	0
1989	4	0
1990	4	0
1991	4	1
1992	4	1
1993	6	1
1994	7	2
1995	10	2
1996	12	2
1997	13	2
1998	17	2
1999	22	2
2000	24	2
2001	24	2
2002	25	3
2003	28	3

20 Irish-speaking families and is being organized by Cathal Ó Donghaile. It would be established on a 52-acre site and plans include a projected education and cultural centre. Still in the planning stage, an application has been made to both the Dept of the Gaeltacht in Dublin and the Northern Ireland Office for £1.8 million towards the cost. Cathal Ó Donghaile told a UK newspaper, "It's a big dream, but it's not impossible. Eventually, we hope to have a cultural centre at the heart of the village and to attract employment and tourists to the area. The centre would be the hub of the village, hosting a Gaelic college, education, music, social, environmental and health programmes. The Irish language is lying

dormant in everyone, and we want to create a stress-free environment in which all sections of the community can enjoy Irish culture." It goes without saying that the proposal by Cathal Ó Donghaile to launch a new Irish-speaking community in Northern Ireland is precisely what is required in Ireland and indeed in all the Celtic countries.

Numbers of Irish speakers

The recent 2001 census revealed 167,490 persons, or 10 per cent of Northern Ireland's population of 1,685,267, as Irish speakers with 75,125 claiming more or less complete fluency. A further 1,450,000 persons declared a much more limited knowledge of Irish. The same census indicated a population of 1,685,267 in Northern Ireland, of whom over 820,000 were Nationalist, or 48–50 per cent of the population. (The 2002 census for the Republic revealed 246,571 persons living in the three Irish-administered Ulster counties of Donegal, Cavan and Monaghan, of whom some 25,000 can be considered Irish-speaking in varying degrees. So, of Ulster's 2 million people, we may reasonably hazard the guess that some 100,000 are Irish speakers). If accurate, this means that about 10 per cent of Nationalists may be considered fair to fluent Irish speakers, a figure that is broadly comparable with the south where in 2002 some 339,000, or roughly 8 per cent, claimed fluency.

The eight stage GIDS scale for Irish in Northern Ireland

A stage-by-stage analysis of recent and current RLS efforts on behalf of Irish in Ulster and their future prospects

Stages 7 and 8: Reconstructing Irish, adult acquisition of Irish as a second language, and cultural interaction in Irish involving adults

Although a significant amount of vocabulary and expressions must have been lost through the demise of Irish as a community language throughout most of Ulster, its position has never been quite as desperate as has sometimes been painted. Extensive written records of Irish in manuscript form from the 1600s, 1700s and 1800s, whether in southern dialects or the Ulster dialect of Irish, are in existence and there is no need to reconstruct missing pieces of the language (as with Cornish). Literature in Irish is now relatively easy to access, along with dictionaries and grammars.

Regarding interaction in Irish involving adults, there is a fairly strong tradition of Irish usage throughout the six counties, whether in the form of "Irish-speaking pub nights" or in the more formal setting of Conradh na Gaeilge classes which never ceased operating in Ulster. In fact it is fair to say that efforts to utilize spoken Irish on such occasions by adults in Ulster were, and are still, more common than similar initiatives south of the border, due to the heightened nationalism of Ulster Catholics.

Stage 6: Establishing the vital linkage with family and community

The importance of the establishment of the Shaw's Road Gaeltacht in west Belfast cannot be overstated, not only for Irish in Ulster. It is the first urban Gaeltacht to be established in Ireland and attempts are presently being made to emulate it eventually in Dublin and Galway (a Cork urban Gaeltacht is already in existence). Irish is the dominant language of the family and is now being intergenerationally transmitted (Irish is now in its third generation of transmission in the Shaw's Road Gaeltacht). An Irish-speaking church, Irish-speaking businesses and an Irish-medium school serve the community which numbers over 1,000. Irish-language signage is everywhere visible and the Irish language is also heard everywhere. While, clearly, the Irish Government, let alone the northern authorities, have yet to endorse such community initiatives as necessary elsewhere in the island, whether on an urban or a rural base, it is quite clear that only through the establishment of such new Gaeltachtaí in eastern Ireland and elsewhere can Irish ever hope to be spoken on a wide scale again, hence careful attention must be paid by Irish RLSers to the strengths and weaknesses of this particular Gaeltacht, in order to learn from its experiences and how to correctly go about the establishment of similar ventures in other Irish cities and towns in the future.

Stages 5 and 4: The attainment of literacy in Irish, learning Irish at school and education in Irish

As mentioned above, classes to improve speaking ability in Irish, as well as literacy in the language for adults, date from 1891 and the establishment of the Gaelic League. Despite the unfriendly political climate in Northern Ireland, Irish-language classes by Conradh na Gaeilge and other Irish language bodies never ceased. As outlined above, Irish was severely limited in the school system after 1922 when the Unionist administration halted many Irish language classes in primary schools and then launched an assault on the Irish language in secondary schools, starting in 1942.

The situation today is far from satisfactory as, out of roughly 330,000 primary and secondary school children in Northern Ireland, only some 3,885 (less than 2 per cent) are able to study in Irish-medium schools. The co-ordinating body for Irish-medium schools in Northern Ireland is Gaeiloiluint, which works closely with the Gaelscoileanna organization in the Irish Republic. Funding, difficulty training needed teachers and lack of real support from the administration remain the chief obstacles in this situation.

Nevertheless, the Irish-medium schools which are in operation in the north are an authentic example of Joshua Fishman's classic "4A" type of school, where the endangered language in question is used for both instruction and administration under Xish auspices. Type "4B" schools are also on the scene in Ulster, as Catholic schools and some state/Protestant schools now offer Irish as a subject.

Stage 3: Irish in the workplace

Effectively, Irish is not used as a full, living language in the workplace in Northern Ireland, with the exception of the small number of cases like the Irish-speaking shops and other business establishments in the Shaw's Road Gaeltacht in Belfast and by the staff administering the Irish-medium primary and secondary schools.

Stages 2 and 1: Irish in the Media, Government and Business

As stated above, Irish is not yet present in business or the worksphere to any great extent, however, it has established a foothold. In government administration, Irish is, in reality, almost absent. For the present, the media scene allows for more optimism. Both the BBC radio and television services for Northern Ireland now broadcast programmes in Irish, particularly for learners. In addition, northern audiences can tune in to Raidió na Gaeltachta and Teilifís na Gaeilge broadcasts from the south, so northern Irish speakers, like those in the Republic, do at least have access to more or less full Irish language radio and television programming. Northern Ireland can also boast an Irish-language newspaper, *An Lá* – no small achievement for the Nationalist community, which numbered 820,000 in 2001. The recent upgrading of *An Lá* to a daily newspaper – in fact the only Irish-language daily in Ireland – is entirely typical of the enthusiasm of the Nationalist community in the north for the Irish language and can only augur well for the future of Irish in Ulster.

Proposals and recommendations for the future in Northern Ireland

The question of where the Irish language in Northern Ireland goes from here is an important one for the Nationalist community, for Unionist supporters of the language, for language activists in Northern Ireland, for Ireland as a whole and indeed for the language movements in all the Celtic countries because of the implications for language renewal at large. It is particularly important for not only the Nationalist political spokespersons but also language agencies in Northern Ireland to have a clear vision regarding where the brunt of future efforts should be concentrated.

Despite partition, the Irish people both north and south of the border have obviously continued to pursue a not entirely dissimilar path of partial promotion of Irish since 1921. That is, where it was judged possible and advisable and where circumstances allowed, Irish has been brought back into society to a certain extent since 1921, both north and south. It has been brought back into the schools (as a subject initially and now, of late, as a medium of instruction for some 7 per cent of schoolchildren in the Republic, although only 1 per cent of children in the north as of 2003), into the public domain and, in the past several decades, the media on a wide scale, with radio and television in both north and south carrying Irish-language programming.

In the case of the north, the goal is to re-establish Irish as a daily spoken language in family, community and social life (a position it occupied until fairly recently) and also to re-establish Irish as a major language of government administration, media and education (spheres not dominated by Ulster Irish since the 1500s). As the Unionist population in Ulster (some 858,000 persons) identify mainly with English and Ulster Scots, we must realize that it is the Nationalist population in Northern Ireland who are the constituency or "target market" for increased Gaelicization. Language activists must also realize that efforts to strengthen Irish among the 820,000 Nationalists of Northern Ireland and 1.1 million Nationalists of the nine counties of Ulster, must be sensitive to the practical concerns, issues, aspirations and even reservations of Ulster Catholics towards the Irish language. Ulster Catholics, like the population of the Republic, clearly have some reservations and fears regarding a full embracement of Irish, despite their (accurate) reputation as eager enthusiasts of the Irish language. Further, this attitude of reserve towards Irish is also reflected in the policies of the SDLP and Sinn Féin – the two political parties who command over 90 per cent of the Nationalist vote – towards Irish (the SDLP and Sinn Féin took 46 per cent of the total vote in the most recent Northern Ireland election).

The goal in the north, as in the south, must be one of bilingualism between Irish and English. At the same time, the SDLP, Sinn Féin and the political parties of the Republic hold positions on the language question which fall far short of building a genuinely bilingual and equally Irish/English-speaking society – in any part of Ireland, (see the party policy papers regarding Irish of both the SDLP and Sinn Féin).

Debate must take place among language bodies in the north and the two Nationalist parties in the north in order to clarify what policies may best be pursued in Ulster to eventually realize the goal of an Irish-speaking Ulster.

The proposals below deal specifically with Northern Ireland; however, it may be helpful to acknowledge here the need for greater future coordination between the Republic and the six counties of Northern Ireland, particularly a coordination of language policy between the three counties of Donegal, Cavan and Monaghan and Northern Ireland.

I) Organizational

I.i) The immediate establishment of an organization, either with or without government support, to coordinate the establishment of new Irish-speaking communities in both urban and rural areas in Northern Ireland. It should be remembered that new Irish-speaking communities have already been established in Belfast and elsewhere. These must be expanded and, more critically, serve as the model for other urban and rural Irish-speaking communities that would eventually serve as the foundation for a new Irish-speaking Ireland.

II) Community

II.i) The establishment of new Irish-speaking communities in each urban and rural community in Northern Ireland, (initially the larger towns but later to be followed by the rural communities and smaller towns of Northern Ireland). New Irish-speaking communities are the most central tenet of stage 6.

II.ii) The establishment of a new organization to assist young families who wish to raise their children in Irish. Existing language agencies are already overtaxed and such a new body, whose mandate is the establishment of new Irish-speaking communities, would signify an unequivocal commitment and link to stage-6 efforts.

II.iii) The mounting of a publicity campaign aimed at young parents to raise their children in Irish and to use Irish at home. Again, priority should initially be given to the larger urban centres such as Belfast, Derry, Craigavon, etc., (also stage 6).

II.iv) A publicity campaign be mounted to attract native Irish-speakers in Britain, the United States and elsewhere back to the new Irish-speaking communities in Ireland, including those being established in Northern Ireland. Financial and political constraints are a consideration here, it is true, but efforts by the Irish Government to attract Gaelic speakers back to Northern Ireland may well have some success in increasing the Irish-speaking population there, (stage 6).

II.v) Learning aids and counselling must be provided to young families who opt to raise their children in Irish. Booklets on parenting skills in Irish, poems, games for children in Irish, prayers, riddles, songs, reading-readiness in Irish, etc. Such services and supplies, so necessary in any serious attempt to rebuild family and community life in Irish, could best be provided by the new organization recommended above – to coordinate the rebuilding of Irish language use at stage 6.

II.vi) Grandparenting and daycare in Irish, free of charge, is another crucial course which must be made available all over Ulster, as the large numbers of middle-aged Irish speakers can be utilized. Such a service might be co-ordinated by organizations such as Foras na Gaeilge, the Ultach Trust or Comhdháil Náisiúnta na Gaeilge but, however linkages are established with older native and second-language Irish-speakers, they provide valuable backup for stage-6 efforts in general.

II.vii) The expansion of Irish-speaking youth groups to every community. Youth groups in Irish are not merely backup for stage 6 but are an actual part of the process of providing an Irish-speaking environment for youth outside of school.

III) Educational

III.i) The continued establishment of new Irish schools in every community by the Gaelscoileanna organization to the point where at least 50 to 60 per cent (and eventually a much higher figure) of Nationalist primary children are using Irish as their primary school language. Protestant children whose parents desire an Irish-language education for their children must also be accommodated. This corresponds to the stage-4 level but is necessary for stage 6 to take root.

III.ii) The establishment of an Irish-medium university in the north, either in Belfast or in Derry. Fairly extensive courses are already taught through Irish at Galway University and at others but the failure to establish an actual Irish-language university during the first 80 years of independence is symbolic of a hesitancy to make a real commitment to the language. Efforts to expand Irish at university level fall within the range of stage 1 and hence are greatly dependent on the success of earlier efforts at the stage-6 and stage-4 levels.

III.iii) The planned establishment of more classes for adults in more Ulster communities to help expand adult literacy in Irish. The organizations which are presently offering lessons in Irish to adults are affiliated with Foras na Gaeilge, Comhdháil Náisiúnta na Gaeilge, Conradh na Gaeilge and the Ultach Trust. A more coordinated and united effort by these organizations to bring Irish to a greater segment of the adult population in Ireland could be mounted, (stages 8 & 5).

IV) Media

IV.i) The further promotion of the new daily Irish-language newspaper in the north (*An Lá*) by perhaps arranging for it to be subsidized by Foras na Gaeilge. This new Irish language daily could possibly be offered free of charge to all organizations and families that request it, (stage 2).

IV.ii) The continued expansion of Irish on BBC radio and television broadcasts in Ulster. An increase in Irish language broadcasts on other television and radio stations should continue and can help reinforce the position of the language in the media, (stage 2).

IV.iii) The extension of RTE and TG 4 broadcasts into the north of Ireland.

V) The work sphere

V.i) A policy of promoting Irish must be extended to the workplace. Sporadic initiatives have been launched in the work place by government agencies but have lacked the permanent resolve that is a prerequisite for success, (stage 3).

VI) Political status

VI.i) The campaign to secure official status for the Irish language in Northern Ireland must be increased and intensified. Only then can Irish language use be extended within the civil service at all levels of administration, whether on a parish, municipal, county, regional or national level in both north and south. Indeed, all of the efforts and recommendations mentioned above will be fortified when official status for Irish in the north becomes a reality in these sectors. Unfortunately, language is a political issue and long-term efforts to strengthen Irish cannot, in reality, ignore the legal status of the language (or lack thereof).

References
(In addition to those listed for Éire)

Boyd, A. (1969) Holy War In Belfast, Republic of Ireland, Anvil Books Ltd.

Canavan, Tony, of the Central Community Relations Unit at a conference organized by Chomhdháil Náisiúnta na Gaeilge in Cultúrlann Mac Adam – Ó Fiaich, West Belfast.

Cathcart, Rex (1984) The Most Contrary Region: The BBC in Northern Ireland 1924–1984, Belfast, Blackstaff Press.

Committee On Irish Language Attitudes Research (CLAR) (1975) Report. Dublin Stationery Office

Education (NI) Order 1998, HMSO, Belfast, Paragraph 89, p.89.

Mac Aonghusa, Proinsias (1993) Ar Son na Gaeilge, Conradh na Gaeilge 1893–1993, Dublin, pp.217–27.

Mac Con Iomaire, Rónán (1999) "Dhá Mhí Fágtha ag Bord na Gaeilge", Foinse, 31 Jan.

Maguire, Gabrielle (1991) Our Own Language, Clevedon, Multilingual Matters.

McCoy, Gordon (1997) "Rhetoric and Realpolitik: the Irish language movement and the British Government", in Donnan, Hastings and McFarlane, Graham, Culture and Policy in Northern Ireland: Anthropology in the public arena, Institute of Irish Studies, Queens University, Belfast.

McDermott, Jimmy (2001) The Old IRA and The Belfast Pogroms, Belfast, Beyond The Pale Press.

Northern Ireland Human Rights Commission (2001) Making a Bill of Rights for Northern Ireland, Belfast.

Ó Cairealláin, Gearóid (1999) "Bord na Gaeilge le scor i mí an Mhárta", An La, 28 Jan.

Ó Muirí, Pól (1999) "Tuarascáil", Irish Times, 3 Feb.

The Northern Ireland Census 1991, Belfast, HMSO, 1992, p.159.

The Northern Ireland Census 2001, Belfast, HMSO.

iii.) Scottish Gaelic in Scotland/ *An Ghàidhlig*

Diarmuid Ó Néill

Ro-ràdh

"CHANEIL CÀNAIN ann dha nach urrainnear rud a dhèanamh". Tha na briathran seo a labhair Joshua Fishman na aithisg iomraitich "Tionndadh Gluasad Cànaine" an 1991 air leth freagarrach air an t-suidheachadh Ghàidhlig RLS an Alba a tha an ceartuair mi-mhisneachail do mhòran luchd-iomairt a tha ag obair às leth na cànaine a dh' aindeoin adhartais an cuid de phrìomh raointean a tha toirt dòchais fhaicilleach a-thaobh na Gàidhlig. Feumar aideachadh gu bheil suidheachadh na Gàidhlig an Alba an-diugh na adhbhar iomagain. Nochd fiosrachadh cunntas-sluaigh 2001 a dh' fhoillsicheadh bho chionn ghoirid gu robh 58,652 an Alba a' bruidhinn na Gàidhlig. Tha seo a' comharrachadh sìor-chrionadh mòr bhon 65,000 luchd-bruidhne an 1991 agus an 88,000 an 1971. Mar sin feumar smaoin chùramach is beachdachadh a thoirt do ro-innleachdan sam bith a chruthaichear airson Gàidhlig an Alba. Tha a' chànain air a bhith crìonadh a-rèir àireamh an t-sluaigh airson ùine mhòir. Am meadhan nan 1700an bha an àireamh còrr is leth-mhillean agus gu mu 1400 bha còrr is leth sluagh na h-Alba a' bruidhinn na Gàidhlig.

'S e taobh eile dhe na duilgheadasan a tha aig muinntir RLS gu bheil an sluagh a tha bruidhinn na Gàidhlig an Alba a' fàs aosda, agus còrr is leth de luchd-bruidhinn na Gàidhlig an cunntas-sluaigh 2001 40 bliadhna dh' aois no còrr. Cuideachd bha na sgìrean an Alba san robh luchd-bruidhinn na Gàidhlig fhathast sa mhòr-chuid an cunntas 2001 nan coimhearsnachdan an ìre mhath dùthchail is iomallach far a bheil fìor chruadal eaconamach a' tachairt riutha cuideachd. A thuilleadh air seo tha sgaoileadh eadar-ghinealach na cànaine san teaghlach, san dachaigh is anns an nàbachd air fàs coimeasach ainneamh.

An suidheachadh na Gàidhlig tha oidhirpean comharraichte muinntir

RLS air tachairt a-mhàin san fhichead bliadhna chaidh seachad. Tha a' mhòr-chuid de dh' iomairtean às leth na Gàidhlig air an cur air chois aig ìre na coimhearsnachd ionadail, chan ann aig ìre àird, fharsaing, nàiseanta air feadh Alba. Tha seo a' nochdadh an sgaraidh san dòigh smaoineachaidh an Alba mu àite na Gàidhlig san riochd nàiseanta.

Translation courtesy of the Gaelic Language Board of Scotland/Bòrd na Gàidhlig

Introduction: "There is no language for which nothing can be done."

These words, spoken by Joshua Fishman in 1991 in his now well-known work *Reversing Language Shift*, are particularly appropriate for the Gaelic RLS scene in Scotland which presently is disheartening for many activists working on behalf of the language, despite progress in some key areas which allows for a cautious optimism for Gaelic. The situation of Gaelic in Scotland today does, it must be admitted, give cause for concern. The census of 2001 showed 58,652 speakers of Gaelic in Scotland. This represents a continued sharp decline from the 65,000 speakers in 1991 and the 88,000 speakers in 1971. Hence, whatever strategies are devized for Gaelic in Scotland must be given serious thought and reflection. The language has been in decline demographically for a very long period. In the mid-1700s the figure clearly exceeded half a million and until about 1400 over half the population of Scotland was Gaelic-speaking.

Another challenge facing RLSers in Scotland is that the Gaelic-speaking population of Scotland is an ageing one, and more than half of the Gaelic speakers in the 2001 census were over the age of 40. In the Gaelic context, serious and significant RLS efforts have occurred only in the last several decades. Most initiatives on behalf of Gaelic have been launched at the local community level and not on a larger national Scotland-wide scale, reflecting the split in Scottish thinking about where Gaelic fits in the national identity.

The historical background of Scottish-Gaelic

The language which is now known as Scottish-Gaelic came from Ireland some time in the late Roman era and was, for many centuries, almost identical to Gaelic as spoken in Ireland, Man and the Irish colonies established in Wales during the same period. The background of Gaelic itself is not well known. Both Britain and Ireland were predominantly Celtic-speaking by the beginning of the Roman era but not exclusively. In Scotland, older languages appear to have persisted in the northwest of the country for some time after the arrival of the Gaels. The problematic Picts seem to have been partly Brythonic-speaking but it is within their territory that inscriptions in stone have been found which suggest the persistence of an unknown and non-Indo-European language into the historical period. In addition, many of the place-names and personal names of the Picts are non-Celtic.[250] Also, to the north and northwest of the Picts, were found other peoples of unknown linguistic affiliation, such as the "Attecotti" of early Irish records, as well as a broch-building people who inhabited Caithness and the Orkneys and who successfully resisted Pictish attempts at conquest during the early historical era.

It was in Argyll that the oldest traditional Gaelic kingdom was established by colonists from Dal Riada in Ulster in the fifth century. It is likely, however, that Gaelic had already been established in this region even prior to the establishment of the kingdom of Argyll. In early Irish literature the Picts of Scotland, as well as several non-Gaelic peoples in Ireland, are referred to as "Cruithne". Just why this is so, is uncertain. It is possible that pre-Celtic peoples of non-Gaelic origin persisted in Ireland just as they apparently did in Scotland to a late date.

Although British or Welsh missionaries, such as St Jerome in the third century, had been attempting for many years to convert the Picts to Christianity, it was St Colomba, who arrived in the late fifth century from Ireland, who was destined to have the greatest spiritual impact. His great mission at Iona would have not only spiritual but cultural impact on Scots, Picts, Britons, Saxons and the other peoples of northern Britain. In addition, not only Iona but the entire early-Christian movement in Scotland probably had cultural and linguistic consequences, in that Gaelic came to be perceived as the vehicle of a superior and literate Christian culture. The consequence, ultimately, was the triumph of Gaelic at the expense of Pictish, Brythonic and the other languages of the north, despite the fact that the Pictish kingdoms retained their military prowess until a late date.

In 844 the unification of the Scottish and Pictish kingdoms under Kenneth Mac Alpin occurred. The Scottish state expanded in the eleventh century to include Brythonic-speaking Strathclyde to the south as well as

English-speaking Lothian to the southeast.

By the early tenth century, Gaelic had come to be the dominant language throughout most of what is now Scotland, even retaking the Hebrides from Norse but the tide was soon to turn against it, as English-speaking Lothian increasingly began to assert its importance within the Scottish state and it would not be long before Gaelic, like Pictish before it, was thrown on the defensive. The problem for Gaelic was that Edinburgh and English-speaking Lothian were more economically advanced than the rest of the country and were a bridge with the great neighbour to the south. Gaelic did, however, retain its predominance in affairs of state, at least until the late-fourteenth century.

The retreat of Gaelic as the common speech of the Lowlands was a drawn-out affair taking several centuries, surviving in many Lowland districts into the 1600's. By 1400 at the latest, however, Gaelic was associated in lowland thinking with the remote Highlands. The union of Scotland and England in 1603 was another event which further accentuated the differences between the tradition-bound Highlands and the rapidly Anglicizing eastern and southern regions of Scotland. The Battle of Culloden occurred in 1746. The event would have repercussions for both Gaelic society and the Gaelic language. Many clans had sided with the unsuccessful Stewart claimants to the British throne. The victorious Hanoverian government took its revenge on the Highland clans.

During the late eighteenth century, many Highlanders began to emigrate, carrying Gaelic to various parts of the world outside of Scotland. The most important of these settlements would prove to be Nova Scotia. Ominously for the language in Scotland itself, Gaelic was, throughout the late 1800s and for most of the 1900s, effectively excluded from the schools and indeed students were punished for using it. It would not be until the 1980s that Gaelic would re-establish itself on a more solid basis in primary and secondary education.

The traditional Gaedhealtachd

There is evidence that, until quite late, Gaelic was still spoken fairly widely, even in the Lowlands. Newspaper advertisements seeking school teachers during the 1600s in Edinburgh often requested a knowledge of "the Erse". Many, though certainly not all of the Lowland Scots who settled in Ulster in the 1600s, were Gaelic-speaking, as has been clearly

Figure 8.1
Gaelic speaking by parish, 1881

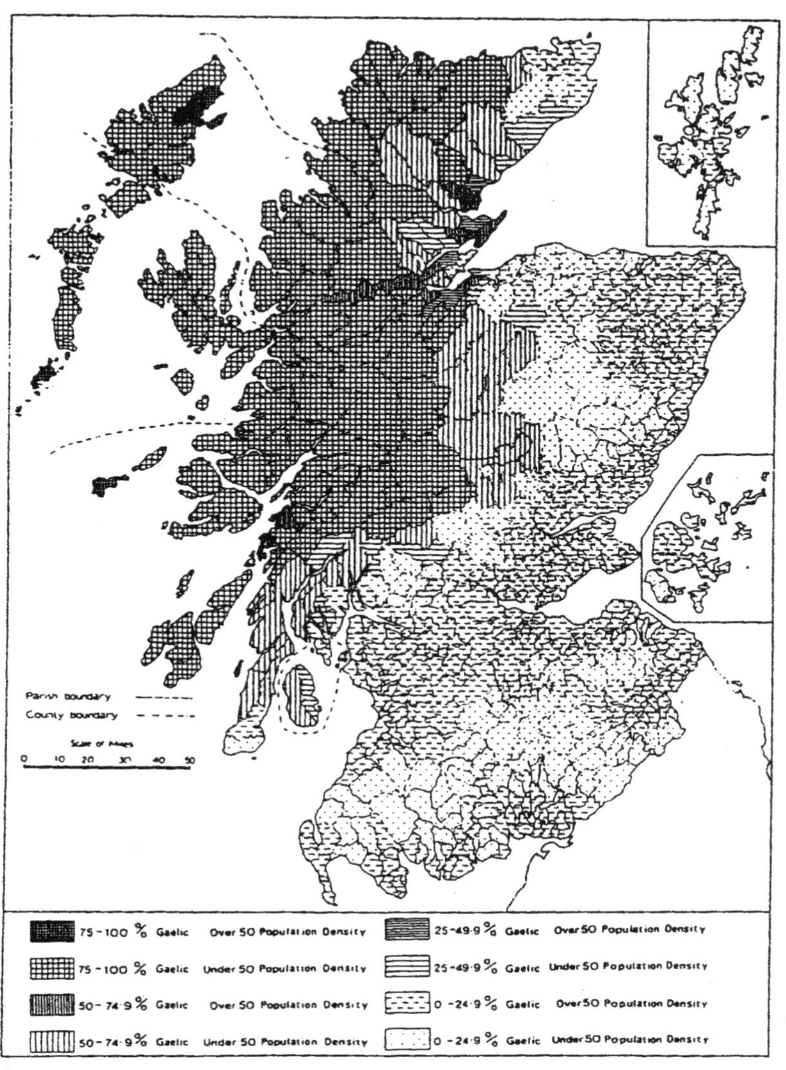

Source: Charles Withers, *Gaelic Scotland 1698–1981,* Routledge Press, 1984

Figure 8.2
Gaelic speaking by parish, 1931

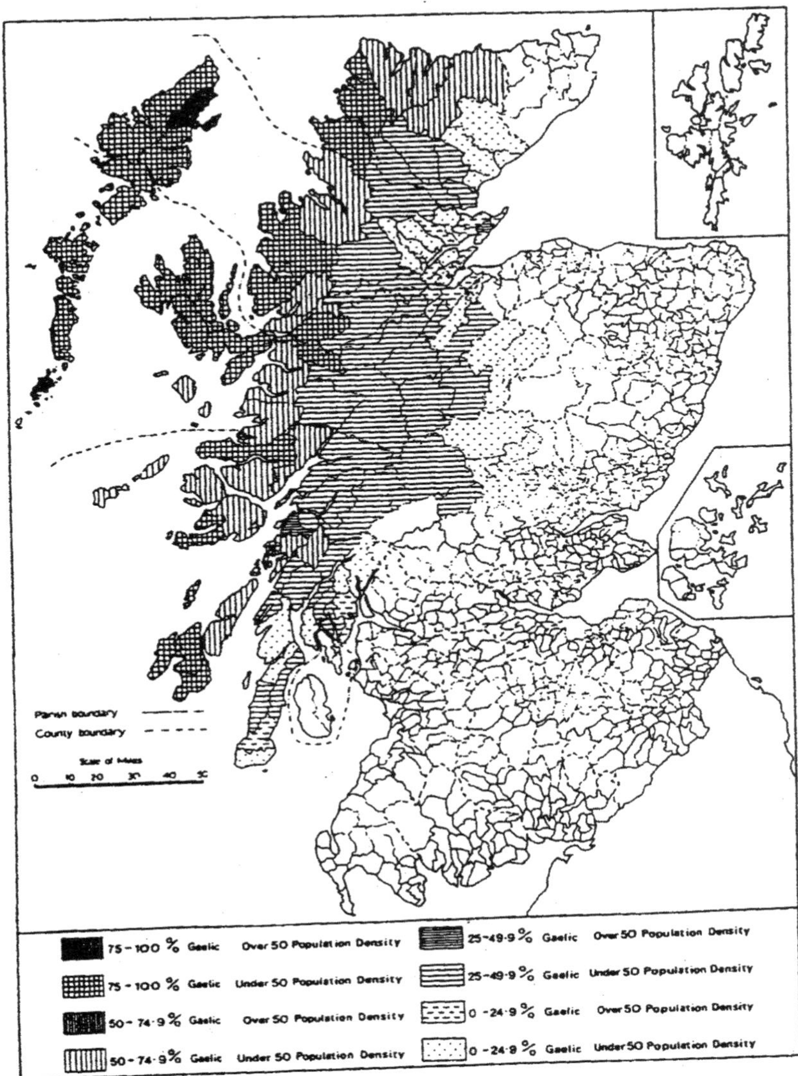

Source: Charles Withers, *Gaelic Scotland 1698–1981,* Routledge Press, 1984

Figure 8.3
Gaelic speaking by parish, 1951

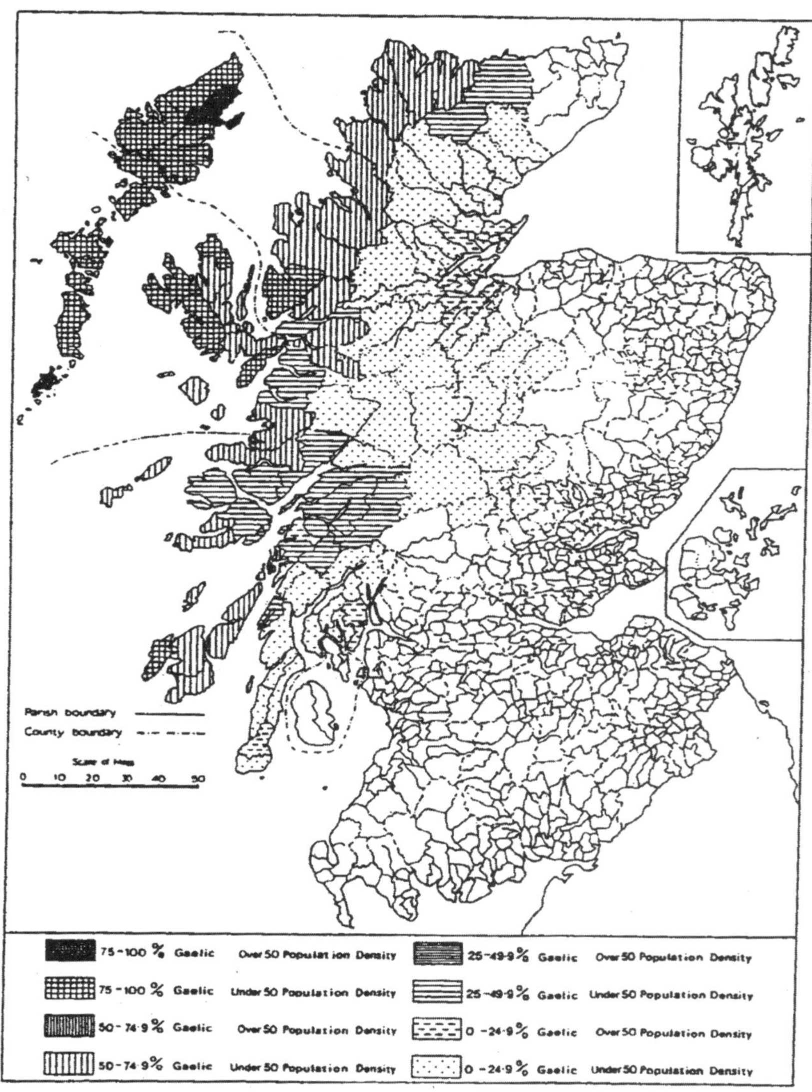

Source: Charles Withers, *Gaelic Scotland 1698–1981,* Routledge Press, 1984

Figure 8.4
Gaelic speaking by parish, 1981

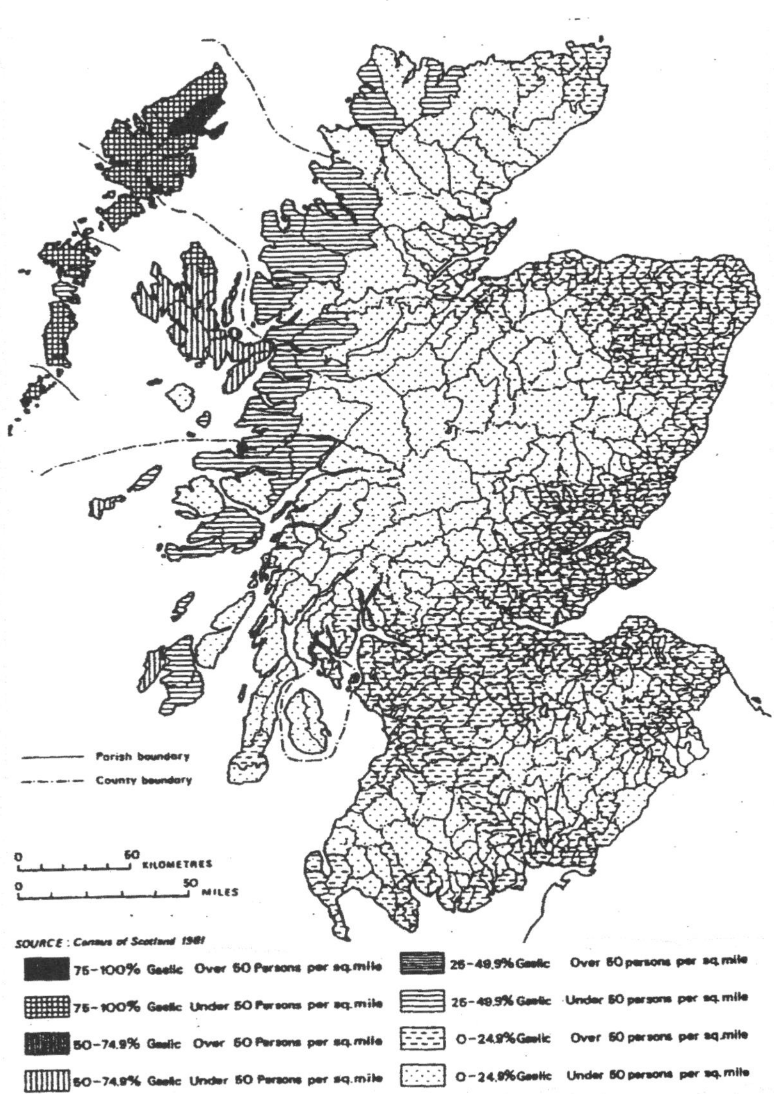

Source: Charles Withers, *Gaelic Scotland 1698–1981*, Routledge Press, 1984

Figure 8.5
Distribution of urban Gaelic speakers, 2001

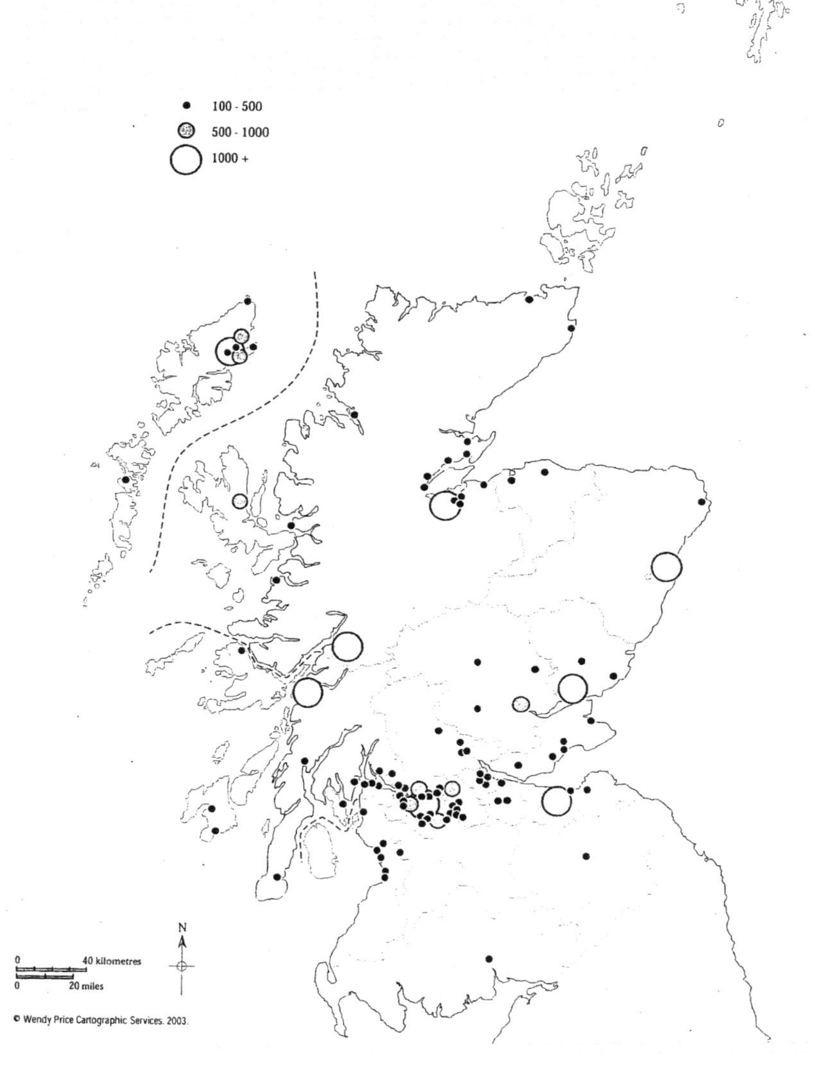

Source: CLI Gaidhlig, Scotland

documented. There is no question that towards 1700 at least, Gaelic was still spoken in districts south of Glasgow, such as Galloway. Clearly, Scots had replaced Gaelic in most of southern Scotland and along the north-eastern seaboard, but not exclusively. It would appear that pockets of Gaelic survived in these regions. These people saw themselves as Scots and Lowlanders, albeit Gaelic-speaking Lowlanders. The exact dimensions of the retreat of Gaelic in the Lowlands are imperfectly known. Gaelic may have been spoken by as many as 500,000–700,000 people in 1740 and, as late as 1900, the Gaelic-speaking districts of the Highlands encompassed half of Scotland, though Gaelic speakers numbered no more than 254,415 in 1891. The clearances and a heavy rate of emigration throughout the 1700s and 1800s clearly lowered the absolute numbers of Gaelic speakers but, geographically, Gaelic was still widely disseminated, even in the early twentieth century. With the First World War came further demographic upheaval as casualties were high among Highland regiments.

Gaelic in the twentieth century

Despite the losses of earlier centuries, Gaelic was still spoken throughout about half of the geographic area of Scotland at the turn of the twentieth century and in most of the traditional Gaedhealtachd. However, during the twentieth century the language suffered some of its most severe attrition. The most recent census, taken in 2001, indicated some 58,652 Gaelic speakers, or 1.21 per cent of the population, down from 65,978 in 1991, or 1.37 per cent and from 254,415, or 6.75 per cent of the population in 1891. Some estimates place the Gaelic-speaking population of Scotland at about 20 per cent in 1800. These recent results contain both good news and bad news for Gaelic. Obviously, such a low figure, not only in the national context but also within the traditional Gaedhealtachd itself, is cause for concern as to whether or not Gaelic can sustain itself for much longer at such low demographic levels. On the positive side, it is evident that the rate of decline of Gaelic has slowed somewhat and that moderate growth in the numbers of urban speakers in places such as Glasgow, Edinburgh and Aberdeen is taking place. This last development is of no small importance. Any future RLS strategy for Gaelic must have an urban base, as well as a traditional one.

Throughout the twentieth century, the decline of Gaelic took place at a moderate rate, unlike Irish in the nineteenth century or Breton in the post-war era. As with Welsh, the 1920s and 1930s saw severe erosion but thereafter the rate of decline seems to have slowed somewhat and in the 1950s over a hundred thousand were still using the language.

Stage-by-stage analysis of current RLS efforts

Stages 8 and 7: Reassembling the language and bringing it to adults, some of whom once learned it and still remember it marginally and others of whom most never acquired it before

Gaelic is a living language and no reconstruction is needed as is the case with some North American Indian tongues. There has, however, been a breakdown of intergenerational language transmission in urban and rural areas, and many adult native speakers, who have ceased to use the language (particularly where the marriage is with a non-Gaelic-speaking partner) in family and community life, still possess fair to fluent speaking ability in the language. Some estimates place the number of people able to understand but not speak Gaelic, in Scotland, in the range of 30,000 to 40,000 (above and beyond the 58,652 Gaelic speakers enumerated in 2001). Hence, like Welsh and Irish, Gaelic has somewhat more depth in Scottish society than the absolute figures would immediately lead one to believe and, by definition, greater potential for advances by an RLS strategy geared towards targeting those with limited speaking capacity but speaking capacity none the less.

We have a fairly good picture of the different dialects of Gaelic, although admittedly our knowledge of the extinct Gaelic dialects of the southern Lowlands which were displaced between 1200 and 1500 is very incomplete indeed.

Traditionally, in Gaelic Scotland, as in Wales and Man, literacy in and learning of the native Celtic tongue was fortified by the use of the Protestant Bible in even the smallest communities and clearly this type of "religious-based" literacy in Gaelic has played a role in the survival of the language until the present (as in Wales), as opposed to the Irish and Cornish cases where English did not encounter much opposition in the field of religious literature. Although during the Reformation in the 1500s many Gaelic books were burned, the language fairly quickly managed to establish a place for itself in the emergent Protestant religious literature and it is to this date that we can credit the establishment of the first authentically Scottish-Gaelic literature, as the local dialects now were written for the first time, in place of the traditional Irish-based standard which had, until this date, been employed throughout Ireland and Gaelic Scotland for over a millennium. It is, however, clear that the Scottish Gaelic dialects, like Manx, must have been divergent from the Irish dialects for some time previous to this date.

There are also many native speakers in the Gaedhealtachd itself who have largely gone over to English, who could yet be recruited back into Gaelic-speaking networks or social groups for adults. Gaelic has many learners and supporters among the non-Gaelic-speaking population, despite traditional stigmas associated with Gaelic. These supporters are a reserve that must be tapped in order to expand the Gaelic-speaking base in the long run.

Generally speaking, however, it is obviously among the English-speaking urban population at large that a greater effort must be made over the next decades with regards to bringing the language to adult learners. This can and must be done in a way that involves larger absolute numbers than has previously been the case. One very recent survey revealed that "32 per cent of respondents were in favour of learning Gaelic", so there is an opportunity among the Scottish population which remains to be addressed but which, nevertheless, offers hope for the future – a situation where far more Scots than many realize, are passive supporters of the language and whose passive support could yet be activated and converted from passive to active support and even usage of Gaelic. Presently, courses for adult learners are available through Comunn na Gàidhlig, Comann an Luchd Ionnsachaidh (CLI), An Comunn Gàidhealach and others. They take the form of correspondence courses, night courses, summer courses, as well as day courses in an increasing number of institutions. It is to be hoped that the newly-established Gaelic Language Board – Bòrd na Gàidhlig will have an impact in this field, as well as others, and will be able to channel badly-needed funds into certain key programmes.

In the above respects, Gaelic essentially occupies a similar position to the other Celtic languages, as well as to other minority languages at large. It has become rather marginalized and limited to rural areas and retains (thus far) only a minor presence on the urban scene.

Stage 6: Establishing the vital linkage with youth, family, neighbourhood and community

As with other languages, this area is crucial for Gaelic. Gaelic-speaking networks, not only for adults but also for families. Before Gaelic can build itself up in higher-order functions, it must first conquer the arena of intergenerational family transmission. As with Irish, Gaelic must also somehow reestablish a presence for itself in the towns and cities of the urban south and east, not just in the rural and remote regions of the northwest. To a limited extent, Gaelic-speaking networks do exist in cities such as Glasgow, Aberdeen, Inverness, Dundee and Edinburgh, where Gaelic speakers and learners gather, either socially or in less structured settings. Indeed, there have been Gaelic-speaking communities in these cities for centuries, as Highlanders migrated to them in search of work. Gaelic, like Welsh, has traditionally been strong in the churches but as church attendance wanes, this area is less and less a safe refuge for Gaelic.

Intergenerational family and community use of any language is difficult to plan and it is still more difficult for fragile minority languages such as Gaelic. As with the other Celtic languages, there are social stigmas attached to the use of Gaelic which must, in the long term, be overcome within Scottish society. These are that "Gaelic is not relevant to modern life" or that "it is a foreign and alien apparition on the Scottish scene". These and many other psychological barriers must be broken down before a campaign can be mounted to restore Gaelic to popular favour and acceptance, a prerequisite for new and successful family, social and community initiatives.

One important new coordinating body on the scene in Scotland is the National Gaelic Parents Association/Comunn nam Parant Naiseanta, which was established in 1994. Among other things, its mandate is to monitor progress in extending Gaelic-medium education. The body has thus far served as an effective link between schools and community regarding extended usage of Gaelic.

Both family and community use must be tackled in the urban arena as well and this will be difficult for Gaelic, for ironically there are now fewer Gaelic speakers residing in places such as Glasgow and Edinburgh than there were a century ago. Due to the limited numbers involved with Gaelic, it may be more realistic to launch Gaelic-speaking networks in the vicinity of new Gaelic-medium schools to be established in the future.

Stage 5: The attainment of literacy, independent of the public education system

Until fairly recently, literacy in Gaelic could *only* be acquired independently of the public education system. Between 1872 and enactment of the Education Act and 1984, when Gaelic-medium education was relaunched, Gaelic was all but excluded from the classroom, both as a medium of instruction and even as a subject of study (which took place but only to a very limited degree and usually at secondary level). Despite the fairly strong historical tradition of Gaelic, literacy weaknesses are apparent in this field today among older speakers, due to the language's long exclusion from this important field. A breakdown of the 1991 figures indicates that only roughly two-thirds of Gaelic speakers were literate in the language. Even worse, only about one-third of children in the present Gaedhealtachd are in Gaelic-medium school units, so there is some question as to whether or not this critical shortcoming is really being tackled in the present. It is certainly an issue which must be tackled in the future. Nevertheless, the figures of literate Gaels would probably be far worse, were it not for the strong tradition in Gaelic Scotland of church literacy among most of the religious sects (Presbyterian, Established, etc.). As in Wales, church-acquired literacy played a role in preserving the native Celtic idiom down to the present day. Not only ministers but most congregation members traditionally acquired and still acquire an ability to read the Bible in Gaelic.[251] Not only have the various churches taught parishioners how to read and write in Gaelic but a majority of churches in the Gaedhealtachd, even today in 2004, still offer church services in Gaelic, thus continuing to provide an important status symbol for an otherwise beleaguered language. For the future, obviously Gaelic language activists cannot rely on the churches alone but, as stated, the situation might be far worse today were it not for this important social bulwark of Gaelic in the past several centuries.

There are various courses available for Gaelic learners. Without doubt one of the areas which must be tackled by bodies such as the new Gaelic Language Board is the establishment of more adult literacy classes, as well as perhaps correspondence courses in Gaelic to cater to the widely dispersed but numerically significant number of persons who would be open to learning Gaelic if the facilities available to do so were there. As stated above, courses for adult learners are presently available through Comunn na Gàidhlig, Comunn an Luchd Ionnsachaidh (CLI), An Comunn Gàidhealach and other groups (correspondence courses, night courses, summer courses etc.). The newly-established Gaelic Language Board, as well as RLS activists at large in Scotland, clearly need to make a breakthrough in this area over the next generation as church-based literacy wanes and the need of parents and community alike for facilities to acquire Gaelic literacy in new, non-traditional urban settings grows.

Stage 4: Education in Gaelic and learning Gaelic at school

If there is one area which truly offers room for hope, it is the RLS arena of Gaelic-medium education (Type 4A schools) particularly at the primary and pre-school levels. Although there is still a long way to go, Gaelic-medium education has clearly made great strides since its (re)establishment in Scotland in the 1980s. At the time of writing, there are now over fifty schools around Scotland which offer Gaelic-medium education in either all-Gaelic establishments or in bilingual streams in English-medium institutions. Perhaps the most important new body in this area is Comhairle nan Sgoiltean Araich – the Gaelic Pre-school Council. Within its first ten years CNSA has established over 140 Gaelic pre-school groups around Scotland, which include over 2,400 children at the time of writing.

In addition, the number of schools offering Gaelic as a subject (Type 4B schools) has tripled since the early 1980s. It is presently at the secondary level of Gaelic-medium instruction that the greatest challenges occur. However, these same difficulties – lack of qualified teachers, insufficient funding, lack of sufficient numbers yet in many areas – are problems that also plague Irish- and Breton-medium schools, as well as those of other minority groups, so it is not an inherently Scottish problem. It is often forgotten that Gaelic, like Manx, was for a very long period employed as the medium of instruction in local religiously administered schools in Gaelic-speaking areas of Scotland until fairly late 1872, to be specific, when the Education Act effectively ushered in a new era of English-only instruction, even in areas where children could not understand English, just as happened in other Celtic countries. There is to some extent a risk in Scotland today that those in the RLS movement may repeat the classic Irish mistake of putting all their eggs in the school education basket in their understandable desire to expand the role of Gaelic in the school system, both as a medium of instruction and as a subject that is taught in the school curriculum.

It remains an area which still needs much expansion. Only about one-third of children in Gaelic-speaking areas are presently attending Gaelic-medium schools, while outside the traditional north-western Gaedhealtachd there is only one completely Gaelic-medium school in all of Scotland (in Glasgow). Clearly, more such schools must be established in other major centres such as Edinburgh, Aberdeen, Inverness, etc. There is room for optimism, however, in the encouraging rise over the past decade of Gaelic-medium pre-school units, which clearly indicates there is a desire for more school services in Gaelic than are presently being offered to parents and children.

In summary, we can say that, as at present, although over 97 per cent of Scottish students are not yet getting exposure to the Gaelic language, whether as a subject or as a means of instruction, the language has clearly made progress in this key area. Generally speaking, the Gaelic RLS movement in Scotland must make headway in the growth of Gaelic-medium schools in both the Gaedhealtachd and the larger urban centres in which are found fairly numerous proactive parents who are open to Gaelic-medium playgroups and education for their children.

Stage 3: Gaelic in the workplace

As with Ireland, English first secured its foothold in the traditionally Gaelic-speaking Highland areas by establishing itself in the towns. By the early 1800s at the latest, English had come to be associated even in Highland minds with commerce, trade and government employment, not to mention the importance English had come to assume regards to overseas emigration to such English-speaking destinations as the United States, Canada and Australia and even internal migration to Lowland towns in search of employment. Although in Canada, Gaelic-language use survived intact on a community basis, the trend even there was clear from the outset.

In Scotland, it is obviously limited in practice to the Gaelic-speaking areas and, even there, seems to take a subordinate role to English, particularly at management levels. Obviously, in more isolated communities where traditional occupations such as fishing, farming and the like dominate, Gaelic is used, but even here English is increasingly intrusive.

In the future, not only the Gaedhealtachd, but urban areas, must be tackled in this respect. Just as Irish cannot in the long run ignore Dublin and Belfast, the very same is true for Scotland. No long-term future for Gaelic can be hoped for unless a greater urban presence is established. In this respect, the Shaw's Road Gaeltacht in Belfast is an example of what must be achieved. It may seem daunting to Gaelic RLSers but unless new Gaelic-speaking urban areas, or at least networks, are established, it is difficult to foresee a breakthrough in the other RLS categories as the traditional Gaelic-speaking heartland continues to contract.

Stage 2: Local governmental services and media

The reality on the ground, even in areas where Gaelic speakers are a majority, is that very few governmental services are available through the medium of Gaelic. Within the Gaelic-speaking areas there is a clear need for more Gaelic-speaking civil servants.

If a more ambitious RLS policy gets under way in Scotland in the future, it is clear that some kind of blueprint, a long-term social plan to train greater numbers of Gaelic-speaking civil servants will be needed, not only for the existing Gaedhealtachd but for any new urban Gaelic-speaking networks which would have an equal need for government services through Gaelic.

In the realm of media, Gaelic has had better luck in the past two decades. BBC Scotland has carried Gaelic-language radio programming since the 1920s. More recently, Radio nan Gaidheal began broadcasting in 1984. Its programme is a mixture of news, music, sports, current affairs and cultural programmes. Initially, the station broadcast only for five hours on the west coast but the service was later extended to all of Scotland. In 1990 the Gaelic Television Committee/Comataidh Telebhisean Gàidhlig was established under the Broadcasting Act. The BBC's Gaelic-language programming includes, like radio, a wide variety of news, sports, current affairs programmes and even a Gaelic soap opera, "Machair". Some 500,000 people periodically tune in to Scotland's Gaelic-language television programmes, a figure far exceeding the country's 58,000 actual Gaelic speakers but perhaps indicative of the numbers of passive but still pro-active supporters of Gaelic, who could yet be mobilized.

As regards printed media, Gaelic-language material is still not plentiful. There is only one Gaelic-medium newspaper at present. However, certain English-language newspapers Gaelic columns.

Although there is not yet a fully Gaelic-language television service in Scotland, such a service in the future will probably be a necessity for a successful RLS campaign in Scotland at large. One would also think that a Gaelic-language daily newspaper and an expanded Gaelic-language presence on the internet would be advisable. Although, as Fishman has already commented, languages such as Basque, for example, cannot realistically hope to compete with Spanish or English in the internet arena. The same could certainly be said of Gaelic and the other Celtic languages.

Stage 1: Gaelic in the higher spheres of work, education and government

Gaelic in Scotland does not hold a strong position in any of these three areas at present. There is some teaching through the medium of Gaelic at some higher institutions of learning but Gaelic has yet to establish or re-establish a working presence for itself in the higher spheres of work, education and government. The three universities in Scotland, at present with the strongest Gaelic-language study programmes, are those of Edinburgh, Glasgow and Aberdeen. Encouragingly, translation facilities are already being established in the new Scottish parliament. A Gaelic Language Bill was passed in November 2004 by Scotland's new, devolved parliament establishing a Bòrd na Gàidhlig that "can require Scottish public authorities to produce and implement Gaelic language plans, and will itself produce a national strategy for Gaelic. It can also provide guidance on Gaelic education."

Recent developments for Gaelic

The role of the Scottish Executive

In 1999 a task force was appointed by the Scottish Executive entitled "Gaelic: Revitalizing Gaelic, a National Asset" to examine the arrangements and structures for the public support of the Gaelic organizations in Scotland, to advise Scottish Ministers on future arrangements, taking account of the Scottish Executive's policy of support for Gaelic as set out in the Programme for Government, and to report by 30 April 2000.

The Scottish Executive and Gaelic

The role of the Scottish Executive is multifaceted but is broadly focused on three areas: broadcasting, education and cultural organizations. In addition, the Executive is committed to achieving secure status for Gaelic and to invest in Sabhal Mor Ostaig, the Gaelic College in Skye.

The budget for 2000–01 was £13.2 million. Out of this allocation £8.5 million was allotted to broadcasting, £2.6 million to education under the specific grants scheme, £605,000 to other educational initiatives, £693,000 to Sabhal Mor Ostaig, and £608,000 to cultural organizations.

Approximately £500,000 is allotted annually by the Scottish Arts Council to projects that are directly or indirectly related to Gaelic. Over the past twenty years there has been an expanded scale of government support for Gaelic. Besides financial support, there have been other encouraging recent developments, including the appointment of a Minister for Gaelic by the Government at Westminster and the continuance of this post by the Scottish Executive, government initiation of and continued support for the Columba Initiative, the first Gaelic debate in the Scottish Parliament, the provision of Gaelic signage and translation facilities in the Parliament building, the appointment of a Gaelic Parliamentary Officer, the start of the project to produce a Gaelic dictionary for use by the Parliament, the establishment of an Inter-Party Parliamentary Committee for Gaelic and the identification of Gaelic education as a National Priority Action Area. A further impetus for development came with the signing by the UK Government of the Council of Europe Charter for Regional or Minority Languages, making provision for the use of Gaelic in defined circumstances in civil proceedings in areas of Scotland where Gaelic speakers form a substantial proportion of the population.

"Gaelic is a precious jewel in the heart and soul of Scotland. It is not constrained within strict boundaries or herded into tight corners. Gaelic is national, European and international. It is fundamental to Scotland; it is not on the periphery or on the fringes. It must be normalized and its rights must be secured." – Alasdair Morrison, MSP, Minister for Gaelic (Debate in Scottish Parliament)

Gaelic in the present

In 1982 came the formation of Comunn na Gàidhlig in order to undertake new initiatives to energise the language. Despite some significant successes, beneath a façade of well-being induced by palliative measures, Gaelic is a critically ill patient on life-support.

Table 8.1

The Gaelic-speaking population of Scotland, 1891-2001

Source: The Celtic Languages, Donald MacCauley

Year	Total Population	Gaelic Speakers	Percentage
1891	4,025,647	254,415	6.75%
1901	4,472,103	230,806	5.16%
1911	4,760,904	202,398	4.25%
1921	4,573,471	158,779	3.47%
1931	4,588,909	136,135	2.9%
1951	5,096,415	95,447	1.87%
1961	5,179,344	80,978	1.5%
1971	5,228,965	88,892	1.7%
1981	5,035,315	82,620	1.6%
1991	4,998,000	65,978	1.37%
2001	5,062,011	58, 652	1.21%

Table 8.2

The growth in Gaelic-medium education between 1991 and 2001

1991	1992	1993	1994	1995	1996	1997	1998	1999	2000	2001
614	824	1080	1260	1456	1587	1736	1816	1831	1862	1859

The statistics tell a story of decline (*see Table 8.1*). The recent census of 2001 revealed the language had fallen to 58,652 speakers. The 1991 census had shown 65,978 Gaelic speakers in Scotland (1.35 per cent of the national population), down from 79,307 in 1981(1.6 per cent) and 210,677 in 1901(5.2 per cent). One frequently hears that the percentage of Gaelic speakers is so low that that any attempt at survival, far less revival, is futile. Less prevalent is the question of why the percentage is so small and what should be done to reverse the decline.

Challenges

The present-day backdrop of Gaelic is that, within an overall ideology of linguistic assimilation and the stranglehold of a dominant language and powerful external forces, Gaelic has been neither an official nor a promoted language. At worst, it was discouraged, sometimes by restrictive legislation including Education Acts, and, at one time, it was even proscribed. At best, it was tolerated by the authorities. The history of the Gaelic language has been a chronicle of dereliction: official negligence; malicious intent; deliberate denial; and, perhaps most damaging of all, benign neglect. The language has suffered from stigmatization and from attrition through outward migration, loss of population and decline of community. But there are encouraging signs that it is no longer being marginalized. Gaelic has an important contribution to make to a socially-inclusive Scotland.

While much is being done by committed and dedicated activists to develop Gaelic, and while significant headway has been made on a number of fronts in recent years, further progress is being quantitatively and qualitatively constrained by lack of resources, lack of focus and lack of language planning. The task force was reminded, by all of the organizations, of the inordinate time and energy they have to expend on raising funds to enable them to remain viable. The situation is compounded by the absence of an overall development policy and helps to nurture and embellish perceptions that the Gaels do not have their act together, that resources are being duplicated, and that public money is not being prudently apportioned or spent. While much of the "Gaelic debate" is candid, open and healthy it occasionally generates more heat than light and the rhetoric sometimes assumes greater importance than the language itself.

"When I think of my tongue being no longer alive in the mouths of men, a chill goes over me that is deeper than my own death, since it is the gathering death of all my kind." – David Malouf, Australian author (1985)

Set against the achievements of lesser-used language communities in other European countries – Wales, Catalonia, Euskadi for example – the level of initiative and provision for Gaelic in Scotland remains startlingly low. While the efforts and accomplishments must be acknowledged and those who spearheaded them applauded, new and bold initiatives are now imperative. A lack of strategy, policy, planning and focus is not the way forward.

There are three basic options confronting Gaelic. The first is to do nothing and let it die quickly. The second is to apply palliative care and delay the demise. The third is radical remedy. If Gaelic is to survive, the third option is the only choice. It's not the easiest option. It requires strong leadership, frank dialogue, sensitive and elegant management, creative vision and a strong institutional structure. The Scottish Executive role in creating and nurturing these features is crucial.

"Ultimately, the issue of Gaelic is not just a Scottish issue. It is an issue of human dignity, of belonging, and of justice." – Comunn na Gàidhlig (Secure Status for Gaelic, December 1997)

Conclusions, recommendations and long-term goals

As we have seen above, Gaelic faces some severe challenges in the twenty-first century, to the point that some question whether promotion or even survival is really even possible. However, the recent census of 2001, despite the decrease it recorded, did indicate an increase in the number of speakers under the age of 14, for the first time in many decades. The numbers of both learners and students in Gaelic-medium schools has increased *(see Fig. 8.7)*. There are actually some indications that the former free-fall of Gaelic is bottoming out and indeed may be reversed over the next two decades, allowing a window of opportunity for a more expanded Gaelic RLS programme over the next several decades. Not only short-term but long-term goals need to be identified and then assigned priority by the RLS movement in Scotland, particularly given its limited financial and human resources. Fishman's old adage of "a bird in hand is worth two in the bush" would be well applied to Gaelic in Scotland today. Clearly, the Gaelic language movement in Scotland possesses limited financial and human resources. They must be concentrated on projects and goals that will yield tangible short-term results and benefits for the language in Scotland today, before larger, more national goals can be pursued.

We have looked at the critical issues which pose a challenge to the survival of Gaelic as a community language in the heartland and they are daunting challenges at that. Proponents of Gaelic RLS need not feel disheartened, however – despite the scale of recent losses revealed by census results over the past several decades. There is at least a new understanding evident in Scotland of the issues that must be tackled, which was not really there prior to the 1980s. As in Ireland, however, Gaelic activists should realize that focusing on the heartland may not be enough any more. In Scotland a breakthrough must be made in urban areas in the next two generations if RLS is to avoid becoming an increasingly academic question, as the rural heartlands will not likely survive the present rate of attrition and contraction for much longer. In Scotland, it is clear that Gaelic activists must somehow establish a presence in the urban south. New Gaelic-speaking communities, or at least networks, simply must be established in Glasgow and Edinburgh, as well as other centres, such as Aberdeen and Inverness. Fishman's advice to the Irish not to ignore the establishment of new, urban-concentrated, family-neighbourhood-community language bases, applies with equal validity to Scotland.

We have seen above how, in Scotland, traditionally, there is a divided tradition with many people not identifying with Gaelic at all. This is a double challenge that RLS movements in Wales and Ireland do not face. This does not make things easy for those who must argue the case for Gaelic, even in the new more Nationalistic Scotland of the twenty-first century. As we have seen, nationalism in Scotland does not necessarily add up to support for Gaelic. Hence, in some ways, Lowland Scotland's rejection of its former Gaelic tradition is reminiscent of the rejection by Navarre of the Basque language and culture, despite the fact that 10 per cent of Navarre's population is still Basque-speaking and the entire province was Basque-speaking as recently as the 1860s.

Thus, in arguing their case for Gaelic, activists must focus on those many Scots of Highland background who do accept Gaelic as part of their identity and, in addition, appeal to those Lowlanders who are favourably disposed towards Gaelic as part of the larger Scottish identity.

Recent developments allow for a cautious note of optimism when we reflect on developments such as the establishment of Bòrd na Gàidhlig, the recent passing of the Gaelic Language Bill, gains in Gaelic-medium education and media, as well as the recent achievement of Scottish devolution itself which has thus far led to some tangible gains for Gaelic, despite scepticism by some Gaelic activists.

Case study proposals and recommendations for Gaelic/An Ghàidhlig

Both long-term and short-term goals

Gaelicization incorporating the principles of Reversing Language Shift.

Specific proposals

This policy of Gaelicization should ultimately entail:

I: the increased Gaelicization of those areas which were until recently mainly Gaelic-speaking (The Gaidhealtachd).

II: the selective establishment of new Gaelic-speaking communities and other Gaelic cultural activities in the towns and cities of the traditionally English-speaking Lowlands (though not the Lowlands as a whole, due to its cultural identity with Scots and English cultural expression).

I) Community

I.i) The establishment of new Gaelic-speaking communities in various areas (initially the larger urban centres but later to be followed by the smaller towns, communities and rural areas of Scotland as a whole) – not only in Highland Scotland but in Lowland Scotland as well, where are to be found many language activists and enthusiasts. New Gaelic-speaking communities are the central tenet of stage 6.

I.ii) The mounting of a publicity campaign aimed at young parents to raise their children in Gaelic and to use Gaelic at home. Again, priority should initially be given to western Scotland but followed shortly thereafter by the urban south, (also stage 6).

I.iii) Learning aids and counselling must be provided to young families who opt to raise their children in Gaelic. Booklets on parenting skills in Gaelic, poems, games for children in Gaelic, prayers, riddles, songs, reading-readiness in Gaelic, etc. Such services and supplies, so necessary in any serious attempt to rebuild family and community life in Gaelic, could best be provided by the new organization recommended above – to coordinate the rebuilding of Gaelic-language use at stage 6.

I.iv) Grandparenting and daycare in Gaelic, free of charge, should be made available all over Scotland, while there is still time to utilize the still-significant number of older Gaelic speakers. Such a service might be co-ordinated by Comunn na Gàidhlig or organizations such as CLI because of their links with adult learners, or even a newly-appointed government body to complement the existing voluntary organizations but, however linkages are established with older native Gaelic speakers, they provide valuable backup for stage 6 efforts in general.

I.v) The establishment of Gaelic-speaking youth groups, ultimately in every community. Youth groups in Gaelic are not merely backup for stage 6 but are an actual part of the process of providing a Gaelic-speaking environment for youth outside of school.

I.vi) A publicity campaign could be mounted to attract Gaelic speakers in England, the US and elsewhere back to the new Gaelic-speaking communities in Scotland. Financial and political constraints are a consideration here, it is true, but the present and past efforts by the Irish Government, for example, to attract Gaelic speakers back to western Ireland did in fact have some success in increasing the Irish-speaking population. Hence, such a stratagem may also secure some success for Scottish-Gaelic, (stage 6).

II) Education

II.i) The continued establishment of new Gaelic-medium schools throughout Scotland. Priority should be given to the western Gaelic-speaking areas where, at present, only a third of primary and secondary school children are enrolled in such schools. Following closely on efforts to reinforce schools in the still Gaelic-speaking districts, should be an even more intensive campaign to launch Gaelic-medium schools in the urban south. Cities such as Glasgow, Edinburgh, Aberdeen, etc. cannot be ignored by Gaelic status planners, particularly as the population of native speakers declines This corresponds to the stage-4 level but is necessary for stage 6 to take root.

II.ii) The establishment of a Gaelic-medium university in the next several decades. It cannot be overstressed how important it is to have such an institution, whether in western Scotland or in the south – where most of the learners and Gaelic enthusiasts are to be found. Efforts to expand Gaelic at university level fall within the range of stage 1 and hence are greatly dependent on the success of earlier efforts at the stage 6 and stage 4 levels.

II.iii)The establishment of summer camps in Gaelic in as many communities as possible, so that Gaelic-language learners everywhere in Scotland have access to summer facilities where they can practise their Gaelic, (this is at the stage 5 level but again is necessary backup).

II.iv)The planned establishment of more Gaelic language classes for adults in more Scottish communities to help expand adult literacy in Gaelic. In Scotland, the number of adult learners is in the thousands. A more co-ordinated and united effort by the language organizations to bring Gaelic to a greater segment of the adult population in Scotland could be mounted, (stages 8 & 5).

III) Media

III.i)The establishment of a daily newspaper in the Gaelic language, perhaps subsidized by the new Scottish Ministry of Culture, (stage 2).

III.ii) The continued expansion of Gaelic on radio and television, with the establishment of an all-Gaelic television service, as opposed to the present limited BBC service. An increase in Gaelic-language broadcasts on other television and radio stations should continue and can help reinforce the position of the language in the media, (stage 2).

IV) The workplace

IV.i) A policy of Gaelicization must be extended to the workplace. A new body to handle status and corpus planning for Gaelic may be the route to follow in assisting organizations, municipalities and private companies which ask for guidance regarding terminology in the Gaelic language. The project by André Lavanant in Brittany to launch new Breton-speaking business enterprises is a good example of what must also be undertaken in Scotland, (stage 3).

V) Political status

V.i) Now that the Gaelic Language Act has been passed, a new clarity should gradually develop, regarding both the legal status of Gaelic and the rights of Gaelic speakers. It is too early to predict how effective the new Bòrd na Gàidhlig will be and how fast the Gaelic language will penetrate into public life and the civil service in particular. At any rate an official admission has been made that Gaelic language planning is important. The conferring of an official, legislative status to the language will certainly expedite the implementation of the recommendations listed above.

References

Ball, Martin J. (2002) *The Celtic Languages,* London, Routledge Press.

Borgstrom, C. H. (1937) "The Dialect of Barra in the Outer Hebrides", pp.71–242, *The Dialects of the Outer Hebrides*, Oslo, Aschehoug.

Dorian, N. C. (1978) *East Sutherland Gaelic*, Dublin Institute For Advanced Studies.

Durkacz, Victor (1983) *The Decline of The Celtic Languages*, Edinburgh, John Donald.

Jackson, K. H. (1953) "Common Gaelic", *Proceedings of the British Academy*, No. 37, pp.71–97.

MacCauley, Donald (ed.) (1983) *The Celtic Languages*, Cambridge University Press.

MacDonald, K. (1986) "Scots Loanwords in the Gaelic Vocabulary of Applecross", *Scottish Language* no., pp.120–5.

MacLeod, M. (1963) "Gaelic in Highland Education", *Transactions of the Gaelic Society of Inverness*, pp.305–334.

MacLeod, Iseabail (1995), "Scotland; A Linguistic Double-Helix", EBLUL pp.12–18.

Shaw, W. (1978*) An Analysis of The Gaelic Language*, England, Menston Scholar Press.

Ternes, E. (1973*) The Phonetic Analysis of Scottish Gaelic*, Hamburg, Helmut Buske Verlag.

Wainwright, F. T. (1955) *The Problem of The Picts*, Edinburgh, Thomas Nelson and Sons, Ltd.

Withers, C. W. J. (1979) "The Language Geography of Scottish-Gaelic", *Scottish Literary Journal* (Language Supplement), pp.41–54.

Withers, Charles (1988) *Gaelic Scotland, The Transformation of a Culture Region,* London, Routledge Press.

iv.) Reversing Language Shift – Gaelic in Nova Scotia

Diarmuid Ó Néill

THE USE OF SCOTTISH-GAELIC in Nova Scotia dates to the mid-1700s when the first Gaels arrived from Scotland. Eastern Nova Scotia came to be the most important and long-lasting linguistic colony established in Canada, although it is often forgotten that Gaelic continued as a community language in use for many generations in other provinces, such as Ontario, Québec, New Brunswick and Prince Edward Island. Indeed, at the time of Canadian confederation in 1867, Scottish-Gaelic, after English and French, was the third-largest language in Canada, with over 200,000 speakers. In addition, Irish was widely spoken at this time by a significant minority of the immigrant Irish population in nineteenth-century Canada, giving Canadian society a Gaelic flavour not seen before or since.[252] In fact, in the 1871, 1881 and 1891 Canadian censuses, Irish and Scottish immigrants were more numerous than people of English, French or United States origin. Broadly speaking, despite the often tragic circumstances of the Highland Clearances in Gaelic Scotland, the Scottish and Gaelic experience in Canada has been a distinctly positive one. From the start, Canadian authorities welcomed and encouraged Highland immigration as a way to populate the severely under-populated British colonies in North America during the late 1700s and 1800s. So, while it is true many Highland Gaels departed their lands under duress during the 1700s, many departures for Canada by the early 1800s were increasingly being made willingly and hopefully, in the expectation of improving one's lot economically.

Figure 9.1
Gaelic in Nova Scotia, 1901

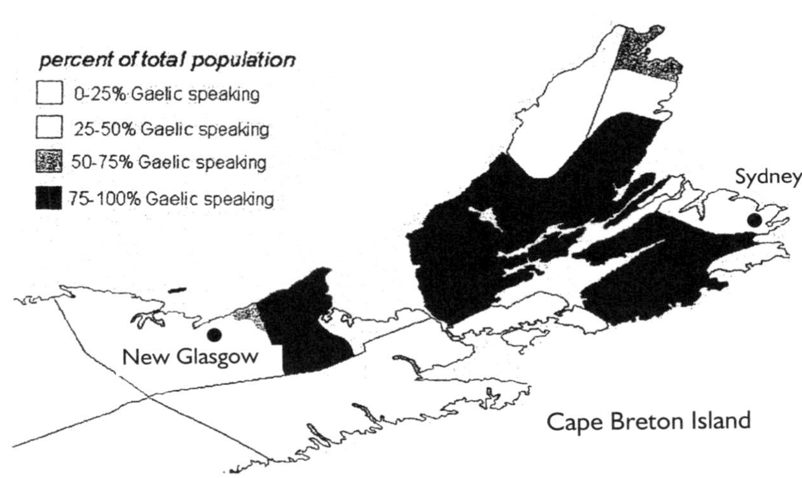

Figure 9.2
Gaelic in Nova Scotia, 1932

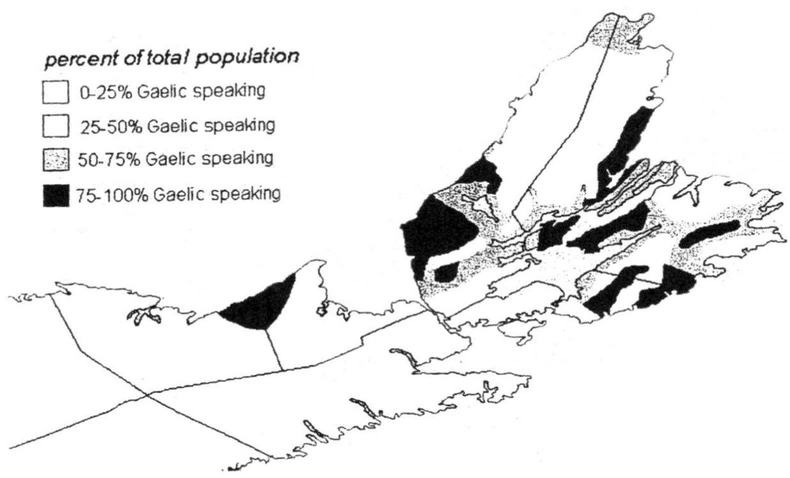

Figure 9.3
Distribution of Gaelic speakers by age group and residence, 1951

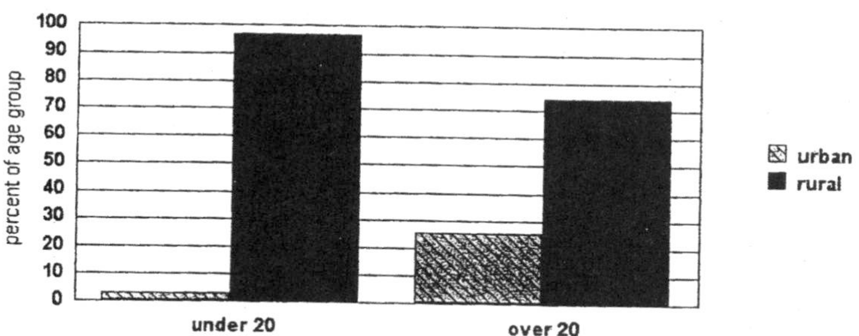

Figure 9.4
Distribution of Gaelic speakers vs total population, 1951

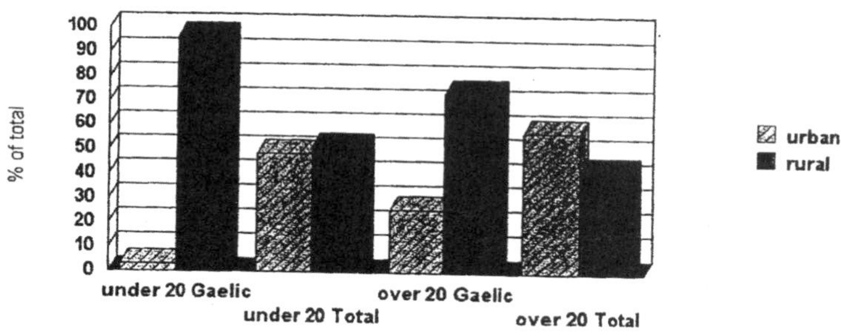

Figure 9.5
Gaelic and French in Nova Scotia, 1871-1991

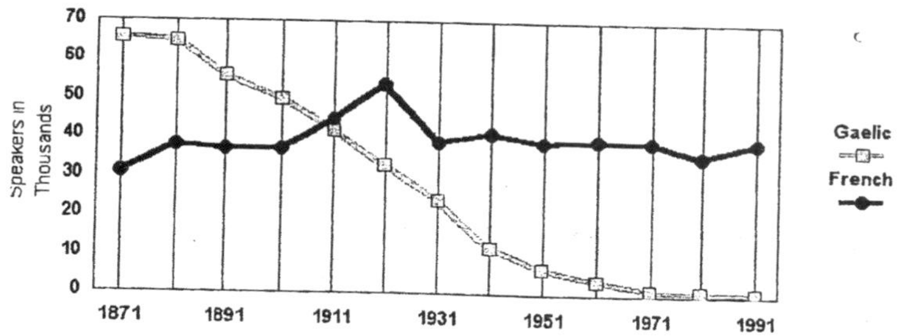

1871-1891 and 1911 estimated for both languages
1921 estimated for Gaelic

In the case of Nova Scotia, most of the Acadian French population was expelled in the mid-1700s to Louisiana and North and South Carolina, opening up new land for colonists from Britain and New England. A significant number of United Empire Loyalists arrived in Nova Scotia after 1780 from the newly created United States, and were joined by successive waves of Germans and Gaelic-speaking immigrants from the Scottish Highlands, adding to the small number of French who remained along with the Native Indian Micmac tribe. A wave of Irish immigrants in the 1840s and 1850s added further to the province's mosaic.

With the exception of the French Acadian population, however, no group was as successful in maintaining its linguistic cohesion as the Highland Gaelic-speaking community, for so long or for so many generations. Gaelic has been spoken in Nova Scotia as an indigenous language continuously from the late 1700s to the present day. Some 80,000–100,000 Gaelic speakers (or one third of the province's population) dwelt in Nova Scotia in the late 1800s. Gaelic is a language in Nova Scotia whose patrimony is not questioned, unlike in Lowland Scotland today (as late as 1931 there were an estimated 25,000 Gaelic speakers, though this would fall to 7,000 by 1951). Add to this the high esteem in which Gaelic is held by even the Conservative political and economic establishment in the province and one could cautiously say that there is probably the potential for an almost Irish-style enshrinement of the language in the symbolic political life of the province, although only 542 Gaelic speakers were recorded in 1991 (and 415 in 2001). Whether or not a Gaelic RLS movement in Nova Scotia could move beyond the tokenism of the Irish Free State of the 1920s, to real restoration, is another question, but clearly there are some opportunities here. There is in fact real reason for optimism in Nova Scotia. In November 2002 the Government of Nova Scotia released the Gaelic Nova Scotia Report which looked at Gaelic cultural traditions in Nova Scotia, as well as the status of the Gaelic language in Nova Scotia and how to improve it.

Perhaps most inspiring for Gaels in the province was the announcement on May 31, 2004 by the Minister for Culture, of $100,000 of funding and a twenty-year programme to promote and revive Gaelic in Nova Scotian society, which raises the issue of possibly enhanced legal status for the language and many other dramatic proposals for the language. The new development strategy is examined below.

Stage-by-stage analysis of current RLS efforts

Stages 8 and 7: Reassembling the language and bringing it to adults, some of whom once learned it and still remember it marginally and others of whom never acquired it before

The living language still exists, although among a small minority of the population. There is no need to reconstruct the language, although most native speakers are elderly. Some linguists speak of a Nova Scotia dialect but it would appear that several dialects of Scottish Gaelic survived the crossing from Scotland; however, this was never a problem since, even in Scotland, the dialects have always remained close enough to ensure mutual comprehension.

Despite the failure of Gaelic to achieve any kind of formal recognition in Nova Scotia or Canada during the 1800s or thereafter, there is a long tradition of Gaelic media in Nova Scotia. From the early 1800s onwards, Gaelic has always been present in the printed media and, for periods, dailies in the language existed. Fairly extensive recordings of the Nova Scotia Gaelic dialects have been made and are on record. As far as bringing the language to adult learners, this is done, not only through evening and correspondence courses coordinated through various school-based initiatives, but also through the Gaelic College at St Anne's in Cape Breton. For any future RLS planning in Nova Scotia it is clear that something more methodical would be needed, in order to achieve the critical mass that is, at present, missing. One possibility would be a campaign directed at those adults who already possess some Gaelic (as well as those who don't) to take part in programmes which promote at least some limited use of Gaelic among adults in certain settings (possibly pub nights, as in Ireland and Brittany).

Stage 6: Establishing the vital linkage with youth, family, neighbourhood and community

Although only 542 Gaelic speakers were enumerated in the province in 1991 and 415 in 2001, it is clear that there are at least 1,500 active learners and past learners with a limited-to-passive command of the language, as well as many more thousands of sympathisers with the language in the province of one million, whose passive goodwill towards Gaelic clearly could be activated. Due to the fact that there are no more than several hundred mainly elderly native Gaelic speakers left in Nova Scotia, any community-based initiatives would literally have to start from scratch and would have to rely heavily on learners, which need not rule out eventual success. If RLS activists and planners in Nova Scotia find the concept of a new urban Gaedhealtachd too daunting, then the concept of new Gaelic-speaking networks in the vicinity of Gaelic-medium schools could theoretically allow Gaelic speakers, parents and children alike, to maximise the advantage of their proximity to one another. It is difficult to see at this point how such an initiative could be mounted anywhere outside of either Halifax or Cape Breton Island itself. Although, as outlined below, such province-wide RLS initiatives may be necessary in the case of Nova Scotia Gaelic, due to the now much-changed demography of the province.

Such community initiatives would have to be actively supported by language enthusiasts with some government backing, who see their identity linked to Gaelic, although they are no longer Scottish but rather Canadian. This would not likely be much of an obstacle, as in Nova Scotia, Gaelic has been less stigmatized than the other Celtic languages and tends to be regarded with respect by even establishment figures.

At the time of writing, no serious efforts in Nova Scotia towards planning for stage 6 have yet been undertaken, however it is clear from the Gaelic Nova Scotia Report and the recently announced Development Plan for Gaelic that there are those who are giving serious thought towards future community initiatives. Governmental and community initiatives aimed at addressing stage-6 issues have not yet occurred but this is likely to change in the future, particularly if the Report is acted upon. It is clear that initial emphasis in Gaelic RLS efforts in Nova Scotia would have to be placed on establishing more extensive young adult fluency (stage 7) in certain areas. This would be a necessary precondition for any stage 6 initiatives which could, nevertheless, still be mounted in Nova Scotia, provided they set realistic goals – such as Gaelic-speaking networks in proximity to any Gaelic-medium schools that are established, rather than new Gaelic communities, which may be too ambitious a goal at this point.

Stage 5: The attainment of literacy, independent of the public education system

In Nova Scotia, as in Gaelic Scotland, a strong tradition of church-based literacy in Gaelic kept the language alive in cultural circles and the media for many generations, despite its near-total exclusion from the schools. At present, about 1,500 students and adults are studying Gaelic – but a greater effort must be made to tie-in these efforts to school literacy and actual community use of the language in order for any future RLS agenda to take hold. As mentioned above, the Gaelic College on Cape Breton is one place which is already promoting Gaelic literacy for adults outside the regular school system. One wonders if the Cornish example might not be relevant here. In Cornwall, as in Nova Scotia, schools in the local Celtic medium are still absent from the scene but Cornish is offered after regular hours at many schools. Until a more thoroughgoing programme to teach adult literacy in Nova Scotia is launched, local schools might be more effectively used to teach literacy in Gaelic to larger numbers of adults at evening classes.

Stage 4: Education in Gaelic

As early as 1879 there were calls in Nova Scotia's parliament to introduce Gaelic into the schools of the province, however it was not permitted as a subject until 1921. This was in response to a petition in 1920 requesting use of the language in schools. The success of the 1920 petition seems to have strengthened the resolve of Gaelic activists somewhat, for by the 1930s calls for a greater Gaelic presence in the schools were becoming more determined and emphatic. By 1938 Gaelic was a recognized subject in Sydney Academy with an enrolment of 50 students. Also in 1938 the Cape Breton County Council adopted the following resolution;

"Now therefore be it resolved that the legislature be urged to provide for the maintenance of a Gaelic teacher in connection with the Normal School at Truro; and thus enable students preparing for the teaching profession to acquire a knowledge of Gaelic for the purpose of teaching it in the schools. Also that Gaelic be prescribed on the curriculum of the evening school for adults."

It is clear from the strident attempts being made throughout the late 1800s and early 1900s to secure a place for Gaelic in the education system, that Nova Scotia society was trying to address the issue of a language which was still very much a reality in the everyday life of the province but which had not secured formal recognition from the English-oriented establishment. These efforts clearly continued well after 1931 when the census indicated Gaelic was rapidly yielding ground to English on all fronts. Indeed, the fact that the 1879 appeal to the Nova Scotia parliament for Gaelic in the schools was actually made in Gaelic, implies that the language was widely spoken in the halls of the parliament in Halifax.

Today, despite the demographic losses of the last half-century, Gaelic is increasingly offered in schools as a regular subject and is also taught through adult-orientated correspondence and summer courses. It has yet to achieve the critical mass, however, that would be necessary among adult learners so as to re-establish the language among other age groups in the population.

Establishing a place for Gaelic-medium education in the present education system is a daunting task. It is a necessary one, however. Efforts to establish Gaelic-medium education are of paramount importance to any successful RLS efforts at stage 6, as well as other critical stages of language renewal in Nova Scotia. It is interesting to note that, traditionally, just as in Celtic countries in Europe, there was also a stigma attached to the Gaelic language's continued use in Nova Scotia society as the twentieth century progressed. This author recalls, several years ago, listening to a native Gaelic speaker being interviewed on CBC television, describing how, when he was attending the local Catholic Primary school during the 1930s, the nuns told him and other students that "they were not good Canadians" because they had continued to use Gaelic despite repeated warnings.

For the immediate future, no new Gaelic-medium type 4A schools are anticipated in Nova Scotia but this could change, as stated above. Such schools, beginning from nursery level through primary and secondary level (as we are seeing happen today in Scotland, the Isle of Man and elsewhere), would be a necessity for any serious RLS programme in Nova Scotia. The announcement on 31 May, 2004 of a new twenty-year initiative for Gaelic specifically addresses the need both for more Gaelic pre-school units, and for more schools offering Gaelic as a subject.

Stage 3: Gaelic in the worksphere

Although Gaelic was, of course, widely employed in the worksphere in

Nova Scotia in the early twentieth century and sporadically even into the 1950s (particularly in the fishing industry but also the logging industry), it has now been many decades since this was the case. There are rare cases where the language is still employed in educational institutions and even in some types of tourist-based businesses but otherwise, Gaelic has now effectively ceased to be used in the workplace in Nova Scotia. On a positive note, however, the Gaelic Nova Scotia Report enlarges at length on the potential for improving tourism and the economy at large in Nova Scotia, through attracting both tourists and Nova Scotians to Scottish- and Gaelic-oriented summer events and year-round events as well. The Report clearly foresees a more prominent role for Gaelic than is presently the case.

Stage 2: Local governmental services and media

At present, virtually no services in Gaelic are provided by any level of government in Nova Scotia. With regard to media, perhaps not surprisingly, due to the large Gaelic-speaking population of Canada during the 1800s, many books and even newspapers in Gaelic did come into existence, particularly in Nova Scotia but also Ontario. From 1892 to 1904 a Gaelic-language weekly, *Mac-Talla*, was printed in Nova Scotia. Many others came and went, *Mosgladh* (by the Scottish Catholic Society), *Teachdar nan Gàidheal* in Sydney, and several others. There has been and continues to be a limited presence on radio. Right now, there is only one Gaelic-language programme on radio. Should any earnest RLS programme ever be mounted in Nova Scotia, it goes without saying that greater, radio and television coverage in Gaelic would have to be included in public broadcasting, directed at both adult and student learners. It is worth saying that a Gaelic-language monthly for Nova Scotia would not be an impossible first step, if subsidized by the government. In fact, it is food for thought for Gaelic activists to suggest that *Mac-Talla* might be relaunched as a monthly or weekly initially, and perhaps later expanded to a daily if circumstances allow.[253]

Stage 1: Gaelic in the higher spheres of work, education and government

It is premature to discuss the introduction of Gaelic into any level of government administration, as the lower-order functions of the language, such as its greater concentrated use in the family-neighbourhood and school arenas, must be tackled first. In the realm of higher education, however, there are clearly opportunities in the present. St Francis Xavier University in Antigonish (established in 1853) clearly has the pre-eminent Gaelic programme in the province and this has been the case all along (it presently has about 200 students in its Gaelic programme). Both it and Dalhousie University in Nova Scotia offer the language as a subject and continue to have little difficulty in locating students who are interested in studying the language. If Gaelic were to be expanded as a medium of instruction at university level in Nova Scotia, it would have to be done within one of the existing universities in the manner of a "bilingual stream", as the idea of a fully Gaelic-medium university in Nova Scotia is unrealistic at this point.

Greater funding for Gaelic programmes began to become available in the 1970s and, in addition, under the Trudeau administration in the 1970s and 1980s the language clearly had a friend in Allan MacEachan who was a leading minister in the Trudeau administration, and also a native Gaelic speaker from Nova Scotia who was well aware of the institutional and financial difficulties faced by the language, and who personally intervened for Gaelic-friendly initiatives on many occasions. His enthusiasm for the language was, and is, entirely typical of the attitude of Nova Scotians of all social rank who wish the language well and want to see it live, even if they are at a loss as to just how this may best be done. It is this natural interest and enthusiasm for the language by all Nova Scotians which must be tapped into and utilized in any future co-ordinated RLS effort in Nova Scotia.

Conclusions and recommendations

The position of Gaelic in Nova Scotia today, can only be described as serious. With only 542 mainly ageing native speakers enumerated in 1991 and fewer still in the ambiguous 2001 Canadian census (which lumped Irish and Gaelic together across Canada), the prospects for the language's continued transmission appear bleak for the twenty-first century (it would appear that, as of 2001, there were 415 fluent Gaelic speakers in Nova Scotia, with 55 located in Halifax). Any successful programme of Gaelic restoration in Nova Scotia rests squarely on strengthening the language at stages 8 and 7 initially but followed closely by further implementation at stages 6, 4A and 4B. Only then could any efforts be mounted at the higher-order levels of government, media and education.

Table 9.1
Canadian census information about Gaelic, Welsh and Breton in Canada in the census years of 1996 and 2001
Source: Statistics Canada

	1996	2001
Speakers of Celtic Lang.	3,980	3,850
Speakers of Gaelic Lang.	2,170	2,155
Speakers of Welsh	1,665	1,615
Speakers of Breton	105	60
Gaelic in Nova Scotia	410	415
Gaelic in Halifax	50	55
Gaelic in Ontario	840	720
Gaelic in Toronto	395	270

Gaelic Nova Scotia 2002–04: a dramatic turn for the better

Gaelic Nova Scotia Report – November 2002

31 May, 2004 – Announcement of a new 20-year Gaelic Development Strategy

Recent developments offer not only cause for hope but even for real language restoration in Nova Scotia. First, came the release in November of 2002 of a study commissioned in 2000 by the government of Nova Scotia which was entitled “Gaelic Nova Scotia: An Economic, Cultural, and Social Impact Study”. It takes stock of Gaelic resources in Nova Scotia. Also, the government began a series of public consultations on various cultural issues, including the Gaelic language. The present Minister of Culture, Rodney MacDonald, who budgeted over $20,000 for the study, certainly did more for Gaelic than any previous minister. Second, came the announcement on 31 May 2004 by the Minister of Culture of a new twenty-year development plan for Gaelic in the province. The minister also pledged $100,000 in funding towards Gaelic-language programmes. This is a dramatic development whose potential impact on Gaelic in the province cannot be overstated. It is treated in a more detailed manner below. To a certain degree, the present state of Gaelic in Nova Scotia is almost reminiscent of Manx Gaelic about two decades ago. This can be said because the language in Nova Scotia still retains hundreds of native speakers and clearly has the potential passive support of many thousands of others. Might it not be possible to establish a Gaelic Language Unit in Nova Scotia along the lines of the Manx Gaelic Language Unit established in the past decade? Such an undertaking would require the appointment of a Gaelic Language Officer or, as is now being proposed, a Minister for Gaelic Affairs in the Nova Scotia cabinet to coordinate efforts for Nova Scotia, as was done in the Isle of Man. The Cornish are preparing to follow the Manx example and appoint a Cornish Language Officer with a fairly extensive mandate. This author thinks that such an initiative in Nova Scotia would be greeted with enthusiasm and real support from Gaelic-lovers and government alike. Not least because, as stated, Gaelic in Nova Scotia is held in high esteem by the "establishment" to a greater degree than is the case even in some segments of Scottish society. In addition, the Manx example is a realistic and pertinent example of how a small but effective unit can actually achieve a lot and get programmes started which later lead to larger widespread endeavours, as was the case with Manx when it spread rapidly throughout the island's schools and is now branching out further into other realms of society.

The Nova Scotia of 2004 is, of course, radically different from the Nova Scotia of the mid-1800s and Gaelic activists have to bear this in mind as they go about status planning for any RLS strategy in Nova Scotia. Apart from the fact that Nova Scotia had a population of 943,000 in the 2001 census, as opposed to 331,000 in the 1861 census, the population today is far more urban than in the earlier period. Many who immediately think of Cape Breton Island as the ideal staging ground for a spiritual rebirth of Nova Scotia Gaelic overlook the fact that the population of Cape Breton is only about one third of what it was in 1901. Gaelic Nova Scotia, like Gaelic Scotland, underwent a certain amount of depopulation as out-migration in the early 1900s to Halifax, Boston and the mills of New England drained the heartland of Gaelic speakers. Clearly, Gaelic RLS in Nova Scotia must encompass Halifax and indeed all of Nova Scotia, not just the traditional eastern bastions of the language in the province. Further, while some one third of the population in 1861 spoke Gaelic and, even as late as the 1890-1910 period, at least a quarter of Nova Scotia's population likely had some command of Gaelic, this is not the case today and any Gaelic RLS strategy is starting from a far smaller base. So long as the goals entertained are realistic, the recently announced RLS strategy for Gaelic in Nova Scotia could work and it most certainly can improve the state of Gaelic in the province.

On 31 May, 2004 Rodney MacDonald, the Minister for Culture announced on Cape Breton Island a $100,000 package of funding over a twenty-year period for Gaelic in the province. The development plan is called "Developing and Preserving Gaelic in Nova Scotia: Strategy for a Community-Based Initiative". Among other things, the Minister announced ambitious plans for an eventual legally enhanced status for the language, possible establishment of a Minister for Gaelic in the provincial cabinet, as well as establishment of pre-school Gaelic units in the province, the expansion of the language in the schools and the promotion of Feisean – community celebrations of Gaelic culture. The Minister commented that "although Scottish-Gaelic is in a perilous state in the province", he is "confident the trend can be reversed".[254]

The new development plan for Gaelic in the province could mark a new threshold for the language and for RLS in the province as a whole, if carried through. It clearly aspires to an eventual restoration of Gaelic to widescale everyday community use, establishment of Gaelic-medium schools, use in the civil service, as well as some degree of legal and official status in the province. To non-Canadians this might sound radical but one must live in Canada with its strong bilingual tradition (English/French) and multicultural value system to comprehend that, in Canada, this is really not radical at all. In addition, Nova Scotia is located right beside New Brunswick, a bilingual province with a French-speaking population of about 44 per cent, while in Nova Scotia itself about 12 per cent of the population is of French origin. In fact, for many generations it has often stuck in the craw of Scottish Canadians that the French language and culture were legally enshrined in both the British North America Act and then the Canadian constitution, while Scottish Gaelic had never achieved any legal recognition even in Nova Scotia where it was, and still is, a daily language of the community. Readers should be aware that attempts were made to secure recognition for Gaelic, not only provincially in Nova Scotia but also nationally on a Canadian level. The most famous, but by no means the only attempt, was made by Senator Thomas MacInnis in 1890 when he introduced his unsuccessful Bill in the Canadian Parliament to have Gaelic recognized as an official language in Canada alongside English and French.

Returning to the new development proposal announced by Culture and Heritage Minister Rodney MacDonald on May 31, 2004, the Minister joined the Gaelic Council of Nova Scotia, representatives from the province's Gaelic community and the Scottish organization, Bòrd na Gàidhlig, to officially release the community-based initiative.[255] "Although we have a long road to travel, today we are putting a sail to the mast," said Mary Jane Lamond, co-chair of the Gaelic Council of Nova Scotia. "We view the development and maintenance of our language skills and cultural events as significant assets to our communities' social and economic future well-being." The council has started work on developing Gaelic resources both locally and in terms of Gaelic-language development internationally. Throughout the community consultations, Lamond noted, people felt there wasn't enough Gaelic cultural content in school. She added that the Department of Education offer a Gaelic Institute for teachers in July at Dalbrae Academy in Mabou. The participants have a chance to gain knowledge of Gaelic art, language and culture which they share with their students province-wide. Considering the importance of the Gaelic resource in the province, the Gaelic Council has requested a minister for Gaelic affairs be established immediately. Council co-chairman Lewis MacKinnon said the release was a great beginning: "We are looking forward to developing links and partnerships with the broader community. This is an exciting time." Hector MacNeil, chairman of the Gaelic Development Steering Committee, said one of the impediments to development of Gaelic in Nova Scotia had been the lack of consensus on how to move forward. "People were working in different communities but without a unified consensus. Today, with the strategy document, we have that consensus and a direction forward." He added that there would be problems and challenges. "The job of the implementation committee will be to put together working groups. These groups will address the various issues brought forward by the community through the consultation process. Issues such as education and how Gaelic is perceived locally and in larger communities. Also, the need for places for Gaelic in our communities where people can speak and live Gaelic." Allison MacKenzie, coordinator of Feis an Eilein in Christmas Island, said the strategy showed government was listening to the wishes of communities. "We've helped illustrate that Gaelic is valuable socially and economically with the Feis in Christmas Island. Also, that pride of place is important and Gaelic is critical to the future of Cape Breton and Nova Scotia. We have a distinct place in the world. We've always known this and now, with this strategy, others will as well." MacKenzie is hopeful there will be increased Gaelic learning materials and help to acquire instructors. Emily Redden, a Grade-11 student at Rankin School in Iona, stressed that with, the absence of Gaelic development, Cape Breton was in danger of being erased from the map of Celtic cultures. Redden, who is a member of the Rankin Gaelic Club, said the work to preserve Gaelic in Nova Scotia should keep youth in mind.

In the public announcement of the new Gaelic initiative which was carried by most Canadian media, including the national newspapers and the CBC, the Gaelic Steering Committee outlined three items of particular importance: i.) the vision, ii.) the mission statement, iii.) the goals of the Gaelic Development Plan For Nova Scotia 2004.

i.) **The Vision**: Our Gaelic language and culture thrive in Nova Scotia. Those things we value are maintained in each community because Gaelic lives.

ii.) **The Mission Statement**: To create an environment that makes Nova Scotia a place where Gaelic language and culture thrive.

iii.) **The Goals**:

1) to increase the number of Gaelic speakers
2) to preserve, maintain, and develop the Gaelic language and culture
3) to encourage and promote all forms of Gaelic cultural expression
4) to strengthen Gaelic communities
5) to develop a place where people can live and work in Gaelic
6) to instil pride and self-confidence within the Gaelic community.
7) to increase public appreciation of Gaelic culture
8) to base the development of Gaelic language and culture in local communities with the support of municipal, provincial, and federal governments.

9) to achieve secure status for the Gaelic language under law in Nova Scotia.

In summary, there we have it: a dynamic, exciting and inspiring example of RLS strategy for Gaelic in Nova Scotia which appears well thought-out and ambitious, considering the daunting obstacles the language faces in the province. It is not, however, all that surprising to those who have encountered Nova Scotia Gaels who clearly and rightly regard their language as entitled to a life and a future equal to any other in Canada.[256]

Notes

At the time of writing, one of the most invaluable sources of information to be had for any student of Gaelic in Nova Scotia is the *Gaelic Nova Scotia Curatorial Report* Number 97, finally published in December of 2002 by the Museum of Nova Scotia, particularly as it deals not only with past-tense scenarios but lays stress on where future initiatives must lie.

Another equally valuable reader for Gaelic students is *Options For The 1990s; Community Initiatives For Gaelic Language and Cultural Development in Nova Scotia*, (Sydney, Cape Gael Cooperative, 1989)

Further suggested reading is *Gaelic in Nova Scotia: Opportunities; The Potential for Gaelic Development in Nova Scotia*, (Halifax, Nova Scotia Gaelic Council Submission to the Department of Education, 1997).

References

(In addition to those listed under Scotland)

Coady, Moses (1939) *Masters of Their Own Destiny. The Story of The Antigonish Movement of Adult Education Through Economic Co-operation*, London, Harper.

Collins, Julie (2004) "New Initiative For Gaelic", *Cape Breton Post*, 31 May.

Cox, Lorraine Vitale (1994) "Gaelic and schools in Nova Scotia", *Nova Scotia Historical Review*, No. 14, 1994, pp.20–40.

Edwards, John R. (1984) *Multilingualism*, London, Routledge.

Kelly, James Colin (1980) "A Socio-geographic Study of Gaelic in Cape Breton." M.A. Thesis, St Francis Xavier University.

Kennedy, Michael (2000) *The Gaelic Nova Scotia Report*, the Government of Nova Scotia (Curatorial Report No. 97).

MacKinnon, Kathleen Lamont (1964) "A Short Study of the History and Traditions of the Highland Scots in Nova Scotia", M.A. Thesis, St Francis Xavier University.

MacKinnon, Kenneth (1975) *Cape Breton Gaeldom in Cross-Cultural Context: The Transmission of Ethnic Language and Culture*, England, Hatfield Polytechnic.

MacNeil, Joe Neil, trans. and ed. by John Shaw (1987) *Sgeul gu Latha (Tales Until Dawn), The World of a Cape Breton Gaelic Story Teller,* Montreal, McGill–Queens University Press.

Sinclair, D. M. (1950) "Gaelic in Nova Scotia", *Dalhousie Review* XXX (Oct.).

v.) The case of Manx Gaelic/ *Yn Ghailckagh*

Brian Stowell

Manx Language Foreword

TA CHENGEYDERYN CUMAADAGH dy mennick gra dy vel y Ghaelg, chengey ghooie Ellan Vannin, "marroo" ny "anvio" as ad coontey dy dooar ee baase ec y traa cheddin as y shenn loayrtagh dooghyssagh s'jerree ayns 1974. Agh ta'n meenaghey shoh jeh baase chengey ro choon, er yn oyr erskyn ooilley dy row rieau sleih ayn dynsee yn Ghaelg dy flaaoil myr y nah hengey oc. Ayns ny feed ny jeih as feed blein hie shaghey er y gherrid, ta'n chengey er ny aavioghey dy mooar, son y chooid smoo lesh cooney argidoil veih Reiltys Ellan Vannin. T'ee goll er ynsaghey ayns ny scoillyn, as, ny smoo scanshoil foast, ta gleashaght possan-cloie Gaelgagh ayn. Ayns 2002, hie ny fraueyn jeh bunscoill Ghaelgagh er cuirr. Hoilshee yn coontey-pobble s'jerree dy vel yn earroo dy Ghaelgeyryn er nirree dy mooar, as keeadane mooar jeu shid nuy bleeaney jeig dy eash as ny sloo.

English Language Foreword

Conservative linguists often describe Manx Gaelic, the native language of the Isle of Man, as "dead" or "extinct", marking the death by the demise of the last old native speaker in 1974. However, this is too narrow a definition of language death, particularly since Manx Gaelic has never lacked a body of people who have learned to speak it fluently as a second language. In the last twenty to thirty years, the language has undergone a significant revival, largely funded recently by the Government of the Isle of Man. It is taught in schools and, more significantly still, there is a Manx language play-group movement. In 2002, an embryonic Manx-medium primary school was set up. The most recent census revealed a big increase in the number of Manx Gaelic speakers, with a large percentage of these being aged nineteen and under.

Manx Gaelic: Its past, present, and future

Historical Introduction

Manx, or Manx Gaelic, is the native language of the Isle of Man, which is a quasi-autonomous British Crown Dependency, strategically situated in the north Irish Sea between Ireland and Britain. The Isle of Man is not part of the United Kingdom of Great Britain and Northern Ireland, nor is it in the European Union. It is likely that a Brythonic (P-Celtic) language was spoken in the Isle of Man (or "Mann") before Gaelic. This is attested by Ogham inscriptions on crosses, the most obvious being at Knock y Doonee in Andreas. Although the names on this stone are Irish, the form in which they are recorded shows Brythonic influence.[257] The "Celtic lake" aspect of the Irish Sea is illustrated by the tradition that a Welsh prince, Gwriad, took refuge in the Isle of Man before the year 825 AD. While in Mann, tradition says that Gwriad had a son called Merfyn known in Welsh history as Merfyn o dir Manaw (Merfyn from the land of Mann). Merfyn went to north Wales to found powerful dynasties there.

It was not until, say, 400–500 AD that Gaelic came to the island, probably with Irish invaders. Old Irish was the ultimate parent of the modern Manx language. Since the language at that stage must have been identical to that of Ireland and Scotland, it is impossible to identify any writings as being discernibly Manx. Mann is mentioned in the Cormac Glossary, in which Senchan Torpeist, a famous Irish bard of the seventh century, is described as visiting the island and admiring its literary school. The stories and cycles in Gaelic culture, like that of Finn and Ossian, must have been recounted in Mann. It is possible that they remained popular through oral tradition among the ordinary people well into the nineteenth century. In 1789, Heywood heard a fragment of an Ossianic poem from an old woman in Kirk Michael, in the north of the island. The fragment Heywood wrote down is now held in the British Museum.

Gaelic culture on the island first came under threat about 800 AD with the first Viking raids. The Vikings eventually imposed themselves as the ruling order, establishing Tynwald, the Norse parliamentary assembly which is the basis of Manx government to this day. But while the Norse had an abiding influence on Manx political and legal institutions, it was the Norse who were assimilated into Gaelic culture, as a list of the Kings of Man shows, with names such as Dónal Mac Teige (1096–98) and

Mac Raghnall (1187–1226). The unique Norse–Celtic crosses of the Isle of Man show clearly the fusion of Gall and Gael, with a bias towards Norse male names and Gaelic female names. It is very likely that in the Norse period the ruling class in Mann was bilingual in Norse and Irish and there was an underclass which spoke only Irish. It is possible that Norse survived in Mann into the fourteenth century. However, Gaelic obviously strongly reasserted itself in Mann, to such an extent that few words of Norse origin can be found in modern Manx. In the end, Manx shows less evidence of Norse influence than does Scottish Gaelic. However, some Norse influence is evident in words such as Manx *giau* (creek) from Norse *gjá*, and *baatey* (boat) compared with Norse *bátr*. Norse also made itself felt in many Manx place-names, for instance Laxey (Laksaa in Manx), from *lax* (salmon) and *á* (stream). Another example is Snaefell (Sniaul in Manx), from *snae* (snow) and *fjell* (mountain).

By the eleventh century the Kingdom of Mann and the Isles had come into existence, the "Isles" being the Hebrides. The kingdom actually covered hundreds of islands, but for administrative purposes the number was put at thirty-two with Mann as the most important. Mann was the centre of the Tynwald assembly, a legislative body composed of twenty-four members, eight of whom were from the Isles. This later became known in English as the House of Keys, probably from its Manx name Yn Kiare as Feed, the Four-and-Twenty.

During the Norse period, the Celtic church was brought to an end in Mann (in 1079), whereby one possible bastion of Manx learning, Maughold Abbey, was eclipsed by Rushen Abbey, which reached the height of its influence in the 1340s. At that time, the Manx must have been separated from the Gaelic hinterland to a certain degree.

The period of Manx independence came to an end in 1266, following the death in 1265 of Magnus, the last King of Mann and the Isles. The kingdom was ceded to Alexander III of Scotland. In 1289, when Edward I took the island for England, there started a protracted struggle for ownership, with Robert Bruce taking it in 1313. In 1346 England retook it for good. In fact, in 1333, Edward III had granted the island to William de Montacute, Earl of Salisbury, who became King of Mann without having to pay homage to the English king. Eventually, in 1405, Henry IV gave Mann to Sir John Stanley, provided he paid homage. Stanley's descendants were to rule Mann for the next three hundred years under the title of "king" or "lord" of Mann.

The constitution of the Norse dynasty survived throughout.

Following the English takeover, presumably, the language of Mann began to diverge from that of Scotland and Ireland. While the island was still almost completely Gaelic-speaking, the effects of being somewhat cut off from the greater Gaelic world must have been compounded by growing trade with England, and the influence of an English-speaking administration.

There would have been no noble patrons of Gaelic culture in Mann at this time, unlike the contemporary situations in Gaelic Scotland and Ireland. So, it would be difficult to imagine the existence of bardic and literary schools in Mann. However, it is virtually certain that folk literature was still being developed in this period, as witnessed by the Manx Traditionary Ballad, which was probably composed some time between 1490 and 1520. This gives a potted history of the island from the introduction of Christianity onwards.

We know very little indeed about English influence on Mann and its language before the Reformation (*c.*1530). When the Reformation was completed in Mann (a process which took some considerable time), the Church of England was the established church. The Manx language must have proved something of a barrier to the Reformation. This, however, had the effect of inspiring clergy to write in the indigenous language of the country and not in Latin, in order to spread the new doctrine. In Ireland, for example, this resulted in the publication of a Protestant catechism in Irish by John Kearney in 1571.

John Phillips, a Welshman who in 1605 became Bishop of Man, translated the Book of Common Prayer. Although this was not published until 1893/4, the translation in itself was a breakthrough for the Manx language. Phillips's spelling brought the comment that "few else of the clergy can read the same book for that it is spelled with vowels wherewith none of them are acquainted". Although it has been said that Phillips's spelling is his own creation and that this influence has distanced Manx from its Gaelic cousins, leaving it as Gaelic dressed up as English, another school of thought argues that this spelling, although not based on the Gaelic system, is based on writing dating from well before Phillips's time. This was a period, it must be remembered, when English was hardly heard or seen on the Isle of Man, except in terms of administration, with the island under the control of the Stanleys, Earls of Derby. Records of Manx ecclesiastical courts, it is argued, would of necessity have included a lot of Manx. Indeed, given that the language was overwhelmingly spoken in Mann for hundreds of years, it is hard not to believe that it was not used as a means of official communication, at the very least by priests and bishops.

There is a slightly mysterious report that Aodh Mac Aingil (1572–1626), a master of literary Irish, a poet and briefly Roman Catholic Archbishop of Armagh, was sent from his native County Down in 1585 to receive part of his education in the Isle of Man. It should be realized that this was a time when it was asserted that the Manx people "most readily conform without a single exception to the formularies of the Church of England". Such things suggest that the situation in Mann was not quite as certain accounts of history would have us believe.

Comments about the Manx language from English sources appeared in the seventeenth century. In Speed's *Theatre of the Empire of Great Britaine* (1611), the observation is made concerning the Isle of Man: "The wealthier sort ... do imitate the people of Lancashire... the commoner sort of people, both in their language and manners, come nighest unto the Irish." James Challoner in 1656, while visiting the island, mentioned that "few speak the English tongue", those few presumably being the townsfolk. And Camden wrote in 1695 that "Their gentry are very courteous and affable, and are more willing to discourse with one in English than in their own language".

In 1627, Yn Stanlagh Mooar (The Great Stanley), or James, Seventh Earl of Derby, became Lord of Mann. As well as encouraging bright Manx youths to attend university in England, James had far-reaching plans to found a university in Mann. It could be that he had been inspired by the establishment of Trinity College in Dublin in 1591. These plans came to nothing because of the English Civil War. In any case, the path had been sketched out for Manx youth in later times: higher education in English culture through the English language.

In England, following the Civil War, it had been the intention to implement plans for a national school system. But when the monarchy was restored, these plans were dropped. By one of those quirks of history with which the Manx are familiar, the idea of schooling for all (in English) was nevertheless retained and acted on in Mann. From 1663 to 1669 Isaac Barrow was both the bishop and governor of the Isle of Man. He was determined to set up an "English school" in each parish in the Island. He commented that the people were "for the most part loose and vicious in their lives, rude and barbarous in their behaviour". He thought the church ministers were "v ery ignorant and wholly illiterate; having had no other education than what that rude place afforded them... I suppose the best way of Cure would be to acquaint them with the English tongue..." It is possible that Barrow's offensive remarks were part of a general reaction to the man who was bishop immediately before him, Bishop Rutter. Rutter is well known to students of Manx for his poem in that language in which he praised the delights of what he saw as the enclosed world of the Manx people and hoped this world was safe from pernicious outside influences. Rutter's easy-going attitudes seem at odds with those of Barrow.

The church schools set up by Barrow saw the foundation of elementary schooling in the island, with English as the medium of instruction. Each church minister was obliged to teach in a school in his own parish, with Barrow seeking to make Mann independent of clergy trained elsewhere. Secondary education began with the Free Grammar School in Castletown, the capital of Mann at that time. Barrow was very much ahead of his time in adopting the policy of compulsory education for all. This policy ran into increasing difficulties towards the end of the seventeenth century, very likely because few Manx people spoke English at that time, although Bird puts forward other reasons in his history of Manx education.

Flowering of the language in the eighteenth century

Thomas Wilson became Bishop of Mann in 1693, when, effectively, Church and State were one body as far as education matters were concerned in Mann. This meant that the bishop had considerable power. By church law, if children did not attend parochial schools their parents could be punished. But Bishop Wilson, whose attitude to the Manx language and other matters was realistic and enlightened, did not preside over a system which was excessively punitive. In 1704 Wilson introduced lay teachers into schools, thus changing his predecessor's policy of having only clergymen as teachers. This caused difficulties because sufficient pay could not be offered to attract suitable lay teachers. There was, in fact, no effective provision for elementary education over the whole island until the implementation of the Education Act of 1872.

In 1707, Bishop Wilson published *The Principles and Duties of Christianity*, which was the first book published in the Manx language. He wished the clergy to be able to use Manx, "for English is not understood by two-thirds of the island".

Now and again we find evidence that English was still the language of a minority of the population. In 1743, for example, when Wilson authorized a teacher to set up a secondary school in Ramsey, it was laid down that the teacher was to "... instruct the children ... in learning the English tongue...".

Wilson's work and his efforts to have the Bible translated into Manx were highly successful. In 1748, St Matthew's gospel was published in Manx. Hildesley succeeded Wilson as bishop in 1755. Hildesley, who was very sympathetic to Manx, did a survey to establish how many of the teachers in the "petty" (parochial) schools could teach through the native language. The Bishop evidently recognized the unreality of a system in which children could not understand the language of their so-called education. The survey showed that instruction was through Manx in only three parishes, with such replies as "The Master of the parish school at Lezayre Church and the Master of the School at Sulby are both foreigners and therefore unable to teach them in Manks".

The action taken by Hildesley was to make available teaching material in Manx and to limit the use of English. In 1758 he urged the clergy to use their "best endeavours to improve the use and practice of the Manx language". By 1763 all the gospels and the Acts of the Apostles had been published. In 1775 the whole Bible, *Yn Vible Casherick*, was finally translated and published. As is evident from the time-span involved, the translation and publication of the Bible was something of an epic. A suitable climax occurred when a Manx clergyman was shipwrecked while travelling to the printer with the manuscript. He managed to hold the manuscript above his head while making his way to the shore and safety.

Other translated religious works, such as *Yn Fer-raauee Creestee* (The Christian Monitor) and Wilson's *Shibber y Chiarn* (The Lord's Supper) were published in 1763 and 1777 respectively.

For a time, it seemed that Manx would become an established medium of instruction in schools. Archbishop Drummond of York was supportive of the policies of Wilson and Hildesley with respect to Manx. In quite a short time, there was only one parish where there was a teacher who could not teach pupils using *çhengey ny mayrey* (the mother tongue).

In 1764, further information on the strength of Manx at that time comes from a paper issued by the Society for the Propagation of Christian Knowledge, in which it was stated that: "The population of the Isle is 20,000, of whom the far greater number are ignorant of English."

But in 1772 Hildesley died, leaving Manx once more in the more familiar situation of being ignored or belittled by those with power and prestige. Within ten years of Hildesley's death, there were only five schools which used Manx to teach catechism and prayers.

In the eighteenth century, Manx and Manx culture began to receive more attention from the outside world. In 1707, Edward Lhuyd, the first true Celtic philologist, published his *Archaeologia Britannica*. This contained a list of Manx words in Lhuyd's own phonetic spelling, making the material of great interest.

Baase Illiam Dhone was also recorded at this time, being a form of eulogy on the Manx patriot, William Christian, executed in 1662. The well-loved song *Ny Kirree fo Niaghtey* (The Sheep under the Snow) which has been dated to about 1700, is the most famous of a variety of songs and poems dealing with local and national events, personalities, love, and so on.

The greatest body of original and uniquely Manx work, which also dates to this century, is known as the "carvals", religious songs sung on a variety of themes, usually around Christmas. Some of these ranged to a couple of hundred verses. In total, about one hundred and fifty carvals were collected, half of which were published by A. W. Moore in 1891 as *Carvalyn Gailckagh*. The carvals lasted as a living tradition into the early nineteenth century.

Mona Douglas describes how "the old Manx people sang as naturally as they talked… At the winter evening gathering of the neighbours round the turf fires certain songs, usually well-known ballads or love songs or sometimes a national song like *Baase Illiam Dhone* would be sung by one person… In other songs, such as general lilts, hymns, carvals, humorous songs and so on, several people, or perhaps the whole company, would join. But the charms and fairy songs and songs of death were not used in these gatherings at all, for it was believed that to sing these in the wrong place and time, and without need might well cause evil happenings."

Dancing, like singing, was an intimate and essential part of old Manx social life. There were various types, such as processionals involved with turf cutting, the fair, and the marching of fishing boat crews. There were reels and rounds, and there were somewhat ceremonial dances like

Mylecharaine's March or Cutting of the Fiddler's Head.

In Mann, the fiddle was the usual accompanying instrument for dancing. In fact, it has been, for the last couple of hundred years at least, virtually the Manx national instrument. Harps and bagpipes, though once possibly as common in the island as in Scotland and Ireland, were not in evidence. In the mid-eighteenth century, a traveller recorded of Manx folk that they were: "Much addicted to the music of the violin, and few there be that cannot make some shift upon it". In 1728, another visitor wrote of how the whole community made a full fortnight's holiday over Christmas, hiring fiddlers and holding dances in every barn, most of them lasting the whole night through. This period from 21 December to 6 January was known as *Yn Kegeesh Ommidjagh* (The Foolish Fortnight) in Manx.

The demise of these practices has been blamed in many ways on "a century and a half of somewhat Calvinistic religious thought" which discouraged the tendency to dancing and singing and made the country folk apt to think of these as unsuitable pursuits for any decent Christian. So, by the end of the nineteenth century, they had virtually lost the gaiety of the eighteenth-century Manx, who sang quite naturally of "fiddling, dancing, singing, playing at cards and praising the Lord", as one carval puts it. Indeed, those that did maintain the dances and songs, most particularly the fishermen (amongst whom the language also maintained itself at the end of the nineteenth century), had resorted to calling the dances "games".

We then have evidence which shows the strength of Manx language and culture in the eighteenth century. Again, in 1796 Waldron in his *Description of the People and Customs of the Isle of Mann*, mentions the great love of the Manx people for music and dancing. He tells how every Christmas fortnight every parish hired fiddlers at the public expense "... and dance and sing the long nights away." Another notable festival was the Mheillea at harvest time.

About 1796, Rev Thomas Christian published an abridged version of *Paradise Lost* in Manx translation in rhyming couplets. This is of interest linguistically, since it provides a significant body of written Manx of the eighteenth century (albeit in translation) which is independent of the Bible. In 1995, under the auspices of the Centre for Manx Studies, Rev Robert Thomson published an edited version of Christian's work, with introduction and notes.

Methodism had a great impact on the island, with mixed outcomes for the language. Wesley greatly approved of the Manx people, seeing them as simple souls. In 1783, Wesley wrote to one of his preachers in Mann saying, "If you would learn the Manx language I would commend you". However, in 1789, he rebuked another preacher, stating that "I exceedingly disapprove of your publishing anything in the Manx language. On the contrary, we should do everything in our power to abolish it from the earth, and persuade every member of our Society to learn and talk English. This would be much hindered by providing them with hymns in their own language".

However, as Broderick has pointed out, Wesley's ministers in Mann saw the situation more realistically and published Wesleyan hymns in Manx in 1795 and in 1799. A strong tradition of lively preaching in Manx was maintained throughout much of the nineteenth century. But Methodism apparently hastened the decline in traditional singing and dancing in the nineteenth century. The Anglican Church also did not approve of some of the traditional festivals, thus having an additional negative effect on the language.

Paradoxically, the flowering of Manx culture in the eighteenth century coincided with the beginning of the decline. Quite often, the demise of Manx as a general community language has been mistakenly attributed to the Education Act of 1872. The fate of Manx had been settled more than a hundred years before that, however, as Broderick has made clear. One event above all others had a great impact. This was the so-called Revestment Act of 1765 whereby the British Government transferred sovereignty from the Duke of Atholl to the British Crown and proceeded to suppress what the British authorities saw as "smuggling" by direct rule.

Broderick comments that "the decline of Manx results not so much from rigorous action against it from within, but from a changing set of circumstances emanating from without". Before the mid-eighteenth century, most Manx people did not need the English language and there was little incentive for foreigners to settle in Mann. The Revestment Act changed all this. By the 1760s, the Isle of Man had become demonized in the British parliament as "that island". From the British point of view, the island was responsible for huge losses in revenue to them. Because of its advantageous tax position, the quasi-independent island was carrying on a flourishing trade in wines, spirits, tea, and tobacco with continental Europe. Attracted by this trade, English merchants had established a significant presence in

Mann, effectively founding Douglas as a town. Since the island was classed as a foreign country with respect to Britain, some of these merchants added insult to injury by receiving monies from the British exchequer for their valiant efforts in exporting goods to a foreign country – the Isle of Man. The goods, of course, were non-existent.

What the British authorities viewed as "smuggling", many Manx saw as legitimate trade on the part of an independent country. The Manx very much resented the Revestment Act, which they called *Yn Chialg Vooar* – The Great Deception. The suppression of "the trade" led directly to poverty and emigration and hence the advance of the English language in Mann. This tendency was enhanced by immigration of people on fixed incomes from north-west England in the period from about 1790 to about 1814. The great depression in the Manx economy after 1765 was followed by a further depression in the period 1825–1837, leading to more emigration of Manx people, mainly to America.

Since English had been confined to the towns, the building of roads which facilitated contact between town and country in the period 1750–1800 also encouraged the spread of English. What had enormous impact, however, was the establishment of regular steamer services between Mann and England in 1833 and the subsequent rise of an enormous tourist industry which eventually saw more than ten times the island's own population arriving as holidaymakers in Mann each summer.

Significantly, a late gesture of support for Manx in schools came from outside the island rather than from inside. A supply of spelling books in Manx was sent to the island in 1821 by the Sunday School Society in London. As the *Manks Advertiser* reported: "It seemed most desirable that the inhabitants should be taught to read their vernacular tongue, which had not been taught to any of the children attending schools, nor for a very long period, (if indeed ever in the schools), a primer or spelling book in Manx having never before been printed. The rich boon was considered a real acquisition, as hereby many children would become enabled to read the Holy Scriptures to their parents in the only language which they understood." The *Manks Advertiser* reporter seems not to have known about Hildesley's work in the schools some sixty years previously.

As well as the spelling books, four thousand copies each of *James Covey* and *Poor Joseph* in Manx had been sent to the island by the Liverpool Tract Society. And the Bristol Church of England Tract Society provided two thousand copies of a tract about preparing for death. A total of about six hundred children received tuition in Manx in seventeen Sunday schools using this teaching material.

But powerful forces were acting against the language. Along with John Wesley, almost all the leaders of Manx society felt that Manx should disappear completely from the face of the earth. Increasingly, English was perceived as the sole medium for gaining advancement, with Manx seen as a bar to progress. If bilingualism was seen as a way forward by some, we have little evidence of this. The almost hysterical attitude adopted by an increasing number of Manx people towards the language was made clear in a letter to the *Manx Advertiser* in 1821. The writer signed himself or herself "A Native", saying that Manx did not deserve to be called a language: "What better is the gibberish called Manx than an uncouth mouthful of course (sic) savage expressions… Abolish the Manx; I would say then, as fast as ye can, ye learned of the country. Judges, Lawyers, Clergy, crush it. Allow no one, not even one of your servants or neighbours to speak one word of Manx; and thus, by degrees, annihilate it."

The man who was Bishop of Mann when Manx was being taught in Sunday schools in the 1820s was strongly against the language. From the minutes of the Standing Committee of the Society for Promoting Christian Knowledge for 13 July 1825, we see that Bishop Murray wrote to that society to state that: "There is no longer any necessity for impressions of the Bible and Book of Common Prayer in the Manks Tongue; but that in the English tongue they are much wanted." Murray also informed the society that the teaching of Manx was forbidden by Act of Parliament! This was fantasy but, given the attitude of the London government to subject peoples, must have seemed plausible. In any case, the teaching of Manx in Sunday schools was not maintained.

In 1840, William Kennish published a powerful poem bewailing the decline of Manx. The poem, which was published in the Mona's *Herald*, is entitled "Dobberan Chengey ny Mayrey" (Mourning the Mother Tongue) and personifies the language as a wretched old woman:

"Lesh ooilley mygeayrt-y-mooie frytlagh as rast."
("Having all her garments tattered and torn.")

Then saying: "Son mish, ta fys ayd, ta scaan y chenn ghlare,
Ec cloan Vannin er my hregeil".

("For know, I am the old language's ghost,
The children of Mannin have left me.")

In 1859, the vicar of Malew, Rev William Gill, said: "The language is no longer heard in our courts of law, either from the bench or the bar, and seldom from the witness box. The courts are indeed still fenced in Manx, according to ancient traditionary form; and the Island laws are still promulgated in that language on the Tynwald Mount, where the last lingering accents of the Gaelic in Manx – once the language of Europe, the universal language of the British Isles – will probably be heard… It is rarely now heard in conversation, except among the peasantry. It is a doomed language – an iceberg floating into southern latitudes. Let it not, however, be thought that its end is immediate. Among the peasantry it still retains a strong hold."

In 1861 in a comment on Cregneash, J. G. Cummings states: "Here the Manx language lingers, and may linger some time longer."

In 1872, Rev J. T. Clarke wrote of "the deadly indifference (of the Manx) in saving their mother tongue from being altogether buried in the grave". This is best summed up by the common quote "*Cha jean ee dy bragh cosney ping er dty hon*" (It will never earn you a penny). Translating from the Rev Clarke's Manx: "It was all Manx they had. And in the time of Deemsters (Judges) Kaye and Crellin, no attorney dare appear before them unless they could plead in Manx". In terms of the church, Clarke wrote that: "During the reigns of Bishops Wilson and Hildesley, no young man could be ordained without his possessing a good knowledge of Manx". Indeed, he speaks of his early days as a minister when he "could only preach in English one Sunday a month".

Clarke blamed increased communication, stating that "The Manx market is brought within five or six hours of the English one and to deal in the English markets it is English and English only (that) Manx people must learn to speak". He also said that all the authorities of the island conspired against Manx – ministers, deemsters and lawyers.

Despite reforms in the House of Keys in 1853 which opened the way to popular elections, and more importantly the act of 1866 which gave the Isle of Man "home rule under pleasure", nothing whatsoever was done to preserve the national language.

From 1875, we get the first reasonably accurate number of Manx speakers on the island. This was from a survey conducted by Henry Jenner, later to lead the revival in the Cornish language. Jenner sent a questionnaire to the island's clergy and estimated from the results that, outside of Douglas, about 12,350 people spoke Manx, or 29 per cent of the population.[258] It was estimated that only about 190 knew no English. The main Manx-speaking region was in the north, but most monoglots lived in the south. There were slight variations between the Manx spoken to the north of the ridge of hills making up the "backbone" of the island and that spoken to the south of this ridge. Of seventeen parishes, only one, Kirk Lonan with 1,850 Manx speakers, considered a knowledge of Manx to be necessary for clergy to carry out their duties.

Very little detailed information is available on the decline in traditional songs. In 1883, Thomas Kermode stated that he had not heard a song sung "for the last forty years".

In 1883 and 1884, a debate between a number of correspondents in *Notes and Queries* gives us the following insights: "The old people, especially in the mountains and other remote regions, still use it, but in another generation it will almost have died out".

"There can be no doubt that the Manx people are thoroughly ashamed of their language... they have heard it constantly ridiculed by English visitors".

A contemporary comment was that those who habitually used Manx were spoken of with contempt by other Manx people who used English only.

It is of interest that the correspondents alluded to areas of Man where the language was still spoken, mentioning the hills, Foxdale mines, cottages near Peel and Cregneash and farms on the west coast beyond Glen Maye, as well as Ronague. In the north, they mentioned the parishes of Jurby and Bride.

The 1871 census registered 13,530 speakers of Manx, 25 per cent of the total population. This figure included 190 monoglots. The 1901 census showed there were 4,419 Manx speakers (8.1 per cent of the total population) with just 59 monoglots. Still, Manx maintained connections with its Gaelic cousins. Nóra Ní Shúilleabháin writing in *Islands and Authors* mentions that: "The Manx fleet (at Valentia) led by the captain's nobby, the John Alfred, were friendly callers and Manx and Irish Gaelic were exchanged and understood. When the cannonading of the Great War was heard we saw their red sails no more".

The emigrating Manx had brought their language with them to the New World. In the nineteenth century, Thomas Quayle established his famous shipbuilding firm in Cleveland, Ohio (it is estimated that about 30,000 people in Cleveland now are of Manx origin). Manx was used in several townships in North Ohio and an area of Pennsylvania was Manx-speaking until the start of the twentieth century. The Rev J. T. Clarke, writing in 1872, mentions meeting Manx people from Cleveland who spoke Manx: "There, 'tis all Manx they have in social meetings, in their daily transactions, in preaching". Indeed, it could be the case that Manx survived longer as a community language in North America than it did in the Isle of Man.

The decline of Manx continued. According to the 1911 census, there were 2,382 speakers, including 31 monoglots. The First World War saw the island lose five per cent of its young men. In 1921, the census figure for Manx speakers had dropped to 915 speakers, including 19 monoglots. This was the last census to record people speaking Manx only.

Official census returns for people having knowledge of Manx are available from 1871, when the number of speakers was given as 13,530 (25 per cent of the population). It is likely that the early census figures underestimated the number of speakers since there would have been reluctance on the part of some people to admit they spoke Manx. This possibly tendency was definitely not there in later census returns, when some people with scanty knowledge of Manx would declare they spoke it, to show their support for the language. At the very least, however, the later census figures indicate the degree of sympathy for Manx as well as giving a rough guide to the number of speakers.

The inter-war years saw more work to save what was left of Manx language and culture, most particularly by that long-lived and inspirational figure, Mona Douglas. But the 1931 census claimed only 531 speakers. Despite the setting up of groups such as Aeglagh Vannin and Caarjyn Vannin, the decline went on. In a letter of 1931, Stanley Hill pointed out a possible way forward: "I am convinced that only the strongest action by Tynwald can now be of the slightest avail. The experience of the Irish Free State in these matters would surely be at their disposal".

In 1941 Mona Douglas lamented, "A modern and alien life is all about us now, and before its onslaught the old Gaelic culture of our land is in danger of being lost".

The study, preservation and development of Manx up until 1990

The nineteenth century saw the publication of Manx dictionaries and other books concerning the language. The Rev John Kelly (1750–1809) had been involved as a copyist in making the Bible available in Manx. Later, Kelly was the author of a grammar and two dictionaries. His grammar was published in 1804, but his trilingual dictionary (English with Manx, Irish and Scottish Gaelic) came to grief in a fire. His other dictionary (Manx-English) was not published until 1866, long after his death.

Kelly's work has been criticised for his fanciful etymology and for his inclusion of non-Manx words in his dictionary. However, his dictionary has been re-published more recently and is referred to by students. Kelly's introduction to his triglot dictionary survived and is of interest in that it seems to apologise for any actions which might apparently hinder the advance of English. Just the opposite, Kelly explains: "It has long been the policy of France to render her language universal. Had a similar policy been extended by this country (England) to Ireland – had books been printed in Gaelic, and Gaelic schools established… the people would have acquired learning by using the English alphabet, they would have read English before they could read Irish… they would have understood English before they had learnt Irish – such a portion at least of English as would beyond a doubt have enabled them… to have diminished, if not altogether to have removed, the deplorable ignorance, poverty and bigotry under which they have so long laboured… This cultivation of the Gaelic language will destroy the language itself, as a living language; but it will have produced the knowledge of a better."

Kelly goes on to claim "the Roman Catholic faith was entirely superseded in Man" by the publication of Gaelic books and by obliging the clergy to understand and use Gaelic. It must be remembered that this was written by an Anglican clergyman living in England shortly after the 1798 rebellion in Ireland. Probably, Kelly believed what he had written. In any case, no matter what he believed, it would have been extremely difficult for him to have produced any work which unreservedly promoted any branch of the Gaelic language.

In the introduction to his excellent Manx–English dictionary of 1835, Archibald Cregeen also produced something akin to an apology. It is more difficult than with Kelly to believe his heart was in this "apology": "I am well aware that the utility of the following work will be variously appreciated by my brother Manksmen. Some will be disposed to deride the endeavour to restore vigour to a decaying language". Cregeen goes on to point out that "There are thousands of the natives of the Island who can at present receive no useful knowledge whatever, except through the medium of the Manks language." His dictionary would not "hinder the progress of the English" but would, in fact, "have the contrary effect".

That Cregeen's heart was truly in his work, however, is evident from his preface to the dictionary: "It is designed to facilitate the attainment of that ancient language... That a language so venerable for its antiquity... should be so generally neglected, is much to be lamented... Whilst the natives of Wales and the natives of North Britain are enthusiastically attached to the language of their forefathers, let it not be said that the natives of Mona regard 'Chengey ny mayrey Vannin veg veen' with disgraceful apathy and heartless indifference".

In 1858, the Manx Society was set up "For the publication of National Documents of the Isle of Man". This society published a valuable series of books, including John Kelly's dictionary in 1866 and the *Book of Common Prayer* in 1893–4. The Manx Society was wound up in 1907, having virtually achieved its aims. In 1896, two important collections of Manx music and songs were published. One of these was *Manx National Songs, with English words, selected from the ms. collection of The Deemster Gill, Dr J. Clague, & W. H. Gill, and arranged by W. H. Gill*. In a very clear way, W. H. Gill intended to appeal to a much wider audience than those interested in the Gaelic past (and present). Words and music must have ended up far removed from the original in many cases.

In the same year, *Manx Ballads and Music* was published. This was edited by A. W. Moore, author of *A History of the Isle of Man* and Speaker of the House of Keys. This book was much closer to the reality of Manx culture. The Manx words of traditional and other songs were given, with English translations alongside. Where possible, musical scores were provided.

Predictably, Gill's book was a huge public success compared with Moore's. Drawing-room arrangements with dashes of sentimentality in the English words were much to be preferred, compared with songs of the people in a language most Manx were desperate to pretend did not exist. Interestingly, a contemporary reviewer savaged *Manx National Songs* and praised *Manx Ballads and Music*. It was to be several decades before the latter book was to be more widely appreciated.

In 1899, Yn Cheshaght Ghailckagh (Manx Language Society) was founded, with A. W. Moore as president. The aims of the society were the preservation of Manx as the national language of the Isle of Man, the study and publication of existing Gaelic literature and the cultivation of a modern literature in Manx. There was an account of the Manx Language Society's first annual general meeting in the journal of the Gaelic League, *An Claidheamh Soluis*. An important member of the society was described as enthusiastically backing the preservation of Manx, but speaking strongly against Manx speakers passing the language on to their children! The Gaelic League reporter commented that after this, Yn Cheshaght Ghailckagh could hardly be taken seriously.

This highlights a common feature of language movements: preservation as compared with revival. Certainly the Manx Language Society has made very significant contributions to the preservation of the language by publishing books on and in Manx. Throughout most its life, it is probably fair to say that the society has veered more towards preservation rather than revival.

Until quite recently, Manx was not really a respectable subject for Celtic scholars to study. Following the emergence of Celtic Studies as an academic subject in the nineteenth century, Manx had to rely to a large extent on the devotion of gifted amateurs and enthusiasts. One exception was Sir John Rhys, who wrote a treatise entitled *Outlines of the Phonology of Manx Gaelic*. This was published with the *Book of Common Prayer* in 1893–4.

The foremost non-professional scholar was John J. Kneen (1873– 938). He did a great deal to bring Manx to the attention of the public by publishing language lessons in newspapers. Among other works, he produced a grammar, an English–Manx pronouncing dictionary and a handbook of conversational phrases. He is also well known for his work on Manx personal names and place-names, for which he was honoured by the Norwegian government in 1930, following recommendations by Professor Carl Marstrander.

Edmund Goodwin published his *First Lessons in Manx* in 1901, a book which generations of Manx learners have relied on, along with Kneen's books. Goodwin's book was revised by Rev Robert Thomson in 1965.

In 1909, the first sound recordings of native speakers of Manx were made by Rudolph Trebitsch.

Several visits were made by philologists to the island to record the speech of the last native speakers. In 1929, Marstrander could find only forty people with some Manx. He was unduly pessimistic in 1934, when he thought there was only one true native speaker left. In fact, in 1946 Charles W. Loch visited the island and was able to produce a list of some twenty native speakers. This number had fallen to ten by 1950 and to seven by 1955, as Professor Kenneth Jackson established. By the time of the next official census in 1961, there were just two native speakers left, as far as was known. These were Sage Kinvig, who died in the following year, and Ned Maddrell, recognized as the last native speaker of what might be called "traditional" Manx. Ned died in 1974.

But before the demise of these native speakers, some crucial sound recordings had been made, using the first commercially available tape recorders. In 1947, Éamon de Valera came to the island on an official visit as Taoiseach of the Irish Free State. He met with Ned Maddrell and, after conversations in Manx and Irish, had his interest suitably aroused to send a sound-recording unit from the Irish Folklore Commission to make significant recordings of Manx from the last native speakers. This intervention by the Irish government highlights the inaction of the Manx government, which, despite individuals in the House of Keys, was quite content to let the language die.

The work of Robert Thomson and George Broderick has done a very great deal to bring Manx language studies to the attention of the international academic community. Works by Thomson such as *A Glossary of Early Manx* and *The Study of Manx Gaelic*, along with his many academic papers have proved invaluable to students. To a large extent, George Broderick has specialized in the Manx of the last native speakers of the "traditional" language, producing the definitive description of this language and giving important analyses of the characteristics of decline of a community Gaelic language.

During most of the nineteenth century and the early twentieth century, efforts to preserve and develop Manx and to use it as an everyday language were seen as unacceptable by most Manx people themselves. At best, the language was considered worthy of study by antiquarians. Many a scholar must have masked his or her true feelings by saying they wanted to learn Manx simply in order to read the Bible in that language.

While linguistic continuity was maintained by those who acquired a fluent knowledge of Manx as a second language, a desire to become a fluent speaker was regarded as a highly eccentric ambition until quite recently. Foremost in changing this attitude was a small group of language activists who came together in the late 1930s and 1940s. They included Leslie Quirk (practically a native speaker), Charles Craine, William Radcliffe, Mark Braide and his brother Tom, Walter Clarke and Doug Fargher. This group used Manx as a living language, while paying great attention to the Manx of the native speakers. In the 1950s, the group made tape recordings of the old speakers to supplement the work of the Irish Folklore Commission, with Douglas Fargher, Walter Clarke and William Radcliffe being particularly active. All this activity was carried out entirely in Manx, which enabled several others, including Brian Stowell and Bernard Caine, to become fluent speakers also.

The contribution of Douglas Fargher from the 1950s onwards was pivotal. He organized adult classes in Manx, published booklets on Manx and was an effective publicist for the language at a time when this often brought ridicule. His great work was the very comprehensive English–Manx dictionary which was published by Shearwater Press with government support in 1979.

Also prominent in the 1950s was John Gell, who, on behalf of Yn Cheshaght Ghailckagh, published *Coraa Ghailckagh* (Manx Language Voice), a magazine entirely in Manx which came out four times a year. This bold initiative came to an end in 1957 when the magazine folded. From 1965 to 1970, a news-sheet called *Credjue* (Belief) was issued by Brian Stowell. In the 1970s, Ian Faulds of Shearwater Press and Mona Douglas published *The Manxman*, a periodical which contained some articles in Manx only.

From the 1960s, there was growing interest in the language. Manx advanced through night classes taught by people who had learnt their Manx from the last of the native speakers. This growth of interest was best shown by the census figure for 1971 of 284 speakers, giving a 72 per cent increase from ten years previously.

Despite the language classes, the language organization, Yn Cheshaght Ghailckagh, remained somewhat moribund until 1972, when Douglas Fargher and others got elected to the committee and started organizing Oieghyn Gaelgagh (Manx Language Nights) in various pubs, and publishing new material.

Following a suggestion by an Irishman in New York in the 1960s, Brian Stowell translated the Irish language course *Buntús Cainte* into Manx, with the assistance of Robert Thomson. This course was used by various adult classes over a period of years, having been revised by Adrian Pilgrim.

The 1970s saw much-increased activity to promote Manx. In 1973, George Broderick published a new English translation from the original Latin of *The Chronicle of the Kings of Mann and the Isles*. This was accompanied by a parallel translation into Manx by Brian Stowell and Robert Thomson. Also in 1973, George Broderick produced the first significant recording of songs entirely in Manx, sung by Brian Stowell.

In 1976, Yn Cheshaght Ghailckagh published *Skeealaght* (Story telling), a collection of stories by four new authors. 1976 also saw the revival by Mona Douglas of Yn Chruinnaght. In the 1930s, Yn Chruinnaght had been a one-day event similar to a country fair. The new event developed into a successful week-long inter-Celtic festival held each July in Ramsey.

In the 1950s, the Celtic Congress had been particularly active in Mann under the leadership of Joseph Woods. Later decades saw the emergence in the island of a highly effective branch of the Celtic League (the political breakaway from the Celtic Congress), led by the trade union secretary Bernard Moffatt. The Celtic League's journal *Carn* regularly carries articles in Manx as well as the other Celtic languages.

Representatives of Cymdeithas yr Iaith Gymraeg (The Welsh Language Society) visited the Island in January 1977 to share their experiences. That same year, other aspects of Manx culture began to come to the fore when the all-male dance group Bock Yuan Fannee was formed. The Manx Folk Dance Society had an appreciably longer history and had carried out invaluable work in restoring and developing Manx dancing. Bock Yuan Fannee demonstrated a new, robust spirit.

By 1978, Manx language radio broadcasts had been increased to one hour per week where previously there was fifteen minutes of Manx per week, or less, on the radio.

Colin Jerry published the first of his booklets *Kiaull yn Theay* (Music of the People) in 1978. These booklets, which give the music for folk instruments and the words in Manx for traditional dance tunes and songs, have played a large part in the revival of Manx folk music and song which has taken place in step with the partial revival of the language. Colin and Cristl Jerry established a regular folk session on Saturday night in Peel which has lasted many years.

Through the 1970s, Yn Cheshaght Ghailckagh began to exert more pressure, and in 1981 canvassed all candidates for election to Tynwald on their stance regarding the language. The response showed a degree of disdain for Manx among the candidates, with 56 per cent of respondents advocating no official support for the language. Yn Cheshaght Ghailckagh commented: "The survey confirms that while the language is not subject to overt oppression, it remains the victim of ignorance and indifference emanating from the highest levels of society. It is self-evident that the language societies in Mann need not look to their own government for support. The outlook remains bleak."

In fact, the government had given some support to the language, in the form of provision of evening classes for adults, for many years. In some schools, ad hoc teaching of limited amounts of Manx was undertaken by interested teachers. In 1982, Manx was offered as a General Certificate of Education subject at Ordinary Level, under the guidance of Robert Thomson, the foremost academic authority on the language. This qualification was taken by adult students until GCE O-Levels were replaced by the General Certificate of Secondary Education (the Isle of Man follows the English education system). For various reasons, a GCSE in Manx was not developed, leaving Manx as the only Celtic language for which formal qualifications cannot, as yet, be taken.

In 1983, the first film to be made entirely in Manx, *Ny Kirree fo Niaghtey* (The Sheep under the Snow), was produced by George Broderick and Peter Maggs of Foillan Films. They produced several other films in Manx, but were very severely limited by lack of funding. Also in 1983, an important conference took place. This was entitled "Manx Gaelic Today" and generated useful debate concerning the state of the language.

In 1984, *Fritlag* (Rag), was published by Bob Carswell, coming out monthly. This publication carried illustrations and new terminology in Manx. Although it eventually folded in 1987, due to pressure of other commitments on the editor, it marked a further step forward in the rebirth of the language. Another step was taken in 1984, when the Isle of Man Bank agreed to accept cheques written in Manx. The bank had changed its mind after protests following an initial refusal to accept such cheques.

For the first time ever, the Manx language was given limited official recognition in 1985 through a resolution of Tynwald. This established

Cooonceil ny Gaelgey (The Manx Gaelic Advisory Council) under the auspices of the Manx Heritage Foundation. The council members were Rev Robert Thomson, Adrian Pilgrim and Douglas Fargher (until the latter's untimely death in 1987). Cooonceil ny Gaelgey has carried out invaluable work in translating the summaries of new laws into Manx each year and providing the Manx titles of government departments for stationery, Manx translations of street names, and so on. The summaries of new laws act as a source of new terminology in Manx.

Yn Cheshaght Ghailkcagh opened its first ever headquarters in 1986 in a former school building at St Jude's in the north of the Island. Since that time, the headquarters has been successfully run by John Crellin and Leslie Quirk, men who have done enormous work for the language.

1986 also saw other developments which raised the profile of Manx. Mactullagh Vannin (Echo of Mannin) brought out a very successful cassette of new arrangements of traditional Manx tunes. Another major conference on Manx was held under the auspices of the Ned Maddrell annual lecture, and Manx Radio broadcast a language course for beginners.

The language movement had found new vigour, while not touching the heights of assertiveness reached by some Welsh activists. More street and road names in Manx were put up, often paid for by Yn Cheshaght Ghailckagh. Bilingual signs began to appear on government buildings. The issue of taking marriage vows in Manx was successfully resolved.

In 1987, building on developments from the previous year, another forum was held, this time focusing on Manx in education. The key address was given by Alun Davies, the Director of Education in the island and a native Welsh speaker. He suggested that he was open to bringing Manx into the schools; historically, it had only been taught sporadically during lunch breaks or after school at pupils' requests.

A stage-by-stage analysis of recent and current RLS efforts on behalf of Manx and their future prospects

Stages 7 and 8: Reconstructing Manx, adult acquisition of Manx as a second language and cultural interaction in Manx involving adults

Although a significant amount of vocabulary and expressions must have been lost on the demise of Manx as a community language, its position has never been quite as desperate as has sometimes been painted. Religious literature in Manx has been relatively easy to access, along with dictionaries and grammars. The tape recordings of old native speakers made from the late 1940s to the early 1960s and associated studies (in particular by George Broderick) have given us detailed knowledge of the Manx of native speakers of the late nineteenth century. Some of these tape recordings are easily available on audio-cassette, and many more will soon be accessible on CD.

In the mid-1990s, it was proposed that the post of Manx Language Development Officer be created to work on language projects which fell outside the remit of the Department of Education. Inside that department, Manx language was dealt with by the Manx Language Officer (see below). Phil Gawne, a prominent language activist and employee of Manx National Heritage, was appointed as a part-time Manx Language Development Officer, funded jointly by the Manx Heritage Foundation and Manx National Heritage (effectively, both arms of the Manx Government). Part of Phil Gawne's remit was to assist people providing Manx classes for adults.

Following initiatives from the Manx Language Development Officer, Phil Gawne, the membership of Coonceil ny Gaelgey (Manx Gaelic Advisory Council) has been expanded and the council made more proactive than reactive. It is now producing lists of recommended technological terms in Manx, as well as Manx translations of street and road names for official use. So far, Coonceil ny Gaelgey has not attempted to standardize the orthography of Manx (which would not be a huge undertaking) or to make recommendations on points of syntax. Meetings of Coonceil ny Gaelgey often involve lively discussion, particularly since there are preservationist members, as well as those on the revivalist wing (with the latter being in the majority). One problem is to get wider dissemination of the council's recommendations among Manx speakers and learners.

Manx classes for adults are generally organized outside the Manx Government's adult education schemes, partly because the fees for "official" classes are regarded as high and partly for social reasons. The "private" Manx classes for adults are generally offered at three or four centres in the island, with nominal fees being charged (to pay for room-hire, typically). The social function of classes often takes precedence over the rapid acquisition of Manx Gaelic – a feature common to adult evening classes in other countries. At any one time, there are up to 150 adults studying

Manx at evening classes.

A support group called Caarjyn ny Gaelgey (Friends of the Manx Language) was set up in the late 1980s by Peter Karran, a member of Tynwald and a great supporter of Manx. This led to the establishment of an important private language centre at St John's, in the middle of the island, where classes are offered at different levels and Manx language events are held. There is another important private Manx language centre at Kirk Michael in the north of the island, based at the local football club and run by Phil Kelly, the present Manx Language Officer for the Manx Government (see below). Also in the north, classes are held at Thie ny Gaelgey, the headquarters of Yn Cheshaght Ghailckagh.

People taking the private classes for adults are often not trained teachers (again a common feature in other countries), and, although a significant amount of modern teaching aids have been produced recently (audio and video cassettes, a CD-ROM, etc.), there is some reluctance to use them and even a tendency occasionally to revert to the old days and inflict reading from the Manx Bible on virtual beginners. In spite of all this, the adult classes do have some marked successes. They could, however, be made much more effective as regards producing more Manx speakers, while retaining the valuable social aspect.

In addition, annual summer schools in Manx were started in 1993 at the Manx Museum in Douglas and have attracted students from around the world.

The General Certificate in Manx has been available as a qualification for adults as well as school pupils (generally aged 15 or 16) since the autumn of 1998. At that time, about 60 adults registered to take this qualification, with 19 of these gaining it by 2001. Shortly, a higher qualification in Manx will be available to adults. This will be equivalent to Advanced Level in the English system (typically, three Advanced Levels with good grades will win access to a university for an 18-year-old).

Manx Radio broadcasts short, simple Manx lessons each weekday morning and these have been very successful as a good public relations exercise (very much needed for Manx) but, obviously, of limited use for serious language acquisition.

An immersion course is being developed for adults associated with Mooinjer Veggey, the Manx language playgroup movement (see below). Such a course will of course be useful to those outside the movement.

There is a growing demand for a correspondence course – something which Manx language activists have been about to produce for many years now. A prime need is to establish learner-friendly drop-in centres where people can go to hear Manx spoken and to speak themselves, rather than keep taking courses in the language with little opportunity to develop skills in speaking it. Manx-speaking weekends are organized occasionally but these tend to be in venues which sympathetic people at present outside the Manx-speaking circuit will find unacceptable, if not daunting. There is still a lingering feeling among older people that you must suffer if you are learning Manx.

In the late 1990s, Phil Gawne, the Manx Language Development Officer, was the prime mover in instituting the now annual Feailley Ghaelgagh (Manx Gaelic Festival), a week-long event designed to bring the language to a wider public by means of public events, talks, song and music. This festival receives significant sponsorship from the private sector as well as from the Manx Government.

Revivalists in the Manx language movement have recently sought to make use of the language at public events (concerts, ceilidhs, lectures, etc.) which are not explicitly involved with the movement. These efforts have had some impact, but it remains the case that quite a few fluent speakers are reluctant to use any Manx outside their own small circle, even though this usage is becoming accepted by more people.

Stage 6: Establishing the vital linkage with family and community

The strength of the old Manx attitude that the language could be studied as an academic subject but should never again be used as an everyday language cannot be over-emphasized. As seen from other countries, the emergence in the Isle of Man of a small number of families where children are being brought up with Manx as well as English would be regarded as an interesting phenomenon. In the context of the Isle of Man, it is almost revolutionary.

Of great significance was the founding in the early 1990s of a Manx-speaking pre-school playgroup called Chied Chesmad (First Step) which organized initially with ten children. Families bringing their children up as bilingual in Manx and English were the driving force here. For the first time in a hundred years, new native speakers of Manx were emerging. In

1996, Chris Sheard and Phil Gawne, two fathers bringing up children with Manx, visited Scotland under the auspices of Yn Cheshaght Ghailckagh to see at first hand the operation of Gaelic playgroups and the progression of children through Gaelic units in Scottish schools. This was taken as a model for action in the Isle of Man.

In the late 1990s, the Manx-language playgroup movement Mooinjer Veggey (Little Folk) took over from the then-defunct Chied Chesmad. Mooinjer Veggey is a private organization which, since the late 1990s with government assistance, has established three playgroups strategically sited in the island, catering for a total of about 60 children aged between two and four. It is the aim that as many children as possible move on from these playgroups to the primary school unit where teaching will be through Manx (see below).

A significant number of parents with children attending Manx-language playgroups would like to acquire varying degrees of knowledge of Manx. It is a major problem how this demand can be met, given that it will be difficult for most of the parents involved to attend the immersion course which is being developed. That this demand exists, however, shows how great the change in attitude to the language has been.

Stages 5 and 4: The attainment of literacy in Manx, learning Manx at school and education in Manx

The attainment of literacy in Manx for adults has been discussed above (stages 8 and 7).

In 1990, the Manx government commissioned a Gallup "quality of life" survey. Thirty-six per cent of the respondents said that they wanted Manx to be taught in the schools on an optional basis, a result which surprised those who habitually ignored or belittled the language. The 1991 census returns gave a figure of 643 Manx speakers in the Island, indicating a significant growth in support for the language since 1971 (data on the language had not been sought in the 1981 census) when the corresponding figure was 284.

Following a decision by the Council of Ministers (the Manx cabinet), a Manx Language Officer and two full-time peripatetic teachers of Manx were appointed. The Manx Language Officer (Brian Stowell) and the two teachers (Phil Kelly and Peggy Carswell) took up these newly-created posts in January 1992. A decision was taken to offer a "taster" Manx course to all pupils aged seven and over (including secondary school pupils) from September 1992. The response was overwhelming, revealing a large, previously hidden desire to learn Manx. About 40 per cent of primary school pupils (with parental approval) indicated their wish to attend Manx classes. In the secondary sector (aged eleven and over) the numbers were understandably less, but, at an average of seven per cent, were still higher than had been guessed at. A total of 1,949 were registered as wanting to study Manx. (The total school population in the island is about 10,000.) The numbers wanting to take Manx could not be coped with and classes had to be delayed arbitrarily for several hundred pupils. In September 1992, about 1,400 primary and secondary pupils started taking classes. At the end of the school year in July 1993, about 1,200 pupils were still attending the Manx classes. Virtually all the dropout occurred in the secondary sector, there being significant resistance to the teaching of Manx in two of the five secondary schools. Not all of this resistance stemmed from hostility to the language per se, but from real problems caused by a very full compulsory curriculum.

Offering Manx in the schools proved to be successful, with almost all pupils showing great enthusiasm for the language. This enthusiasm was shared by native Manx and recent incomers alike. When a proposal was put to Tynwald in January 1996 that the number of Manx teachers operating in the schools should be greatly increased, this proposal was lost by just one vote. In the accompanying debate no anti-language sentiments were voiced, even by known opponents of Manx.

Teaching material for the schools' programme was created from scratch, producing the course *Bun Noa* (New Base or New Meaning) along with an audio-cassette and computer software for teaching.

In spite of an overcrowded and over-prescriptive curriculum (controversially introduced from England in 1990), optional Manx as a subject has shown it has solid and lasting support. In 1996, Brian Stowell retired and Phil Kelly took over as the government's Manx Language Officer. Since then, another full-time peripatetic teaching post was created for Manx, giving a team of four in the Department of Education (the Manx Language Officer and three teachers). At present (2001), about 800 pupils take Manx at any one time, the vast majority of these being in the primary schools. This does not show a drop in demand for Manx. Rather, it reflects an undesirable trimming down in the number studying Manx to enable the

Manx language team to cope more easily. (Initially, the tactic was to offer Manx to every pupil who wanted it, in the hope that a sufficient number of teachers would be appointed to meet the demand. This did not happen.) The timetabling of Manx in many schools remains unsatisfactory, particularly in secondary schools. However, a further step forward was taken in 2001 when Tynwald passed a new education act under which it is now a legal requirement for the Manx Government to make provision for teaching Manx in its schools.

Since 1997, pupils in the five secondary schools under the Manx Government have been able to take the General Certificate in Manx. As anticipated, uptake in the schools for this qualification has not been as high as for adults (because of an overloaded and prescriptive school curriculum and some timetabling difficulties). Nevertheless, up to ten pupils per year are opting to take the General Certificate.

In the early 1990s, discussions took place over the foundation inside a primary school of a Manx Gaelic unit in which Manx-speaking children would be educated through Manx. The foundation of such a unit was one of the proposals in a major report on Manx submitted to Tynwald by the Manx Department of Education in January 1996. Finally, thanks to the persistence of Phil Gawne and others, it was agreed to incorporate a Manx Gaelic unit inside Ballacottier School, on the outskirts of Douglas. This unit started up in September 2001, initially with eight children, representing a great advance for the Isle of Man.

Stage 3: Manx in the workplace

Effectively, Manx is not used as a full, living language in the workplace in Mann, with the exception of the small number of cases like the Manx Gaelic Unit inside the Department of Education.

Stages 2 and 1: Manx in the media, government and business

Manx Radio broadcasts three programmes per week which have significant Manx Gaelic content, giving a total broadcasting time of about four hours per week. Some of this is funded by the Gaelic Broadcasting Committee, a quasi-government body set up in the early 1990s to oversee and promote radio broadcasting in Manx. The original intention was for the Gaelic Broadcasting Committee to be a statutory body, but Tynwald decided to make the committee advisory-only. By an act of Tynwald, radio broadcasters operating from the Isle of Man are now legally obliged to include a certain proportion of Manx Gaelic programming in their output. However, it has been demonstrated that the Manx Government's Telecommunications Commission (a regulatory body) could permit radio broadcasters to operate with zero Manx Gaelic content if broadcasts are directed outside the Isle of Man. Manx Radio's station identification has been in Manx and English for some years and the station also broadcasts frequent short lessons in Manx, as mentioned above.

The Isle of Man does not have its own television service but is served (badly) by stations in Britain, meaning that there are no programmes in Manx. Possibly the island will have its own service in the near future, but very strong representations will have to be made to get any programmes in Manx.

There are three newspapers in the Isle of Man, all weekly and all owned by one company which is based in Britain. The newspapers are reasonably sympathetic to the language, so there is on average at least one short column in Manx per week. The problem is not so much that the papers are reluctant to print material in Manx but the difficulty of finding people who can write Manx well and supply material week after week. However, the management of the newspapers remains unduly suspicious of copy written in Manx only, much preferring bilingual copy.

Manx Gaelic has a reasonably good presence on the internet. However, although the percentage of Manx households connected to the internet is significantly larger than the United Kingdom average, few of the older language activists have this facility. But the Isle of Man, through the heavy investment in information technology in its education system and the growth of its finance industry, is well prepared in general for future developments in this area.

Language activists in other countries may well describe the usage of Manx in government and business in the Isle of Man as "tokenism" and "cosmetic". But Manx had gone down so far, that this is generally not the view in the Isle of Man itself. At the open-air Tynwald ceremony each fifth of July, the reading out aloud in Manx of the summaries of laws passed in the preceding year is a practice that was never discontinued. This has kept the Manx public aware of the existence of Manx and provided valuable new vocabulary and terminology for the language. All departments of the Manx Government now use stationery which is bilingual and many notices on official vehicles, etc., are bilingual. It has recently been reiterated that

Table 10.1
Resident population by knowledge of Manx Gaelic and area of residence, 2001

Area of Residence	Speaks, Reads or Writes Manx Gaelic	Speaks Manx Gaelic	Writes Manx Gaelic	Reads Manx Gaelic
Towns				
Douglas	589	516	125	178
Ramsey	152	139	86	106
Peel	97	88	53	59
Castletown	59	57	34	38
Villages				
Port Erin	76	70	31	42
Port St Mary	46	42	34	38
Laxey	18	16	9	15
Onchan	140	123	61	87
Parishes				
Andreas	31	23	16	21
Arbory	39	35	20	21
Ballaugh	20	18	11	15
Braddan	47	42	22	31
Bride	18	17	9	10
German	28	28	15	21
Jurby	32	32	16	20
Lezayre	34	32	22	24
Lonan	30	28	17	20
Malew	47	42	24	32
Marown	38	37	20	25
Maughold	13	11	8	10
Michael	37	37	20	26
Patrick	43	43	25	33
Rushen	38	34	20	27
Santon	17	17	8	11
Total	1,689	1,527	706	910

Figure 10.1
Percentage of resident population with knowledge of Manx Gaelic

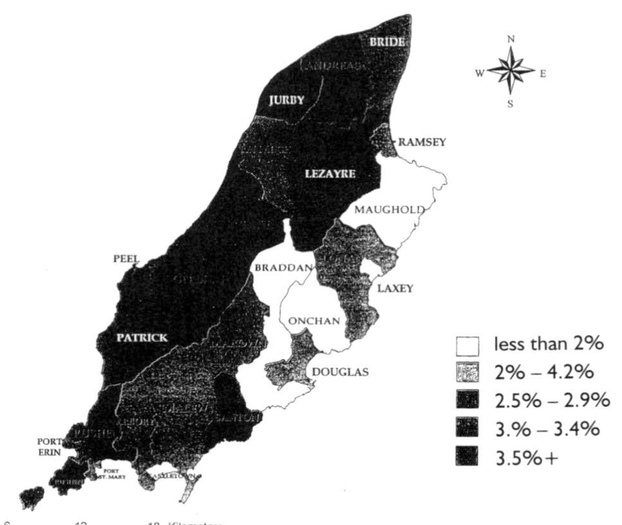

oaths can be taken in Manx in law courts.

The Manx Language Development Officer, Phil Gawne, finalized a comprehensive plan of action in 2001 for Manx Gaelic, mainly involving the Manx Government.[259] This plan calls for continued (and increased) financial support for the Manx language playgroup movement, Manx-medium education, a more secure position for Manx as a subject in schools, more use of Manx in government circles, along with other proposals. In the 1980s, Tynwald had, in fact, approved the recommendations of a sub-committee calling for formal support for Manx and for increased use of the language in government departments. Some of this sub-committee's proposals were implemented, but by no means all. In 2001, it was decided not to submit Phil Gawne's plan to Tynwald for approval, but to prioritize actions and attempt to deal with these pragmatically.

The rapid growth of the finance industry in the Isle of Man and the consequent, relatively huge influx of people to work in the booming Manx economy, led to an increase in the token use of Manx to emphasize the separate identity of the Isle of Man and of Manx products. A notable instance of this was the request by the Manx branch of a South African bank to translate the preface to one of its documents into Manx for display at headquarters in South Africa. Outlets of large UK firms in the Isle of Man such as Marks & Spencer and Tesco have felt the need to put up some notices in Manx, and, in an insular supermarket war, a Manx supermarket firm has used notices in Manx to appeal to the loyalties of Manx customers. It is interesting (and predictable) that recent incomers generally understand that Manx Gaelic can have market appeal, much more easily than older, dyed-in-the-wool Manx politicians, some of whom are still carrying the psychological baggage that the language is a shameful secret!

For some years now, token announcements in Manx have been made on aircraft operated by Manx Airlines. These announcements were discontinued at one stage but re-introduced after complaints by members of the public.

A finance act recently passed by Tynwald finally regularized the position over cheques written in Manx. It is now the case that any bank registered in the Isle of Man must honour such cheques. In reality, since cheques were first used in the Isle of Man, certain people have always written them in Manx. However, some bank workers would occasionally raise questions about cheques made out in Manx.

Concluding remarks

In many reference works, Manx Gaelic is described as "dead" or "extinct".[260] However, remarkable things are happening in the Isle of Man. Since the 1950s, attitudes to the language have changed a great deal, possibly due in no small measure to the dying-off of an older generation who had been brought up to despise the language of their ancestors. In the 1950s, letting slip the dread secret that you were learning Manx would often elicit the passionately hostile spitting out of: "Manx? That was never a real language!" Even now, some very old Manx people will give you the modified form: "Manx? That was never much of a language...".

About a hundred years ago in the Isle of Man, the World Manx Association was formed, taking as a theme the words of the Manx poet T. E. Brown: "Whate'er is left to us of ancient heritage...", referring to what was then perceived as the remaining scraps of Manx heritage. T. E. Brown also referred to Mann as being "lost in the Empire's mass". Almost all Manx people at that time had firmly rejected their native language but nevertheless wished to proclaim themselves Manx. Manx "dialect", or Manx English, was seen as an acceptable badge of identity in place of Manx Gaelic. What would those people (and T. E. Brown) make of an increasingly Anglicized Isle of Man which has become a significant international finance centre, where the Manx-born are in a minority, where the population is growing rapidly because of an economic boom in the early years of the twenty-first century which brings negative unemployment, where Manx English has greatly declined and Manx Gaelic is growing in strength?

In his introduction to the first published volume of a new history of the Isle of Man, John Belchem, Professor of History at Liverpool University, wrote: "The growth of the finance sector has brought significant demographic change: native-born Manx are now (just) in the minority. At this point Manx Gaelic has become politically correct and socially desirable, available even at nursery school, a fashion which seemingly unites natives and new arrivals. Now all-but indistinguishable in its daily speech patterns from the north of England, the Isle of Man, enmeshed in multinational finance, is seeking a symbiotic public language to secure its distinct identity. It is this complex and symbiotic cultural context which has also stimulated interest in Manx studies and led to this New History."

Talk of "fashion" and political correctness will not endear him to conservative Manx people, but Belchem's message shows the change in attitude that has taken place concerning Manx Gaelic. However, the language movement started from such a low base that an enormous amount needs to be done. Since 1992, several thousand young people have gained some knowledge of the language, but the vast majority of them are being lost to the language on completing their school courses. There is an overriding need to provide many more social occasions where people of all ages can meet to hear Manx spoken and practise speaking it themselves. Also, children who are being brought up with Manx need to be convinced this is not a language unique to their household.

The 2001 census showed a relatively huge increase in the number claiming to speak, read or write Manx Gaelic. This was 1,689, with 46 per cent of these being under the age of 19, the total number being over ten times the lowest number recorded (165 in 1961). 1,689 represents 2.2 per cent of the population of the Isle of Man, this having risen to 76,315 in 2001 as a consequence of the economic boom in the Island.

Among adults there is a demand for Manx which is not being met, partly because of poor teaching. This is a particularly crucial point in the case of parents of children who are attending Manx-language playgroups.

Above all, while due homage must be paid to the Gaelic-speaking past and the way of life then, Manx needs to shake off the death-laden aura of permanent mourning for its demise as the main community language in the Isle of Man. A general revival of Manx is unlikely, but there is no doubt that an increasing number of people want to use it in their everyday lives. To prosper in relative terms, the Manx language movement has to be open and inclusive. The movement must also retain a strong belief in the bottom-up approach, and appreciate that transmitting the language to the very young is a top priority.

In 2003, the Isle of Man government formally extended the Council of Europe's European Charter for Regional or Minority Languages to the Isle of Man. This was a significant step for Manx Gaelic, since the fact that the Isle of Man is not part of the European Union means that there has been a tendency for the language to be overlooked in international affairs.

Proposals and recommendations for the future of Manx-Gaelic

Phil Gawne: Yn Greinneyder, or Facilitator For Manx

Objectives For Manx Gaelic (to December 2004)

1. Provide information, advice, guidance and support to new parents on the advantages of early bilingualism, ensuring that materials supporting the use of Manx in the home and at pre-school groups are produced and distributed to parents through the IOM hospital maternity wing, to all Manx speakers and learners and to all relevant health visitors and mid-wives.

2. Support the development and expansion of Manx pre-school groups, ensuring the highest standards of language transmission are obtained and establish a secure funding source for all Manx pre-school groups.

3. Ensure that parental demand for Manx-medium primary education is met by supporting the Manx-medium primary class and providing educational and financial support to parents.

4. Ensure that adequate numbers of teachers and language workers are available in the future through the development of a "one year to fluency" immersion course for teachers, nursery nurses and all adult learners and through the development of retraining programmes for unqualified Manx speakers.

5. Provide a secure status for the language, ensuring that this status is adequately maintained by establishing an advisory body for language planning and policy for Manx Gaelic, which would also adopt the role of main funding organization. To be effective, such an agency must employ at least one full-time equivalent language development post.

6. Ensure that opportunities exist to raise children's awareness, knowledge and general understanding of Manx as widely as possible throughout the school system. Do everything to ensure that increased levels of

staffing are provided for the Manx language programme, ensure that all schools timetable optional Manx for years 3 – 7 and ensure that the TCG (GCSE equivalent) is offered by all secondary schools.

7. Offer the new ATG (A-level equivalent) to adults and as a language option to year 12 in secondary schools.

8. Increase the success rate of adult learners by raising the standard and quality of provision at this level by ensuring that teacher training courses are available and establishing a centrally based national resource centre for material for all learners

9. Develop and expand the use of Manx in the public, private and voluntary sectors through the production and distribution of marketing materials aimed at increasing the profile of Manx in business and government.

10. All government departments to ensure that all new and replacement signs erected follow government policy which recommends that all street name signs, village and town boundary signs are bilingual, except where the traditional Manx name is the accepted form, and encourage local authorities to follow this recommendation.

11. Extend community-based language activity through the development and implementation of a comprehensive programme of events for speakers and learners.

12. Implement practical measures to raise the status of the Manx language, including: the IOM Post Office Authority to adopt as official policy that all Manx Gaelic-addressed mail to be delivered as quickly and efficiently as English-addressed mail; IOM Post Office Authority and IOM Treasury to have drawn up and implemented a strategy for the inclusion of some Manx Gaelic on all stamps, coins and bank notes; and Manx Heritage Foundation and other appropriate organizations to have developed a support structure for Manx-language internet providers.

13. Ensure language planning is effective and up-to-date by scrutinizing and adopting international minority language initiatives and treaties. IOM Government to have formally requested that the UK Government extends the provisions of the European Charter for Regional and Minority Languages to the Isle of Man.

14. Develop and standardize terminology and translation with Coonceil ny Gaelgey (official translation service) undertaking widespread promotion of its services and producing specialized terminology dictionaries to be widely available and free on the World Wide Web.

15. Provide a more Gaelic influence on the accent of spoken Manx and ensure that good standards of Gaelic usage are maintained by releasing tape or CD recordings of native Manx speech and through expansion of Manx Heritage Foundation's Manx language writing fund.

16. Produce a development strategy for Manxlanguage broadcasting and publication in all currently available media.

Notes

1. Recommended reading for students of the history of the Manx language is this work by Belchem, J. (ed.) (2000) *A New History of the Isle of Man: Volume V: The Modern Period 1830–1999*, Liverpool University Press.

2. Of particular relevance to this article on Manx see Fishman, Joshua, *Reversing Language Shift*, Clevedon, Multilingual Matters, 1991, particularly its introduction which provides ideological clarification as to the why of language restoration.

3. Of no less importance is the second Fishman volume, hence see Fishman, Joshua: *Can Threatened Languages Be Saved?* Clevedon, Multilingual Matters, Clevedon, 2001.

4. "Manx-Gaelic At the Turn of the Millennium", Stowell, Brian, *Carn* 116, 2001, p.12. For the first time since the mid 1800s, Manx is now being employed as a medium of instruction in Manx schools. Church-run Manx-medium schools were shut down in the 1800s by the British Government and the new Manx-medium primary school at Ballacottier which opened its doors in September 2001 is a symbolic landmark in Manx cultural history which cannot be overstated. More will follow.

5. For a generalized look at the recent political and linguistic changes in the Celtic countries, see *Celtic Dawn*, Peter Berresford Ellis, Y Lolfa, 2002. It goes far towards explaining both the historical background of Celtic nationalism as well as its present state of evolution.

6. Also see *The Celtic Revolution*, by Peter Berresford Ellis, Y Lolfa, 1985 (first printing) for an account of the historical background of each of the six Celtic nations.

References

Baker, C. (1993) *Foundations of Bilingual Education and Bilingualism*, Clevedon, Multilingual Matters.

Bird, H. (1991) *An Island That Led – The History of Manx Education* (Vol. 1) Isle of Man, Hinton Bird, Rushen Vicarage, Port St Mary.

Belchem, J. (ed.) (2000) *A New History of the Isle of Man* (Vol. V) The Modern Period 1830–1999, Liverpool University Press.

Broderick, G. (1991) *Language Contact in the British Isles: Proceedings of the Eighth International Symposium on Language Contact in Europe*, Douglas, Isle of Man, 1988.

Cooke. P. (1993) "Globalization, economic organization and the emergence of regional interstate partnerships" in C. H. Williams, (ed.) *The Political Geography of the New World Order*, London, Wiley, pp.46–58.

Council of Europe (1992) *European Charter for Regional or Minority Languages*, Strasbourg, Council of Europe.

Dorian, Nancy C. (1988) *The Celtic Languages In The British Isles*

Durkacz, V. E. (1983) *The Decline of The Celtic Languages*, Edinburgh, John Donald.

Fishman, Joshua (1991) *Reversing Language Shift*, Clevedon, Multilingual Matters.

Fishman, Joshua (2001) *Can Threatened Languages Be Saved?*, Clevedon, Multilingual Matters.

Grin, F. (1996) "Economic Approaches to Language and Language Planning", *International Journal of the Sociology of Language*, Vol. 121, pp.1–16.

Hechter, M.(1975) *Internal Colonialism: The Celtic Fringe in British National Development*, London, Routledge.

Heusaff, Alan (1998) *Carn 105*, Dublin, The Celtic League.

Kinvig, R. H. (1975: 3rd ed.) *The Isle of Man: a Social, Cultural and Political History*, Liverpool University Press.

Kneen, John (1990) *English–Manx Dictionary*, Isle of Man, Castletown Press.

Kneen, John (1978) *Manx Idioms and Phrases*, Yn Cheshaght Ghailckagh.

Minority Rights Group (1991) *Minorities and Autonomy in Western Europe*, London, Minority Rights Group.

Mlinar, Z. (ed.) (1992) *Globalization and Territorial Identities*, Aldershot, Avebury Press.

Ó Cuiv, Éamonn (1998) Speech, International Conference on Language Legislation, Killiney, County Dublin, 15 October 1998.

Ó Rahilly, T. F. (1972) *Irish Dialects Past and Present*, Dublin, Institute For Advanced Studies.

O'Riagain, P. (1992) *Language Planning and Language Shift as Strategies of Social Reproduction,* Dublin, Instituid Teangeolaiochta Eireann.

Rayfield, J. R. (1970) *The Languages of A Bilingual Community*, The Hague, Mouton.

Saunders, G. (1988) *Bilingual Children: Guidance For The Family*, Clevedon, Multilingual Matters.

Stowell, Brian, "*Manx-Gaelic At The Turn of The Millenium*", Carn 112, p.12.

Thomson, R. L. and Pilgrim, A. J. (1988) *Outline of Manx Language and Literature*, Isle of Man, Yn Cheshaght Ghailckagh, St Jude's.

IV. Conclusion

What is the Way Forward?

Diarmuid Ó Néill

IN THIS WORK, we have looked at the six Celtic languages, their historical background, their present circumstances, their individual positioning according to the GIDS scale and at some very specific proposals and recommendations made regarding each of them.

We must never lose sight, however, of the ultimate objective of revival efforts on behalf of all six languages which now go back almost a century and a half. Increasingly, a consensus is emerging among Celtic language activists that intergenerational transmission and family and community use are the critical areas which must be tackled. The goal, of course, which we are seeking is nothing less than full-scale normalization of Celtic speech in the Celtic countries, or re-vernacularization of the Celtic languages, as Joshua Fishman would put it.

The Celtic world is a diverse one, not only politically and linguistically, but also because language revival efforts in each country are at different stages of a hopefully similar process which, in the end, will lead to successful language renewal and rejuvenation. Is there really a chance that the Celtic languages will re-establish themselves on a significant scale as normally-spoken vernaculars in their own countries, in spite of the severe dislocation they have undergone in recent centuries? The ways and means do exist to reverse language shift. The question is, will they be applied and, if applied, will they be applied in as thorough a manner as is necessary to achieve the critical mass[261] that would achieve a bilingual society in each of the Celtic countries?

At present Ireland, Wales and Brittany have made the greatest strides towards laying the foundations for successful wide-scale re-vernacularization of the Irish, Welsh and Breton languages. Irish-, Welsh- and

Breton-medium education have made the most widespread increases in absolute numbers but also proportionally and on a national basis. At present, Welsh-medium primary education accounts for about 20 per cent of students in Wales, Irish-medium education continues its slow but steady increase both proportionally and absolutely and, presently, 6 per cent of primary students in the Irish Republic and about 1.5 per cent in Northern Ireland are being educated through the Irish language, while Breton-medium education will, within a year or two, account for about 5 per cent of all primary students in Breizh Izel, the traditional Breton-speaking region. The present figure of 2.5 per cent of all primary students in Brittany as a whole may not seem impressive but one must bear in mind the severe political and financial constraints bearing down on the Breton-language schools which make its growth quite impressive indeed. Manx-medium education is now a reality, with 15 students now enrolled (2002/03 school year) in the first Manx-medium school. Scottish Gaelic-medium education has continued to expand in the younger age brackets but nationally only one school has been established outside the traditional Gaedhealtachd (in Glasgow) and, in the traditional Gaelic-speaking region of the north-west, only about one third of the local children are being educated through Gaelic so, in addition to tackling the urban south, there is also a need to confront the low percentage of children in the Gaedhealtachd itself (an irreplaceable human resource for the language) who are being educated in Gaelic-medium schools. This issue is part of the larger RLS issue of where Gaelic fits in Scotland – only in the traditional Gaedhealtachd, or in a national context? Cornish-medium schools do not yet exist but on 5 November, 2002 the UK Government included Cornish within its definition of the European Charter of Minority Languages by signing the Charter for Cornish. This will lead inexorably to Cornish being introduced in the schools as both a subject and a medium of instruction.

However, there arises the question again; can a clean break with the past be made by Celtic language activists with the old tactic of producing Celtic-speaking students, whether through the school system or through adult courses, with insufficient thought given to the next stage of language planning which must inevitably follow – the congregation of these new Celtic speakers into new Celtic-speaking families, networks and indeed new communities?

None of the language agencies working for the promotion of the Celtic languages has yet adopted anything remotely resembling a blueprint for the widespread re-establishment of Celtic-speaking communities, whether it is Foras Na Gaeilge in Ireland, Ofis ar Brezhoneg in Brittany, the Welsh Language Board in Wales or any other language body, voluntary or government-sponsored. Paradoxically, such new Celtic-speaking communities and networks are a reality – in all six Celtic nations. Whether one is referring to the new Irish-speaking communities of Belfast, and Cork or to the Cornish-speaking networks which have slowly formed in the past two generations, or to the new Breton-speaking networks which have formed in proximity to the new Breton-medium schools of Diwan, Div Yezh and Dihun in the larger towns and cities of Brittany, one is discussing a phenomenon which is a reality.

Achieving the critical mass which is necessary to involve a much greater percentage of the population at large would require the kind of language planning which only an organization specifically dedicated to the establishment of new Irish-speaking or Cornish-speaking or Breton-speaking communities can provide. If this step – stage 6 in the GIDS scale – is not effectively tackled, then it is unlikely that the Celtic languages will be able to maintain their present tenuous hold as spoken languages in those districts where they are still the everyday language – western Ireland, northern and western Wales, western Brittany and the Western Isles of Scotland, for more than another two generations at most. In addition, if stage 6 of the GIDS model is not tackled successfully, the success of more advanced stages, such as 5 through 1, are open to question. The Celtic languages cannot make any impact in the worksphere or in government administration and higher education if they cannot build a more secure foundation for themselves in family and community life.

An admonition for Celtic language activists – the need to organize Celtic-speaking communities on a much wider scale

In summary, let it be said that the most important message of this study is a call to language movements in all six Celtic countries to establish an organization in each which is dedicated to the establishment and fostering of new communities in its respective Celtic language, in the same manner that organizations to promote and expand new Celtic-medium schools were established, such as Diwan and Gaelscoileanna. This is a "five minutes to midnight" reminder that the establishment of new Celtic-speaking communities, or the failure to establish new Celtic-speaking communities, will make or break the future survival of the Celtic languages.

Will the Celtic languages really thrive once again?

Alba/Scotland

Scottish-Gaelic seems, on the surface, to be in desperate straits but one should not underestimate the influence that resurgent Scottish nationalism may have on the language movement and also the determination of Gaelic activists to pull their language out of the fire. Gaelic activists often point to the detachment of many Lowlanders, including Nationalists, towards Gaelic and, while they are correct, the general feeling is that a rising tide lifts all boats, so a more self-governing Scotland may yet prove to be a more "Gaelic-friendly" environment than the completely centralistic state which has governed Scotland for the past 300 years and which, in reality, strives for the assimilation of the Celtic languages rather than their continued survival. Important lessons have been learned from past mistakes and there is an increasing realization that Gaelic must look to the urban south for new speakers, rather than continuing to rely on the Western Isles alone to carry the torch. Just as with Irish, it remains to be seen how successful urban revitalization of Gaelic in Scotland will be – and yet there is no question that it is a key element in the equation.

In the meantime, Gaelic-medium education continues to expand at a moderate rate. Gaelic is now used in broadcasting on both television and radio. Publishing still suffers, however, from a limited market. To a certain extent, one could say that Gaelic is present at almost all of the eight stages of the GIDS scale, if only in limited geographical and social groups. Comunn na Gàidhlig is the main Gaelic-language body in the voluntary sector. In addition, there is now a Scottish government minister whose portfolio includes Gaelic so, clearly, the establishment of the new Scottish Parliament has brought some positive change, although some Gaels would contest this – in the true combative Celtic spirit!

Alba Nuadh/Nova Scotia

If Gaelic in Scotland is imperilled, this fear is greatly multiplied for Gaelic in Cape Breton and Nova Scotia. In Nova Scotia, any attempt to re-vernacularise Gaelic among wider sectors of the population must first tackle the basic stages of the GIDS scale, from 8–5, before anything more ambitious may be attempted. In the Nova Scotia context, with only 452 speakers in 1991, as opposed to roughly 80,000 in 1890, Gaelic is a language which has clearly suffered massive erosion. Gaelic RLS advocates in Nova Scotia must focus on the basics. In this case, pre-school immersion in Gaelic, the establishment of Gaelic-medium schools, the expansion of adult courses in Gaelic, before higher level functions can be conquered.

Fortunately, Gaelic has some friends in the government and the release of the *Gaelic Nova Scotia Report* on 12 November, 2002 by the Nova Scotia Government, at last sees some official recognition of the problem.

Breizh/Brittany

Numerically, Breton had 700,000 speakers as recently as 1970, although this has fallen to 304,000 in 2003. Breton has factors working in its favour and against it. Public opinion is solidly behind the new Breton-medium schools established since 1977 (Diwan, Div Yezh and Dihun) which, although still only with 8,877 students (2003/04 school year) in their charge, are an important symbol of the determination to keep this language alive. In addition, the continued expansion of publishing in the Breton language, a new Breton-language television station Télé Breizh, numerous radio stations which broadcast in Breton, as well as greater social planning launched by such bodies as the Office of the Breton Language. Particularly worthy of mention is the present Ya d'ar Brezhoneg (Yes to Breton) campaign launched to increase use of Breton in businesses and in the workplace.

At the time of writing, however, the heavily symbolic crisis over whether or not Diwan was/is to receive public funding has concluded. The reader will recall how the French Council of State vetoed an agreement between Diwan and the French Education Ministry in the autumn of 2001 which would have integrated Diwan with the public schools – and public funding. In November of 2002 the French Council of State brought down a final ruling against public integration with Diwan, dashing the hopes that France was becoming a more pluralistic and democratic society. This chapter is yet another indication that sociolinguistic planning not backed up with political clout is, in effect, impotent. On 30 May, 2003 the Cultural Council of Brittany announced that it would bring charges against France in the

European Court of Human Rights in Strasbourg over the issue so, at the time of writing, this chapter is not yet finished.

Breton sociolinguistic planning in the future may be forced to put more and more emphasis on political status to ensure hard-won gains are not undermined by a less than friendly political environment.

Cymru/Wales

The present state of Welsh gives reason for both optimism and concern. At present strong numerically, Welsh appears on the surface to have made it relatively intact into the new millennium. However, as the rapid collapse of Irish in the 1840s and Breton in the 1960s show, there is no safety in numbers. In 2005 there is, in areas of south-western Wales, the problem of Welsh speakers abandoning Welsh, and then there is the problem of a flood of monoglot English-speaking incomers who are not assimilated, settling in most areas of the traditional Welsh-speaking heartland. In addition, there has been a constant haemorrhage of Welsh speakers who have gone over to English monoglotism during the twentieth century. The 1911 census recorded a high of 977,000 speakers.[262] In 2001 the figure was about 580,000. By the 1960s the Welsh were sufficiently alarmed to produce Saunders Lewis's famous 1962 broadcast "The Fate of the Language" which many regard as a turning point in the Welsh language movement.

Since then, although we have witnessed continued language loss, we have also seen important developments such as Welsh-language television and radio, as well as a dramatic expansion in Welsh-medium education to roughly 20 per cent in 2003. Also of great importance are the campaigns that have been mounted in the public sector by the Welsh Language Board, encouraging greater use of Welsh in the family and elsewhere in society. So, clearly, Welsh has factors working for and against it. Welsh has a chance to stabilize and survive, just as other endangered languages in the recent past, such as Hebrew, Québec French, Basque and Catalan. The establishment of the Welsh Assembly in 1998 indicates that Welsh nationalism is not dead either and this can only be a healthy development, as we have seen elsewhere the price paid by threatened languages with no political champions to back them up.

Argentina

The position of Welsh in Argentina is, of course, vastly different from Welsh in Wales but even here there is room for optimism. Several thousand have some knowledge of Welsh with varying degrees of fluency. The circumstances are different but the GIDS scale still applies to this situation also. Welsh has to be maintained at the community and family level if long-term survival is to be ensured.

More particularly in this case, Welsh must tackle the erosion it has suffered among the younger age sectors who have gone over almost entirely to Spanish. However, as Welsh is still widely employed by those over 40, there still exists the option of utilizing older speakers for re-vernacularization efforts.

Éire/Ireland

In the case of Ireland, it must be stated that the main existing language bodies do not at present support the establishment of new Irish-speaking communities. Both the government agency Foras na Gaeilge – the new all-Ireland language body and Comhdháil Náisiúnta na Gaeilge, the voluntary language body for the Irish Republic, continue to support the present policy of Irish by choice. This is an error on their part. It does not arise out of antipathy to the Irish language (as with the hostility of Paris to the Breton language) but rather a failure to recognize that the goals and policies pursued by the Irish Government since 1921 towards the Irish language can no longer be considered appropriate or effective policies (not in the Republic and certainly not in the more challenging arena of Northern Ireland).

Foras na Gaeilge, the new language body for both the Irish Republic and Northern Ireland, is a child of the Peace Accord in Northern Ireland. As well as the promotion of the Gaelic language in both the north and south of Ireland, it is also charged with the promotion of Ulster Scots (introduced into Ulster in the 1600s by Scottish colonists), a speech which is very closely related to Scots or Lallans, the Anglo-Saxon dialect where it was first established by Saxon invaders in the fifth century and developed through the centuries into a speech which was kindred to, but not the same as, English. The mandate of Foras na Gaeilge is also to promote the Irish language in both parts of Ireland. As we have seen in the section on Northern Ireland, this task was rendered well-nigh impossible until the present, due to obstruction by the British Government and the Unionist administration in Ulster. It is legitimate to ask whether the new language body is up to the task of promoting Irish in Ulster – something ardently desired by the majority of the Nationalist population of Ulster (roughly 50–55 per cent of the people concerned). Hopefully, Foras na Gaeilge will have an impact.

On the surface, it would appear that things have taken a turn for the better with the establishment of Foras na Gaeilge. Its budget was set to increase from £13 million in 2001/02 to £17 million in 2002/03 but a cut of £2 million was announced in late 2002, raising questions in many quarters yet again about the Irish Government's real level of commitment to the Irish language. The objectives of the body are greater status, acquisition planning, greater usage, communications improvements, as well as more accurate planning and research. Foras na Gaeilge takes the sensible approach of promoting one dialect throughout Ireland (still an issue on occasion, due to the traditional rivalry between the Ulster dialect and the official standard dialect of the Republic, as well as resentment in the Gaeltacht towards "Dublin Irish". That is, the standard dialect of Irish developed in the 1940s based on the west-central Irish dialect of Connemara in Galway although also influenced strongly by Munster Irish, which at that time possessed a far greater body of written literature than the other dialects). This has at times been a contentious issue, with language activists in the north favouring the Ulster dialect of Irish for publishing, as well as in media such as radio broadcasts; but most language activists are in agreement that the Irish language movement can afford the luxury of only one dialect. Other objectives of Foras na Gaeilge include complete working and official status for Irish in the European Union and also in Northern Ireland.

Another important issue is the Irish Language Bill which has now been published under the new name, The Official Languages Bill. It initially met with dissatisfaction. However, following negotiations with the voluntary language bodies such as Comhdháil Náisiúnta na Gaeilge, a compromise was reached which was acceptable to both the Government and the language bodies. Some of the initial criticisms had been that the bill left too much power at the discretion of the Minister for the Gaeltacht – and hence other politicians – rather than enshrining it as legislation with teeth which could be enforced in the courts by the average citizen. Regarding the use of Irish in court, even in the Gaeltacht the Bill had been very vague about this right. Even after the amendments, the private sector is not really tackled as regards the promotion of Irish in the workplace (giving us a clue as to what worries the establishment in Dublin). Interestingly, Foras na Gaeilge felt obliged to criticise the bill at first, as possibly reducing the legal status of the language. It still remains to be seen just how effectively the Bill which has been passed allows Irish speakers to uphold their rights in court.

On the positive side, Irish-language radio and television services and printed media are now a reality. In addition, the Gaelscoileanna Irish-medium network is proving to be a great success story. However, all of these isolated strands have yet to be woven into one thoughtful, cohesive and effective language strategy.

In summary, it must be reluctantly said that both Foras na Gaeilge and Comhdháil Náisiúnta na Gaeilge are still not entirely marching in the right direction. The true goal of the Irish language movement today remains what it was in the nineteenth century, when it was epitomized by the Gaelic League, and that is the restoration of Irish as a national language in the everyday life of Ireland where it is spoken as commonly as English. Half measures which do not address the question of making Irish a family and community language again everywhere in Ireland cannot set the tone for a future trek back to an Irish-speaking Ireland. What is needed is a body or organization with an ideology to match which can provide real vision and guidance at this critical crossroads for Irish. Such a body has yet to appear on the scene in Ireland.

Kernow/Cornwall

Cornish, the last remnant of British Celtic in south-western Britain, remained in daily use till the mid-1700s and probably early-1800s in isolated fishing villages in western Cornwall. The modern revival got underway in 1904, spearheaded by Henry Jenner but it is important to remember that Cornish probably never ceased to be spoken and remained in limited use throughout the nineteenth century. A language without the financial resources available to Welsh and Irish and without the residue of native speakers that Irish, Gaelic, Breton and Welsh still possess, the Cornish have nevertheless made great strides and are clearly planning to advance much further. Although dialect standardization remains a problem as there are three vying for support in Cornwall, the question of dialect also plagued the Irish and Bretons until they eventually accepted a standard.

Cornish has not yet been introduced into the schools, either as a subject or as a medium of instruction – but this is inevitable, eventually, and Cornish teachers are already preparing for it. The goals of the Cornish language movement, as elaborated by Wella Brown of the Cornish Language Board, are ultimately 1) for Cornish to be as widely used as English in Cornish society; 2) the inclusion of Cornish in the European Charter of Minority Languages; 3) the appointment of a Cornish Language Officer; 4) the establishment of Cornish at all levels of the educational system; 5) training courses for teachers; 6) broadcasting opportunities in radio and television and 7) greater funding for research and funding of Cornish.

While these are arguably long-term goals, Cornish language planners clearly have in mind a thriving and not merely living Cornish language in the future which will take its rightful place at all eight stages of the GIDS scale, a position not occupied by Cornish since the Saxon conquest in the tenth century. Two important recent developments have taken place regarding Cornish. Firstly on 5 November, 2002 the United Kingdom government signed the European Charter of Minority Languages to include Cornish and in May 2004 it was announced that preparations were being made to introduce Cornish into the public schools as a regular subject for the first time.

Mannin/The Isle of Man

Manx Gaelic has gone from virtual extinction in the 1940s to having 1,689 speakers according to the 2001 census. It is now a regular school subject available to many, if not all, who desire to study it. A Manx-medium school is now in operation. Manx can be heard on the radio and seen in newspaper columns, even if no Manx-language daily yet exists. Publishing in Manx is on the upswing as demand for dictionaries, school texts and other literature increases.

While the Manx Government has partly facilitated this progress and recently signed the European Charter of Minority Languages to ensure inclusion of Manx, it is essentially the people and the voluntary sector of the Manx language movement, rather than its thoroughly Anglicized establishment, who have saved Manx from oblivion. They aim to do more than that, as Phil Gawne makes clear in his outline of goals for the future, which include more pre-school groups, more Manx-medium schools, more social planning aimed at greater bilingualism in new families, increased adult learning of Manx, increased use of Manx in the economy, and the list goes on.

The Manx are realists and do not foresee a Manx-speaking society in the near future. If they continue to make the same kind of progress they have been making, a society where Manx is on a par with English is not out of the question in the future.

Can the Celtic languages be restored?

One would like to give an unqualified "yes" in response to this question. However, languages can die. Sumerian, Gaulish, Etruscan, Pictish and many others are no longer with us. There is another kind of death, where a language is officially used, but where it has lost its cohort of first-language speakers. If the Celtic languages are to avoid this fate, the establishment of new Celtic-speaking communities is all the more important. Provided the six languages in question do focus on the critical stage 6 of the GIDS scale and later build upon it in the higher order stages, from 4 through 1, they can re-establish themselves in lost territory. It is also important for each language to select goals that are realistic. Obviously the Cornish do not have the financial resources of the Welsh or the Irish. In addition, Breton is more constrained politically than Welsh or Gaelic or Irish, so it must set more limited status goals for itself which, for example, cannot for the foreseeable future include official status (a Breton goal nevertheless). The four Celtic languages which find themselves more constrained for financial and political reasons: Breton, Cornish, Manx and Gaelic must focus initially on the lower-order stages; 8 – 5, more adult literacy, more community use, some school use, etc.

At present, it is only Welsh and Irish that can pursue linguistic expansion at all eight stages of the GIDS scale. Both have achieved greater political autonomy, both have hundreds of thousands of literate speakers, both have the financial resources and, most importantly, both countries have not accepted absolute English linguistic dominance, advanced as it is in both Wales and Ireland. They have opportunities to advance which other threatened languages do not. Indeed, it could be said that Irish is presently within striking distance of re-establishing itself on a wide scale as a community language, a position it has not really occupied since the pre-First World War era. For all six Celtic languages to advance, they must better come to understand their strengths and weaknesses as they lay out their future strategies for what will be six new success stories in the field of sociolinguistics in the new millennium.

Endnotes

[1] "Language shift" is the term used for describing the change in language use from a threatened language to a dominant one. Reversing this shift is a primary concern of those committed to the threatened languages, and the theory of Reversing Language Shift is being constantly developed by sociolinguists and those responsible for language planning.

[2] It is ironic that the Scottish-Gaelic tradition in Nova Scotia, while not dominant, is very much a part of the mainstream identity of Nova Scotia in contrast to the Gaelic Highland tradition in Scotland.

[3] Taken from Fishman, J. *Reversing Language Shift*, Multilingual Matters, Clevedon, 1991, p. 395.

[4] These would be called "state" schools in the UK.

[5] In May of 2004, plans were announced to prepare for the introduction of Cornish as a subject into the regular curriculum of public schools.

[6] Here I am taking Fishman's direct advice to me, see Fishman, 1997. He also avers that "Williams tells us less than he easily could about what it is that Welsh and other nationalists "feel" about the Welsh language, why they not only champion it but why they adore it, what qualities they believe that it, and only it, possesses, and what more responsibilities they are convinced are owed to it and why". (1997, p.148).

[7] See Waldo Williams, *Dail Pren*, Gwasg Gomer, (Llandysul, 1956) and for an appreciation of his work Ned Thomas, "Waldo Williams – In Two Fields", in Hans-Werner Ludwig and Lothar Fietz, (eds.), *Poetry in the British Isles*, University of Wales Press, (Cardiff, 1995), pp.253–66; see also Tony Conran, *The Peacemakers: Selected Poems of Waldo Williams*, Gomer Press, (Llandysul, 1997). W. R. Evans, *Awen Y Moelydd*, Gwasg Gomer, (Llandysul, 1983). W. R. was my headteacher at Ysgol Gymraeg y Barri.

[8] Here the Welsh language movement is defined, in broadly social as opposed to narrowly linguistic terms, as the organized attempt to promote the interests of Welsh speakers in the life of the nation. In focussing on the ideas of Saunders Lewis and Gwynfor Evans, my approach parallels Fishman's advice to adopt a rather more

phenomenological approach to language and nationalism.

[9] The Welsh translations were sponsored for two reasons: to seal the populace within a Protestant state for fear of Catholic incursions and to diffuse the spread of English, because side by side with the Welsh version, a copy of the English version was placed in each parish church so that those reading them might "by comparing both tongues together soon attain to a knowledge of the English tongue", quoted in Davies (1993), p.24.

[10] See W. T. R. Pryce and C. H. Williams. "Sources and Methods in the Study of Language Areas: A Case Study of Wales", in Colin H. Williams, (ed.), *Language in Geographic Context*, (Clevedon, Avon, 1988), pp.167–237.

[11] On religious influences, see R. Tudur Jones, *Ffydd ac Argyfwng Cenedl*, (Abertawe, 1971); R. Tudur Jones, *Yr Undeb: Hanes yr Undeb Annibynwyr Cymreig*, 1872–1971, (Abertawe, 1975).

[12] Some of the leaders include the Rev Michael D. Jones, who led a small exodus to Patagonia in 1865 to establish a Welsh migrant community, known as Y Wladfa; Emrys ap Iwan, the first minister of religion to appear before a court of law and insist on the primacy of the Welsh language in legal proceedings in Wales; Dan Isaac Davies, the HMI for Schools who advocated a greater use of Welsh-medium education; Thomas Gee, the publisher of such ambitious multi-volume Encyclopaedias as "*Gwyddoniadur*" and advocate of mass circulation periodicals in Welsh; and two members of a most influential family, O. M. Edwards, the university teacher, writer, publisher and first Chief HMI for schools in Wales, who sought to establish a more tolerant approach to bilingualism by attacking the injustice associated with the Welsh NOT within the school system. His son, Sir Ifan ab Owen Edwards established Urdd Gobaith Cymru (The Welsh League of Youth) in 1922 which has become the largest mass movement in Wales encouraging children and young adults to develop skills, competence and leadership qualities in a variety of contexts, principally community work, eisteddfodau, and sporting achievements.

[13] The original aim of Plaid Genedlaethol Cymru was "to keep Wales Welsh-speaking. That is, to include (a) making the Welsh language the only official language of Wales and thus a language required for all local authority transactions and mandatory for every official and servant of every local authority in Wales; (b) making the Welsh language a medium of education in Wales from the elementary school through to the University". Quoted in A. Butt Philip, *The Welsh Question: Nationalism in Welsh Politics*, 1945–1970, University of Wales Press, (Cardiff, 1975), p.14; see also D. H. Davies, *The Welsh Nationalist Party* 1925–1945, University of Wales Press, (Cardiff, 1983).

[14] Nationalism is not an autonomous force, and we should be careful not to interpret individual nationalist activists as agents of a transcendent ideology, but rather as part of practical politics. Nevertheless, the ideological agenda set by early nationalists did construct a set of national goals and provide a context within which one could measure the success of the national programme for the survival of a distinct Welsh identity.

[15] Particularly significant in this respect was the work of D. J. Davies whose admiration for Scandinavian social credit policies, economic cooperation and

decentralisation of power were reflected in a series of publications such as *The Economics of Welsh Self-Government* (Caernarfon, 1931) and, together with Noëlle Davies, *Can Wales Afford Self-Government?* (Caernarfon, 1939). For a critique of the class versus nationalist appeals see J. Davies, *The Green and the Red: Nationalism and Ideology in 20th Century Wales*, (Aberystwyth, 1980).

[16] In this respect, there are many parallels to be explored between idealists such as Saunders Lewis and Sabino de Arana, Valenti Almirall, Yann Foueré, E. MacNeill and Éamon de Valera.

[17] "The Principles of Nationalism", delivered at Plaid Cymru's first Summer School in 1926. For development of his ideas, see the collections S. Lewis, *Canlyn Arthur*, Gwasg Gomer, (Llandysul, 1985) and S. Lewis, *Ati, Wyr Ifainc*, Gwasg Prifysgol Cymru, (Cardiff, 1986).

[18] See Lewis, 1975, p.7. For a variant on the same theme, see also Bobi Jones, *Crist a Chenedlaetholdeb*, Gwasg Efengylaidd Cymru, (Pen-y-bont ar Ogwr), 1994.

[19] Quoted in D. G. Jones, "His Politics" in *Presenting Saunders Lewis*, J. R. Jones and G. Thomas, (eds.), University of Wales Press, (Cardiff, 1973), p.33.

[20] These conflicting interpretations are summarized in the exchange, which took place in the pages of *Y Llenor* in 1927, dubbed by W.J. Gruffydd as a struggle between Reaction and Revolt. At the root of the debate is a profound difference between idealism and pragmatism, in spiritual as in socio-political affairs. Whereas Lewis's ideas are based on a pristine conception of what Wales could and should be, Gruffydd, and those he represented, portrayed Wales as it was, and wanted to advance Wales into a co-equal, fully recognized partnership within the British state, wherein Welsh distinctiveness might be secured.

[21] In displaying an idiosyncratic admixture of his aesthetic and ascetic strains, his principled objection to crude materialism, as revealed in his opposition to the slogan "Bread Before Beauty", did not play very well before a Welsh audience mired in a period of acute economic depression, and enamoured by the appeal of socialism. Although many have described him as revolutionary or visionary, it would be more accurate to describe him as a political idealist, disdainful of colleagues who would quibble at the lack of pragmatism of many policies he advocated. A younger generation of Welsh scholars is today far more critical of his role and long-term impact on the national movement.

[22] For these allegations see D. H. Davies, op. cit. pp.109–116. A re-examination of the relationship between Fascism, anti-Semitism and the views of Saunders Lewis and his colleagues is available in R. M. Jones, *Ysbryd y Cwlwm*, Gwasg Prifysgol Cymru, (Cardiff, 1998), pp.324–35.

[23] His father, Daniel Evans, was a department store owner and a deacon at Tabernacl Independent Chapel, Barry, Glamorgan, then one of the most Anglicized, thriving towns in Wales. Never fully conscious of his nationality until he went up to Oxford, and re-learned Welsh, he was always something of an enigma, simultaneously embodying and standing apart from mainstream Welsh culture. In protest at the jingoistic justification of the Second World War, he preached pacifism in his

home-town main square among other places and shunned the armed forces for a life as a market gardener in Llangadog, then steeped in Welsh rural culture. For details see G. Evans, *For the Sake of Wales,* (Bridgend, 1996).

[24] Of course, several valleys in the Peak District and in the Pennines were also converted into reservoirs, but that did not figure prominently in Welsh discourse.

[25] G. Evans, *Non-violent Nationalism,* Fellowship for Reconciliation. (New Malden, 1973).

[26] D. Fennell, "Where it went wrong: The Irish language movement", *Planet,* 36, (1977); R. Hindley, *The Death of the Irish Language,* Routledge, (London, 1990) gives a pessimistic and, many would argue, flawed account of the real situation.

[27] Evans, op. cit. p.15.

[28] See J. Davies, op. cit., 1981; 1985; and C. H. Williams, op. cit., 1982; 1994. For an insightful treatment of the relative failure of the notion of community defence in mobilizing support for nationalism, see L. McAllister, "Community in Ideology: The Political Philosophy of Plaid Cymru", Ph.D. Thesis, University of Wales, 1995.

[29] For example, Cynog Dafis chaired the Post-16 Education Committee while Rhodri Glyn Thomas chaired the Culture Committee. Both were leading advocates of the emphasis on increased bilingualism within the Assembly and in the Government's eventual statement on its language policy, as detailed in Iaith Pawb, (2003).

[30] Since the Acts of Union of England and Wales, 1536 and 1542, the Welsh language had been proscribed as a language of officialdom and thus did not benefit from being institutionalized in the affairs of the state. For details on relevant legislation before the Welsh Language Act of 1967, see D. B. Walters "The legal recognition and protection of pluralism", *Acta Juridica,* (1978), pp.305–26.

[31] For an authoritative account, see C. Dafis, "Cymdeithas yr Iaith Gymraeg" in *The Welsh Language Today,* M. Stephens (ed.), Gomer Press, (Llandysul, 1973). Cynog Dafis has recently retired as an influential Plaid Cymru member of the National Assembly and former Chair of the Education Over-16 Committee of the Assembly.

[32] However, there is a strategic qualifier to this, for recall the last impulse of the "Fate of the Language" BBC (Cardiff, 1962) lecture: "The language is more important than self-government. In my opinion, if any kind of self-government for Wales was obtained before Welsh is admitted and used as an official language in local and national administration in the Welsh-speaking areas of our country, then the language will never achieve official status at all, and its death would be quicker than it will be under the rule of England."

[33] In discussing contemporary causes such as student rebellions in France and the US or the anti-Vietnam war campaigns, K. O. Morgan argues that "the Welsh language movement had virtually nothing in common with any of these overseas movements; but in so far as it inspired the young and seemed to appeal to traditional folk culture in contrast to the shoddiness and false glamour of commercialized capitalism, it helped speed on militancy", *Rebirth of a Nation: Wales 1880–1980,* University of Wales Press, (Cardiff, 1981), p.385.

[34] See C. H. Williams, "Non-violence and the Development of the Welsh Language

Society, 1962c. 1974," *Welsh History Review,* 8, 4, (1977), pp.426–55; C. H. Williams (ed.), *National Separatism,* University of Wales Press, (Cardiff, 1982), esp. pp.145–66; also C. H.Williams, Christian Witness and Non-Violent Principles of Nationalism in Kristian Gerner et. al. (eds.) *Stat, Nation, Konflikt,* Bra Böcker, (Lund, 1966), pp.343–93. On a more personal note, within the University of Wales, Swansea, branch of Cymdeithas yr Iaith in the late sixties to the mid-seventies, there was a great deal of support for parallel campaigns such as the Anti-Apartheid movement and the Third World First movement. Indeed, several student leaders such as myself were active in all three without there being any hint of contradiction either of method or purpose.

[35] This is not to deny the structural tension inherent in the relationship between Plaid Cymru and Cymdeithas yr Iaith, as illustrated in periodic demands that the latter adopt a lower profile during UK election campaigns for fear of damaging Plaid's electoral performance. A second illustration is the personal cameo provided by the different trajectories taken by Gwynfor Evans and Meinir Evans (father and daughter), for details see G. Evans, *For the Sake of Wales,* Welsh Academic Press, (Bridgend, 1996), pp.196–99.

[36] On migration, see the collection Ll. Dafis (ed.), *Yr Ieithoedd Llai: Cymathu Newydd-Ddyfodiaid, Cydweithgor Dwyieithrwydd yn Nyfed,* (Carmarthen, 1992).

[37] "The Fate of the Language" lecture was aimed at Plaid Cymru, not at the mobilization of a new language movement. However, there was a growing tension throughout the sixties and seventies between cultural nationalists, such as Adfer and Cymdeithas yr Iaith, and constitutional, parliamentary nationalists such as the Plaid Cymru leadership. For an insightful overview of the growth of the Welsh Language Society, see Dylan Phillips *Trwy Ddulliau Chwyldro*, Gwasg Gomer, (Llandysul, 1998).

[38] The Hughes–Parry Report (1965) on the status of the Welsh language received general support for the principle that the language should enjoy "equal validity" with English for official, governmental and legal purposes. Cledwyn Hughes, Welsh Secretary of State for Wales in the Wilson Cabinet, warmly endorsed the Report and, in time, the principle of "equal validity" was incorporated in the 1967 Welsh Language Act.

[39] For discussions of this theme, see C. H. Williams, "Minority Nationalist Historiography", in R. Johnson et al, *Nationalism, Self-Determination and Political Geography,* Croom Helm, (London, 1988); see also D. Z. Phillips, *J.R. Jones,* University of Wales Press, (Cardiff, 1995) and R. M. Jones, *Ysbryd y Cwlwm,* Gwasg Prifysgol Cymru, (Caerdydd, 1998).

[40] Out of this crisis of confidence there emerged a more convincing adherence to non-violent methods, as a result of the influence of Ffred Ffransis, and a distancing of dissenting groups such as Adfer, the Free Wales Army and other factions.

[41] In reality, of course, many friends of the Society, such as Alwyn Rees, worked tirelessly in encouraging the Welsh bourgeoisie and cultural establishment to stand shoulder to shoulder with the Society. Not such a difficult task as might be imagined, for many were naturally sympathetic and/or connected with the protestors either

as parents and relatives or former teachers and current lecturers. The Society might be likened to an advanced guard preparing the way for reform, which has been galvanized by the Welsh bourgeoisie. The historical record shows that, often, the Language Society's claims of its own role and success are widely exaggerated. In addition to the bureaucratic-technical intelligentsia, we should also recognize the work of sections of the Labour Party, especially in relation to the implementation of bilingual education and the advocacy of Welsh language rights.

[42] For a summary and analysis of the campaigns and incidents with which it was connected in its first decade 1963–73, see C. H. Williams, op. cit. (1977) Table 2 and pp.439–54.

[43] See E. Thomas, *The Welsh Extremist,* Y Lolfa, (Talybont, 1971); Williams, C. H., "Non-violence and the development of the Welsh Language Society", *The Welsh History Review,* 8, 4, (1977), pp.426–5.

[44] Adfer, translated as Restoration, had as its aim to restore and empower the communities which comprised a Welsh-speaking heartland. For a lively debate on its aims and effect see R. Tudur Jones, "The Shadow of the Swastika" and E. Llewelyn, "What is Adfer?" in I. Hume and W. T. R. Pryce (eds.), *The Welsh and their Country,* Gomer Press, (Llandysul, 1986), pp.234–43, and pp.244–52.

[45] Adfer and Cymdeithas Tai Gwynedd, among others, sought to reinvigorate declining villages and appealed to sympathisers to forgo their easy existence in the Anglicized suburbs of Welsh cities and return to the heartland. Although the call may have gone largely unheeded, the pressure points they identified have been subject to recent planning legislation and to the formation of linguistic enterprise initiatives such as Antur Teifi and the various Mudiadau Iaith, see below.

[46] Fishman's GIDS framework has not been influential in Wales and is being used here at the request of the editor. The lack of impact derives from three factors. First, Welsh developments predate most of Fishman's prescriptive analysis. Secondly, critics in Wales, such as Glyn Williams (1999), have demonstrated that Fishman's programmatic, evolutionary account of social change is inherently consensual and conservative, it fails to give full weight to the historical power relations inherent in the language struggle. Thirdly, several influential analysts are critical of Fishman's misrepresentation of the Welsh, Quebécois and others' experience and consequently treat his generalizations and models with a great deal of caution. See Williams and Morris, 2000; Castonguay, 1994.

[47] Morris (2000) notes a number of obvious flaws with this present system. Until the release of council circular FE/CL/98/38 (this circular released on 25 March 1998 informed consortia members that the Council has henceforth decided to: (i) re-emphasize that all funding to institutions for Welsh for Adults provision is conditional on institutions participating in and adhering to the relevant consortium strategic plan; and (ii) tie part of the programme area weighting (PAW) to consortia activity, p.219), there had been little that the funding council could do, should a consortium member choose to ignore the local development plan and compete for students (i.e. finance).

[48] The general aims of Mentrau Iaith would be to create social conditions that will

nurture positive attitudes towards Welsh and an increase in its general use; to normalize the use of Welsh as a medium of social and institutional communication; and to highlight the close relationship between language and attitudes which relate to quality of life issues, the environment and the local economy.

[49] How long it might take to achieve this so that the community is willing to shoulder the responsibility – and whether or not as a result of this transfer the related abolition of the Menter will cause harm to the language – is hard to answer and will vary according to each situation.

[50] Let me illustrate: for example, the Ruthin area was chosen because of these indicators:

"the age profile of Welsh speakers, which reveals lower numbers in the key 25–44 age group, suggesting, in turn, problems in the transmission of Welsh between the generations;

"the results of consultations and meetings with local people and key organizations, including the County Council and the local Menter Iaith;

"the responses from focus groups with young people in the area, work undertaken jointly with S4C" (WLB, 2003).

[51] Increased resources have enabled the WLB to monitor the implementation of these schemes more effectively. The Board believes that effective monitoring is crucially important to ensure that Welsh-language services are being properly and fairly offered to Welsh speakers.

[52] For further details visit www.welsh-language-board.org.uk.

[53] In consequence, Wales has experienced both grass roots, largely parental movements in favour of extending bilingual education, and a smaller number of movements which, are nevertheless often well organized and which oppose such an extension on the grounds that it limits their natural rights as British citizens.

[54] Were it not for the dedication of committed schoolteachers and their parent associations in promoting bilingual education, the Welsh language would today be in a parlous state.

[55] For an analysis of bilingual education as a social phenomenon see C. H. Williams, *Addysg Ddwyieithog yng Nghymru Ynteu Addysg ar Gyfer Cymru Ddwyieithog,* Canolfan Astudiaethau Iaith, Bangor, May, 1988; ibid. "Agencies of Language Reproduction in Celtic Societies", in *Maintenance and Loss of Minority Languages,* Willem Fase, Koen Jaspaert, Sjaak Kroon, John Benjamins, (eds.), (Amsterdam, 1992), pp.306–29. See also Colin Baker, (ed.), "Bilingualism and Bilingual Education", Special Issue of *Education for Development,* Vol. 10, No. 3, 1987.

[56] This was certainly the case until relatively recently, and even today certain local authorities are reluctant to service the demand for bilingual education in their areas. It also increased the determination of those parents who, angered by the perceived injustice in the educational system, became involved in broader linguistic and political issues.

[57] See G. Humphries, "Polisi Iaith Awdurdod Addysg Gwynedd – Adolygu a

gweithredu ym 1986", *Education for Development,* Vol. 10, No. 3, (1987), pp.7–23. For an excellent overview of the system up until the early eighties, see Colin Baker, *Aspects of Bilingualism in Wales,* Multilingual Matters, (Clevedon, Avon, 1985).

[58] It is now possible to teach a wide range of subjects including Maths and Science, Design and Computing through the medium of Welsh. Currently, all, save a few opt-out schools in the secondary sector, are required by law to teach Welsh to pupils in the lower forms.

[59] This is a field which Maite Puigdevall i Serralvo and I are researching in connection with Menter a Busnes, see Puigdevall i Serralvo and Williams (2001).

[60] The chief organizational characteristic of Welsh-medium publishing is its dependency upon grant-in-aid from public coffers. A third of all books are school texts or children's books, initially dealing with Welsh themes by Welsh authors, but increasingly translating the more popular English-medium stories, reference books and visually stunning discovery and factual/documentary guide books. Adult books are dominated by literary conventions which prize verse, prose, Eisteddfod competition winners and the like, reflecting the niche market of Welsh-medium publishing. Rarely would one find a Welsh translation of a highly popular English novel, for it makes little economic sense. It is more probable that contemporary drama, rather than novels would be translated, in part because it is related to performance and in part owing to the probability of its having been commissioned for television or radio.

[61] Up to 1982, some ten per cent of programmes were transmitted in Welsh, with the effect that those who preferred not to watch Welsh-medium output had their television sets tuned permanently to English transmitters in the Mendips, Shrewsbury, Kidsgrove and Chester. In consequence, one had the continuing anomaly that very many households in Wales received their daily diet of regional news and accompanying programmes from a neighbouring region across the border. This also limited the appeal and impact of English-medium programmes produced in Wales, and, of course, diminished the potential revenue derived from commercial advertizing. Both sides of the "linguistic divide" were thus profoundly unhappy with the situation. However, identifying the problem is one thing, acting to redress it is quite another, especially when there are huge political and financial implications. Turning aerials to receive English-based programming may also be interpreted as a partial rejection of identification with Welsh issues.

[62] For his own account of this episode, see Gwynfor Evans, *Bywyd Cymro,* Manon Rhys, (ed.), Gwasg Gwynedd (1982) and in translation by Meic Stephens under the title *For the Sake of Wales,* Welsh Academic Press, (Bridgend, 1996). His argument in favour of a separate channel is set out in Gwynfor Evans, *Byw Neu Farw? Y Frwydr dros yr Iaith a'r Sianel Deledu Gymraeg,* (1980).

[63] This is part of a wider debate concerning the language policies of both S4C and the BBC, and has another dimension as regards the attempts to modernize Welsh, which some argue is the transmission of Anglo-American values and culture through the medium of Welsh.

[64] Bwrdd yr Iaith Gymraeg, *Adroddiad Blynyddol a Chyfrifon, 1997–98,* Bwrdd yr

Iaith Gymraeg, (Caerdydd, 1998).

65 Under the spirit of the 1993 Act, the Board has also developed partnerships with the 22 Unitary Authorities through Rhwydwaith (Network), with the Welsh Consumer Council, the Welsh Council for Voluntary Action and with a range of private sector organizations. During the financial year 1997–97, grants totalling £2,254,792 were distributed under the Board's main grants scheme to organizations as varied as the National Eisteddfod, the Welsh Books Council and Shelter Cymru (Welsh Language Board, 1998).

66 Annual Report of the Welsh Language Board, (Cardiff, 1998). In order to increase opportunities the Board proposes to, among other things, agree Welsh language schemes with public organizations; to encourage providers of public services to regard the provision of high-quality Welsh-medium services on a basis of equality with English as a natural part of providing services in Wales, and encourage Welsh speakers through effective marketing initiatives to make full use of the services available through the medium of Welsh.

67 J. E. Hughes, *Canllawiau Ysgrifennu Cymraeg,* Bwrdd yr Iaith Gymraeg, (Caerdydd, 1998).

68 The Board has committed itself to undertake research into the holistic analysis of Welsh-speaking communities; to formulate effective action plans for addressing potential problems in conjunction with key players across all sectors; to discuss the role of unitary authorities in initiating and co-ordinating language policies; to assess the effectiveness of existing community-based initiatives (such as Mentrau Iaith), as a means of promoting the use of Welsh and their usefulness as a model for facilitating the creation of new, locally-run initiatives.

69 Research conducted on behalf of the Welsh Language Board by me and Jeremy Evas analysed the deficiencies of language agencies and investigated how communities devise strategies to overcome the absence of routine exposure to domains and networks which reinforce Welsh, see C. H. Williams and J. Evas, *The Community Research Project,* The Welsh Language Board, (Cardiff, 1997). The four areas surveyed were Dyffryn Teifi, Cwm Gwendraeth, Cwm Aman and Mold.

70 There remains a crucial sociolinguistic question. If provision is increasing apace in most domains, what of the actual usage, status and application of bilingual skills in the market place? Here again it is possible to exaggerate the significance of bilingualism as a daily phenomenon, for it depends a great deal upon what meaning one reads into various developments and situations.

71 This was significant in two respects. The long-term aim of the cultural nationalist programme was to establish some form of self-government, as a response to the democratic deficit in Wales. Secondly, the Assembly operated from the beginning as a bilingual chamber.

72 Catalonia is the best European example of linguistic normalization. Four elements characterise the process. At the political, administrative level a new language regime was ushered in by the Autonomy Statute of 1979, which established by Decree 115 in 1980 the Direccío General de Politica Lingüistica, and by Decree

220, 1980, within DGPL the Servei de Normalització de l'Ús Oficial de la Llengua Catalana and the Servei d'Assessorament Lingïstic. Subsequent laws included the Llei 7/1983 de Normalizació Lingüistica a Catalunya, and Llei 20/1987, which created Institució de les Lletres Catalanes. Secondly, there is a very active marketing and promotional campaign using popular slogans denoting the role of Catalan in education: La Premsa a l'Escola, Catala a l'Escola, Contes a Cau d'Orella, and in civil society, La Norma, catala cosa de tots, El Catala depen de voste, Es nota prou que som a Catalunya? Thirdly, wide-ranging reforms within education provided for the socialization of Catalan youth and of migrants from regions of Spain and North Africa e.g. Convocatoria Oposicions BUP, FP (which involved the testing of oral and written comprehension of Catalan from 1981 onwards) and the Decree 18/1986 whereby all teachers contracted by public examination must demonstrate their knowledge of Catalan comprehension and expression. Fourth, the media blossomed, both in terms of Catalan editions of Spanish newspapers e.g. El Pais, from 1982 onwards and the establishment of an Autonomous Third Channel TV3 which broadcast regularly from January 1984 and which was supplemented after the Telecommunications Act of April 1988 by a wider range of broadcasts, both on T.V. and radio.

[73] C. James and C. H. Williams, "Language and Planning in Scotland and Wales", in *Planning in Scotland and Wales,* H. Thomas and R. Macdonald, (eds.), The University of Wales Press. (Cardiff, 1997), pp.264–303.

[74] The Assembly's recruiting policy and training programme could also impact on the public sector and especially local government. Currently there is an acknowledged shortage of competent accredited translators, experienced language tutors, and skilled bilingual administrators and technical specialists. The training infrastructure for a bilingual workforce is woefully inadequate. The skills gap in the workplace needs to be addressed urgently if the relationship between the Assembly and the rest of the public sector is to operate harmoniously.

[75] It is imperative that both the university system and the training of professional specialists take due regard of "need" and not just "historical demand" (which is skewed in favour of English) and attend to the very real employment and training needs of creating a bilingual society. In addition, strong positive messages on the societal value of bilingualism will not go unheeded within the private sector, and surely this is how cultural development takes place.

[77] For British emigration patterns into Argentina during the nineteenth and twentieth, centuries, see Andrew Graham-Yooll, *The Forgotten Colony: A History of the English-Speaking Communities in Argentina,* 1981. An updated version of the book appeared in Spanish: *La Colonia Olvidada: Tres Siglos de presencia británica en la Argentina*, Buenos Aires, 2000.

[78] The background to the cultural changes in Wales during the century preceding the Patagonian venture can be found in Geraint Jenkins, *The Foundations of Modern Wales 1642–1780*, 1987. For the new sense of national identity with regard to the Patagonian venture, see Glyn Williams, *The Welsh in Patagonia*, "Establishing the Settlement-Ideological discourse", but also the sense of "Britishness" which

coloured the nationalism of the nineteenth century in Wales, R. Tudur Jones, *Yr Undeb: Hanes Undeb yr Annibynwyr Cymraeg 1872–1972,* 1975.

[79] Several monographs on particular communities have been published including: *The Welsh Way: Oral History in the Long Creek Welsh Community in Iowa, 1995;* Evan E. Davies (ed.), *Our Heritage: Early History of Tyn Rhos Welsh Congregational Church and Its Neighborhood* Ohio, 1979. More general histories of the Welsh diaspora include: Myfi Williams, *Cymry Awstralia*, 1983, Chamberlain, M. E. (ed.), *The Welsh in Canada*, 1986, Carol Bennett, *In Search of the Red Dragon: The Welsh in Canada*, 1985.

[80] R. Bryn Williams, *Y Wladfa*, Cardiff, 1962, p.19.

[81] See William D. Jones, *Wales in America, Scranton and the Welsh, 1860–1920*, Cardiff, 1993, "Y Gymraeg a Hunaniaeth Gymreig mewn Cymuned ym Mhensylvania" in Geraint H. Jenkins (ed.), *Iaith Carreg Fy Aelwyd: Iaith a Chymuned yn y Bedwaredd Ganrif ar Bymtheg*, Cardiff, 1998, where he quotes for instance Rowland T. Berthoff (British Immigrants in Industrial America 1790–1850) who states that although anxious to preserve their language in America, they tended to assimilate rapidly, given their higher social status compared with many other immigrants. For a more regional approach, see Anne Kelly Knowles, *Calvinists Incorporated: Welsh Immigrants in Ohio's Industrial Frontier*, Chicago, 1997. Questions regarding national identity of the Welsh in America were discussed in the Welsh language newspaper of North America, Y Drych, for which, see Aled Jones, Bill Jones, *Y Drych and American Welsh Identities 1851–1951,* Cardiff, 2001. See also Glyn Williams, "Incidence and Nature of Acculturation within the Welsh colony of Chubut: A Historical Perspective", *Kroeber Anthropological Society Papers*, Spring, 1968.

[82] For the background and early history of the Welsh colony in Patagonia, reference can be made in the first place to R. Bryn Williams, *Y Wladfa*, Cardiff, 1962, which concentrates mainly on the period up to *c.*1920. For a more sociological approach, the reader should consult Glyn Williams, *The Desert and the Dream (A Study of Welsh Colonization in Chubut 1865–1915*), Cardiff, 1975 and *The Welsh in Patagonia (The State and the Ethnic Community*), Cardiff, 1991. The early years of the colony were chronicled by two of the foremost participants in the Patagonian venture: Abraham Mathews, *Hanes y Wladfa Gymreig yn Patagonia,* Aberdâr, 1894, translated into Spanish under the title *Crónica de la Colonia Galesa de la Patagonia*, Buenos Aires, 1995, and Lewis Jones, *Hanes y Wladfa Gymreig,* Caernarfon, 1898, also available in Spanish as *La Colonia Galesa,* Rawson, 1993.

[83] For further material regarding the early stages in the history of the colony and the period leading up to the voyage of the *Mimosa* (1865), see Elvey MacDonald, *Yr Hirdaith* Llan-dysul, 1999; a short history concentrating on the period 1865–69 was published by Thomas Jones, Glan Camwy in serial form in the Welsh-language newspaper *Y Drafod* in 1926. For a recent Spanish translation, see Fernando Coronato, *Historia de los Comienzos de la Colonia en la Patagonia,* Trelew, 1999. Published reminiscences by several of the members of the original *Mimosa* contingent also give insights into the hardships and cohesion of the early colony. See in particular John Daniel Evans, *El Molinero,* Buenos Aires, 1994. The writings of others who arrived

in the following two decades are extremely valuable sources for the development of the colony. See William Meloch Hughes, *Ar Lannau'r Gamwy ym Mhatagonia,* Liverpool, 1927; William Casnodyn Rhys, *La Patagonia que canta,* Buenos Aires, 2000; for the period 1875–1902 *John Coslett Thomas, Hunangofiant,* Paul W. Birt (ed.), (forthcoming).

[83] For the most detailed chronological history of the town 1886–1942, see Matthew Henry Jones, *El Desafío Patagónico,* volume 1(1886–1903), volume 2 (1904–1913), volume 3 (1914–1923), volume 4 (1924–1933), volume 5 (1934–1943), Trelew, 1997.

[85] *At Home with the Patagonians,* London, 1871. John Daniel Evans, in particular mentions that he had read the book before beginning his period of exploration into the hinterland, see Clery Evans, *John Daniel Evans, El Molinero.*

[86] For this critical period of colonial expansion towards the west, see R. Bryn Williams op. cit., chapter XI "Lledu'r Ffiniau"; Glyn Williams op. cit. chapter 6, "Expanding the Horizon", chapter 7 "Cwm Hyfryd"; John Daniel Evans, pp.38–130; John Coslett Thomas, An Autobiography, chapter XII "Exploring the Interior", chapter XXII "Going Up Country", chapter XXVI "Up Country Again". Reports were written by several of the Welsh participants in the two expeditions led by Governor Luis J. Fontana in 1885 and 1888, apart from those included in John Daniel Evans, *El Molinero*, see also William Lloyd Jones Glyn, "Ysbeithio neu Archwilio Patagonia", *Y Drafod*, October–December 1930; John Murray Thomas, "John Murray Thomas' Diary of the Expedition to the Andes", *Camwy*, Gaiman, November 1985. For the history of the founding of the Andean Colony and the 1902 Plebiscite which ensured the legal borders between Chile and Argentina in Spanish, see Virgilio González, *El Valle 16 de Octubre y su Plebiscito,* Trelew, 1998, see also *El Regional* (Edición especial) "La Colonia 16 de Octubre", Gaiman, July 1975.

[87] This was the origin of the ill-fated expedition led by John Daniel Evans "El Baqueano" in which four Welshmen on their return from the upper reaches of the Chubut River were attacked by natives who had themselves recently been the victims of army intrusions into their territory as part of the wider policy of clearing the native population from Patagonia. Three of the Welshmen were killed in what became known as Dyffryn y Merthyron (Valle de los Mártires).

[88] Virgilio González, *El Valle 16 de Octubre y su Plebescito,* 1998.

[89] See Lewis H. Thomas, "From The Pampas to the Prairies: The Welsh Migration of 1902", in *Saskatchewan History,* Winter 1971, vol. XXIV; Robert Owen Jones, "From Wales to Saskatchewan via Patagonia", in *Celtic Languages and Celtic Peoples,* pp.619–643,

[90] Glyn Williams, "The Welsh in Patagonia", p.40; also by the same author, "The Welsh in Patagonia: A Demographic Note" in Norsk Tidsskrift for Sprogsvidenskap 1969, p.238 where he states: "Knowing that Welsh immigrants to Patagonia virtually ceased in 1911, we can now state that no more than 2,300 Welsh people ever emigrated to Patagonia".

[91] William Meloch Hughes, *Ar Lannau'r Gamwy ym Mhatagonia*, p.149.

[92] Ibid., p.p.44, 45.

[22] See in particular Robert Owen Jones, "Yr Iaith Gymraeg yn y Wladfa", in Geraint J. Jenkins (ed.), *Iaith Carreg Fy Aelwyd*, Cardiff, 1998, "Language variation and social stratification: Linguistic change in progress", in Martin J. Ball (ed.), *The Use of Welsh*.

Important information about lexical variations and the evolution of "Patagonian" Welsh are to be found in Gareth Alban Davies, "Iaith y Bobl" pp.62–85, in *Tan Tro Nesaf*, Llandysul, 1976.

[94] Robert Owen Jones, *Hir Oes I'r Iaith: Agweddau ar Hanes y Gymraeg a'r Gymdeithas*, Llandysul, 1997, p.310–311.

[95] This tendency had been noted by William Meloch Hughes in his volume of reminiscences of his life spent in the colony between 1881 and 1925, *Ar Lannau'r Gamwy Ym Mhatagonia*, Liverpool, 1927.

[96] John Daniel Evans quotes verbatim comments made by his contemporaries which are clearly the spoken Welsh of the Rhondda area. His manuscript writings from the period 1915–1917 also reflect some of his own inherited phonology of South Wales.

[97] John Coslett Thomas, *Autobiography*, (English translation) Winnipeg, Manitoba, 1994, p.56.

[98] Nonconformist chapels in Wales usually had either a name taken from the Bible e.g. Bethesda or Bethel; or took a local geographic name, e.g. Pendre.

[99] It is noteworthy that the continuum of Sunday school instruction, which would have been known to all of the *Mimosa* contingent, is seen at work even during the voyage to Argentina in 1865 before being re-established within a short period in Patagonia itself. See the diary of Lewis Humphreys published in Welsh in *Y Drafod*, 15 April, 1910, and in Spanish translation in Matthew Henry Jones *El Desafío Patagónico*, vol. 2, pp.151–154.

[100] Clery Evans, *John Daniel Evans, El Molinero*, Buenos Aires, 1994 (second edition), pp.25–26.

[101] R. Bryn Williams, *Y Wladfa*, pp.155–8.

[102] This had arisen as a result of the demographic changes in the valley whereby the town of Trelew was increasingly becoming a Spanish-speaking centre in the area. Resistance to Spanish in earlier years should also be understood in terms of language as the bearer of cultural and religious values, and in this sense, those who spoke Spanish ("Lladinwyr") were viewed as having a value system quite different to that cultivated by the Welsh.

[103] John Coslett Thomas, op. cit., "Chubut" p.55.

[104] R. Bryn Williams, *Y Wladfa*, p.199.

[105] William Meloch Hughes, op. cit, "Ym Myd Addysg", pp29–35; *A Orillas del Rio Chubut*, pp.33–38.

[106] For examples, see Edi Dorian Jones, *Fotografías: Capillas Galesas en Chubut*,

"Contacto gales-aborigen en las capillas", pp.35–37; John Coslett Thomas, op. cit., "Indians of Patagonia", p.113, Matthew Henry Jones, op. cit., vol I, p.65 where the chief Kingel is mentioned as one who learned to speak Welsh. Further details are to found in R. Bryn Williams, op. cit., p.265–6.

[107] William Meloch Hughes describes the mixed character of Trelew where Welsh, Italian and Spanish inhabitants lived in harmony, *Ar Lannau'r Gamwy*, pp.201, see also John Coslett Thomas, op. cit., "Gorlifiadau (Floods)", pp.255–270.

[108] H. S. Ferns, *Britain and Argentina in the Nineteenth Century*, Oxford, 1960; see also Andrew Graham-Yooll, *The Forgotten Colony*, 1981.

[109] Matthew Henry Jones, op. cit., tomo I, pp.39–40.

[110] John Coslett Thomas, op. cit., p.252.

[111] John Coslett Thomas, op.cit, p.187, p.242. In the later reference Thomas states, "That school was of course a Welsh school, and it was established after Eluned Morgan gave up her English school".

[112] Robert Owen Jones, *Hir Oes i'r Iaith*, Llandysul, 1997, "Y Gymraeg ym Mhatagonia", p.317.

[113] R. Bryn Williams, *Y Wladfa*, p.271.

[114] R. Bryn Williams, *Crwydro Patagonia*, 1960.

[115] Matthew Henry Jones, op. cit., tomo III, p.8.

[116] Matthew Henry Jones, op. cit., volume III, p.15.

[117] Ibid., p.8–9. The College also held evening classes for the learning of English.

[118] Ibid., p.8. The majority of those quoted have Welsh surnames.

[119] For recollections of school life in the schools of Patagonia during the first half of the twentieth century, see Guto Roberts and Marian Elias Roberts (eds.), "Fy Ysgol i", pp. 40–83, in *Byw ym Mhatagonia*, Caernarfon, 1993; for a history of Bryn Crwn school (1896–1968), see *Escuela No.39 de Bryn Crwn: Un Recuerdo*, Rawson, n.d.

[120] Matthew Henry Jones, *El Desafío Patagónico*, tomo I, p.33; also *Ar Lannau'r Gamwy ym Mhatagonia*', William Meloch Hughes op. cit., p.108; Abraham Mathews, *Hanes y Wladfa Gymreig yn Patagonia*, Aberdâr, 1984, p.p.99–101; R. Bryn Williams op. cit., pp.186–189, et passim., Glyn Williams, *The Welsh in Patagonia*, pp.38–40; pp.106–108, et passim.

[121] Robert Owen Jones, "Yr Iaith Gymraeg yn y Wladfa" p.292 in Geraint Jenkins (ed.), *Iaith Carreg Fy Aelwyd: Iaith a Chymuned yn y Bedwaredd Ganrif ar Bymtheg*, University of Wales Press, 1998.

[122] Glyn Williams, op. cit., p.106.

[123] William Meloch Hughes, op. cit., "Ym Myd Masnach", p.116.

[124] For the circumstances surrounding the liquidation, see R. Bryn Williams, op. cit., p.279–282.

[125] Glyn Williams, *The Desert and the Dream*, Cardiff, 1975, p.165.

[126] Ibid., p.165.

[127] For the early history of *Y Drafod*, see: Matthew Henry Jones, *El Desafío Patagónico*, vol. I, p.43–45; R. Bryn Williams, *Y Wladfa*, p.198, and by the same author *Rhyddiaith y Wladfa*, passim, Eluned Morgan, *Y Drafod*, 18 January 1918, and for comments regarding language use in the paper, see Glyn Williams, *The Welsh in Patagonia*, p.248–249.

[128] Matthew Henry Jones, op. cit., p.45.

[129] Other newspapers were available and arrived on the ships and packets from Buenos Aires. Some members of the Welsh élite subscribed to and contributed to the English-language press in Buenos Aires, notably *The Standard* that began publication in Buenos Aires in 1861. This newspaper often ran articles by the leaders of the colony including Lewis Jones and John Murray Thomas.

[130] Osian Hughes, *Los Poetas del Eisteddfod*, p.13; R. Bryn Williams, *Awen Ariannin*, pp.12, 22–42.

[131] Matthew Henry Jones, op.cit., vol 1, p.47.

[132] Matthew Henry Jones, ibid. The mixed choirs were made up of 60 to 80 voices each. The three choir directors at this time were T. Dalar Evans, John Carrog Jones and Llewelyn Williams.

[133] Matthew Henry Jones, op. cit., vol I, p.51.

[134] See example in Matthew Henry Jones, op. cit., vol 1, p.58.

[135] See in particular Glyn Williams, *The Welsh in Patagonia*, chapter 3, "'Socio-religious Organization".

[136] In the early period, amongst the most influential were Abraham Matthews, John Caerennig Evans, D. Casnodyn Rhys, Lewis Humphreys and David Lloyd Jones.

[137] Edi Dorian Jones, *Fotografías: Capillas Galesas en Chubut*, 1999, Trelew, pp.195–6.

[138] Ibid., p.127–128.

[139] Ibid., p.131.

[140] Ibid., p.131.

[141] Matthew Henry Jones, op. cit., vol. II, p.210; III, p.234; IV, p.200.

[142] Compiled by Matthew Henry Jones op. cit., vol. III, p.229. The list is no doubt incomplete but gives a clear picture regarding the small number of Welsh-owned small businesses in the town.

[143] *Y Drafod*, 28 July 1892. The numbers for Rawson/Trelew are: Argentines: 489; British: 347; Italian, 145; others: 45. In Gaiman the figures are: Argentines: 368; British; 713, others: 28. The previous census of 1881 revealed that in the colony there was a population of 1,010 of which there were 806 Welsh, 177 Argentine, English 4, Irish 3, Italian 4, Spanish 3, North Americans 3, Germans 3, French 4, Austrian 1, Chilean 1, and Danish 1. Also, Matthew Henry Jones, op. cit., vol. I, p.158. Some Afrikaaners also came after the Boer War.

[144] John Coslett Thomas, op.cit., p.257.

[145] Glyn Williams, *The Desert and the Dream,* Cardiff, 1975, p.172.

[146] Approximately 1,000 Welsh immigrants arrived between 1886 and 1911. On the basis of this and other statistics, Glyn Williams estimated that no more than 2,300 Welsh people ever immigrated into Patagonia, Glyn B. Williams, "The Welsh in Patagonia: A Demographic Note", in *Norsk Tidsskrift for Sprogvidenskap*, p.238, 1969, Supplementary Volume.

[147] Glyn Williams, ibid., p.179.

[148] A sense of stagnation in the Welsh life of the colony during the late 1920s and 1930s can be felt in the letters of Eluned Morgan to the Rev William Nantlais Williams, Dafydd Ifans (ed.) *Tyred Drosodd: Gohebiaeth Eluned Morgan a Nantlais*, Pen-y-Bont ar Ogwr, 1977.

[149] *Y Drafod*, "A Adawn ni y Wladfa?" (Shall We Leave Patagonia?), 22 September 1913.

[150] Matthew Henry Jones, vol III, p.161.

[151] Ibid., p.37.

[152] Ibid., vol. V, p.16.

[153] Osian Hughes., op. cit, pp.64–65

[154] Matthew Henry Jones., op. cit., vol. IV, p.245.

[155] For more personal recollections of the Eisteddfodau of this period, see *Byw ym Mhatagonia*, ed. Guto Roberts and Marian Elias Roberts, "Atgofion Eisteddfodol" pp.125–144.

[156] As an example of language and the Eisteddfod, the programme for the 1999 Eisteddfod, divided into youth and adult sections, demonstrates a clear desire to give as much room to the Welsh language as possible. The two sections are divided into recitation (including choral competitions), literary competitions and translations. Interestingly, the translation competitions had included English, French and Italian as well as Spanish and Welsh. The main literary prizes reserved the "chair" for a Welsh poem and the traditional "crown" for a Spanish poem.

[157] J. Fishman, *Reversing Language Shift,* Clevedon, 1991.

[158] M. G. Mulhall, *Handbook of the River Plate for 1875*, Buenos Aires, p.48.

[159] The most graphic account of the Welsh involvement in this colony can be found in John Coslett Thomas, *Autobiography*, Winnipeg, Manitoba, 1994, chapters 16–22.

[160] For a full description of the history and present situation of this and other colonies, see Ramón Gutierrez (ed. et al), *Habitat e Inmigración: Nordeste y Patagonia,* "San Jerónimo. Enclave Suizo en Territorio Santafesina», Buenos Aires, 1998, pp.15–49.

[161] Ibid., p.30.

[162] Ibid., p.44.

[163] Joshua Fishman (ed.), "Sociolinguistics", in *Handbook of Language and Ethnic Identity*, 1999, p.158.

[164] Joshua Fishman, *Reversing Language Shift*, 1991, chapter 14.

[165] Joshua Fishman, op. cit., 1999, p.153–4.

[166] Ofis ar Brezhoneg released a new estimate of 4,123,795 inhabitants for Brittany in April 2004.

[167] The Breton language and other minority languages are not recorded in the French census, so studies of the language are forced to rely on estimates, such as those made recently by Ofis ar Brezhoneg.

[168] At the time of writing, in mid-2004 the French Government has not ratified the full European Charter and relations between the state and minority-language schools have clearly become more tense.

[169] The exact eastern limits of the Breton language in the medieval period are uncertain but place-names suggest that it was spoken considerably farther east than today. Indeed, parts of western Loire–Atlantique were Breton-speaking into at least the 1920s and possibly even the 1950s in isolated cases.

[170] Although no census statistics exist to record the decline of Breton, recent estimates suggest it has been catastrophic since 1970 when well over 500,000 employed the language, to the present where daily speakers may number no more than 50,000, as opposed to the 304,000 who have some knowledge of the language.

[171] Out-migration became particularly severe in the post-war period with about 500,000 leaving for work in Paris, Belgium and Canada during the 1950s alone. The Canadian census of 1996 recorded 105 Breton speakers in Québec and 155 in Canada.

[172] The Breton situation, like Irish and Basque, can, according to Joshua Fishman, in *Reversing Language Shift*, be salvaged only through concentration of speakers in the family, community and neighbourhood arena.

[173] Philip Payton, (1996) *Cornwall*, Fowey, Alexander Associates, pp.91, 93.

[174] Kenneth J. George (1986) "How many people spoke Cornish traditionally?" in *Cornish Studies 14* (1986) Institute of Cornish Studies, Redruth, pp.67–70.

[175] e.g. Nicholas J. A. Williams (1995) *Cornish Today*, Sutton Coldfield; Kernewek dre Lyther, pp.77–80, and (forthcoming) "Middle and Late Cornish" in McCone, K. *Compendium Linguarium Celticum*, Reichert Verlag.

[176] Payton, op. cit., ch. 6, pp.119–148; Jon Angarrack (1999) *Breaking the Chains*, Bodmin, Quill Distributors/Stannary Publications, p.50.

[177] A. L. Rowse (1941) *Tudor Cornwall*, reprinted 1990, Redruth, Dyllansow Truran, p.9; and Paul Hodge commenting at Focus Group meeting Sat 19 Feb 2000 at St Austell Church Rooms on: Jon Angarrack (1999) *Breaking the Chains*, Bodmin, Quill Distributors/Stannary Publications ISBN 09529313 11, pp.51–52.

[178] Oliver J. Padel (1975) *The Cornish Writings of the Boson Family*, Redruth, Institute of Cornish Studies.

[179] P. Berresford Ellis (1974) *The Cornish Language and its Literature*, London, Routledge & Kegan Paul, p.166. A. S. D. Smith (1947) *The Story of the Cornish*

Language, its Extinction and Revival, Camborne, Camborne Printing and Stationery Company, pp.9–10.

[180] George, op. cit. p.70.

[181] Derek R. Williams (1993) *Prying into Every Hole and Corner: Edward Lhuyd in Cornwall in 1700*, Redruth, Dyllansow Truran, ISBN 1 85022 066 2; Simon James (1998) *The Atlantic Celts – Ancient People or Modern Invention?* London, British Museum Press ISBN 0-7141-2165-7, pp.44–46.

[182] William Pryce (1970*) Archaeologia Cornu-Britannica*, Reprint Redruth, Dyllansow Truran. P. Berresford Ellis (1974) *The Cornish Language and its Literature*, London, Routledge & Kegan Paul, pp.120–124. (He cites Thomson, mine engineer of Truro, William Bodinar, fisherman of Mousehole, father of Sir Joseph Banks in 1791, John Nancarrow of Market Jew, Jane Cock and Jane Woolcock also of Mousehole.)

[183] Thomas Shaw (1991) *A Methodist Guide to Cornwall*, London, Methodist Publishing House, p.31.

[184] Ronald M. James (1994) "Defining the Group: Nineteenth-Century Cornish on the North American Mining Frontier" in Philip Payton (1994) *Cornish Studies* (Second Series) Exeter, Exeter University Press, pp.32–47.

[185] Philip Payton(1999) *The Cornish Overseas*, Fowey, Alexander Associates ISBN 899526-95-1

[186] Philip Payton, ibid., p.174

[187] P. Berresford Ellis, op. cit., p.129.

[188] Shaw, op. cit., p.31.

[189] Henry Jenner (1877) *An Early Cornish Fragment*, London, Athenaeum No 2614 (1 Dec 1877) pp.698–699. Also a modern study: Lauran Toorians *The Middle Cornish Charter Endorsement – The Making of a Marriage in Medieval Cornwall*, Innsbruck: Innsbrucker Beitraege zur Sprachwissenschaft, herausgegeben von Wolfgang Meid ISBN 3-85124-622-5.

[190] Bottrell (1870–1883) *Traditions and Hearthside Stories of West Cornwall*, three volumes, originally published by author at Penzance, reprinted: Llanerch Publishers, Lampeter 1993 ISBN 1-86143-001-9, 1-861-43-002-7, 1-86143-003-5; Robert Hunt (1865) *Popular Romances of the West of England*, 3rd. edition 1930, London, Chatto & Windus.

[191] I am indebted to Dr Amy Hale, Institute of Cornish Studies, Truro, for the reference to: Mrs Frank Morris (1898*) Cornish Whiddles for Teemn Time*, London, T. Fisher Unwin (The Children's Library). See especially pp. 155, 213–215.

[192] e.g. parish history by Rev E. G. Harvey (1875) Mullion, Truro, Lake. Chapter on "Old Cornish Language", which contains Lord's Prayer and Apostles' Creed in Cornish and local place-name meanings. (Reported in *An Gowsva* 12 Haf/Summer 1999) Portreath, Spyrys a Gernow, pp.6–7.

[193] Henry Jenner (1904) *A Handbook of the Cornish Language*, London, David Nutt.

194 Henry Jenner (1875/6) "The Manx Language: its Grammar, Literature and Present State", in *Transactions of the Philological Society*, 1875–76, p.172.

195 Amy Hale (1997) "Genesis of the Celto-Cornish Revival? L. C. Duncombe-Jewell and the Kowethas Kelto-Kernuak", in Payton, P. (ed.) *Cornish Studies*, second series No. 5 (1997) Exeter, University of Exeter Press, pp.100–111.

196 Conversations in their homes with Richard and Ann Jenkin, 21 Feb 2000, and G. Pawley White 27 Feb 2000.

197 Henry Lewis (1923) *Llawlyfr Cernyweg Canol*, Aberystwyth. It was reprinted in 1946. A German translation has appeared: Stefan Zimmer (1990) *Handbuch des Mittelkornischen*, Innsbruck: Innsbrucker Beitraege zur Sprachwissenschaft, herausgegeben von Wolfgang Meid; and an English translation, edited by Glanville Price, 2001.

198 R. Morton Nance (1923) *Cornish for All – a Guide to Unified Cornish* (Third edition 1958) Penzance, Saundry, for Federation of Old Cornwall Societies.

199 This circle certainly included Smith (Caradar) and Nance (Mordon), F. B. Cargeeg (Tan Dyvarow) who ran a correspondence circle, Dr Hambly of Tyr ha Tavas, Peggy Pollard (Arlodhes Ywerdhon), Edwin Chirgwin (Map Melyn), E. G. Retallack Hooper (Talek), D. H. Watkins (Carer Brynyow), Mrs Phoebe Proctor (Morwennol – Nance's daughter and probably the first person to have been brought up with Cornish in the twentieth century), W. D. Watson (Tyrvab), R. St V. Allan-Collins (Halwyn – who had taught Cornish in London), and Richard Hall of St Just. (source: Berresford Ellis, op. cit., ch. 7.)

200 A. S. D. Smith (1947) *The Story of the Cornish Language – its Extinction and Revival*, Camborne, Camborne Printing and Stationery Co. Ltd., p.20.

201 P. Berresford Ellis, op. cit., ch. 7.

202 Inglis Gundry (1966) *Conow Kernow – Songs and Dances from Cornwall*, St. Ives, Federation of Old Cornwall Societies.

203 Merv Davey (1983) *Hengan – Traditional Folk Songs, Dances and Broadside Ballads Collected in Cornwall*, Redruth, Dyllansow Truran ISBN 0-907566-71-5.

204 Cowethas an Yeth Kernewek (1984) *Kernewek Hedhyu – Report on the State of the Language*, p.12

205 Wella Brown (1961) "Stuth an Yeth Kernewek yn jeth Hedhyu", paper to Celtic Congress, Lannion, quoted in Philip Payton and Bernard Deacon (1993) "The Ideology of Language Revival" in Payton, P. (ed.) *Cornwall Since The War*, Truro, Dyllansow Truran, p.278.

206 E. G. Retallack Hooper (Talek) (ed.) (1964) *Kemysk Kernewek – A Cornish Miscellany*, Camborne, An Lef Kernewek.

207 P. Berresford Ellis, op. cit., p.194, citing personal letter of 19 July 1972.

208 Bernard Deacon (1996) "Language Revival and Language Debate: Modernity and Postmodernity", in Payton, P. (ed.) (1996) *Cornish Studies* (Second Series) No. 4, Exeter, University of Exeter Press, pp.88–106 (see Note 1 on p.103).

[209] P. Berresford Ellis, op. cit, p.194 quoting Thomas's speech to Celtic Congress at St Ives, April 1963.

[210] Ken George (1986) *The Pronunciation and Spelling of Revised Cornish*, Saltash, Cornish Language Board.

[211] Ken George (1995) "Which Base for Revised Cornish?" in Payton, P. (ed.) *Cornish Studies* (Second Series) Three, Exeter, University of Exeter Press. pp.104–124. Ken George (1998) *Gerlyver Kernewek Kemmyn an Gerlyver Kres, Cornish–English, English–Cornish Dictionary*, Seaton, Kesva an Taves Kernewek ISBN 0-907064-6; also see: Ken George (1993) *Gerlyver Kernewek Kemmyn: An Gerlyver Meur*, Saltash, Kesva an Tavas Kernewek; Ken George (1995) *Gerlyver Kernewek Kemmyn: Dyllans Seradow Sowsnek – Kernewek*, Kesva an Tavas Kernewek.

[212] Richard Gendall (1990) "The Language of Cornish People" in *Old Cornwall*, Vol. 10, No. 9; Richard Gendall (1991) *The Pronunciation of Cornish*, Menheniot, Teere ha Tavaz; Richard Gendall (1994) *1000 Years of Cornish* (Second Edition), Menheniot, Teere ha Tavaz;

[213] R. R. M. Gendall (1991) *A Students' Grammar of Modern Cornish*, Menheniot, The Cornish Language Council; R. R. M. Gendall (ed.) (1992/5) *A Students' Dictionary of Modern Cornish, Part I English–Cornish* (Fourth Edition 1992, corrected 1995) Menheniot, Teere ha Tavaz; R. R. M. Gendall (ed.) (1997) *A Practical Dictionary of Modern Cornish, Part One; Cornish–English.* Menheniot, Teere ha Tavaz; R. R. M. Gendall (ed.) *A New Practical Dictionary of Modern Cornish, Part Two: English–Cornish*, Menheniot, Teere ha Tavaz; Richard Gendall (2000) *Tavaz a Ragadazow – The Language of my Forefathers,* Menheniot, Teer ha Tavaz.

[214] Wella Brown (1961) "Stuth an Yeth Kernewek yn jeth hedhyu", paper to Celtic Congress, Lannion, quoted in Philip Payton and Bernard Deacon (1993), "The Ideology of Language Revival" in Payton, P. (ed.) *Cornwall Since the War*, Truro, Dyllansow Truran, p.278.

[215] Bernard Deacon, op. cit., pp.277, 286–7.

[216] Wella Brown, Denise Chubb, Ray Chubb, Neil Kennedy, and Jane Ninnis (1991) *The Cornish Language*, joint publication of Cornish Language Board, Agan Tavas, Dalleth, Cossell an Tavaz Cornoack, An Gressenn Kernewek, Kowethas an Yeth Kernewek.

[217] Philip Payton and Bernard Deacon, op. cit., pp.287, 290; and Bernard Deacon (1996) "Language Revival and Language Debate: Modernity and Postmodernity", in Payton, P. (ed.) (1996) *Cornish Studies* (Second Series) Four, Exeter, University of Exeter Press, p.106 (note 75).

[218] Payton and Deacon, Deacon, op. cit.

[219] Glanville Price (1998) "Modern Cornish in Context", in Payton, P. (1999) *Cornish Studies* (Second Series) Six, Exeter, Exeter University Press, pp.187–193.

[220] Jon Mills (1999) "Reconstructive Phonology and Contrastive Lexicology: Problems with the Gerlyver Kernewek Kemmyn", in Payton, P. (1999) *Cornish Studies* (Second Series) Seven, Exeter, University of Exeter Press, p.193–218.

[221] N. J. A. Williams (1995) *Cornish Today: An Examination of the Revised Language*, Sutton Coldfield; N. J. A. Williams (1996) "Which Cornish?" A talk given at Lostwithiel on 6 September 1996 (author's publication) N. J. A. Williams (1996), "Linguistically Sound Principles: the Case against Kernewek Kemmyn" in Philip Payton (ed.) *Cornish Studies* (Second Series) Four, Exeter, Exeter University Press, pp.64–87; N. J. A. Williams (1998) *Cla 'pya Kernewek: An Introduction to Unified Cornish Revised,* Hayle.

[222] Neil Kennedy (1996) "Cornish Today: a Modern Cornish Perspective" in Philip Payton, (1996) *Cornish Studies* (Second Series) Four, Exeter, Exeter University Press, pp.171–181.

[223] Henry Jenner (1904) *A Handbook of the Cornish Language*, London, David Nutt.

[224] P. Berresford Ellis (1974) *The Cornish Language and its Literature*, London, Routledge & Kegan Paul ISBN 0-71007928-1, ch. 7.

[225] Brian Murdoch (1993) *Cornish Literature*, Woodbridge, Boydell & Brewer.

[226] Richard Gendall (2000) *1000 Years of Cornish* (Second Edition) Menheniot, Teer ha Tavaz, pp.14–15.

[227] Tim Saunders (ed.) (1999) *The Wheel – an Anthology of Modern Poetry in Cornish 1850–1980*, London, Francis Boutle ISBN 0-9532388-7-3.

[228] Tim Saunders (1999) *The High Tide – Collected Poems in Cornish 1974-1999*, London, Francis Boutle ISBN 0-9532388-6-5.

[229] A. S. D. Smith (1947) op. cit., p.14. The persons named are: Henry Jenner, Richard Hall, W. D. Watson, R. Morton Nance, and R. St. V. Allan-Collins; Berresford Ellis, op. cit., pp.158-160. Gorseth records communicated by Treeve Crago, Gorseth Archivist, March 2000.

[230] Wella Brown (1981) "Stuth an Yeth Kernewek yn jeth hedhyu", paper to Celtic Congress, Lannion July 1981 in Payton (ed.) (1993) op. cit., p.278; and State of Language Statistics for 1999, communicated by Jane Ninnis.

[231] Berresford Ellis, op. cit., p.168.

[232] Joshua A. Fishman (1991) *Reversing Language Shift – Theoretical and Empirical Foundations of Assistance to Threatened Languages*. Clevedon, Multilingual Matters ISBN 1-85359-121-1, pp.87–107.

[233] Berresford Ellis, op. cit., p.166; A. S. D. Smith (1947) op. cit., gives a figure for 1933 of classes held in "seven Cornish towns" involving 60 students, p.17.

[234] Berresford Ellis, op. cit., p.158.

[235] Kowethas an Yeth Kernewek (1984) *Kernewek Hedhyu: Deryvas war Stuth an Tavas – report on the State of the Language,* p.27. (The items are alphabetical in Cornish.)

[236] Ibid., p.21.

[237] *State of the Language Statistics 1999*, communicated by Jane Ninnis; and graphs prepared by Wella Brown. Both sources are acknowledged with many thanks.

[238] *State of Language Statistics 1999*. The apparent decline should be read with caution. Over time, numbers have tended to fluctuate year on year.
[239] Ibid.
[240] In his 1991 work *Reversing Language Shift*, Joshua Fishman accurately commented on the sense in the Irish language movement that more might have been achieved during the period 1921–1991.

[241] In the recently published work *Lost Languages*, Robinson 2002, the issue of such non-Indo-European languages as Etruscan and Basque is explored at length.

[242] In *The Age of Arthur*, Morris gives a detailed backdrop of the evolution of post-Roman Britain and its implications for the future Celtic nations.

[243] One of the more detailed explanations of the linguistic complexities caused by linguistic change in pre-famine Ireland is provided in the opening chapters of Miller's *Emigrants and Exiles*.

[244] Hindley accurately draws attention to the massive undercount of Irish speakers in the 1851 census in *The Death of The Irish Language*.

[245] In *Reversing Language Shift* in 1991, Joshua Fishman comments on the failure of the Irish government to carry out the critically important Community Projects proposal during the 1980s.

[246] The author interviewed representatives of Gaelscoileanna, Foras na Gaeilge and Comhdháil Náisiúnta na Gaeilge in 2003 and was briefed on present policy planning.

[247] Surveys carried out by the Gaelscoileanna organization indicate over 30 per cent of young Irish parents as supporting the enrolment of their own children in Irish-language schools. Such positive manifestations of support for Irish suggest the language may have lost some of its past stigma with the young.

[248] This painful period is at last being examined thoroughly in such recent works as *The Old IRA and the Belfast Pogroms* by J. MacDermott.

[249] For a thorough and more lengthy treatment of the important Shaw's Road Gaeltacht, see Gabrielle Maguire's *Our Own Language* by Multilingual Matters in 1991.

[250] Debate still rages about the linguistic affiliation of the Picts. While the records suggest both Brythonic and Gaelic influence, the presence of non-Celtic personal and place-names and even words does indeed suggest the persistence of older cultural and linguistic elements. This is what one would expect under the circumstances and this is what one finds when any study is made of records such as the Pictish king lists, for example. The first Bishop of Argyll in 565, Itharnon, was a Pict who bore a non-Celtic name just as did many Pictish kings of the period, such as Bliesblituth and Uscombuts. Records from this period in Ireland suggest the same scenario, a predominantly Celtic-speaking society with fragments of an older culture and even language still present.

[251] In addition to spreading Gaelic literacy in the reformation period, the churches also created the first authentically Scottish–Gaelic literature, as opposed to the

previous literature which was based on the standard Irish dialect employed previously by Gaelic Scotland for over a millennium.

[252] Both in Canada and in the United States in the nineteenth century, Irish and Scottish immigrants and their representatives tended to downplay linguistic differences in the interest of social and communal advancement but contemporary sources confirm the widespread, continued use of Irish and Gaelic throughout the 1800s in cities such as New York, Boston, Halifax and Toronto – of a Gaelic America, we could accurately say.

[253] The weekly Irish-language newspaper *An Lá* (The Day) has recently been upgraded to a daily from a weekly, partly because of increased government funding from the Irish Government (as is also now happening in Nova Scotia) but also because of increased demand. It is seen by many people in Ireland as a national newspaper. The Irish-language weekly *Foinse* based in County Galway is also government-subsidized.

[254] See the *National Post* (of Canada), 1 June, 2004, p.10 for details of the Minister's anouncement.

[255] See the *Cape Breton Post*, 1 June, 2004 for further details of the Minister's anouncement.

[256] The author has encountered many Nova Scotia Gaels in Toronto and well recalls an encounter in the mid-1970s when on a tram in Toronto he enquired of two women, what language they were speaking? to which they responded "Gaelic", as "they were from Nova Scotia".

[257] Like Scotland and parts of Wales, Man was heavily colonized by Gaelic speakers in the late Roman and post-Roman periods.

[258] There is every reason to believe that Manx, like Irish, was massively undercounted in the late 1800s and early 1900s in the various census counts, due to the stigma of poverty and backwardness associated with the language.

[259] The flowering of the Manx language movement over the past decade is truly phenomenal when one looks at the expansion of the language in the schools as a subject and much more recently even as a medium of instruction.

[260] It is remarkable how frequently remarks have been made about the "extinction" of Manx in spite of the fact that the language is clearly expanding as a spoken medium in the present and never lacked fluent speakers at any point in time.

[261] In all six Celtic communities, Celtic-speaking networks are continuing to form and evolve but there still remains the question of just how extensive this phenomenon must become in order to amount to real revival.

[262] It is likely that Welsh speakers, like Irish and Manx speakers, were significantly undercounted in the various censuses of the late 1800s and early 1900s, although this cannot be proven scientifically.

Index

Y

Some other books of interest:

Spreading the Word: The Welsh Language 2001
John Aitchison & Harold Carter
A new, comphrhensive study of the Welsh language: an authoritative, essential work of reference.
0 86243 714 8
£8.95

Celtic Dawn
Peter Berresford Ellis
A fascinating history of the various movements that have campaigned for pan-Celtic unity.
0 86243 643 5
£9.95

Land of My Fathers
Gwynfor Evans
An uniquely comprehensive, illustrated history of Wales written by Wales' foremost political figure of the twentieth century.
0 86243 265 0
£12.95

The Pan-Celtic Phrasebook
Liam Knox
Compare essential phrases in Breton, Gaelic, Irish and Welsh; with translations into English and French.
0 86243 441 6
£5.95

For a full list of publications, send now for our free, full-colour catalogue or simply surf into our website:
www.ylolfa.com
where you can order on-line.